LEGAL STREET SMARTS

How to Survive in a World of Lawyers

D1399689

LEGAL STREET SMARTS

How to Survive in a World of Lawyers

DENNIS M. POWERS, J. D.

Foreword by
Harry N. MacLean, Esq.

INSIGHT BOOKS
PLENUM PRESS • NEW YORK AND LONDON

Library of Congress Cataloging-in-Publication Data

Powers, Dennis M.
    Legal street smarts : how to survive in a world of lawyers /
Dennis M. Powers ; foreword by Harry N. MacLean.
        p.   cm.
    Includes bibliographical references and index.
    ISBN 0-306-44760-6 (pbk.)
    1. Attorney and client--United States--Popular works. 2. Lawyers-
-United States--Fees--Popular works. 3. Law--United States--Popular
works.   I. Title.
KF311.Z9P69 1994
347.73'077--dc20
[347.30777]   94-28828
                                                        CIP

ISBN 0-306-44760-6

© 1994 Dennis M. Powers
Insight Books is a Division of Plenum Publishing Corporation
233 Spring Street, New York, N.Y. 10013-1578

An Insight Book

Printed in the United States of America

Dedication

To My Wife, Judy,
My Daughter, Kim,
My Son, Dennis II,
My Mother, Dorothy, and
All my family and friends.

Foreword

Legal Street Smarts is a remarkable book. When Dennis Powers first asked me to read the manuscript, I worried that it might be either another "How To" book for people wanting to draft their own wills or another book bashing lawyers and advising people how to get around the legal system. How wrong I was. What I found instead, and what the reader will find, is a thorough, clearly-written book showing people how to make the legal system work for them. Rather than condemn or complain about the system, Powers demystifies the law and lawyers and educates the reader on how to be a sophisticated consumer. *Legal Street Smarts* should be a part of every American home library, along with the *Encyclopedia Britannica*, a *Webster's* dictionary, and the *Physicians' Desk Reference*.

Law and medicine share one thing in common: an arcane, esoteric language that serves to exclude the consumer and imbue the practitioner with an air of expertise, perhaps even infallibility. A businessman consulting a lawyer on a product liability case is likely to be talked to in something akin to a foreign language. The legal consumer is on the outside looking in and unless he takes on the daunting task of self-education, that's where he will remain. It amazes me that so many Americans, who insist on thinking for themselves and demand strict accountability from those whose goods and services they purchase in other areas of their life, have tolerated their position on the outside of the law and the legal system. It is, after all, your legal system and the lawyers (and judges) are working for you.

Legal Street Smarts was a book waiting to be written. Powers, an insider, understands how the system works and, with amazing clarity, he has translated the mass of principles and procedures into a language and format that the average American can understand and work with in his or her daily life. The fact is, many legal issues that come your way can be handled without formal legal advice. Did you receive a notice of a tax audit? Curious about the benefits of Chapter 11? Confused about no-fault insurance? In the past, your options were to continue wondering or to turn to the expert. Now it is possible to educate yourself and learn the basic strategies for legal problem solving.

As a lawyer myself, I found perhaps the most fascinating chapter to be on the selection of a lawyer when the use of one becomes inevitable. The lawyer, like the doctor, has always controlled this relationship, from beginning to end. You, as the client, pretty much did what you were told and paid the bill. Now, as an educated legal consumer, you enter the lawyer's office to interview him; you come with a list of questions about his experience with this type of problem, how he bills for court time, how much he charges for copies, what happens if the case settles, etc. When a lawyer hands you a fee agreement to sign, you thank him and take it home to review it. You comparison shop, just like you would for a car, a computer, or a home.

One last word. You'll find that you don't have to wait until you have a legal problem to find this book useful and interesting. Once you see the ease with which Dennis Powers lays out the intricacies of various areas of the law, such as contracts or bankruptcy, it is tempting to pick up the book and read it from front to back as an educational adventure.

Harry N. MacLean,
Attorney

Preface

Litigating differences as a way of solving disputes continues to spiral upwards in this country. The numbers of attorneys increase, nearing one million now, and the outburst in lawsuits and conflicts increase the odds of you being involved in one, whether or not you already have been. People more and more demand that they have a right to compensation for nearly any form of infringement, whether real, imagined, or even fair.

The problem is not just the risk of a high, adverse judgment, but also that the cost of defending or bringing a lawsuit can have as much an adverse affect on a person, his family, and savings. Anyone with assets to protect is a potential victim of these trends, the odds being that a lawyer already has billed you for expensive services or a costly problem requiring one will occur in the not-too-distant future.

Early on in my career, I saw the need to control the high costs of legal compliance, agreements, and disputes, especially when disputes boiled over into the courtroom. The costs of the attorneys, although the work was necessary and adequate, was staggering. It was necessary for clients and attorneys to develop a close working arrangement, oriented towards solving legal problems and disputes in the most cost-effective manner—and that wasn't being done.

Many lawyers don't approach clients with a view to giving them the best value, as the training they receive goes against this. What's income to them is an expense to the client. What's a few days in court can be a disaster for the client. And many people don't know that this can be controlled, not to mention the ins-and-outs of how to do it. *Legal Street Smarts* was written for this purpose and to give you an edge in surviving this as best you can when it's your turn.

Although lawsuits are expensive, almost prohibitively so depending on the dispute, the current glut of attorneys is bringing about changes that only can benefit the general public. Fixed fees and other more consumer-friendly billing approaches are being used by lawyers no matter where they practice law. Even though these aren't widely known, they are being discussed by attorneys, even recommended by bar associations to their membership. The new value-billing approaches, along with how to get them, are discussed in detail in this book.

Even in this litigious environment, there still are a number of ways people can safeguard their assets. Preventive steps can be taken to lessen the risks of entering into the litigation abyss. These are simple steps that are only a matter of common sense, whether it's taping an exposed electrical wire or knowing what your insurance covers before there's a problem. The beginning chapters address what's within your control.

There are a number of areas people neglect in their everyday lives or in which they have difficulties that can end up involving expensive attorneys, stress, and hits on their wallet—all avoidable if handled differently in the first place. Whether it's when the IRS sends you an audit letter, you're thinking about a living trust for estate planning reasons, or having temporary financial problems, there are tips and approaches to take that can save you tens of thousands of dollars, or more, in costs and legal fees.

The beginning and middle chapters of this book outline hundreds of ways to minimize legal fees, stress, and problems in these everyday areas—whether it concerns the running of your business, hiring a contractor, or buying insurance. As part of this, a number of questions are discussed and answered. When do you need an attorney or should you do-it-yourself? How do you find the right attorney at the right cost? What should you do when facing the problems that happen to everyday people?

If you're now facing a lawsuit or a dispute, whether you've had experience before with attorneys before or not, then go directly to Chapter 14 and on. The costs and whether you win or lose depend many times on what you do in the very beginning. You need to decide how important the lawsuit is, whether it involves your business or personal life, and whether to handle it yourself. These considerations are set forth at Chapter 15 and on.

However, you can make decisions which turn out horribly simply because you haven't been through the system before, relying entirely on your attorney, or weren't familiar with what was going on. There are alternatives to solving your dispute, not involving the slow, expensive approach taken by our civil courts, and Chapter 16 should be turned to directly in that event. Finding the right litigation attorney is explained, and what to do immediately after being sued, in the following chapter.

It turns out that many people, even after being billed by a lawyer or going through the courts before, swear that they'll never go through that headache again. However, they find themselves once more in a similar predicament, this time with a different problem and different facts. The ways to avoid the unpleasant cost surprises and specific litigation cost-control tips are presented in the last chapters, along with a discussion of your consumer rights and what to do if your current attorney has done a lousy joy or has billed you an out-of-this-world amount.

In short, this book is the product of years of experience, interviews with experienced attorneys in specific areas, and hundreds of client and lawyer observations. If you have any need for legal services, or think you might, then this book has been written for you, the client and consumer who pays the bills.

This book is not intended to give legal advice for any particular problem, situation, person, or entity, and you are specifically advised to consult the expert opinion of legal counsel and/or a tax professional for your specific questions. This is what lawyers call a disclaimer. And they're needed now.

Acknowledgments

Although the opinions in this book are solely the responsibility of the author, this is to thank Sandra Caton, Dennis Iden, Stewart Holden, Chuck Harris, Bill Paynter, Myles Dresslove, and Bob Smith, all of whom reviewed certain chapters with insightful comments and invaluable, professional help. Peggy Smart, David Chambers, Jean Hopeman, Patt Wardlaw, Ed Powers, and George Forrester, also reviewed the manuscript, and I am grateful for their assistance. I wish to thank my agent, Jeanne Fredericks, and my editor, Frank Darmstadt, who were supportive from the very beginning in making this project a reality. This is also to thank the hundreds of clients and friends who over the years provided the stories, impetus, and experiences that ended up in this book and have ended up helping others. There are too many to name, and you know who you are. My best to all.

Contents

The Continuing Crisis

The courts are used now to solve every imaginable type of problem with the cases litigated reaching into areas rarely considered in years past. Lawsuits are filed against vacation-property owners and summer camps in rural areas over insect bites, whether by a bee or a tick with Lyme disease. Fights over the valuation of frequent flyer programs occur in divorces and disputes with the airlines. Litigation takes place over who owns the rights to sunken treasure underneath the sea or who was at fault when a high school or college student becomes injured or sick. Hotels are suing when group reservations are canceled.

People sue over as many rights as they feel they own, whether it's logging trees or leaving the forests alone, not smoking or smoking, not smelling perfume, the right to a particular job, or even over a baby conceived by another. This isn't to say such rights aren't important, because they are. The problem is that this depends on which side you're on with both sides feeling they're right. However insubstantial a case may be, a lawyer can be found to file a lawsuit.

There are over 20 million civil lawsuits now filed annually in this country's state courts (including divorce, probate, and small claims court cases)—up from 14 million a decade ago. Because of our highly individualistic society and our proportionally much larger number of attorneys, there are 30 times as many lawsuits per capita in the United States as in Japan. Nearly one-half of the companies in various surveys report having discontinued at least one product line specifically because of concerns over product liability lawsuits.

Lawyers in turn have been battling an image problem for years—not, as might be expected, as the consequence of taking on unpopular positions for clients but, rather, for the size of their bills. An American Bar Association-commissioned survey, conducted by Peter D. Hart Research Associates in 1993, found that the more contact people have with lawyers, the less favorably they look upon them. The major complaints about attorneys were that they made too much money (63% of those surveyed), were greedy (59%), and charged excessive fees (55%). People aged

45 to 59, the upper middle class, those with high incomes, the highly educated, and those understanding the legal system were the most likely to view attorneys and the legal system negatively.

"What do I think about our legal system? I think the only way you win is to stay out of it," observed one college instructor who had been through the courts. "If I had known it would cost me three times more and take that much longer to sue from what my attorney had first estimated, I wouldn't have started the lawsuit, much less continued on with it," concluded a veteran of the legal wars. "When I was sued, I felt like a victim. I discovered how easy it is to find lawyers and file lawsuits, whether the case has merit or not. None of this has to do about fairness," said another. Experiences such as these have become commonplace in a legal system and society seemingly out of control—indeed, they have reached crisis proportions.

Nor is this crisis a recent development. The number of civil cases filed in federal courts over a 40-year period increased five times faster than the US population. The number of civil cases filed in state courts increased twice as fast. However, the federal court filings were based on the 40-year period ending in 1980, and the number of state court filings was only for the 10-year period ending in 1975. Since then, the number of lawsuits has continued to spiral upwards without abatement and doubled again.

Groups of trial attorneys routinely target areas for litigation in their meetings, swapping experiences on expert witnesses, common defenses, and settlements. Specialized litigation groups have been formed to focus on such targets as dentists, pharmacists, computer vendors and even manufacturers of bicycles and car batteries. Class action suits, generating lucrative fees for the attorneys with expectations for the claimants, are brought in every possible field from water hookups, checking account fees, and trust management to business acquisitions and sales of securities. "Fear of being sued keeps companies in check from making bad products or taking the public for granted," said one litigator, repeating an argument used often by the trial attorneys. "You do make a lot of money, as well. It's why I'm there," the attorney admitted when questioned further.

The magnitude of the legal costs following these increases in the number of lawsuits is staggering. Legal scholars researching the area of torts (the "wrongful" act by one party against another or property) have concluded that the legal and compensation costs for such claims and litigation is well in excess of $100 billion each year. This staggering sum doesn't even include the unnecessary laboratory testing and medical precautions taken by health care providers to protect themselves from lawsuits. According to a Tillinghast study, tort costs (including legal defense, claims handling, and administrative costs) have risen 400 times since 1933, four times faster than the overall economy.

Not limited to negligence claims, the litigation explosion continues to be fueled over time by three basic factors—the ever-increasing numbers of laws at the local, state, and federal level creating even more rights; the "me too" or "I'm a victim" complex prevalent in our society; and the number of attorneys beating the bushes trying to earn a good living.

The Laws

As if the spiraling increase in the number of laws, regulations, and codes being enacted every year by legislatures and governmental agencies (whether federal, state, or local) weren't enough, the loose drafting of these laws further complicates the problem. Although the intent of these statutes is to protect the overall good of society, whether by prohibiting sexual harassment or increasing environmental protection, the problem is that these laws are broadly defined using words such as "good faith," "reasonable under all the circumstances," and "not unduly burden-some,"—all terms subject to varying interpretations depending on the particular facts. Attorneys, who are paid to argue any position equally well, then use these ambiguities in their lawsuits for results never intended by the legislators.

For example, the Superfund (or the "Comprehensive Environmental Response, Compensation, and Liability Act") was created by Congress to identify and clean up environmentally hazardous waste sites. Considered a controversial program since its inception, the Superfund has been dubbed another "retirement program for the attorneys" by its critics. Cases such as that of the Girl Scouts who had disposed of garbage into a campsite dumpster, without knowing someone else had dumped contaminated waste there also, litter our courts. Often, purchasers of property, whether individuals or small businesses, buy land only to discover the previous owner has left behind wastes covered by the Superfund's provisions. The legal expenses in the battle over who is responsible for these costs usually are more costly than the cleanup or even the value of the land. What is clear in study after study is that the attorneys have made more money over cases such as these than has been used to clean up the environment.

"Me too" and Victims

We live in a society marked by dissension and disagreement. The development of a "me too" attitude that denies even the possibility of one's own culpability has become prevalent. It's always the other person's fault. People are less likely to take responsibility for their actions, and the chance to make some money (when guided by an agreeable lawyer) is rarely turned down, regardless of the reason or cause.

A victim's mentality has developed and become pervasive in this country. Rather than saying "that's life," when confronted by adversity—or even petty inconvenience—people are suing instead, saying they've become a victim through the actions of someone else. People have lost their sense of humor or ability to put things in perspective, and often hurt feelings, rather than actual damages, have become a legitimate reason for suing. Parents of third graders are suing other kids, teachers, and school boards on grounds of sexual harassment over what was considered normal playground behavior 10 years ago. People today don't take "no" for an answer when a club, school, company, or civic organization says they aren't being admitted. It is the group or organization that is somehow at fault, and the denial becomes a matter to be litigated.

Everyone wants equal rights (a very laudable concept), but equality means different things to different people. Some feel equality means being able to walk nude down the middle of the street; others feel equality means being given a student loan (whether they're qualified or not). Attorneys love it when others feel they've become victims and walk into their offices—it generates business, and more business means more money. Everybody wins except society. "Vexatious lawsuits and frivolous litigation have become a respectable venture in this country," commented one defendant who beat off a marginal lawsuit at considerable expense.

My favorite case concerns the individual who applied as a transfer student to a midwestern university, requesting that the school ignore his D average because he had a learning disability. When his application was rejected, he sued the university for $500,000 for pain and suffering, alleging that the university had violated his rights as a disabled person under the Americans With Disabilities Act ("ADA"). Another person alleged that her pet iguana had suffered a broken back when under a veterinarian's care and sued for $1 million as compensation for the emotional stress she suffered. A football player sued his university for not letting him be the starting quarterback as allegedly promised.

Or how about the injured passenger in a car accident who wanted to bring a lawsuit against someone to pay for her medical expenses. Although difficult to prove, it appeared that a tire on the car blew out. She couldn't bring an action against the car's driver because he didn't have any money or insurance. Her attorney thought about suing the car manufacturer (the entity with deep pockets) on a negligent design of tire theory, but a later investigation proved that the design was more than adequate. So she decided to sue the only person left, arguing that the last person who had serviced the car was responsible for the accident by not keeping the tire pressure high enough.

In fact, "Searching for people with assets to get is as important as determining who could be at fault," observed one astute trial attorney. There is a provision in the law called *joint and several liability*. This means that if you're proven to be at fault to any extent then you can be held responsible for all the damages. For example, if you had lent your car to someone who later became drunk and caused an accident, you could have a problem. If an attorney could prove you were 10% responsible under that state's laws (let's say, the attorney argued successfully that you knew the driver would drink, whether that was correct or not), then you could be held responsible for *all* the damages. Theoretically, you could sue for contribution against the driver, but if there were no assets, you would be out of luck.

Then there is *comparative negligence*. Even the greater negligence or fault of the person suing isn't a bar to recovery. For example, the drunk who crashes a car and sues the manufacturer alleging the car wasn't safely designed can still prevail (although the amount of damages caused by the drunk's conduct won't be awarded). In years past, the contributory negligence (or the fault of the person suing that contributed to the cause of the accident), could be a complete bar to any recovery. That isn't the case now.

Suing others has even become a way to earn a living for a few. One such person filed over 30 lawsuits in 15 years, alleging injury from personal assaults, automobile accidents, and falls on store floors, among other claims. A disgruntled businessman sued over 40 defendants, including the state's Attorney General, policemen, detectives, and county officials over his arrest and conviction for carrying a concealed weapon, blaming that conviction (among other reasons) for his business downfall.

Litigation isn't about fairness or jobs or what's in the best interest of this country. It's about attorneys earning the best living they can. It's about clients and people who want to be compensated for their injuries, slights, and misfortunes, no matter how unrealistic or small. It's also about doing whatever you can to avoid becoming another victim of this process.

The Ever-Increasing Numbers

It's no secret the number of attorneys has been increasing; however, the extent of this growth is surprising, even to lawyers. The proportion of attorneys to the general population, historically constant since 1860, has skyrocketed over the last 20 years to the point where there is now one lawyer for every 300 people in the United States—double what the ratio was a generation ago. The American Bar Association counted 325,000 lawyers just 20 years ago, 540,000 in 1980, and 750,000 in 1990—a growth rate of 40% in the last decade alone.

But let's not stop there. There were over 900,000 attorneys in 1994, and the best estimate is that there will be more than 1,100,000 by the year 2,000. The numbers continue upwards, driven by the 35,000 law students who graduate each year, attracted by the high income potential of the profession.

Even the number of law schools has increased over the last 10 years, and applications to law schools have increased as well, averaging over 85,000 each year. Law schools don't limit their enrollments, and state bar associations don't dare employ stricter admission tests because of the number of lawsuits filed by prospective attorneys. Over three-fourths of the attorneys polled in a recent California Bar poll answered "yes" to the question, "Are there too many lawyers in the United States?"

Where Are They?

Not all attorneys work in private practice. A California Bar survey indicated that 14% of its members worked for the government, and 7% were corporate in-house attorneys. Nationally, it's estimated that two-thirds of all attorneys are in private practice.

Not surprisingly, lawyers are unequally distributed across the country— North and South Dakota, as expected, have less than 10,000 each, whereas 139,000 (or nearly one in seven) practice in California. The number of attorneys in California alone grew by 42% in 5 years, according to the California Bar Association. The thickest congregation of lawyers is in Washington, D.C., which, if it were a state, would rank seventh in lawyer population. Concentrations are found in the states of New York, Texas, and Illinois, in addition to California, which isn't surprising given their large metropolitan areas.

This doesn't mean that less-populated states don't have concentrations of attorneys. The migration of citizens and companies to Washington, Oregon, Colorado, Idaho, Texas, Montana, and various southern states has been accompanied by increased numbers of lawyers, as well. There are few states that haven't experienced an increased growth in attorneys on a per capita basis.

The Roaring '80s Led to the Scrambling '90s

To understand what's happening now, you only need to look back at the roaring '80s. It was an unreal time—a decade that produced many sloppily structured, bloated businesses, which included the law firms that had grown fat on their work. Those times are over with the following downsizing by businesses and companies bringing about a similar decrease in the legal business once enjoyed by the attorneys. As the legal work declined and numbers of lawyers increased, a nationwide consolidation also took place in the legal industry.

Downsizing became the in-house "buzz word" for powerful law firms as well as for their clients. Law firms shed lawyers and paralegals, froze salaries, and splintered into smaller firms. Firm after firm reduced ranks, consolidated, or even disappeared as their attorneys left or were forced out. Eighty per cent of large law firms had associate layoffs, and 50% had some layoff of partners in 1992. Ninety-five per cent of *those* firms had *already* laid off associates (with over 50% having laid off partners) in the prior year as well. As just one example, Johnson & Gibbs had more than 300 attorneys at the end of 1990. By the beginning of 1993, the Dallas, Texas law firm had reduced its size to barely 200 lawyers by reducing hiring, laying off both partners and associates, and general attrition. A Philadelphia law firm similarly reduced from over 155 attorneys to 75.

Law firms did more than reduce staff. They stretched how long it takes to become a partner, pressured for more billable hours, raided competitors for specialized partners, hired marketing and public relations directors, and worked harder to please clients with better service and more competitive rates. They diversified by expanding into non-legal businesses, such as consulting, escrow closings, and tax advice. Law firms are now managed as any other business, diving into bankruptcy when times get tough and suing one another over who has to pay the bills.

Lawyers and their firms, even with the national economic recovery continuing during 1994, showed they realized that higher productivity and work efficiency was the key to higher profits. The average profits per partner at the largest law firms increased 3.5% during 1993, which was the best result since 1989. This increase has been attributed to the better use of computer technology and the cuts in costs and people made in previous years, but the result was accomplished with less attorneys—not through price or total billable hour increases. In fact, various law firms have reported that their hourly rates haven't been increased for 3 to 4 years and that some cutbacks in personnel were still occurring in 1994. The legal profession will never be the same.

There's Competition Now

Income-squeezed law firms, who once specialized in defense or litigation on behalf of their clients in specific areas, now work both sides of the fence—they'll defend or sue for anyone who can pay the bill. Law firms are scrambling for clients, and marketing has become a high priority. Attorneys are bombarded with articles and seminars on "How to Improve Short Term Profits," "How to Survive the Legal Recession," "How to Successfully Market Your Practice," and "Improving Your Cash

Flow." The role of the law firm marketing director has expanded, and cost consultants are being hired by small and large law firms alike. Law firms have even banded together into marketing associations.

Partners are pitching themselves in practice sessions, even requiring weekend work sessions to learn the basics on winning and wooing new clients in every state. Sales training, public relations, and advertising firms are being retained by law firms for advice on gaining new clients. Attorneys use brochures, public relations and advertising companies, seminars, mass mailings (depending on what their state bar allows), and mass media advertising in newspapers and on radio and television to find new clients. The legal business is just that—a business.

Lawyers are analyzing their computer systems and usage in the quest to become more cost effective. In the "good old days," attorneys could simply send one-line bills for six-figure amounts. Now, law firms are being questioned on their billings, being forced to submit detailed bills, estimate budgets and plans, and are increasingly having to submit bids for the business of large companies. Lawyers are now being forced by their clients to be more accountable for cost, quality, and time efficiencies.

The economic downsizing of law firms in combination with increasing numbers of new attorneys has resulted in increased competition for jobs across the country at law firms, in the government, and in public-interest entities. Lawyers are working as "temp-attorneys" for law firms and companies with only a temporary need for more staffing. When the particular project or case they are working on is completed, they're back out looking for work. Temporary employment agencies similar to those that service secretarial skills have sprung up that specialize in legal placements from San Francisco to New York City. It is increasingly difficult for newly admitted lawyers to secure work or establish a successful practice.

At the same time, low-price legal clinics, legal plans, and the do-it-yourself movement have all invaded the traditional practice of law. Cut-rate legal clinics have adopted volume discount pricing in their marketing, hoping that more profitable business will be generated by clients with personal injury or more complex needs. The attorneys retained are generally employees, are paid a salary, and can be fired as any other worker.

The growth of legal plans continues, as more attorneys arrive but try to hold onto high hourly charges. Legal plans offer prepaid legal services, usually charging a small monthly fee, which allow a purchaser to use a minimum amount of time for consultations and services. Anything over these limits is charged a lower hourly rate, sometimes one-half of that charged on the going market by other attorneys. The lawyers with such plans are typically sole practitioners who reduce their normal hourly rates to gain more work through the plan.

The rise of the do-it-yourself market has been evidenced by both books and seminars. Although the movement was first oriented toward "writing your own will," "doing your own divorce," and "how to win in small claims court," the subjects have escalated into actual estate planning, federal income tax matters, suing in higher courts other than just small claims, collecting judgments, and other complex areas. The advantage generally cited is being able to avoid the cost of expensive lawyers. The disadvantage is that the law by itself is complicated—reading difficult subjects and taking the time to do what is recommended, especially if you have a good paying job, may not be worth the time. You could also make a critical mistake.

This competition for business, added to the current legal surplus, results in a boon for the consumer. There's a greater pool of qualified and specialized attorneys for the price and work needed to be done. You just need to persist in finding and negotiating with the attorneys who want your business.

Consumer-Oriented Value Billing

The survey results and public complaints haven't fallen on deaf ears. The American Bar Association and individual state bar associations are recommending that attorneys use more consumer-oriented or value billing approaches with their clients. One midwestern bar association panel told its closed-door membership that they needed "to think more about what the client wanted or run the risk of not being paid." Two thousand miles to the west, a California continuing education meeting concluded with the warning that, "consumer-oriented billing isn't the wave of the future. It's what smart attorneys are doing now."

In fact, value billing (fixed price contracts, blended rates, and modified contingent fees with lower costs) are being used in many situations by law firms and their larger volume clients in place of the open-ended, fixed fee. Smaller law firms and sole practitioners are using fixed fees for matters that previously weren't subject to such cost limitations.

When supply overtakes demand, the consumer benefits. Clients want value, and value is determined by the price they're willing to pay or the method of billing used—not the law firm's open-ended, uncertain hourly cost. Firms are being forced to sell their services on the basis of value to the client rather than solely on providing a service without regard to cost.

This doesn't mean that law firms and lawyers don't try holding to the open-ended hourly rate—they do, regardless of where they are. They will still try to bill for one hour's work at a rate that is more than some people can make in one day. However, as attorneys compete harder for a shrinking market, there will be those who would rather work for less than stare out the window with nothing to do.

Not only is value billing motivated by increased competition; it's also brought about as law firms become more cost efficient. A cost-efficient law firm is motivated to use fixed-fee billing when it can produce the service in less time. Drafting a contract that once took 20 hours, but can now be completed now in 10 by using standard provisions and a systematic approach to word processing, is more easily quoted on a fixed-fee basis.

Fee competition will increase further as clients treat legal services more and more as a commodity. "I know that I will lose business if I don't take into account what my clients can afford or will pay. It wasn't like that 5 years ago," commented one seasoned attorney. The sophistication of clients, coupled with increased cost efficiencies of law firms, will move lawyers to emphasize value billing over standard hourly rate billing over time.

The benefits of such legal competition and bidding wars, now experienced by larger companies and wealthy individuals, are possible even for the smallest consumer of legal services. The practice of using a fixed fee for simple wills, collection matters, and uncomplicated divorces already is filtering into more complex matters and litigation. There is definitely a buyer's market for legal services if you know what to do and carefully shop around.

ADRs Are Becoming More Widely Used

Despite "fast track" civil litigation procedures (the rules requiring lawsuits to move faster through the system), the courts have become bogged down by the rash of cases, especially criminal and drug-related ones, that have flooded the system. Because of the priority for speedily determining the charges against an accused, civil cases are repeatedly bounced by the more-important criminal cases to be heard in the future. The courts, with overburdened judges, overworked staff, and limited funds rarely are able to afford modern technology and can't dispense efficient, fair justice.

The increase in delays, expenses, and complexities of litigation has brought about the increased use of mediation, arbitration, and other ADRs (alternative dispute resolution techniques) which are quicker and more cost efficient. The accelerated growth of ADRs has forced the larger law firms to create such departments and gain expertise in this area for competitive reasons alone. If you live in any metropolitan area, or close to one, it would be uncommon not to have attorneys and firms specializing in providing ADR services. It's simply a question of time before most disputes will be forced to be decided by these approaches, given the distinct disadvantages of litigation as a way to resolve disputes.

Specialization and the Quest for Growth

The need to specialize has increased, regardless of whether attorneys work for a law firm or practice by themselves. The law is too sophisticated and complex for any one attorney to understand its many different areas. The number of attorneys practicing alone, historically about one-half of all lawyers, has decreased because of the increasing complexities of the law and the need to share rising overhead. The increase in numbers of law firms, in turn, has allowed attorneys to specialize further in narrower fields within such firms.

The quest for growth today is similar to prospecting in a gold rush. As merger and acquisition, real estate development, and business contract work declined, law firms and attorneys began marketing aggressively into the newer growth areas of bankruptcy, environmental law, technology, international law, and elder or "senior citizen" law. This further forced attorneys to specialize in one field over another. Litigation continues to increase, as lawyers and clients create more theories or causes of action, regardless of the economic times.

However, as one "hot" area begins to cool down as a result of the numbers of attorneys entering that market, the lawyers search for other areas in their quest for business gold. The practical realities of practicing law, unfortunately, very rarely involve issues of justice. "Justice is whether you win or lose when you're the client. It's getting paid when you're the attorney," observed one client who had several experiences with lawyers. This is a business, after all.

Attorneys Are Seeing the Picture

Prospective lawyers continue to be attracted in large numbers by the money that can be made. It isn't until later that they experience the long hours, personal sacrifice, and bruising conflict inherent in this way of earning a living. However, the average income of those who practice law is leveling off, and the profession is turning out to be a less desirable way to earn a good living. Midcareer change counseling is offered by various bar associations and fee-charging consultants alike as one response to this phenomenon.

Eighty-one percent of the respondents to a California State Bar survey found the use of hardball tactics and uncivil behavior growing among attorneys. Seventy per cent answered "Yes" to the question: "If you had an opportunity to start a new career now, would you take it?" Only one-third of the respondents to a recent American Bar Association survey indicated themselves to be completely satisfied with the practice of law. One lawyer put it succinctly: "Look at the numbers of attorneys with drug abuse, alcohol abuse, and divorce problems. You'd think that many of them don't like their jobs."

Yet the number of attorneys who leave the profession each year doesn't significantly offset the large numbers of law school graduates who arrive each year—it takes courage to leave the high income potential for a more peaceful existence. This writer personally knew lawyers who left the profession to become a cabinet maker, an antique store operator, a commercial real estate developer, an author, a legal expense auditor, a bed-and-breakfast owner, a sales representative, a community fund raiser, an investment banker, and to take various business or executive positions. Since the market for legal services is already oversaturated, these lawyers only kept the surplus from swelling even more.

Balancing the Problem

The problem is real. Litigation continues to increase, and every individual or family will be faced by at least one legal controversy that threatens personal assets during a lifetime. Like it or not, you will need to deal with an attorney at some time, and this can be expensive—whether it's a divorce, over financial problems, or when someone else blames you for his or her problems. Nearly two-thirds of those surveyed in the 1993 American Bar Association study had retained a lawyer for at least one legal matter during the past 10 years.

The changes that have taken place in the legal profession are extraordinary and extensive. The wide use of computerization, paralegals (nonattorneys used for legal services), and advertising gives back some power to the consumers. The increasing number of attorneys, decline in the proportion of general practitioners and rise of the specialist, growth of cut-rate legal clinics, and heightened consumer awareness are changing the old ways of billing—the open-ended, hourly rate is being replaced by more consumer-oriented billing practices.

The softness of the market for legal services is both a boon and a bust. Attorneys eager for work take those cases at the bottom of the barrel that should be left alone. On the other hand, clients can negotiate with them over their fees.

What Happens

Although people blame attorneys, judges, and legislators for creating today's risky legal environment, it is also as much their own fault. Since many aren't willing to take responsibility for their own acts and even want to earn a little more money given the opportunity, the game of sue or be sued continues. Other than the devastating effects this has on those ensnared in the courts (including the growing risks of being caught yourself), the effects are seen further in the increasing costs and unavailability of insurance coverage, among other consumer problems.

You read about another seemingly ridiculous lawsuit in the newspaper and wonder how this could have happened. Let's take a look at two cases that can reveal a few of the reasons.

First, we consider the situation of a teenager whose car is hit by a drunk driver, and whose father is subsequently sued by the drunk driver's estate. Second, we explore the case of an older couple being sued by the younger buyers of their house. The problems shown by these examples occur all too frequently across the country.

The Drunk Driver

The wife of the deceased driver, worried over how to cope with the mounting bills, is consulting with her attorney after the accident. She shows her attorney, Ken, a copy of the accident report. Buried in a section is the notation that the vehicle driven by the teenager "may have been speeding." The wife tells the lawyer that although her late husband did drink now and then after work, she "just couldn't believe Jim would have been drinking that night." This is true—Anne still can't believe her husband is a dead drunk driver. Ken's case load is a little low this month, so he says he'll think about it, calls up another lawyer, and obtains the name of an accident investigator.

Meanwhile, the teenager has recovered from his injuries after a hospital stay. The family is happy their son is now well and that the medical bills are covered by medical insurance. Tony will be able to move back to his apartment, register for his first junior college classes, and begin working again. He had moved just a few months ago to a nearby city to live with a friend after graduating from high school. He loved living close to his parents, and they were on very good terms. It was the all-American family.

The father contacted his insurance agent to see about getting Tony's car replaced—it had been totally wrecked when the drunk ran the red light that night. The agent tells Mr. Stephens that Tony's policy had lapsed because of nonpayment of the premiums. Although not happy with this, Stephens decides to contact an attorney to sue the driver's estate. The attorney tells him she will take the case on a contingency fee, but the father wants to think about that. He didn't like the idea of having to run to a lawyer in the first place, and if it hadn't been a drunk driver who had smashed into his son, he probably would have left it alone. The widow, he was thinking, probably had more than enough problems at that time.

A few weeks later, the accident investigator tells attorney Ken, "The kid was probably speeding. But it was quite likely that drunk Jim was the one who had sped through the red light." Ken isn't interested in the case at this time, primarily because the young driver doesn't have any assets. He's been in the business for 20 years and knows that liability is simply how a jury or judge looks at it; if there's no money to be found, then his time will be wasted. And in this business, time is money.

However, the investigator tells him the car registration was in both the son's and father's name. The father apparently had cosigned his son's bank loan and his name appeared on the title and registration. A sobbing Anne quickly pointed out "that must mean something." Attorney Ken now becomes suddenly interested, as he had been wondering how to find a connection between the accident and someone who had money—after all, business is business.

In this particular state, being on the registration alone was enough reason for Mr. Stephens to have a separate but equal liability for his son's actions. At least, it was enough to get it to the jury. "There must be an insurance policy in force," Ken concludes. "That means there's a way to be paid," he says smiling.

The investigator points out that the high alcohol level in Jim's blood, as shown in the accident report, means he had been drunk when the accident occurred. "Someone made a mistake at that laboratory," Anne immediately protests. "Jim never went drinking on a Wednesday night. He had his Thursday managers' meeting in the morning. There's been a tragic mistake."

Ken has heard enough. "We have a shot at this," he concludes. "Our state allows for comparative negligence...most of them do." Anne and the investigator draw closer. "That means," he continues, "that Jim's negligence, or fault, doesn't mean he....I mean you, Anne, as his closest heir, will be barred from collecting. His fault in being drunk will be proportioned against the fault of that kid, which then goes on to the father. What do you think, Billy, can we reconstruct that the kid drove through the red light on the way home and caused the accident?"

"Bit of a problem, but possible...anything's possible," answered the investigator.

"Which means we contest that Jim was drunk on the night of the accident. The lab made a mistake. We maintain the kid caused the accident by driving through the red light. You know, a jury might hold each of them 50% at fault. Maybe 25% against the kid and 75% against us, if we can't control who gets on the jury. But here's your husband, a vice president at our largest employer in town," he says turning to Anne. "Smashed down in his prime, and you have small children to raise. That can't be allowed. I think a jury would understand that," he says in a quieter voice.

"How much do you think we can get?" Anne says.

"Worth at least a million...maybe two. If we get a verdict that just says Jim was 75% responsible, at one million we get $250,000. With a two million verdict, we get $500,000."

"What do I get if you settle first?" Anne says. It was a practical question.

"Probably less, but enough. There will be more than enough for your kids. My office charges a one-third contingency, which means we get one-third of whatever we get for you, assuming no trial. We get nothing if we can't win something. There are costs, of course, and we'll need to discuss that. If you have some problems in paying, we might be able to loan it against what's received from the settlement. You won't be out a dime. What do you think?"

"Where do I sign?" she asks, looking into her purse for a pen. A standard form agreement is placed in front of her. "Poor Jim," she sighs, as she signs her name. "If he only knew....If he only knew."

The complaint was drafted, filed, and served against the shocked Stephenses. It was only later that Ken discovered there was no insurance, but in conducting an asset check, the attorney discovered the Stephenses had stocks, bonds, and equity in the family home. Anne decided to continue with the action.

The same attorney who would sue Jim's estate on a contingency told the Stephenses she had to charge her normal hourly rate of $200 per hour to defend against Anne's claims. She estimated this cost would be at least $50,000, but she also believed the insurance agent had an obligation to notify the father before the policy lapsed when the son missed the premium payments. There were some problems with this action, because the son had moved to his own place, but it was good legal practice to cover all the bases.

Consequently, she brought a separate suit against the agent and insurance company, telling the family that this would be on contingency with no charge for her time. However, they would need to advance the costs for the depositions, transcripts, witness fees, court costs, and court reporters, which she estimated to be about $15,000. They had the money and readily agreed, because they reasoned that none of this would have happened if the agent had told them when the policy was about to lapse. Mr. Stephens knew he would have paid up the policy.

It was 3 years later, after $75,000 in legal expenses and no resolution of the claims by the widow Anne that Mr. Stephens threw in the towel. The lawsuit against the insurance company had been settled out of court for $35,000, of which $25,000 went to the attorney for costs and her percentage. The remaining $10,000 was paid back to the attorney in partial settlement of the legal fees owed for the defense against the claims of widow Anne. The couple filed for divorce and Mr. Stephens moved out of town.

After selling the family home in a bad real estate market and paying taxes on the gain, there was nothing left. The remaining stocks and bonds had been used to pay for divorce attorneys and some of the remaining bills. There was just enough left over to pay for a Chapter 7 liquidation and eliminate the claims of the widow.

Anne received nothing, and was left feeling bitter about the system and what she considered to be a grave injustice—she had been counting on that money as only fair compensation for losing her husband. Attorney Ken never was reimbursed the $20,000 in costs advanced for accident re-creations, court reporters, depositions, expert witness fees, and court costs. He decided not to pursue that further, as Anne was in no mood to pay these costs and couldn't pay them if she had wanted to.

"It was part of the game," attorney Ken reflected philosophically. "You win some and lose some. But at least my time didn't cost me anything, and I had other paying clients...It was a crap shot. The wife told me the same thing 3 long years ago. But I needed one to pay for the kids' college costs."

Selling a Home

George and Joanne had been looking forward to selling their house and retiring to Arizona. George had just retired from the computer company where he had worked for the last 25 years. The couple listed the home with a real estate agent. When the agent asked them how big the property was, George answered it was "over 2 acres as the crow flies," but he didn't really know. He remembered that was what had been told to them when they had bought it 10 years before. When asked again, he told the agent "2 plus acres." She walked through the house, liked it, and set a sales price of $300,000 for the house and property. It was located in a nice, wooded area and looked down on the twinkling lights of a nearby small city. Although the house was in good condition, and had never caused them problems, the couple decided to repaint the house inside and out to give it "that extra good look" to help market it.

A young couple, Sue and Tim, came through an open house, liked the house, and wanted to see it again. They called up the real estate agent and made an appointment. At the last moment, the agent couldn't make it, and so the couple met with George at the property for a walk-through. Having lived only 3 miles away, Sue and Tim knew the area was subject to sliding and had even backed away from buying a house in the area the month before because of their concerns over soil instability. However this house was different, they decided, as it didn't overlook a cliff.

Joanne was in the kitchen, as George showed Sue and Tim around the property. In response to their questions about the foundations, George proudly showed them his "movable foundation." This was a series of jacks under the house that could be adjusted to keep the house in perfect alignment, whether it was raining outside or not. George was a "tinkerer" and felt that his solution was perfect. It had worked for years without problems since Tom, a soils engineer, had recommended it to them in his report.

Everyone peered underneath the house, although nothing could be seen because of the darkness. Tim asked, "What's a movable foundation?"
"It's adjustable. If you want to realign it, you just adjust down here....No problems, no matter what." He didn't say anything else, because he thought everyone knew that jacks would be involved. They said nothing further and walked on.

The young couple looked around, and liked the property. The house was built on a hill which gently sloped down to a secluded area. It was perfect, but a little small, they thought.

They asked how much property was included, and George answered it was "over 2 acres as the crow flies." They looked at the flyer which said that there were "2 plus acres." The couple bought the house, George and Joanne moved to Arizona, and everything was perfect. Or so everyone thought.

Several months later, Sue and Tim concluded they had bought a lemon. They didn't like it. The house was smaller than they had originally thought and colder during the winter. They liked the first house they had been living in more. To make matters worse, the house creaked at night.

Tim discovered the jacks while looking under the house one Saturday morning. He didn't like that. He didn't know what a movable foundation was, but he never could have imagined it was a series of jacks set at various places underneath the house. Sue became suspicious and called in a surveyor. The surveyor reported that the acreage was 1.3 acres, slightly under one acre if you eliminated a hiking trail easement that went through their property. It looked like two acres, given the small canyon below, but looks were deceiving.

George was surprised to hear from Sue and Tim at first and then became dismayed when he heard their complaints. He had always thought the property was a little over 2 acres and thought they knew about the jacks. Besides nothing ever needed to be done with the jacks except for an adjustment "of an eighth of an inch or so." Sue and Tim angrily and abruptly cut off their conversation.

A friend referred Sue and Tim to an attorney who said this looked like a clear case of fraud. Sue especially worried over the creaking in the house and told the lawyer about the small cracks that were developing inside. "Obviously," the attorney concluded, "the sellers had painted over the cracks to hide the settling in the house. The soil instability was the reason for the jacks. What a crazy thing to do. And to lie about it as well. What crooks."

The lawyer told Sue and Tim he would take the case on a contingency, but they would be responsible for the out-of-pocket costs such as expert witnesses, depositions, and filing fees. He cautioned Tim and Sue that this could be expensive because of the technical nature of the case. George would get his soil expert saying that everything was fine, and they would have to get their expert to give a different conclusion. However, the lawyer was confident they would win, especially since the acreage had been misrepresented. Tim and Sue could elect before trial whether they wanted substantial damages or a rescission whereby George and Joanne would have to take the house back. The real estate agent, her company, the soils engineer (Tom) who had done work 10 years ago on the house, and George and Joanne were all sued by the attorney on behalf of Tim and Sue. All of these people needed to hire lawyers to defend them.

George had a mild heart attack when he received the complaint and summons. He didn't know what to do about the costs of defending this nightmare. Joanne suggested they contact their insurance agent who had sold them their homeowner's policy when they were living in the house. The company's agent wasn't sure whether the policy would apply in this case and turned it over to the carrier for a determination.

After threats by their attorney that they would sue, a settlement was worked out with the carrier. The insurance company would defend the case at its expense under the homeowner's policy, but George and Joanne would assume any out-of-pocket damages awarded by the court or in a settlement. All other parties would be responsible for their own legal costs of defense, sharing in any liability or damages as determined later.

Their attorney advised in the beginning that George and Joanne could rescind the transaction, give back all their money, and take back the house. This was quite early in the lawsuit, before any real expense had been expended by either side on the case. After an agonizing decision, they agreed to let the lawyer make that offer.

Tim and Sue's attorney had warned them that they might not win anything with their lawsuit; however, he also advised, "Depending on what the expert witnesses discover, there could be substantial damages. It's hard to say until we hear back from them. In any event, you should be able to give the house back in return for everything you paid....We got them on that point." Then the offer to rescind the deal came in. Tim and Sue turned the offer down, believing that their monetary damages would be large enough to buy another house, rent out the one they were in, and end up with two houses rather than only the one now owned.

The cracking that had appeared through the new paint wasn't severe, although the experts disagreed over what would happen next. Apparently, the dry seasons and heavier than average rains afterwards had caused more cracking than normal. The expert witnesses on both sides gave their reports, were examined later in depositions (informal questioning and answering under oath in the attorneys' offices), and took potshots at each other's conclusions. They were in total disagreement. A total of four expert witnesses were hired and produced expensive reports. All of the parties were examined in long, extensive depositions.

The case approached the trial date, and the judge in the mandatory settlement conference (the meeting held before trial to determine if the case could be settled) put hard pressure on the attorneys to settle. This meant in turn that the attorneys put pressure on their clients to settle, at least depending on what each lawyer believed to be best for his or her particular client.

George and Joanne—especially George, who seemed to have aged overnight—were worn down by now. George had always lived an honest life, or so he thought, and couldn't believe he was accused of fraud or could be asked such harsh questions.

Tim and Sue had discovered that the engineers now had a bill of $20,000 and that the out-of-pocket costs for a trial would be as much. The risk of not getting anything for their troubles, not to mention the greater than anticipated costs, began looming in their minds.

The attorneys finally arranged their settlement—3 years after Tim and Sue had met first with their attorney. Neither side liked what they heard. The lawsuit would be settled by George and Joanne taking back the house, assuming the bank loan, refunding in total what had been paid down or put into the house by Tim and Sue, including a sum for damages. This monetary package totaled $125,000. The judge approved the settlement, and the defendants began fighting among themselves as to who was responsible for what.

George and Joanne ended up paying $50,000 of this, with the rest assumed by the other defendants. They received the house back, but couldn't sell it without coming up with some system to replace the movable jacks (although this had been working except for the slight cracking). One of the recommendations would cost $175,000 for a permanent solution. The net effect was that when the house was finally sold, George and Joanne had in total (including what was originally received in the sale to Tim and Sue) what they had paid down for the property years ago, not to mention a big bill from their accountants, and the loss of all their equity in the house.

Tim and Sue were unhappy because nothing was received for all that trouble, and they had lost money. Their attorney received $50,000 under the terms of the contingency agreement (which was the "damage" award); they received their $50,000 down payment back without interest; the remaining amount of $25,000 was earmarked for their out-of-pocket expenses. Unfortunately, they would be $10,000 short after paying the engineers.

Every attorney was paid in full. Every other person paid or lost. All except for the savvy old engineer, Tom, who said he couldn't afford an attorney. He represented himself, telling the attorneys he had nothing even if they proved he was somehow at fault, and went about his life. He was never bothered, although he had made the original suggestions to George on what to do about the house. Not having money has its advantages also.

What Could They Have Done?

There are many things about life that can't be changed—accidents do happen, events occur out of our control, and we can't plan the perfect life. However, there are steps people can take in narrowing down the risks and liabilities that face them every day. Much is done every day as a matter of common sense.

In our first case, it would have been nearly impossible to prevent the accident from occurring as it did, unless the father had never allowed his son to drive. However, he should have checked on the insurance policy coverage for his son, who surely knew that his policy had lapsed and should have alerted his father. It's true there are a lot of "should haves" and "could haves" here—most lawsuits involve them.

The father could have anticipated the risk of not having insurance and checked on it. He could have called a lawyer and asked about the problems in that state with co-registration with a teenaged driver. The father could have told his son to give him the money to pay for the insurance. He could have sent a letter to the agent, putting the agent on notice to alert him if the son missed a payment—all this would have made his case against the agent and carrier stronger.

In the second case, the homeowners could have hired a home inspection service for a report concerning what was needed to be disclosed or fixed up on the house. They could have shown such a report to the buyers. George should have gone out of his way to ensure that any buyers knew as much as possible about the house before they bought it. He should have put all of these disclosures in writing. Although this can cause problems when selling a house, it is better to make such written disclosures than to go through what George did in his retirement years.

Further, George shouldn't have assumed nothing could go wrong in the sale of the house, especially given its importance to his retirement plans, and he should have taken steps to safeguard the sale from any problems. Although George could have checked ahead as to whether the homeowner's policy covered the sale of their home, the problem is these policies typically don't cover fraud or misrepresentation—a central part of the complaint made by Tim and Sue's attorney.

All parties could have been more careful in selecting their attorneys, especially in monitoring the high fees and costs, and they could have pushed for fixed fees or at least estimates to keep the legal fees within acceptable limits. Unfortunately, people tend to pay more attention when shopping for a refrigerator or a home addition than they do to how their attorneys charge in a lawsuit.

Both defendants should have called their attorney in the very beginning to find out how to avoid any problems with a retirement sale or the liability and insurance coverage for a teenager. The "5-minute" phone call could have saved tens of thousands of dollars for both defendants.

Another critical area lay for both defendants in not realizing the weaknesses of their cases. Tim and Sue became captivated by making more money. If they had accepted the initial offer to take back the house, they would have come out ahead by not wasting years of emotional agony, getting out of the house much sooner, and having their down payment earning a return for that time. It's possible they would have received more by countering the original offer when it was first made. Although Mr. Stephens was caught in the system, he might have been better off saving his money by declaring bankruptcy before incurring large legal bills, a lot of stress, and a divorce.

What Can Be Done?

There are a number of techniques that can be used by people to take control over these problems rather than simply becoming victims. They involve several basic areas and a variety of techniques, all of which are discussed in detail throughout this book.

The Basic Control Areas

✔ Anticipating problems in advance and taking preventive steps.
✔ Utilizing cost-effective insurance.
✔ Hiring the attorney before there's a problem.
✔ Being sure agreements are in writing and understood before signing.
✔ Not ignoring taxes and your estate matters.
✔ Knowing what to do when times become tough.
✔ Understanding what can be done with common business problems.
✔ Realizing the times when you should hire a lawyer.
✔ Managing your attorney and costs when you do hire a lawyer, including those costs for your business.
✔ Knowing what to do when faced with a potential legal problem.
✔ Understanding how to find the right litigation attorney and to control these costs tightly.
✔ Understanding what can be done if you lose a lawsuit.

Anticipate Some of the Areas

Anticipating problem areas doesn't mean sitting up at night, worrying about the ways attorneys and clients can get into your bank accounts should something go wrong. It means taking common sense steps to lessen the chances of disputes or accidents occurring, whether this involves your family or others. Taking action to remedy problem areas gives you a better case should something happen and there is a lawsuit. There are a number of areas that illustrate this, and you will think about others with your own situation.

It Starts at Home

It makes sense to inspect a house before the purchase. Walk through at least twice looking for what you'll have "to live with," inspecting carefully all wiring, plumbing, bathrooms, roof, and other likely problem areas. Look carefully at the land, fences, trees, and shrubs for any evidence of flooding, erosion, slides, and even where children could play and become injured.

Your real estate agent probably recommended that you hire a professional, whether a roofer, termite inspector, or home inspection service before buying your house. Realtors have checklists to use in identifying areas to watch out for in your locality. Rather than listening to the owner's claims as to how great the property is, use these checklists and inspections first. The more care taken in knowing the property's condition before purchase, the less problems with repairs afterwards and the less likely the need to consult an attorney. There's no need to take on problems that could have been avoided in the first place.

Look closely in each room and outside for areas a child or pet could get into, especially electrical plugs, exposed wires, pesticides, and flammable materials. Smoke detectors and fire extinguishers should be installed and operable (you may even qualify for a premium reduction on your homeowners policy). Frayed electrical cords and appliances that tend to "short out" need to be repaired or replaced, and draperies shouldn't be next to radiators. Combustible materials such as cleaning solvents and paints shouldn't be stored where a fire or explosion could occur. Electrical and gas appliances need checking to be sure they're in proper working order.

If you already own a house, then it makes sense to inspect it now before there are problems. The same checklists used for purchasing a home can be used for checking out areas when you've been living there for years. Looking for these areas isn't being slightly paranoid; it's simply what should be done anyway. You want your house to be safe for you and your family.

Broken steps, holes in your yard, and any potholes in the driveway should be repaired. If you have a swimming pool or gullies where children could wander in and become hurt, you would want that broken fence or gate to be repaired so no one can come in without permission. Any tree branches overhanging your neighbor's property could be trimmed, and places where the property forces rainfall onto your neighbor's property could be regraded. "Knowing the property inside and out before sale or purchase avoids unpleasant surprises later—especially when you could have used that information to negotiate a better price before," observed one real estate agent.

Home Liability

A common liability problem with home ownership occurs when a workman, guest, or even a trespasser becomes injured on your property. You should check to see where visitors could slip on carpets, walk through clear plate glass windows, "slip and fall," or trip on steps. Although it's impossible to anticipate every way someone could become hurt on your property and sue you, the obvious areas to be repaired would be the ones most likely to cause problems.

The host liquor liability problem creates one of the larger risk areas. The facts are simple—a drunk guest drives away from your party and injures someone else in an automobile accident. You're sued for supplying the drunk with drinks. Although "host liquor" liability laws vary from state to state, the problem is that the liability in such cases is usually greater than the homeowners policy limits (given coverage). This doesn't mean you must stop giving parties where alcohol is served, but you should check on your homeowners policy when you do, as well as keep car keys away from a friend who has had too much to drink. Serving drinks with moderation is always advisable.

Another frequent source of lawsuits is the sale of property to a buyer who discovers problems later. Consider getting a termite or home inspection report before you place your house on the market—knowing about any problems before the buyer does can only help. "The last thing I need is having the buyer contacting me, or suing me, down the road after I've spent the money. Repairing what needs to be done also makes it easier to sell in a bad market," said one owner of several rental properties.

There's a fine line between what you should or shouldn't disclose. If it would be reasonable to assume a problem would occur if a situation is not corrected, then you should disclose it. For example, if your roof has leaked in the past, then obviously that should be disclosed *if the leak hasn't been repaired.* The problem is that people don't do this, since they don't have the money or feel it would jeopardize the sale. In such a case, you should find a good lawyer.

Different People

"Some people seem to always end up in disputes and problems. They blow up, swear, and make everything worse. Sometimes a simple apology could have ended the matter in the beginning. But these people are never wrong and want to get even...and get into another lawsuit," said one lawyer matter-of-factly. If you have bad relationships with neighbors, then it's only a matter of time before something boils over, especially when someone has a hot temper. But having bad relationships with your neighbors doesn't have to be that way. Unless they're always out of control, you could "let bygones, be bygones." Or ignore the S.O.B. Although this is easier said than done, it can preserve the neighborhood peace.

If you have a teenaged driver, then there are special risks. The statistics indicate that it's far more likely a teenaged driver will have an accident than older parents (and the costs of the premiums paid bear this out). You'll want to set rules on the driving of the car as well as take the keys away if these rules are violated.

If you own a dog that has nipped at you before, then you shouldn't be surprised when it bites a neighbor's child. People love their animals, and this is another hard situation. However, at a minimum, you'll need to keep these pets isolated when problems are suspected.

Check Your Insurance

The ownership of property by itself, whether a house, car, or rental units, creates areas of personal liability. This liability exists whether the ownership is by an individual, business, or nonprofit organization. Although you want a safe house and car and rental properties that don't create problems, this doesn't always turn out to be the case. You can inspect and repair areas brought to your attention, but then an unexpected injury occurs. Someone trips on the carpet in your office. Or your dog bites a neighbor without warning.

Attorneys these days aren't letting the marginal cases pass by—there are too many attorneys and not enough good cases. Lawyers are in the business to make money, and they can be very creative when thinking up new areas of liability when there's money to be made.

That is why having adequate insurance coverage in place is so important, whether at home or in your business. Although insurance is covered in the next chapter, you'll need to be sure the appropriate property damage and liability coverage is in place for all owned or leased assets. As a preventive measure, all insurance policies should be reviewed to ensure coverage is in force and adequate in terms of current replacement cost, including any additions and remodeling. Umbrella or excess liability insurance coverage should be considered should you have assets needing protection.

If you receive an invoice or a change on your coverage that you don't understand, then take the time to call your insurance agent and discuss what's happening. Insurance companies make mistakes too. If you own rental properties and sell one, for example, then review the paperwork received from the insurance company as to the cancellation. You don't want to discover that the agent or company canceled the insurance coverage on the wrong property, and you've just had a loss on the retained property.

If You're Renting

The same approach can be used when you're renting. Although problems with unreasonable people can't be avoided, there are steps that can be taken. First, be sure you can afford the place you are looking at. Then, do a walk-through with the landlord before moving in, writing down what you accept and what the landlord promises to repair. Note any damages down so that you won't be held responsible for that later.

A written lease agreement should be discussed and signed by both parties. This would set down the rent, utility payment responsibility, cleaning deposit (including whether it's refundable), security deposit, who makes repairs, and the other concerns that everyone has when moving into a new place. Any additional landlord rules and regulations that are agreed upon should also be in writing, so that the lease sets down the entire understanding between both landlord and tenant. If you are using a form lease, then be sure that all the blanks are filled.

You should consider purchasing renter's insurance. Confirm everything in writing, whether you agree to paint the house for one month's reduced rent or the landlord agrees to a pet living in the house. It doesn't take much time to do this, and taking these steps does minimize later problems.

Your Outside Activities

Unfortunately, individuals these days must be careful with their volunteer activities. Whether it's a fund-raiser or a civic outing, more and more lawsuits these days involve ordinary citizens simply helping out their community. This liability can be personal and attach against your individual assets. As the first line of defense against this is insurance, then be sure the organization has sufficient liability insurance in place to cover your activities. Such insurance not only covers liability (pursuant to the policy), it also includes the cost of your legal defense (again, subject to the provisions).

If you serve on the board of directors of an organization, then review the insurance coverage very carefully. Being on the board of directors makes an especially tempting target for lawyers and their injured clients. For example, if the board of directors gave the okay for a fund-raiser where someone was injured, you can bet that the directors will be sued individually (as well as the charity) for that decision. Why? Attorneys like to sue as many people as have some connection to the accident. A few might have "deep pockets," and this means more pressure to settle on more favorable terms. As one trial attorney commented, "The more people added to the lawsuit, the more likely the attorney and client gets something in return for all the effort."

The problem is that affordable insurance in many cases isn't available for these organizations and their sponsors. If there's no available insurance coverage, then you either assume the risk or don't work for the charity or civic organization. However, before you decide not to volunteer your time or decline that offer of board membership, you might consult an attorney as to the risks and what is generally done about covering liability problems in your particular situation.

Personal Finances

If you pay attention to your personal finances, then problems with creditors and dealing with attorneys can also be controlled. A review of your finances informally on a quarterly basis and in more detail at least every 6 months should be conducted to be sure everything's on track, no matter how much or little you earn. By monitoring income, expenses, bank borrowings, and credit card usage, you can cut back before it is too late. You need to react quickly when what's coming in isn't equal to what's going out.

By not putting all your saving eggs in one basket, maintaining a liquid "rainy day" fund, and watching your lifestyle, it's possible to keep the necessary control over your finances. Obtain credit cards and unsecured credit *before* you need them—but don't use them unless you're in a financial crunch. In these times, however, financial problems can occur no matter what you do. When such problems do occur, cut your expenses to the bone (and see Chapter 10 for further details).

Avoid the "I can't believe it's real" investment or "get rich schemes." If it sounds too good to be true, then it usually is. Should you want a financial counselor or investment advisor, remember choosing one carefully saves consulting an attorney later. As financial planners at this time aren't generally required to be licensed (unless they sell stocks, bonds, or limited partnerships on a commissioned basis), you need to rely carefully on the recommendations and experiences that others have had with that person. The education and experience of that financial planner should be discussed candidly. As important is the method of compensation. If the planner is compensated by a commission based upon the product sold to you, then there's a built-in bias to sell those specific products (no matter what he or she says). If that person receives a straight fee for advice, with no "bonuses" for what's sold to you, then this problem can be avoided.

Another illustrative area involves taxes. Advanced tax planning during the year can alert you to potential tax problems that are coming up. You shouldn't wait until the last moment to confer with your accountant as to how much is due—by then it's too late to take any steps to minimize such problems. When considering a major step, such as selling a piece of property or stock, consider the tax consequences before you take that action. Should you spend the money received without knowing how much is owed, you could receive a large tax bill for those transactions later without having the money to pay for it.

Keep detailed records such as receipts, canceled checks, and pictures of casualty losses as long as possible. Document the existence of large deductions as well as can be done—just in case an IRS audit letter is received in the mail.

Remember that the IRS can audit for years past. By staying on top of all tax requests and demands, not ignoring them but following up and trying to solve them, you can avoid the surprise levy. The IRS should be taken seriously—prepare in advance for all meetings and follow the other suggestions discussed in Chapter 8.

Your death also involves the payment of taxes. Estate planning shouldn't be put off, regardless of the size of your estate. It begins with preparing a will and can increase to the use of trusts, powers of attorney, and living wills (see Chapter 9). To avoid later expensive proceedings, costs, legal problems, and taxes, you need to understand what happens in this area. When the subject under consideration is your personal finances, knowledge is definitely power.

Your Business

Personal liabilities from your business can arise in many areas—for example, guaranteeing a business loan separately by personal signature; operating a business as a sole proprietorship or general partnership rather than as a corporation; or being the responsible party in causing business payroll taxes not to be paid. Aside from knowing when to contact an attorney for advice on such areas of personal liability, your business also can practice preventive law. Preventive law is just that—by taking actions before a lawsuit can be brought, you can minimize the likelihood of ending up in court or, if sued, increase your chances of winning the case. An unsolved business problem usually is the reason for a business lawsuit. Let's say you're experiencing constant turnover with your work force. If you simply

A Matter of Common Sense

The area of anticipating legal problems is one involving common sense. When you do things that just make sense, usually you're taking steps that preclude legal problems. Let's say you're living with someone. If you wrote an agreement now, signed by both of you, as to who was responsible for what bills and who owned what, there would be fewer hassles should you split up later. Fewer hassles means it's less likely expensive attorneys need to be hired later. Such steps also increase your chances of winning should you be sued.

Although it's impossible to guard against everything that happens in life, at least dealing with what's controllable can make your life easier. If you live in a flood district and your neighbor has flood insurance, then why not consider it? If your neighbors say they'll sue you if something happens again, then take them at their word.

The goal is to consider practically what could happen and then do something about that concern. Then forget it. There's no need to worry about what randomly might happen in life—much isn't within our control. However, it also doesn't make sense to ignore what's in front of our own eyes, and then be sued or damaged by what could have been avoided in the first place.

keep replacing workers, it won't be long before an attorney writes a letter on behalf of some worker whose rights are alleged to have been violated. It's a quick trip to the courthouse from that point. If you had a system to hear and solve the reasonable complaints of your work force, then by cutting down on employee turnover, you would also be cutting down on the likelihood of being in an expensive lawsuit.

There are problem areas even when working for someone else. Driving your own car on company business without the requisite insurance coverage can result in an uninsured problem for both you and the company. Signing the checks when federal payroll taxes aren't paid can subject you to personal liability for the unpaid taxes, even if you're only an employee. Knowing when there could be a potential problem allows you to take the right steps to rectify it first.

To avoid duplication, a number of business strategies for anticipating and dealing with business problems before they become legal disputes aren't included here. Chapter 11 goes into great detail on the various business areas subject to preventive law approaches. Any company that anticipates and deals with such potential legal fallout ahead of time will always be in a stronger competitive position.

The Cost-Effective Use of Insurance

Everyday living by itself involves the chance of injury or loss. Fires, earthquakes, hurricanes, tornadoes, floods, thefts, and accidents, not to mention increasing litigation and economic reversals, are risks that all of us face. This doesn't mean you should worry about what could happen in the future. But it does mean you should look at what insurance is available to cover these unexpected problems.

Insurance is the first line of defense. People can choose which of the risks in their daily life they're concerned about and those that they aren't, then insure against what seems most likely based on what can be afforded. To do this, you need to know what insurance policies cover or exclude. Not knowing what's covered in your insurance policies substantially reduces their value.

An insurance policy is a legal contract between you and the insurance company where the insurer, in return for your payment of the premium, agrees to reimburse you for a specific, defined loss suffered during the policy's life. There's a limit to the amount of money any insurance contract will provide for a covered loss, called the policy limit, and the policy term lasts typically from 6 months to 1 year. Should a covered loss occur, then the insurance company will reimburse you pursuant to the policy's terms.

Insurance is designed to guard against losses along two basic lines. Property insurance provides protection against damage or loss to *your* possessions, whether involving your home, farm, crops, or even business. Liability insurance covers your legal responsibility to others for *their* property damage or bodily injuries.

The types of insurance that can be bought are staggering. Specific insurance is available on cars, airplanes, boats, condominiums, jewelry, computers, antiques, ranches, office buildings, and shopping centers, to name a few. Insurance is available for aviation, ships and their cargoes, burglaries, robberies, extortion, and even kidnapping. There are life insurance, health insurance, various bonds (or guarantees of performance), worker's compensation (payments to employees injured on the job), malpractice insurance (liability insurance for professionals such as doctors and lawyers), title insurance (protection against undisclosed title defects), and even federal insurance against nuclear accidents. And this is only a partial list.

It is theoretically possible to obtain insurance against whatever risk you could possibly worry about. That is, if you didn't have to worry about the cost and had an unlimited pocketbook. Many of us don't have this luxury. As one insurance agent has observed, "Paying premiums these days involves how much you can afford, while paying all your other bills."

People generally don't worry about insurance if they have nothing to protect. If you've just graduated from college with only debt and a diploma gained so far, then the need for insurance won't be nearly as great as if you were 50, owned a home, and had retirement assets to protect. It would be practical to disregard insurance protection if you're the starving college graduate, but foolish if you're an older person looking toward retirement.

People differ in the level of risk they are willing to assume. Where one worries over what could happen to his or her assets, another simply believes it won't happen. An insurance agent told me about an elderly woman who had inherited eight rental houses when her husband passed away. Neither had believed in insurance, and once the bank loans had been paid off (the banks had required sufficient fire and liability insurance to protect their loans), the couple simply had let the insurance policies lapse. They then pocketed the insurance premiums and hadn't incurred a loss to date.

No responsible advisor could recommend that anyone else do this. It simply makes sense to pay $400 per year, let's say, to protect a $200,000 investment from loss, not to mention against the risk that a tenant slips in the shower and brings a $1,000,000 lawsuit. However, the point was made that we're dealing with a very subjective area.

Rather than not insuring at all, you can decide how much of a loss you will accept. Insurance policies generally provide for a deductible, or that amount the insured pays, along with a maximum limit on what the insurance company will pay. Any loss under the deductible limit, or over the maximum limit, will be paid by you. In return, you pay a lower premium cost over a policy that doesn't have such a deductible or maximum limit in place.

For example, if you have a $500 collision deductible on your car, then you'll pay for the first $500 of the repair cost. If your house is insured for $100,000, but it will cost $150,000 to rebuild, then you lose $50,000 if it burns to the ground. The process of using higher deductibles, lower maximum limits, or even no insurance coverage at all, is called self-insuring. This is a fancy word that simply means you pay for the cost of any loss not covered by the insurance.

The cost of saving insurance premiums can be enticing when viewed over a number of years. If you believe you are a careful driver (and hit-and-runs would be rare), then a higher deductible would be in order. For example, saving $75 per year in premium costs for 10 years, by increasing your deductible to $500 from $200, would put $750 in your savings account—provided you didn't have a loss against these self-insuring savings. All of us balance the amount of protection desired (and premium cost) versus the amount of risk assumed (and costs "saved").

The assets most of us want to protect from loss and liability are our cars and houses. In the great majority of states, it is illegal to drive without the state-mandated level of automobile insurance. Further, lenders require property insurance to the amount of their loan or guaranteed replacement cost with liability protection under the standard homeowners policy (generally $100,000, but this differs from state to state).

It Starts with the Insurance Agent or Representative

Insurance is marketed to consumers either directly by the company or indirectly through insurance agents and brokers. Insurance companies that sell direct, either from their home office or through a company agent, are called *direct companies* or *direct writers.* Companies that market through independent agents, not having their own sales staff or agents, are designated as *agency companies.* Independent agents typically represent several insurance companies. As both direct writers and agency companies, including independent agents, compete strongly for business, you'll hear many competing claims as to which one is best.

There is no rule of thumb when making this decision other than first talking with friends and business associates for their recommendations. Interview several (in person or by telephone) as to their knowledge, the financial strength of their recommended insurance companies, the premium costs, and recommended ways to reduce premium costs without sacrificing basic coverage. "Select the person who seems to be knowledgeable and be sure that person is willing to spend the time necessary to explain what's best for you," explained one agent.

It is important, whether buying insurance for the first time or not, to use a person who seems to know what he or she is talking about. The agent should be able to point out a variety of coverages and alternatives for each insurance need you have. It's better if the person has this knowledge, along with the competitive rates, rather than simply being the only agent you know from the Rotary Club or Chamber of Commerce.

Automobile Insurance

No matter where you live, standard automobile insurance is comprised of six different coverages. Take a look at the premium breakdown of your last personal auto policy invoice. These categories, when added up, comprise the bill.

1 *Bodily injury* is liability insurance in case an accident is caused by you and another person is injured or killed.

2 *Property damage* covers the liability when another's property, whether a car, house, building, shed, or even back fence, is damaged by you.

3 *Medical payment* is the amount of coverage for medical, hospital, and funeral expenses for you and your family, regardless of who is at fault.

        4   *Uninsured motorist* pays for your injuries if the accident involves an uninsured motorist (one who has no automobile insurance in effect at the time of the accident).

        5   *Comprehensive* coverage is brought into play when your car is damaged by an event not involving a collision (e.g., falling tree limbs, earthquake, riot, a thief breaking a window or stealing the car, flood, and so on). This insures against damage not caused by your driving and is also called "OTC" or "Other than Collision" coverage.

        6   *Collision* covers the damage to your car caused by a collision with an object, whether it is another car or your neighbor's back fence. This is damage caused by driving, regardless of whether it's your car or another driver's.

The first two areas, bodily injury and property damage, represent insurance for liability you may have to *others* for an accident caused by the operation of your car. The last four provide insurance coverage for *your* hospital bills and car, depending on how the accident occurred or if by an uninsured motorist.

Some of these insurance areas are required to be in effect at predetermined minimum levels by state law, and these amounts vary widely from state to state. The amount of coverage of each, including the amount of the deductibles, can also be set by state law. This area is treated later in the chapter.

Aside from the six areas listed above, a driver can obtain additional coverage at a higher premium for underinsured motorist coverage (where your damage over and above the underinsured driver's coverage is paid up to the decided amount), rental reimbursement (renting a car while yours is being repaired), and towing (covering the cost of towing your car for repairs), among other available special coverages. Additionally, insurance companies provide discounts, depending on the individual insurer, for nonsmokers, antitheft devices, air bags, good driving records, age (usually over 50 but under 70), car-pooling, multicar discount (where your family owns more than one car insured by the same carrier), and multipolicy discount (where the insurer carries all of your important insurance requirements).

Fault versus No-Fault

States using a fault system with car accidents depend on determining liability based upon fault—whoever's at fault is the one who pays. This means that the insurer of the person who caused the accident pays for the damages. Provided you didn't cause the accident, the other driver's insurance company pays you. However, as those involved in any accident have differing views as to who was at fault, it becomes necessary in numbers of cases to sue to determine who was actually at fault. This system of liability requires a court determination or settlement agreement as to fault, including apportioning this where states allow comparative negligence (any award is reduced by the percentage a driver is found to be at fault, but such fault is not a complete bar to recovery). Thus, large court costs, expensive attorney fees, long delays in the judicial process, and a long wait before a decision are common problems in these states.

Concerned over these problems, Massachusetts in 1970 became the first state to enact a no-fault automobile statute. Since then, a total of 23 other states have followed. Michigan and New York enacted the laws that reach furthest in making compensation payable irrespective of fault, whereas 14 states (including

Massachusetts) have more limited no-fault applications. Eight other states, such as Delaware and Oregon, have very limited no-fault benefits and allow injured parties to sue as desired. Thus, nearly one-half or 24 states have some form of no-fault approach to traffic accidents.

The objective in no-fault states is to reduce the number of lawsuits and pay accident bills promptly, regardless of fault. The no-fault system requires each person's insurance company to pay for the medical bills of its insured without regard to whose fault the accident was; lost wages, medical bills, nursing costs, and other damages are also provided without regard to who caused the accident. Since lawyers and lawsuits cost a lot of money—attorneys charge on average one-third of any recovery with as much as one-half of any award going to the attorneys and legal costs, *not* to the victims—it can be seen that no-fault states have a distinct advantage. And the statistics bear this out.

The ability to sue when there is a "serious" injury has been preserved even in no-fault states. It was decided that a person who lost both arms or became a paraplegic, for example, should have the right to sue for compensation over and above what was provided for in the standard no-fault policy. Since serious injuries and/or wrongful death are still the subject of litigation in no-fault states, you should understand what your state provides as well as how adequate your existing automobile insurance coverage is.

Bodily Injury and Property Damage Considerations

Both bodily injury and property damage coverage will pay for damages assessed for other persons or property injured by your driving. Such coverage is, of course, limited by the policy amounts and deductibles chosen (although liability coverage usually isn't subject to a deductible).

This coverage also pays for the legal costs to defend you against any claim or lawsuit that arose from the automobile accident. Such costs *are* considerable, and it's not uncommon for the costs of a legal defense to be even greater than the awarded damages. An attorney charging $200 or more per hour in a nonserious accident doesn't have to put much time in legal paperwork and court appearances to quickly exceed the costs of the injured party's demands.

However, such insurance and legal defense coverage only applies if the driver is covered by the policy. The standard automobile policy generally provides that the head-of-household driver, members of the driver's family living with that person, and anyone with that person's permission to drive the insured vehicle will be covered (but check your policy for the details). This even includes situations when a car other than the insured vehicle is being driven, provided it's being driven with the owner's permission.

All this sounds reassuring at first, but each accident has its own set of facts on whether coverage is present. For example, what if your son took the family car, let a friend drive it, and there was an at-fault accident? If your son didn't have your permission or wasn't licensed, then the insurance company could deny coverage. You, as well as your son, could be held responsible for all the damages and defense costs. Even if your son had permission and he were properly insured, some states provide that an insured driver has no authority to allow others to drive the car.

Again, you could be held liable for the injuries and legal costs. It's highly recommended that you check out exactly what situations will and won't be covered under your policy, especially when others could be driving your car.

Bodily Injury and Property Damage Required Limits

All states require a driver to maintain certain automobile insurance as a condition to drive legally in that state. Although there are states that require much less, most states require the driver to maintain what's called 20/40/10 or 25/50/15 coverage. The first figure refers to the minimum insurance coverage for *one* person injured by your driving. The second figure reflects the minimum insurance coverage for *all* persons injured in an accident. The third figure states the minimum allowable insurance carried for property damage.

Thus, 25/50/15 means that the driver in that state must carry insurance with *at least* $25,000 coverage for one person, $50,000 for all persons injured in an accident, and $15,000 coverage for property damage. The insurance company in this case would pay up to $25,000 for each person hurt in an accident caused by you, but it wouldn't pay more than $50,000 per accident, no matter how many people were killed, maimed, or injured in that accident.

It is easily seen that what's required by a state is far below the levels a prudent driver would want to have, as car accidents can cause damages substantially more than these financial responsibility requirements. If you're held to be liable for causing an automobile accident, then you're responsible for the medical bills, hospital and surgery expenses, lost wages, long-term care, and even pain and suffering. A serious accident, when you are underinsured, will bankrupt you! You will be held responsible in such a case for the entire amount to the penny over what your insurance doesn't cover.

Most insurance agents recommend 100/300/25 *at a minimum*, or $100,000 per person bodily injury insurance coverage with $300,000 bodily injury coverage in total per accident and $25,000 property damage coverage. And even this may not be the best coverage, given that serious injuries and the attorneys' desire for the highest recovery usually end up in higher awards. When you have assets to protect, it may very well be worth the extra premium expense to increase coverage limits or obtain an umbrella policy.

The Umbrella Policy

An umbrella or excess liability policy comes into play after your normal auto or homeowner's insurance has been exhausted. For example, if you have a standard $300,000 auto liability policy and a $1,000,000 umbrella policy, and a $900,000 judgment were decided against you, then you would be covered. The first $300,000 of the judgment would be picked up by the auto policy with the remaining $600,000 paid by the umbrella policy. You would be protected to a total of $1,300,000. Anything over that would be your responsibility from your personal assets.

The cost of an umbrella policy is relatively low, as it is not used until after the prime coverage has been exhausted. The cost of a $1,000,000 umbrella policy can be as low as $200 per year, provided it's issued by the same company that insures your cars and home. It's generally required that you insure all your cars and your home with the insurance carrier that underwrites the umbrella policy.

It can be tempting to save $200 per year for 10 years (or $2,000) and not purchase an umbrella policy. However, if the value of your personal assets after liabilities is greater than $100,000, then the idea of an umbrella policy should be explored (the annual cost in this case would be 2% of such value). Although this is a personal consideration, the greater the value of your assets, the greater the reason to purchase this cost-effective tool.

Premium Trade-Offs

There are various areas you can discuss with your agent to save costs. For example, collision and comprehensive insurance provide for deductibles (bodily injury and property liability coverage don't). When a new car has been purchased or lender financing used, then high deductibles aren't desirable or even allowed (due to the lender's requirements). However, as your car becomes older, the reasons for carrying collision and comprehensive coverage diminish. As the car's value fades over the years, it is possible for the cost of repairs to be even greater.

Accordingly, the insurance coverage for the 10-year-old car purchased for your daughter should be different than that for your new Cadillac. You might decide on a $250 dollar deductible for both collision and comprehension (or higher depending on your assessed risk of having an accident) with your Cadillac, but you might sharply increase these deductibles, even eliminate collision protection on your older car. Remember that most insurance companies will allow you to eliminate collision but still require comprehensive coverage to be kept in place.

Another consideration involves the medical payments coverage when you currently have good health insurance. If not required by your state's law, then you could delete this coverage to save costs. However, remember that your health insurance only pays for those who are covered by that plan—nonfamily members won't be. Let's say, you were driving your car with your brother and had an accident. Your brother's medical bills wouldn't be covered by your health plan. He *would* be covered by the medical payments coverage on your car policy, subject to its provisions and dollar limitations. If you were at fault in the accident, then the liability portion of the insurance would cover your brother but that forces him to make a liability claim on you personally.

Homeowners Policy

Years ago, homeowners had to buy insurance in pieces—a fire policy for protection against fire; a liability policy in case someone was injured on the property; and endorsements for theft, vandalism, and liability off the premises. These protections now are incorporated in one basic homeowners policy that excludes business and automobile coverage. These must be covered by separate policies.

Homeowner policies provide a basic protection against loss to your home, unattached structures on the property, personal property, additional living expenses in case of a loss, and personal liability coverage. However, it is as important to know what isn't covered, or is limited as it is to know the areas that are covered. This should be discussed in detail with your insurance representative.

Your Home

Protection against loss to the actual dwelling, as well as attached structures such as a garage, is included in a homeowners policy up to the coverage limits. Most policies cover detached structures, such as a shed or garage, up to 10% of the dwelling cost. Trees, plants, and shrubs are generally included, as well.

> The basic rule is that a house and any other structures should be insured for their replacement value, not their market value. These two concepts can provide for quite different valuations for the same house. The market value of a house is the price it will sell for on the open market at today's prices. The replacement value is what it will cost to rebuild your house should it be destroyed by fire or another covered event. For example, an older house in a small community might sell for $100,000, but it might cost well over $150,000 to be rebuilt. A house in a surging real estate market might sell for $200,000 but cost less to be rebuilt. In either case, insuring the house at its replacement value can avoid a very unpleasant surprise.

Although many policies provide for an automatic increase in coverage each year to meet the effects of inflation, it's best to be sure your policy is updated annually to avoid becoming underinsured. The problem of being underinsured is more than one of not having enough insurance money to rebuild. It can also reduce the amount of insurance coverage and badly penalize you.

Let's say your house has a $200,000 replacement cost. Again, this isn't market value but the cost it would take to rebuild your house. It's a new house, the fire department responds quickly, and you're certain the house wouldn't completely burn down. You've decided to save on the insurance premiums by insuring the house for only $100,000.

Even if you are right, you'll be wrong. If you arrange for only $100,000 coverage, instead of the required $160,000 (80% of $200,000), then the insurance company generally will pay only 50% ($100,000 carried of the $200,000 total replacement cost) at best. Thus, whether your claim is $10,000 or $100,000, you will receive only 50% of your claim. This "coinsurance" concept carries into all property insurance, even business insurance, and should be reviewed quite carefully with your insurance representative.

Insuring only for what the lender requires, usually the amount of the loan, results in the same problem. Additionally, over time the loan is paid down while your property increases in value. You will become underinsured and subject to the coinsurance rule if you don't also increase your coverage.

Insurance companies don't usually pay replacement value on losses unless you carry coverage for at least 80 percent of the actual replacement value of your house. Although carriers generally refuse coverage unless 100% or full replacement value is carried, some homeowners say their house is less expensive to replace so that the premiums are lower. If less than the required 80 percent is carried, then the amount of reimbursement is proportionately reduced from what should have been carried. Otherwise, people would greatly underinsure, pay small premiums, and then receive full payment for the actual amount of their losses.

Personal Property

The contents of the house are generally covered, such as furniture, rugs, curtains, appliances, dishes, silverware, and clothing, but usually not less than 50% of the limits on the house. Thus, a $200,000 policy usually carries $100,000 in coverage for your personal property. Coverage of personal property applies to losses off the premises in addition to inside or around the house. If your suitcase is stolen while you are traveling overseas, then your insurer will reimburse you for the costs of replacing the suitcase and its contents. All such coverage, however, is subject to limits and conditions, and you will need to read your policy carefully. There are several areas to be especially wary about:

✔ It's very difficult to reconstruct losses in case of a fire, burglary, or other covered loss. Claims become hassles when supporting invoices and photographs don't exist to prove ownership or establish the purchase price. "I had all my valuable possessions burned in the fire, from the fine silver and linens to family heirlooms. I had to hire an attorney when the insurance company didn't believe what I said the losses were. I couldn't prove it and finally had to accept less. Then there were the legal fees," said one who went through this.

An inventory should be taken to document all your possessions, showing the date of acquisition, cost, as well as a picture. Photographs of large-ticket items especially should be taken, as well as clusters of items in various rooms, with as much detail shown as possible. "When possible, I highly recommend taking a home video of the contents of your house and all important possessions," said one insurance agent. "This personal inventory should be updated from time to time as new possessions are purchased with all records stored in a safe place," she added.

✔ As with the dwelling itself, personal property coverage can either be actual cash value or replacement value. Although this is more expensive, typically adding about 10% to the premium cost, insuring at replacement value pays dividends when there's a loss. Rather than receiving the cash value of your 10-year-old radio at garage-sale prices, replacement value pays for the purchase of a new one of like kind and quality. But be careful, as insurance companies do limit replacement compensation to the cost of repairs or a stated multiple of actual cash value (typically four times such value). Sophisticated electronic equipment such as computers, printers, and software should be discussed with your agent as to replacement cost and even special endorsements (but these usually carry a $5,000 loss limit).

✔ The limits on personal property coverage should be reviewed carefully. Most policies, for example, limit the loss to $1000 on money, bullion, and securities, as well as to $1000 (ranging from $500 to $2000) for the loss by theft of jewelry, watches, furs, and other expensive items. You'll be shocked to discover that the loss of your favorite painting or diamond ring, each valued at over $10,000, is so limited. This problem is addressed by purchasing a special *personal articles floater* endorsement (also called "*scheduling*" such specific property).

Expensive possessions, such as oil paintings, guns, jewelry, camcorders, and cameras, should be insured by this endorsement or specific listing. The coverage "floats" with you, no matter where you are (although property away from home is usually limited to 10% of your personal property coverage). If you travel a lot, or your child is heading off to college with a computer, stereo, and TV, then look into this further. When students live in off-campus housing, however, you may need to buy a separate renters policy instead.

Additionally, basic policies don't cover you against accidental loss, such as when your diamond ring slips into the garbage disposal or disappears while you are swimming. A floater covers nearly every loss, including accidental loss, and there's no deductible. Premiums range from $1 to $2 per $100 insured value, and coverage is generally itemized individually with valuations supported by an appraisal or sales slip, thus minimizing problems when documenting a claim.

✔ Your pet dog, cat, or canary isn't covered if it becomes injured or dies. Nor does a homeowners policy cover what your pet does to your property (i.e., chewing up your expensive draperies). However, your liability to others for what your pets do will be covered under the "liability to others" coverage (i.e., your dog chews up the neighbor's leg).

✔ Although a homeowners policy may cover certain small boats and sailboats (but check the small print first), it won't cover larger boats or airplanes. Any boat or airplane insurance coverage should be discussed directly with a marine or aviation insurance specialist. Further, snowmobiles, motorcycles, and minibikes are generally excluded from coverage, as well as rental property (i.e., the tent and party chairs rented for your party or the carpet cleaner used to clean up).

✔ Most policies restrict coverage for loss due to burglary, theft, and vandalism if a house has been vacant for 30 days or longer. If you are leaving for an extended vacation, then talk with your insurance representative regarding what to do.

✔ Don't forget your deductible. The trade-off between the deductible amount and premium cost is again present. Let's say you decide on a $500 deductible to save on costs. Regardless of your policy limit, you still will be out of pocket by the amount of that deductible or $500.

Additional Living Expenses

This coverage, also known as loss of use, pays for your increased living expenses when your house is unlivable due to a covered loss. This reimbursement is limited to what it costs over and above what you would "normally" spend on food and lodging. It won't pay for the best, five-star rated hotels and restaurants in your area, but it will pay for ordinary hotel and restaurant bills, deducting what your normal food and lodging expenses would have been.

Most policies limit reimbursement to 20% of your home insurance coverage. For example, if you own a $200,000 policy, then this provision normally pays up to $40,000 of your "extra" living expenses while your home is being rebuilt. If you had been renting out a room before the loss, then this provision generally covers your loss of rental income during this period.

Important Noncoverage

A standard homeowners policy has disclaimers buried in its boiler plate so that it doesn't cover every type of disaster. Although losses from fire, lightning, windstorm, explosion, riot, and vandalism are covered, nearly all homeowners policies exclude any coverage, for example, for damage or loss from earthquakes, landslides, and floods. Over three-fourths of all losses to homes will be uninsured just because of these exclusions.

To the victims of the California earthquakes (San Francisco in 1989 and Los Angeles in 1994) and the July 1993 Mississippi River flood, this is a very real consideration. You will need a separate policy if you live in areas prone to earthquakes, flooding, earth movements, or hurricanes.

Flooding deserves special mention. Unless special flood insurance has been purchased, you're not insured if a river or street drain overflows into your home. However, you generally are covered if the damage is caused from *inside* the house, such as when a water heater bursts or a washing machine overflows. If you live in an area prone to flooding, whether caused by rivers overflowing or hurricanes, then insurance will be made available for purchase as part of the flood insurance program administered by the Federal Emergency Management Agency (FEMA). The cost of such premiums is the same whether you buy the insurance from a private carrier or FEMA directly.

An important consideration these days, especially with the increase of home offices, is that business activities conducted in your home put all aspects of your policy at risk—whether the dwelling, contents, or liability-to-other provisions. The homeowners policy is designed for personal and not business uses. Insurance companies typically deny claims under homeowners policies if business usage is involved, even when it's a part-time business activity, unless there's a special endorsement or separate policy as to the business use. It makes no difference whether the commercial activity is consulting, computer programming, sales, or even child care. You should consult your agent for a business endorsement if property used in business is kept at home, especially when expensive computer equipment is involved or liability claims can be high (such as with child care, even though carriers are cutting back such coverage).

Personal Liability

It's far more likely you'll face a problem involving an attorney than have your home gutted by fire. A most important provision of homeowners insurance is the protection given against lawsuits and claims made by others against you or your family members for any bodily injury or property damage allegedly incurred. This coverage is not subject to a deductible, as the property coverage portion is, and pays both for the costs of your legal defense along with any damages agreed to or awarded by a court, up to the policy limits.

There are limits, as with all insurance coverage, and you will need to check any potential exclusions with your insurance agent. If you are aware of a stated problem, such as a leaking propane tank or septic tank and the neighbors are complaining, then you need to be careful—pollution, for example, is one area that may not be covered.

A misconception held even by some attorneys is that this protection is localized to your home and actions on your property. That isn't the case. This insurance covers liability claims, whether or not you were in your house or miles away. For example, if you dropped an antique statue at an exclusive store miles away, then the personal liability coverage can cover that unless you dropped the statue on purpose.

The liability coverage is commonly understood in terms of traditional home activities. If your dog bites a neighbor two blocks away or you hit a softball through your neighbor's window, it's easy to see you'll be covered. A delivery person trips over a crack in your sidewalk or your burning leaves set the neighbor's garage on fire, and you are covered. If you regrade your property, which causes heavy rains to flood your neighbor's property later, you will normally be covered.

However, the courts and lawyers, as with everything else, have been busily expanding into areas beyond what was intended. Although definitely a minority position, some states have forced insurers underneath homeowners policies to accept coverage for libel, slander, and invasion of privacy litigation. Lawsuits have been filed against insurers in any number of areas, including claims that home-owners policies should defend and pay claims alleging that the policyholder infected another with the AIDS virus, herpes, and other contagious diseases.

Actions have already been brought in various states against insurers to stand by their policies when the policyholder received an adverse court judgment for child abuse. Although intentional conduct is usually excluded from coverage, there have been cases where children have sued their mothers over negligently failing to protect them from the alleged sexually abusive acts of their fathers. In a Minnesota case, the mother was found jointly liable for part of a $2.4 million jury award against the father. In a Texas case, the mother was found 50% liable for a $3.4 million judgment against her and her husband.

The Exclusions

Years ago, the general rule was that no coverage would exist for any loss that was intentionally caused. That rule now is riddled with exceptions. Coverage has been upheld for assault and battery, child molestation, sexual abuse, and even tossing a valued object up and down so that it shattered, based on the rationale that, although the conduct was intentional, the policyholder didn't intend the damage.

A California case has held that although the insanity of the policyholder *isn't* a defense in a civil action for assault and battery (the policy excluded liability coverage for intentional acts and the insured had committed the assault and battery while insane), the insured's insanity precluded the exclusion from being enforced. The insurer had to defend and pay up.

Another exception in the boiler plate to personal liability coverage is the business pursuits exclusion. This exclusion has been rigidly enforced by the courts, provided the business was a continued or regular activity of the insured. If the activity isn't one associated with the insured's usual business pursuits, then the exclusion is generally not enforced. However, although this is the general rule, it isn't always the case. Courts have denied coverage, for example, when the insured occasionally baby-sat and received payment for the services.

> Whether an insured is doing business part-time or not is a question of fact to be resolved by the courts. Given the high risk of these activities causing a loss of insurance coverage, it's advisable to add on a business endorsement or a separate business property and liability policy, after consulting with your insurance agent.
>
> Keep in mind that homeowners insurance covers basically nonbusiness-, nonautomobile-related claims. It doesn't cover financial obligations, federal or state tax claims, or contract disputes. For example, if you don't pay a friend the money he lent you, your homeowners policy doesn't cover you. Being sued while you are working for a nonprofit organization usually isn't covered either.

Should you move from your house to another but aren't able to sell the old one, you may decide to rent it to others. You will need to cover your landlord's liability, as a homeowners policy does not do this. Property held for rent must have separate personal liability coverage, in addition to fire protection, either tied to a new homeowners policy by way of endorsement or a separate policy. An umbrella policy is specifically advisable should you own rental properties.

Another exclusion increasingly used occurs when a homeowner hires someone to work in or on the house and there's an injury. For example, you hire someone to trim the trees around your house and that person touches high-voltage wires, or the roofer falls through your roof. If the workers don't have worker's compensation or similar insurance insuring their injuries and damages, then you could be held responsible for them. And it makes no difference whether they're watching your child in the house or repairing the roof outside. Check whether or not you need workman's compensation insurance or an endorsement to your homeowners policy to cover this before allowing the work to proceed.

If a lawsuit is filed against you, whether it alleges intentional conduct or not, you should as a rule bring your homeowners policy with you to the attorney's office. Don't listen to the insurance agent if he tells you that you're not covered, as that advice may be wrong. Coverage has been upheld by the courts when only part of the complaint, and at times when none of the allegations, state a cause of action that would be covered by the policy. The costs of defending a lawsuit and potential damages often run into hundreds of thousands of dollars. The cost of a consultation is minuscule when compared against this risk.

The Umbrella Policy

The disturbing rise in high dollar judgments mandates that you look closely at excess liability or umbrella policies. As in the case of automobile policies, the standard liability policy is simply not adequate these days. As homeowners policies typically limit liability to $100,000, it's easily seen such protection isn't sufficient. An excess liability carrier not only has the duty to defend to its excess limits (some cases hold it had to defend when the underlying insurance didn't), but it also can have somewhat broader coverage than the underlying policy. Given the cost effectiveness of a $1,000,000 umbrella policy (generally around $200 per year), a homeowner with any assets to protect should consider purchasing such a policy.

Premium Considerations

As with automobile insurance, there are a number of discounts that are available when you are purchasing homeowners insurance. Age (retired and/or over 55), nonsmoker, use of smoke detectors and/or burglar alarms, and multi-policy discounts are available, depending on the carrier. Again, the trade-off is between the extent of your insurance coverage and any deductibles versus cost. Although this is a personal decision to be discussed with your agent, it is recommended that you keep in place extensive liability coverage, along with an excess limits policy when appropriate.

Renter's Insurance

Renter's insurance is a form of homeowners policy, but it doesn't include property coverage for the dwelling since the property is owned by someone else. Whoever owns the real property has the primary responsibility to secure the insurance for the basic structure. It does provide personal property, additional living expenses, and personal liability to others coverage. You would purchase a renter's policy whether you rent a house, apartment, or a condominium. Personal property, whether in a home, apartment, or condominium, can be damaged or lost by fire, explosion, a hot water tank bursting, theft, and any number of other ways. These losses should be insured against as indicated in the discussion on homeowners policies. The same personal property concerns apply with renter's and condominium policies—do the standard limits of these policies cover the value of the personal property you own and your life style? Do you want to insure for replacement value or actual cash value? Again, a personal inventory should be in place with supporting invoices, pictures, videos, and updates.

Personal liability protection is also as important as your property coverage. Although the landlord will obtain property and personal liability insurance on the dwelling, a tenant still has risks, contrary to what you would expect. Let's say John, currently renting a house from Anne, was cooking one evening. The phone rings, and he walks to another room to answer a telephone. As he talks on the phone, the pan burns and starts a fire that guts several rooms inside the house. The damage is estimated to be $45,000 to restore everything to the condition it was before the loss.

Anne's landlord insurance pays for the cost of the repair and damages. However, John is shocked when he is later sued by Anne's insurance carrier for causing the fire and damage. Insurance policies contain a standard clause, called a *subrogation clause*, which allows an insurance company to be repaid any monies paid out on a claim by suing the persons responsible for causing that damage. If John doesn't have renter's insurance, then he will have to pay the judgment, including his extensive attorney's fees, from his own pocket and assets.

This personal liability coverage, when present, is being broadened by the courts. It's not limited solely to risks occasioned by living in an apartment. Should you be sued by another person over any matter, whether involving bodily injury, property damage, or not, then see an attorney specializing in insurance defense for an opinion as to the coverage of your renter's policy.

Standard renter's policies usually don't include coverage for improvements paid for or made by you to the property. Although this consideration generally arises with condominium ownership, you should be aware that an endorsement needs to be arranged to cover such improvements in case of a loss. The provisions as to additional living expenses will be slightly different from what is contained in a homeowners policy, and you should check this with your agent.

Condominium Insurance

Although renters don't own the structure they live in, condominium owners experience a different situation. In some cases, the condominium or co-op association owns more than just the common areas (the swimming pool, landscaping, recreational facilities, heating and air conditioning, exterior walls, roof, basement, and areas as stated in the association's charter, by-laws, or papers) of the project. These projects may own the interior walls, wiring, plumbing, fixtures, and built-in appliances, for example, to the point where the condo owner is only responsible for any personal property used or stored on the premises. Because of these differences, a condo owner should be sure that his or her individual policy covers what the association's policy doesn't.

A condo or co-op owner needs to use the same considerations as if he owned a house—the questions of replacement cost versus cash value and coinsurance provisions. If the owner insures a condominium for $75,000, where its replacement value is $150,000, then the carrier will reduce its coverage substantially in case of a loss. Many policies would provide in this case that an actual loss of $25,000 would be reimbursed by the lower of $12,500 less the deductible (only 50% of the required coverage was being carried) or actual cash value (its cost less what has depreciated to date). This outcome would be a nasty surprise.

Again, the same considerations apply when you are reviewing a homeowners policy. Ask under what circumstances you'll be covered for property loss or lawsuits and at what level. Consider an umbrella policy. Once the policy limits for property and personal liability have been set, then determine what deductibles you want. Ask for a commercial rider if you are planning to conduct a part-time or full-time business from the premises. The limits on your valuables and any computer equipment, for example, need to be discussed, and a personal property floater should be obtained when these are not sufficient. If you are remodeling or adding a room within the owned structure, then be sure these additional costs are insured. The applicable discounts, such as nonsmoking, age, smoke and burglar alarms, and multipolicies, need to be assessed before you decide on one carrier over another.

Charitable and Community Activities

Your homeowners or renters policy rarely covers lawsuits and claims resulting from your community and charitable activities (however, always check in case of a lawsuit). The particular organization, whether the Girl or Boy Scouts, your church or synagogue, Chamber of Commerce, the local high school, or whatever, will need to have its own insurance covering the acts and activities of its employees and volunteers.

> Fund-raising activities are a consistently litigated area by plaintiff attorneys, and it makes a difference as to how the charitable organization conducts such activities. There's an understandable difference whether funds are raised by selling cookies or by sponsoring a triathlon or high-speed bike race. However, you need to know how well the association's insurance provides coverage on your activities before you decide to work with it or serve on the board of directors (where the legal exposure is even greater).

Such groups always need to have their own insurance covering their buildings and facilities, in case there's a fire or someone slips and falls, in addition to a liability policy covering their activities. Unfortunately, it makes no difference these days for whom you work. High school volunteers have been sued, and cases range from athletes who injure themselves on the playing fields to drama coaches for showing "bias" in selecting contest participants. Substantial damages have been sought and awarded in a number of these cases. Elementary and junior high school students are suing principals, teachers, and anyone they feel is responsible for alleged sexual harassment by other students. Whether a religious institution, the United Way, or a Chamber of Commerce, all have been sued for a variety of reasons, and in many cases all of the individuals associated with the event or happening have been sued.

Business Insurance

Since homeowner and other similar policies don't cover your business activities, separate business insurance needs to be in place to cover such operations. Owners of small businesses have a personal liability for uninsured business losses and liabilities when they don't enjoy the protection of a bona fide, corporate form of organization (and even then there are exceptions as discussed at Chapter 11).

Let's say you own a computer software company as a sole proprietor (where you own the unincorporated business by yourself). If an employee is driving his or her own car to make a marketing call on a customer and is involved in a car accident, then you can be held personally liable. You, as the owner of the business, are responsible for the actions of your employees while they're conducting company business. If you don't have a business automobile liability policy that covers all owned, nonowned, and rented cars used in your business, then you are subjecting yourself to this liability.

If you own a bakery, and a fire occurs on the premises, a similar problem arises. If a worker is burned in the fire, and you don't have worker's compensation insurance, then the business is liable for the medical bills and payments pursuant to your state law. If you own the business by yourself or as a general partner (where you manage the business but have partners), then this responsibility also will be a personal liability. Since your homeowners policy doesn't cover business operations, the uninsured loss would be your personal loss.

Depending on the type of business conducted, owners can insure a variety of business assets against loss from fire, employee theft, burglary, and other covered events. The assets covered, depending on the specific policy, can range from the building, warehouses, and sheds to accounts receivable, inventory, computer equipment, vehicles, furniture, and supplies. Insurance is available on tenant improvements, inventory in transit, loss of rental income (if rental property is involved, whether it's a building or equipment), and even reconstruction of accounts receivable in case of a loss. This insurance is still vulnerable to the coinsurance problem detailed previously when the owner underinsures the value of the property and there's a loss. Such insurance needs to be reviewed carefully for its exclusions, and damage by outside floods and earthquakes are typically excluded.

Liability Coverage

Again, liability insurance provisions are quite important, whether purchased separately or in a package. As with the homeowners policy, companies are able to purchase liability coverage for their operations with property protection in a

Business-owners Package Policy (BPP). This liability protection can be purchased separately in a commercial general liability (CGL) policy. The liability policy typically provides defense costs and damages when the company is legally responsible for a bodily, property, or personal injury sustained by a third party who doesn't work for the business.

Bodily injury involves the accidental injury to a person, whereas property injury involves any accidental damage to real (such as a building) or personal (such as equipment) property caused by the insured. The term "personal" injury refers to the damage to another company's or person's reputation (including invasion of privacy). The standard policy provides protection against claims made against the company resulting from its advertising of goods and services, such as slandering another company's products in such advertising.

General liability insurance covers both legal costs and court judgments or settlements with the claimant. It will generally cover claims stemming from the ownership or control of the company's premises and those due to conduct of its business. Coverage is normally present, for example, when a customer slips and falls on a slippery floor while selecting a dress in a clothing store, or when a fire starts, and a customer is injured while trying to escape the flames.

The Exclusions

This general liability coverage doesn't include product liability—the claims by consumers who used the product and were injured or incurred damage—that product manufacturers face. Nor does the standard liability coverage include professional malpractice or service liability, such as that faced by doctors, dentists, and lawyers for mistakes made in their line of work.

Automobile liability is excluded from the general liability coverage, as that is covered under a business automobile policy. Any claims by employees for injuries are excluded, as these are handled by separate worker's compensation policies. Claims involving sexual harassment or discrimination on the basis of sex, race, color, age, and the like are excepted from standard coverage. Commercial claims due to note defaults, breach of contract, and contract disputes aren't covered. Additionally, you should consider purchasing an umbrella or excess liability policy to increase the liability policy limits from what is stated in the standard policy.

Most smaller businesses such as a clothing store, barbershop, book store, florist shop, yogurt store, or a video mart are insured under package policies or BPPs that are a bundling of various policies. This package generally will include building and general contents, glass breakage, crime (both on and off premises), damage to signs, business interruption (loss of profits due to a covered loss), relocation expense (when the premises can't be rebuilt quickly enough), and general liability.

As with any insurance policies, the exclusions should be looked at closely, as well as what deductibles and overall coverage is best for your business. The standard policies typically don't include coverage for loss of valuable papers (such as those found in an architect's office), property belonging to employees, data processing records, satellite dishes, property held for others (such as found in an appliance repair shop or dry cleaner's), and fine arts.

Various businesses also are quite distinct and need specialized coverage or various changes and endorsements to the standard policy. For example, restaurants (food handling and liquor liability problems), construction companies (equipment, construction, and employee liabilities), computer software (defective product problems), trucking companies (vehicle maintenance, varying state regulation, and different products being transported), and hotels (claims from guests due to security, fire, and safety considerations) all have varying requirements that need to be covered by insurance tailored directly for them.

Product Liability and Malpractice Insurance

Although the general liability coverage, with endorsements, can handle the requirements of most businesses, the problems faced by manufacturers over product liability (usually not covered or excluded, depending on the risk) and service providers for malpractice are separate problems. It's impossible for a person to insulate himself or herself from this, regardless of how many warnings, instructions, or disclaimers of liability are used, or of how simple and safe the product or service is.

For example, a small, plastic toy is swallowed by a small child, and a lawsuit is brought alleging the failure to warn that children could become injured should they put the toy in their mouths. Or a chemical used in your manufacturing process is determined later to cause cancer in laboratory animals, and lawsuits are brought alleging its toxicity with a rash of consumers who now have ailments allegedly from coming into contact with it. Although product liability insurance can be cost prohibitive, it should be considered by every manufacturer. The ability to sleep at nights is one good reason. The problem, however, is that this insurance is quite costly when it's even available.

Professional liability insurance is an absolute necessity these days if you're an insurance agent, real estate broker, accountant, attorney, doctor, dentist, engineer, or other professional. The rule is now very simple—if there has been an injury or loss, the professional will face a claim, whether or not a mistake has been made. However, this liability is not limited to just these professions. Malpractice insurance (which is professional liability insurance) is being purchased these days by tanning salons, priests, day-care operators, masseuses, dog groomers, veterinarians, and a variety of service professionals who deal with the general public.

The problem is that claims can be made years after the work or service was performed. The building designed by the architect 15 years ago is gutted by fire or a floor collapses. A person treated for one illness by a doctor years ago is diagnosed years later as actually having had another. Sexual abuse charges are made against a priest 20 years after the alleged offense. Since the 1970s professional liability insurance has been written primarily on a claims-made basis—the policy in effect at the time the claim actually is made will be the one that covers it.

As with product liability insurance, professional liability insurance is expensive, subject to numerous exclusions and conditions, and may be written with a high deductible along with a high premium. States require such insurance to be carried by certain professionals, and this coverage is specifically excluded from all homeowners policies. Where the risk of damage is quite high, such as with doctors, dentists, and engineers, the cost of such insurance can be extraordinary. However, it can be more reasonable when the risk of a claim is lower, such as with veterinarians and dog groomers. Even if you don't feel you need this insurance, it may be worth looking into—just in case.

Generally

Although business owners are risk takers, they have to consider what can go wrong, especially when employees are involved. It's a fact of life that complete insurance coverage for all the risks you face is either too expensive or not available. However, what's important is to know what insurance is available, what are the most likely risks your business faces, and then to make a reasoned judgment as to what insurance coverage is necessary. It's better to spend one afternoon a year with your agent or broker with follow-up telephone calls, than to receive one bad phone call after an uninsured loss has occurred.

Other Insurance

Insurance can be used for any number of situations. Life insurance is a major industry product used to protect dependents from the untimely death of the one who earns the money. Life insurance is used in estate planning, as a forced savings or investment program, providing for the cashing out of a small business owner's interest, and in many other applications.

Health insurance is a prime concern for individuals and the nation. Without it, given a major illness or uninsured accident, a person's savings can melt down to nothing. Even with a national health care plan, there will be continuing considerations for every person who has assets to protect.

Disability income insurance, providing you and your family with a monthly income if you become disabled and unable to work for an extended time period, is another industry product. Most people are better protected against death with life insurance than they are against disability and disability income insurance.

A form of disability income insurance is worker's compensation insurance. This coverage, mandated by all states, is paid entirely by the employer for the benefit of the employees. Should an injury or illness occur on or due to the job, then the worker is automatically covered. Benefit payments, in the form of a lump-sum or weekly payments, are made pursuant to state law and procedure.

Specific insurance is available for any number of activities and properties, as mentioned throughout this chapter. There's insurance to cover injuries and death when you are flying, traveling to another country, or taking a white-water river trip, although your health insurance policy should cover the medical bills. There is insurance available on baggage, pets, and even burial costs. You can buy single-event insurance to cover your liability for a party, wedding, or a community event. If you're worried about some exposure, no matter how off-beat, the insurance industry will find a way to insure it.

What's Needed Overall

Whether you have or require insurance for your home, personal activities, or business, there are several, general rules:

1 Find a good insurance agent, broker, or representative and spend time with that person discussing your needs. Finding a knowledgeable insurance agent is as important as securing the right attorney for a lawsuit. At times, you can pay an insurance consultant for advice on the necessary insurance coverage and costs but still be ahead because of the discounts arranged in your coverage.

2 Be honest with your representative and don't withhold facts to get a lower premium. If the loss is large enough, the carrier may withhold coverage based on your fraud and misrepresentation in securing that low-cost insurance. If you decide to underinsure (which isn't recommended), then don't be surprised when the carrier cuts the expected reimbursement by the percentage difference.

3 Review all insurance policies, whether personal or business, to know what is or isn't covered *before* a loss occurs. You should know the amount of each insurance, the coverage, exclusions, and deductibles. Know whether or not you're in a no-fault automobile insurance state and the steps to take if there's an accident.

4 Change your insurance coverage and records as your life changes. If you discover that your property is worth more than originally thought, then increase your coverage limits accordingly. Property should be added to insurance policies as acquired. It's too late to think about this after the loss has occurred.

5 Review in detail all insurance at least annually. Be aware that possessions increase in value due to inflation over the years, whereas the same value still sits on the policy as first listed.

6 Keep good records. In case you forget what actual coverage is in place, there should be a record in case a loss occurs. Inventories, receipts, invoices, pictures, and descriptions of all property should be kept in a secure location. The actual policies, endorsements, and correspondence should be filed in one central place. A good habit is writing down the notes of conversations with agents as to the requested coverage, start date, premium amount, and coverage limits, then following up if the anticipated documentation doesn't follow in timely fashion.

7 Bring all liability policies with you when consulting an attorney over a lawsuit, especially when you've been sued. Consulting an insurance defense specialist can pay dividends when there's any question as to coverage.

What if You Have a Claim?

✔ Notify your insurance agent *immediately* after the fire, accident, theft, or receiving the lawsuit—most policies bar the insurance company from having to cover a loss or claim when the insured has been tardy, and the courts generally uphold such denials. "The sooner, the better. Call first, and always follow up in writing," said an agent. "The companies are tough on this one," she added. In the case of a theft or burglary, also report the incident to the police. You'll need the police report to file along with the insurance claim.

✔ As insurers typically require written, documented proof of any loss, include as much information as soon as possible in writing. However, take the time to determine the full extent of the damage, including noting all facts that support that the claim is covered by the applicable policy.

✔ If repairs are needed to prevent further damage to the property, then quickly take all reasonable steps necessary to do so. Any insurance coverage on that loss is jeopardized if the property deteriorates further when you had the ability to control further loss. Notify your agent and/or the regional claims manager about the steps being taken, being sure to save all receipts for later reimbursement. Permanent repairs shouldn't be undertaken until an adjuster has viewed the damage, as carriers generally won't reimburse claims when they don't know what it first looked like.

✔ Keep a written record of your claim. A written, follow-up letter on the claim is proof you submitted it in a timely manner. Always keep the original documents, such as medical bills, repair invoices, and payroll stubs (proving lost wages), and send only copies to the carrier. Copies can become illegible, and the originals are the best evidence of your case in the event there's a later dispute with the carrier.

✔ Stay on top of the claim. If you don't hear from the company, then call your agent and/or the insurance company to find out why there's a delay. Follow this up with a letter. Many states have enacted laws mandating the time by when a claim must be investigated, responded to, and even settled.

If a lawsuit has been filed against you, then keep the insurance company informed of any developments that come to your attention. One of the policy provisions is that the insured will cooperate fully with the insurance company on any claims.

What if There's a Problem?

Insurance companies are in business to make money. Cases that aren't clear cut will more than likely be denied. Also, the sheer size of an insurance company and numbers of claims being processed builds in further delays and errors.

It's well-settled law that an insurance company must exercise good faith in its handling of your claim. The insurance policy is a legal contract between you and the company, and the courts have held that carriers cannot simply turn their backs on an otherwise valid claim. This applies both ways—the insured also must exercise good faith when submitting claims, avoiding fraud and lying.

There is a conflict built in from the beginning. You want to be reimbursed what makes you entirely whole—after all, look at all the premiums paid over the years just for this coverage. The insurance company, on the other hand, wants to adhere to the strict limits of the policy and contain its losses. This difference in approach builds in differences, not to mention that whether a claim is covered can turn on facts both parties dispute or on paper-thin applications of the law. State courts can take entirely different positions when interpreting the same policy provision and similar facts.

Let's say there was a fire in your house, damaging the insides extensively and destroying valuable computer equipment. It will take $15,000 to replace the equipment (bought 5 years ago for $7500) and another $15,000 to repair the interior damage.You are a computer programmer for the Ace Software Company, attach your business card when submitting your claim, and order the new computer equipment you've always wanted.

The first shock is when the claims investigator tells you the house was underinsured by 50% of its replacement value and only one-half of the damages will be covered. The second shock comes when they discovered you used the computer equipment entirely for business, part for the Ace Software Company and part for your own clients after hours. They've told you that your policy, in any event, only provided reimbursement at actual cash value for the old, depreciated computer equipment (worth now $3,000 after deduction for that wear and tear).

The bottom line was that they denied the claim for the computer equipment. After the $500 deductible on property damage to the house, they offered you $7,000 (50% of $15,000, then subtracted the deductible). You will be out-of-pocket $23,000. You remember telling the insurance agent that you wanted the computer equipment "covered" under your homeowners policy. Thinking that it was, you never checked it further. You disagree totally with the insurance company's assessment as to the replacement value of your home.

Or your son was riding on a lawn tractor, playing with a friend on the seat. The friend pushed too hard, and your angry son hit him hard on the shoulder, pushing his companion down on the ground. Unfortunately, his friend was injured (a broken shoulder) and the medical bills amounted to $2,500. The parents want to be reimbursed for their medical bills, and you file your claim. However, it's denied by the company, because they decide that your son intentionally pushed his friend, thus causing the damages. Intentional conduct is not covered by your homeowners policy, they explain. Your son says that he was angry, but he didn't intend to hurt his friend.

Although the majority of claims are handled quickly and without problem, disputes arise when you don't know exactly what's covered. The first problem could have been avoided in the first place by simply checking. However, controversies also arise simply from a difference in looking at the problem, as in the second situation.

If you aren't satisfied with the results, don't run to an attorney first. Operate quickly to avoid any possible legal action being barred by a statute of limitations (where you lose the right to sue if an action isn't brought within a certain time period).

If a claim is denied or delays continue in its processing, then call the agent and complain, asking for the company's claim supervisor. After discussing your position with the agent and company, then follow that up with a letter that further explains your position. If after discussing the situation or receiving the agent's and/or carrier's response, you're still not satisfied, then call or write your state's insurance department. A copy of this letter should be sent to your agent and carrier. Although state insurance departments are slow, they typically are quite consumer-oriented. If necessary, consult an attorney and have that lawyer write a threatening letter to the insurance company.

You will need to assess the insurance company's position versus the cost and time involved in contesting it. If the amount contested could be brought in small claims court, then consult Chapter 17 and bring that action. If the amount contested is larger, then consult an attorney and consider demanding that the matter with your insurance company be arbitrated or mediated (see Chapter 16). If that's refused, then consider legal action (see Chapter 15 on determining the cost effectiveness of such a move) should the company be showing bad faith in its handling of your claim.

If the dispute is over value alone (and not coverage), then you generally will be required to use an appraisal process first before being able to file a lawsuit. Upon an election by either the company or the insured, this process requires the insured (at his or her cost) to hire an appraiser with the company hiring a second one (at its expense). These two appraisers select a third, disinterested "umpire." The recommendation of any two who agree sets the value, the company and insured sharing the cost of the appraisal process and the third appraiser.

In the first case, an attorney should be consulted as to that state's insurance laws and cases as they apply to both denials. A demand letter could be sent by the attorney, and the carrier may agree to an arbitration or mediation, even a combination involving the appraisal process. However, before deciding on any legal action, the ability to win with those facts and the law should first be decided with an attorney. In the second case, small claims would be appropriate if no response has been received in a few months from the state's insurance department.

What if Your Insurance Company Refuses to Defend You?

The duty of the liability insurer to provide a defense at its cost for an insured has been the subject of constant litigation—nearly as much as over the denial of property coverage and insufficient claim payments. The cost of a legal defense can range from tens of thousands of dollars to six figures and more. The cost of the attorneys alone can easily be more than the first settlement offer by the suing party or even the damages awarded by the court.

The insured must provide the carrier with prompt notice that an insured loss has occurred. If notice in accordance with the policy's guidelines isn't given, then the insured can be barred from taking the case any further. However, a number of courts have declined to forfeit the insured's rights unless it was proven that the untimely filing of the claim was prejudicial to the insurance company's rights. When an exact time for response isn't stated in the policy, then this timeliness is a question of fact to be decided by the jury as to what was reasonable under the

> The courts consistently have held that the insurer's duty to provide a legal defense is broader than the responsibility to pay the damages awarded against an insured. Some courts have decided that this means the duty to provide a defense exists even in instances in which the insurance company wouldn't be obligated to cover the damages—although this is a definite minority position.

circumstances. The courts do support the rule that each carrier must make reasonable and good faith judgments over whether to prepare for a defense by initiating an investigation or other activities that would be reasonable under the circumstances.

It must appear that the claim is actually outside the policy coverage for a carrier to incur no legal liability when turning down the claim. There can be no question about coverage when the lawsuit alleges claims that *all* fall within the insurance policy's provisions. More frequently, claims that are beyond the scope of the insurance coverage are included in lawsuits. The general rule is that insurance companies aren't relieved from their defense responsibilities when the complaint includes *at least one claim that's within the scope of the policy.*

Lawsuits at times don't make any accusations within the policy's liability coverage, and insurance companies routinely deny these claims. The state courts have split as to whether carriers can refuse coverage by only looking at what's stated in the lawsuit—those states that disregard the complaint hold, among other decisions, that the insurer must make at least an investigation and determine from all the facts whether there's a duty to defend within what's stated in the policy.

Sometimes the insurance company in "close" cases will compromise or agree to defend but not (or decide later) to be responsible for any awarded damages. For example, a divorced woman was sued by her ex-husband for libel and slander. Although she was initially turned down she persisted, and the insurance company agreed later to defend her at its cost under her renter's policy, but declined to pay any damages awarded against her. "I wouldn't take 'no' for an answer. I consulted with an attorney after the first turndown, then said I was planning to sue them and argued the points told me by the lawyer. I don't know if I would have sued them if they hadn't made the offer. But you have to make a stand," she said.

The problem is when you're declined coverage, whether or not it was wrong, you must consult an attorney in deciding whether to file a lawsuit against the insurance company over its decision. This is separate from the lawsuit or claim in

> An insurance company may be liable for damages if there's a breach of its duty to defend. If the company wrongly refused to defend or honor the claim, then the insured generally will be entitled to be reimbursed for the defense costs, in addition to any damages awarded up to the policy limits. Additionally, courts have also awarded punitive damages, or additional damages, when the refusal of the insurance company was judged to be particularly wrongful or in bad faith.

which the carrier declined responsibility. After deciding what to do with the first lawsuit or loss, you must determine the approach as to the carrier.

An Overview

Having effective insurance in place can make a difference, but the cost of covering everything isn't affordable to most of us. It is simply a bet whether some calamity or event will happen or not.

For example, the great 1993 Mississippi River flood caused widespread destruction in several midwestern states. Only 5% of the households living on those flood plains had flood insurance. High costs and a false sense of security had convinced the other 95% to go without insurance. In fact, many farm and home-owners had canceled their insurance just before the floods, although they had had policies in force for years, because of the need to save money and the belief that the problem wouldn't occur. It had been over 100 years since the last flood of such proportions. Then the rains came.

The same situation exists with respect to earthquakes, hurricanes, car accidents, and lawsuits. As with life itself, you just don't know what will happen. When insurance isn't in force, then you win when nothing occurs. You lose, if it does. You try to make the best decision possible based on what's thought likely to happen and the amount still left in your checkbook.

5

Selecting and Consulting the Right Attorney Beforehand

The "five-minute phone call" to your lawyer is the best investment you can make with an attorney. Whether for business or personal reasons, it's better to ask about legal problems before signing a real estate listing agreement or volunteering time for a nonprofit organization when there's no insurance. Such preventive medicine is always less costly over the long run.

"A client contacted me about a proposed partnership agreement," an attorney reflected. "After discussing what would happen when more money was needed, it turned out the potential partner was trying to pull a fast one with 'weasel wording' and gain control, then kick the other out. My client dropped the discussions and later found a more suitable financial partner." Another client contacted a second lawyer over the filing of a lawsuit. Although he was not happy when informed it was barred by the statute of limitations (the time period within which a complaint must be brought), at least his money wasn't wasted by following the advice of the first lawyer contacted.

We've said this before, but it needs emphasizing. Using an attorney for a brief telephone call, or even an hour-long consultation, isn't designed to add revenues to the pockets of attorneys. Far from it. Instead, asking about questions when you're charged by the minute makes far more sense than being charged by the day when you are in litigation.

Large or Small Firm?

The first decision is whether you want to employ a large or a smaller law firm for your legal work. There are various advantages and disadvantages based on the size of the law firm that's chosen.

Large law firms typically enjoy a good reputation built up through providing good, quality service. However, the quality of the service for you will depend upon who works on your problems and the amount of time spent by junior associates. Large firms generally have a tier structure usually comprised of junior and senior associates who report to junior and senior partners. The general rule of thumb is that associates are priced so that one-third of their billings covers their salary, one-third covers the firm's overhead, and the remaining one-third goes to the profit being distributed among the partners.

Senior partners interface with the more important clients; junior partners and/or senior associates perform the more complex legal tasks, interface with most clients, and supervise the associates; junior associates generally conduct document inspections, routine depositions, routine motions, document drafting, and legal research, not usually spending much time with important clients.

Associates can charge $100 per hour and up in an increasing series of hourly rates based on the seniority of the lawyer, all the way up the pyramid to the $400 or so per hour charged by the senior partners of the largest law firms in major metropolitan centers. The lower hourly rate charged by associates reflects their limited experience and skills in contrast to more senior associates and partners, who bill at higher rates.

Be careful that you're not paying for the education of these associates, their turnover, and their lower quality of work. Associates and junior partners are pressured to meet billable hour quotas typically averaging 2,000 hours per year, and it has been this way for years. This billing level is at a minimum and doesn't leave much room for error. Billing 40 hours for 50 weeks doesn't leave much time for lunch or dinner either, especially when there's competition for work among law firms. This also motivates some attorneys to bill for work not done, to charge two clients for the same work, and even to lie about the actual amount of time. This doesn't mean such practices occur in any particular law firm, but it is a temptation when lawyers who don't meet their expenses will be soon gone.

Individuals and companies employ large firms for their contacts, whether it be for access to regulatory decision makers, politicians, or venture capitalists. A large law firm does have a "one stop," full service capability to meet your specialized requirements, usually without regard to the type of problem—you don't need to be referred to another law firm in another part of town. Such large law firms typically have the resources to meet emergencies, as they aren't dependent on any particular attorney being available.

However, small firms typically charge less and provide more personalized service. Their billing rates generally are less because of lower overhead, fewer attorneys working on the same matter, and not as much pressure to meet billable hour quotas. The partner you talk to is the one you'll be working with, as distinct from the "rain maker" or marketing partner in a larger firm who sells you on the firm, then turns the work over to another attorney.

Large variances in fees can be expected, all depending on the size of the firm you retain. One sole practitioner reported his bill to bring about a settlement in a litigated case was $12,000. The large law firm's bill for the other side was $60,000. Although you can be overcharged by any attorney, no matter what the size of the firm, the amount charged will be less when the hourly rates are lower.

Smaller firms are more likely to work with a smaller client in budgeting, billing, and cost-control matters (although this does depend on how hungry they are). A large firm, even when wanting your business, may not want to work as closely in keeping your fees under control because of the larger office overhead, partner needs for income, and less personal service. The larger the size of your legal requirements, however, the more likely the larger law firm will work with you.

A small firm doesn't provide a "full service" ability and may occasionally need to refer a particularly complex problem to a tax specialist or specialized litigator. Small law firms do network among other small firms for specialists in those areas that complement their own services and won't steal their clients.

The decision on which size of firm to choose depends on what you're comfortable with. You may desire the prestige of a large law firm and be willing to pay more for that. On the other hand, you might be more comfortable with a small law firm where you know everyone. You'll need to decide what's important for you, just as you do when you're hiring someone for your business or to work on your home. *Martindale-Hubbell*, a legal directory discussed later in the chapter, can be consulted as to the size and background of the attorneys working for a given law firm.

Establish What You Need

Today's legal environment is too complicated to entrust all your requirements to one attorney. The law changes too frequently for one attorney to handle your will, divorce, business contracts, and litigation needs. You'll be paying for the attorney's education on your specialized needs in those areas that a lawyer usually doesn't handle. You must shop for a specialist for each specific need you have.

Ask yourself what's needed first by listing the specific problems that need to be solved, the potential legal problems, and any specialized requirements. If you need an estate plan, then you'll be looking for estate planners. If you've been sued, then defending the lawsuit is to be done. Set down the facts that brought about your problem, assemble all the documents pertaining to it, and begin the process.

Generally, the same attorney isn't good for doing both transactional (contractual or noncourt) matters and litigation (arguing in court), even when in the same general field of law. The personalities required are quite different—negotiating contracts requires a detailed, fact-oriented person with a personality allowing for compromises and agreements to be reached. Litigators are paid to stand up in court and argue whether certain facts and laws are true, simply depending on which side they're on. The more aggressive personalities are the winners in court. This doesn't mean a flamboyant personality wouldn't be good drafting a will, but you usually don't find such attorneys doing that. As one estate specialist said, "A transactional attorney is motivated to being accurate and not having later problems with the deal; the litigator is more concerned with beating the other side."

Preparing a will or an estate plan, of course, is quite different from defending a lawsuit over an automobile accident. The attorneys selected should have an ability in the specific need you have. Where more than one problem is needed to be solved, then you might consider a larger law firm. Remember there's no assurance that the specialists found in a larger law firm are the best for you. Talk to both a large law firm and a smaller one if you can't make up your mind.

Also, businesses have specialized requirements for their attorneys. For example, a computer software start-up venture has different legal requirements than a company manufacturing bikinis. The bikini company may have problems with suppliers or immigration compliance problems. The computer venture will need equity raised, securities registered, and protection of software innovations. Your specialized requirements should be thought about first.

The Search for Names

It's not possible to interview qualified candidates unless you have their names. *Technology Executive Roundtable* surveyed 126 high-technology companies with an average $5 million in sales and 50 employees as to how they chose their attorneys— 45% had received references from a business acquaintance, 21% by other references, 19% had conducted their own study, 11% had been referred by their accountant, and 4% by their banker.

Similarly, most people find their lawyers through personal networking with business acquaintances, other professionals, friends, associates, or anyone else known in their world. Bankers, accountants, rotary members, church members, and any other contacts will have ideas on names to follow up.

The problem with referrals is that, although you have a name, there's no assurance that the attorney will necessarily be good with your problem. It's better if the referring person previously retained the attorney for a similar matter with a good experience, rather than merely remembered that person from the yacht club's annual dinner.

Look around your office building, or close to your work, and see if any attorneys or law firms are located there. Walk into a nearby law office even if they don't do your type of work, and ask the legal secretary who does. Keep your eyes open as you walk to lunch. But remember you're only looking for names to interview; you're not trying to hire the first lawyer who'll take your case.

Although ethical rules in all states forbid attorneys from directly soliciting clients (such as by telephone or in the hospital ward), lawyers are allowed by a Supreme Court decision to advertise to the general public. Law firms have accordingly been making use of brochures, direct marketing and public relations efforts, seminars, newsletters, and even television advertising in their quest for new clients in today's competitive market. There are private, for-profit referral firms advertising on television, in newspapers, and in the yellow pages.

Attorneys advertise heavily on TV, in large yellow page ads, and by mass mailings. This form of advertising is generally oriented toward the mass market for simple divorces, drunk driving defense, wills, trusts, personal injury, and bankruptcy matters. These problems occur with the general public more regularly than other matters and are more amenable to volume processing and lower, fixed fees. For example, you usually don't find a civil defense attorney advertising this way to the general public, although you might see a criminal defense attorney advertising for drunk driving defense work. Drunk driving defense is a volume or repetitive activity (many people need it and most are plea-bargained), whereas the cost for civil defense work is higher and not usually amenable to volume advertising.

Another way of locating attorneys involves contacting the lawyers' referral department at your local or state bar association. Normally, these attorneys will be listed under their specialty, such as business, wills, or divorce work. These services require little or no experience or specialty requirements in order to be listed, but they do require the lawyer to be a member of the local bar. In some states and counties the attorneys pay a fee for the listing, and many bar associations require listed attorneys to carry minimum levels of malpractice insurance.

Attorneys use a legal directory entitled *Martindale-Hubbell* when looking for a lawyer to refer a client to over a matter located in another area or state. This is a multivolume set that lists attorneys in the United States by city and state, although it is generally limited to cities of more than 10,000 people.

The listing of all attorneys is in the blue pages of *Martindale-Hubbell*; however, the white directory with the more detailed information is only for those firms that have paid a fee for that inclusion—if attorneys aren't listed in the white directory, this doesn't mean that they aren't practicing law. The white directory includes the college and law school attended, age, honors, professional associations, representative clients, and even specialties that the firm practices in. Further, it lists ratings based upon recommendations made by other attorneys and judges in the same city as to the lawyer's legal ability, adherence to ethical standards, and professional diligence. This is a quick way to secure names of attorneys to interview and to check out names already found. Your local county law library, generally open to the general public, should have a copy of *Martindale-Hubbell*.

The Interview

Once the names of prospective attorneys are in hand, you should interview them initially over the phone. Tell the attorney how you were referred and briefly

The actual interview should cover nine specific areas: a detailed conflict check; the lawyer's experience with your problem; the firm's computerization status; internal staffing; time availability; cost and expense considerations; billing procedures; malpractice coverage; and compatibility.

describe the problems you need solved. Ask the lawyer if there would be any conflict of interest from the law firm's having previously represented any of the other parties involved in your matter. State that you're looking for long-term professional representation for your matters on a cost-effective basis. Then ask if that attorney has the time to handle your problem effectively. *Be sure to determine that the initial consultation, which will also include your questions* and *information about fees, is on a courtesy, no-charge basis. It's typical for attorneys not to charge for the initial consultation.*

Conflict Check

Confirming that the law firm hasn't represented any other party connected with your problems should be done in the beginning. A law firm cannot previously have represented one party in litigation and then represent the other in another adversarial matter. Although it is possible for a lawyer to represent two such parties in non-litigation or contractual matters, provided the written consent of both has been gained, this consent may be difficult to aquire.

Experience

How experienced the law firm is in your matter, what their success rate has been, and how specialized they are in such matters are all quite important for you to determine. If your problem is defending lawsuits, then you want to know how many trials or arbitrations they've had with your problem. If it involves estate planning, then the time spent and numbers of problems handled similar to yours should be checked out.

You should ask the attorneys what problems they see with your case and if there are alternative, nonlegal methods to handle it in a cost-effective way. A problem with many attorneys is that they only see legal solutions to problems. It isn't their fault, because they've been trained to do this. A lawyer who also can see non-legal ways to solve your problem is preferable to one who can't.

For example, if a friend owes you money, you might not need the lawyer to send a series of threatening letters. It may be better to be informed about the law and try to work it out first. See if the attorney describes practical payment programs, rather than the usual approach of threat, suing, and court. After all, you're not interested in suing your friend, you just want to be repaid.

If you feel the local newspaper didn't treat you right, perhaps even libeled you, it may be better if the attorney can get a more favorable article or a retraction published, rather than suing the paper that week. Rather than enter into a long agreement with legalese, it may be preferable to use a simple letter agreement. Instead of suing a party outright, it may be possible to use mediation or arbitration. For example, mediation in divorce and custody matters is being increasingly used in place of the traditional, two attorneys-slugging-it-out-in-court approach.

Business problems, as well as personal situations, are best solved with a business solution—whether it's collecting money, getting a supplier to take back poor quality goods, or resolving a customer's complaint. Remember that using the courts is only one of several ways to solve a problem, and it's an expensive one at best. See Chapter 11 for alternative approaches to use in specific business areas.

Attorneys also can be certified as specialists in fields of the law ranging from family law and federal income taxes to criminal law. This certification is granted according to your state's laws and can be based on the number of years of experience, having taken required courses, and having passed an examination. If you see this designation, then ask what the state requirements were.

Computerization Status

Attorneys and law firms should be computer literate and efficient in word processing, and you should view their operations closely, even by walking through the word processing center with the attorney. Most agreements, pleadings and motions, opinion letters, and routine correspondence have formats and entire paragraphs identical to those in other similar documents. Continuing Education of the Bar, Judicial Council forms, and fill-in-the-blank forms are widely available for any attorney. Software programs in bankruptcy, tax, collections, estate planning, loan documents, and even pleadings (the court documents) are widely available. There are document assembly systems that even allow attorneys to create and amend their own forms. Ask what types the law firm is using.

The cost saved by utilizing such form agreements and documents can be passed onto you. When this isn't present, then you will receive larger than necessary bills, time delays, and even mistakes. Larger law firms even are hiring law school graduates as systems and applications managers, not to automate their clerical tasks, but to develop document assembly and written agreement systems.

Staffing

It's important to meet and assess the experience level of the attorney who actually will be working on your case, especially when with larger law firms. Is it the attorney you were referred to or an associate subject to another's review? The law firm should have a formal training program in place for their associates and not rely on their gaining experience by working on your project. Be careful with this, as you want the best available services for the fees you will be paying.

Time Availability

The law firm should be frank about its ability to meet your requirements in a timely matter. You need to determine, especially with smaller law firms, whether the lawyers have large clients or cases that would make meeting your timing difficult. If you are dealing with a sole practitioner, then ask what backup arrangements are made when that attorney goes on vacation or becomes sick.

Cost and Expense

A frank discussion as to the firm's costs, expenses, and billing procedures should take place. Although this can be intimidating, remember that we are talking about how much you will be paying. If you'll negotiate cost when buying a car, then you should at least look into this with a lawyer. As one client commented, "I didn't want to talk about costs at first, because I needed help and didn't want an argument. However, that changed as soon as she told me what her hourly rate was."

Even if you are nervous, discuss the firm's hourly rates for paralegals, associates, and partner levels, trying to secure a fixed fee or a not-to-exceed written estimate. Ask questions as to how the firm charges for soft costs such as postage, copying, word processing, overtime, and computer research. What fractions of an hour do they bill? What's their policy when charging for travel, out-of-town requirements, and time in court (such as waiting to be heard or traveling a distance for a short hearing)? Do they require a retainer?

Ask if they use value billing such as fixed price, blended rates, and modified contingency fees (see Chapter 12 for further details). Informal estimates should at least be made of the hours and overall cost. Normally, nonlitigation matters are easier to estimate. However, even litigated cases should have a time and cost estimate range or a litigation plan and budget (see Chapter 19).

Billing Procedures

Determine how frequently the attorney or firm bills and the format of that billing. The law firm should tell you whether it bills in a detailed way allowing you to monitor the specific costs of your work. Ask the attorney for a copy of a standard billing form and go over it in detail with him or her. (See Chapter 12 for more details.)

Malpractice Coverage

Attorneys wince at this consideration. Malpractice coverage is expensive, riddled with exceptions or noncoverage, and may not even be affordable. However, every law firm and attorney should have malpractice insurance coverage for the work they perform. The absence of such a policy could indicate they either can't afford it or can't obtain it because of serious mistakes made in the past. Some states require that the presence or absence of malpractice insurance be disclosed in a written fee agreement. However, you can't depend on this and should always ask about it.

Compatibility

You'll be working with these people on personal, confidential matters. *If you don't like their manners or appearance, then consider whether you should be working with them at all.* It may be that their experience makes you want to overlook such personality considerations, but if the "bedside manner" turns you off, then you shouldn't hire that lawyer. Perhaps you want one who is more intuitive or even understanding. You may have a preference for a female over a male, or vice-versa.

Teamwork also is a little used, but important concept. Solving your problem in a cost-effective way requires the two of you working together. You will need to bring to the attorney's attention the necessary facts, even making decisions together as to whether you sue or what legal procedures can be afforded. Being incompatible or not getting who you want only means more problems further down the road.

Tell What You Want

The attorney should be told what you want to accomplish. For example, if you want to sell your house to a friend, tell the attorney that being protected is most important, but that you don't want to become enemies in the process. If writing up a business agreement needs to be completed, then tell the lawyer you can't afford an expensive contract and ask how that can be accomplished.

The level of risk you're willing to assume is another area. If the opposing party is threatening to sue you, tell the lawyer whether you can handle being sued or not. Businesses have similar considerations—a quickly rising software development company will have a different set of goals, risk levels for decisions, and even culture than a long-standing, manufacturing company that stamps out tools and dyes. Production, retirement, employment, financial, and even trade secret policies will be different.

The only way you can receive satisfactory service is to tell your attorney what type of service you want. If you want to know about the developments of your case as they occur (which most clients do, a desire some attorneys ignore), tell the lawyer in no uncertain terms that you want to know what's happening. If you want a low cost, then tell what you're prepared to pay and for what services.

Once you have discussed these factors, thank the attorney for his or her time (it's his or her only asset). Tell the lawyer you'll call if you have other questions. Eliminate immediately any lawyer who hedges on working with you on controlling costs or who is unwilling to discuss such fees other than saying, "I bill on an hourly basis of $200 per hour—that times the number of hours is your bill."

Write down Your Observations

Write down any other observations or details immediately after the meeting. Determine if the person you talked with was the firm's salesman or a competent and qualified attorney—there's a big difference. If you detected selling and smoke, limited observations as what to do about your problem, or talk about how effectively others can handle your job, then you were talking to the salesman. You need to interview the one who'll be doing the work.

Think about the character of the person you just met. Did the attorney seem to be truthful and honest? Did he or she appear competent, understand the law and facts, and show an understanding and interest in your case? Did the lawyer show "street smarts" and understand that problems need to be solved without breaking the deal or creating a worse problem? For example, an attorney who says "We'll serve the lawsuit by next week," may not be as appropriate as the one who says, "I haven't taken your case yet. What if you tried talking to the other party this way..." After this discussion, this attorney might then say "The most cost-effective way of handling this case would be to....But if that doesn't work, then we could try this...then this..."

Note how the office was running when you first came in. Were the secretaries, paralegals, and other attorneys busy? Did the work environment appear to be professionally run? Pay attention to how lavish the office and surroundings appeared—you may be paying for these excessive, plush surroundings. If you have the time, call the state bar association and determine that the law firm and its attorneys are in good standing with no disciplinary proceedings pending or completed.

Interview Several

Although it's time consuming, take the time to interview a number of law firms—the more the better—and get second opinions. Talking to several law firms and attorneys gives you additional insight into your case, not to mention providing backups. If your initial selection doesn't work out, or there's a problem that the selected law firm can't handle, you already will have interviewed the next lawyer to retain. Don't hire the first attorney you see until you determine he or she can meet your needs better than anyone else interviewed. Wait until you've seen them all.

They're All Different

"It was the luck of the draw," said one satisfied client as to picking the right attorney. "The hard thing is to get the one who will charge fairly and do a good job." This is all too true, but they are out there. You just have to work to find them, and your success rate also depends on what you need to have done. A successful, eastern real estate developer said, "For deals you need someone who's honest and will say whether he or she has worked before on that type of problem. As important, your attorney needs to understand the give-and-take of negotiations and not turn the other party off or lose the deal. You don't want him to be reinventing the wheel or reworking the deal at your expense. He needs to have experience in keeping deals together but protecting you at the same time."

If you want a litigator, then you aren't as interested in keeping a deal together—but you do need someone who can solve your problem. Most attorneys are trained well in the law, but some always seem to be more successful than others. If working with a lawyer for the first time, you won't know that person's particular strengths and weaknesses.

Assessing personalities is a good part of the decision. Attorneys come in different breeds—some are "pit bulls" and others "peacemakers." Generally, you want an attorney who'll work for early settlements and discuss the different ways that the problem can be solved. However, keep the "pit bull" in mind when the opposing party thinks its case is a "bet the house" problem.

There are important questions to ask and answer in making a decision, and they're also very difficult to determine. You'll have to rely on your "gut" in evaluating an attorney, just as you do with any other important decision.

Review the Results

Analyze the results of your interviews, and determine whom you want to hire, then negotiate for the best deal. Even after deciding on the one you want, don't always tell the person you've accepted him flat out. Call back and say you're interested in retaining that firm, but that you have a few questions to ask about costs. Then negotiate the best deal you can.

Try a Test Case

Consider giving a favorably interviewed law firm a minor "test" case on which to work, if you have other legal problems. You then can assess whether you like their service, personality, work quality, and cost effectiveness. However, this should be balanced by the realization that attorneys also know when to be on their best behavior. It's how a law firm handles your repetitive matters that is important, but a test case allows you to see how one performs under actual conditions.

Use More than One

Consider employing more than one law firm for different projects if you have the work and especially if you own a business. In fact, most large companies retain several law firms, as they receive economies from the fee competition and have backups in case one firm can't handle something. Law firms tend to work harder when they know a competitor is already performing work for the client. A business can pick among varying specialties for any legal problem. In fact, this trend has become so widespread that the largest companies now are cutting back from retaining 100 or more different law firms to more manageable levels.

Law firms always try to convince you to give them all your work. What supplier doesn't? However, having a number of vendors for your business works in other areas, so why not here? Large companies also retain law firms, paying large retainer fees, just to keep the best law firms for them in the event of a "bet the company" lawsuit. In small cities, you can freeze out the other party from the best representation in both business and personal matters.

In a city of 100,000, located in what was otherwise a rural area, a dispute arose between the sellers and buyers of an office building. The sellers knew that the buyers were planning to sue them for fraud, and they interviewed the top litigators in their area for representation. Even though they only selected one of those seen, all of the interviewed firms took the position that there was a conflict of interest when later contacted by the buyers. The sellers had kept in touch with the nonselected law firms, saying they might need a backup, and the buyers had to scramble to find an attorney. The buyers were frozen out of the top firms, and it was confirmed later that the seller's reason for contacting all the law firms was to create this scenario. This isn't to say that all law firms will turn down business when first contacted by the opposing party. However, it does make attorneys think about conflict of interest problems, even when interviewed but not retained.

The "Beauty Contest"

An example of what happens with a surplus of attorneys is called the "beauty contest." This is legal jargon for the bidding contest among law firms for a large company's business along the rules established by that company. For example, one real estate development and investment firm arranged a beauty contest where a few law firms even offered to do free legal work for a shot at the main part of the work, consisting of a series of large complex office leases. Three law firms then competed in the final round for the main work, supplying the company with staffing plans and offering significant discounts from their normal fees. Each was handed a few leases to do on a trial basis at their bid rate. The company then selected the firm it felt was best and most cost competitive.

The process of using beauty contests involves gathering the names of candidates, usually conducting preliminary telephone interviews to narrow down the candidates, and then the final round of in-person interviews. At times a questionnaire is used to narrow down candidates to the final round after the initial telephone interviews. The winner generally has a chemistry with the client, an enthusiasm for the project, shows initiative (one actually went down to the courthouse and secured a copy of the complaint to research before the interview), and discusses creative approaches in the interview. All this is in addition to being cost effective. As one disgruntled attorney said, "Every time in-house counsel sees the law firm, it seems that there's a beauty contest." What law firms go through to get business these days!

It's a judgment call as to which lawyer gives the best value, especially when you haven't worked with one before. But you need to weigh what's being received for a price, because you can't get your money's worth if you don't.

Getting the Best Value for Your Money

You can limit costs and increase value by limiting the extent to which you use an attorney, if hiring one at all. It may be that after interviewing a few, you've decided the costs are too high. Or you might want to "do-it-yourself" as a challenge.

Let's say you want a will. There are a number of do-it-yourself books on the market that can be bought and consulted. If your estate is uncomplicated, then you could consider doing it yourself. However, whatever you do will take time. You can either talk to attorneys and pay the extra money to have them do it or you can read extensively, then try to do it yourself. This will depend on you, as it will take your time to read the books or attend the seminars, then do the work. If you find that you don't understand it, or don't even want to do it, then you'll shop around for the best price to have an attorney do it.

There are legal clinics, advertising by newspaper, the yellow pages, and television, that will handle everything from divorces to wills and drunk driving cases. Check their costs against what the attorneys quote you over the telephone. Browse through a book store and see if you want to buy a book telling you how to do it yourself. You can even check the county law library for forms and the law when the do-it-yourself books don't specifically treat your state.

However, if your situation is complicated, then you'll want to consult an attorney. Try to obtain a free consultative session where you can show what you've done and ask for the lawyer's recommendations. For example, if you read an estate planning book and decide you need a trust, then see if you understand how to use

Getting the Best Price

As discussed in Chapters 13, 19, and 20, you get the best price by shopping around. Basically this is no different than buying a car. Attorneys will try to argue that their services are personal and that it's difficult to price a product, especially when litigation is involved. This can be true—but comparison shopping also involves deciding on what's received for that price and from whom you buy.

Be sure to discuss frankly with each attorney what you can afford. You don't have to pay just what's billed by the hour each month, as there are the alternative billing approaches (see Chapter 12). If not, try to pay a set amount each month, regardless as to the monthly invoice, as paying for any services involves terms as well as the price. *It is quite possible to set up an installment plan, not to mention receiving a break on any interest charged (and see if this can be eliminated).* You can't lose by trying this before hiring any one attorney.

You Want Value

The lowest cost doesn't necessarily mean you'll receive your money's worth. You need to consider the source before taking the lowest price, and this isn't any different than reviewing the experience and what's included in a low bid to repair your roof. It's better to pay a little more for shoes that last years, than to pay less for shoes that wear out 6 months later.

For example, hiring a recent law school graduate with low fees could be fine if you have a simple collection matter that doesn't represent most of your net worth. If you have a "bet your house" lawsuit, then you're better off avoiding the inexperienced attorney. The preparation of a simple will or divorce could be given to the lower bid, but be sure that the attorney has done this before. For more complicated matters, you should consider the more expensive specialist.

the forms that are included. If you don't, and have assets such as equity in your house, then you should consult an attorney.

As the money involved in your situation increases, then it's more likely you'll talk to an attorney. For example, if you're lending $2,000 to your brother, then handling the matter yourself shouldn't be a problem. However, if you are lending $15,000 secured by your brother's car, then you should consider talking to a lawyer.

You will be trading off the cost of someone else doing it versus your time. It's always more expensive when someone else does something, whether it's painting your house or trimming your trees. As attorneys are much more expensive, you might think about doing the work yourself, but first look at all the options.

6

Get It in Writing (and Understand Your Rights)

Contracts and agreements take place every day. Let's say you tell a friend "If you buy lunch today, I'll buy it the next time we're together." Your friend buys lunch; he'll be expecting you to do the same the next time. This is a contract.

You say to your veterinarian, "I don't have any money today, but if you give my cat the needed shots, I'll come down tomorrow and pay you." As soon as your cat has been given its shots, your veterinarian has accepted the offer for you to pay him. That's also a contract.

A contract is an agreement between parties that creates obligations on both sides. If one party breaks his or her promise, then the other has the right to force the first party to perform or receive compensation for that breach. In both cases, you have an obligation. If you don't buy lunch the next time, your friend could sue you if he must pay again (but more than likely you'll just lose a friend). The veterinarian can sue you if you don't pay for the shots.

To have a valid contract, you need to have a valid offer, an acceptance, consideration (or value), and legal enforceability. If required by law, then the contract also must be in writing to be valid.

An offer is a promise conditioned upon an act, not acting, or another promise. For example, if you say "I'll pay $10 if you walk across the Brooklyn Bridge," then get ready to pay when your friend does it. In that case, the promise was conditioned upon an act—walking across the Brooklyn Bridge. If you say, "I'll pay you $10 if you don't walk across the Brooklyn Bridge," then pay up when your friend walks away, then turns around to you with one hand held out.

Suppose you say to a friend "I'll pay you $10 for that old stove in your barn," and your friend answers "Okay. I'll sell it to you at that price." You have a contract based on two promises—one to pay $10 for the stove; the other to accept $10 for it.

These examples show the differences between two types of contracts. Some contracts involve an offer where the acceptance is implied by an act (walking or not walking across the Brooklyn Bridge). This is called a *unilateral* contract in the law—the person making the offer (the promisor) doesn't receive a return promise, but wants an act to be done instead under the offer's terms. If your friend just stands there, then there's no contract. Once the walk has been completed, the offer has been accepted, and the act has created a duty for you to pay the money. If you don't pay up, then your friend can sue you for not performing.

Other contracts involve both parties making promises to each other, such as with the contract for selling the stove. This is called a *bilateral* contract by the law, as the second party agreed by promising to sell the stove at that price. A bilateral contract is characterized by a promise for a promise; the unilateral contract is evidenced by a promise for an act.

If the response to your promise had been "I'll only sell it (the stove) for $20," then there would be no contract. That was a counteroffer. There is no contract until there exists a meeting of the minds as to the price acceptable to each party.

Most important agreements involve bilateral contracts—buying a car, leasing an apartment, selling your house, and borrowing money all involve promises by both the buyer and seller, landlord and tenant, or lender and borrower. Aside from the requirement of an offer and an acceptance, there must be some consideration or value.

In a bilateral contract, each party promises to do something for the other, expecting to receive something in return. That is the consideration or value. In our example, you wanted to own a stove, and your friend wanted the money. If the price is agreed upon (let's say $20), then there's a deal.

However, the law doesn't worry about the amount or fairness of the consideration, unless there's fraud or some element of bad dealing. If the stove had been worth $200 (you knew your stoves), then that contract wouldn't be set aside just because you received the better deal. However, if you told the other party that the stove was worthless (and you were a recognized expert in old stoves), then the court probably would set the deal aside based upon fraud or misrepresentation.

Even if you have the required promises, acceptance (or meeting of the minds), and consideration, the contract must be enforceable. Enforceability under the law takes many forms. For example, both parties need to have the *legal* capacity to contract, and the subject matter of the contract must be legal as well.

People who are minors (under the age of 18), mentally ill, or under the control of a guardian are deemed not to have the capacity to contract. Minors must take steps to disaffirm the contract, but they do remain liable for the agreement until such actions are taken. Although this area is governed by state statute (some contracts, such as life insurance with minors, are generally upheld), the concept is that people must have the ability to understand the nature of their acts. If you were dazed by a knock on the head or semiconscious from an overdose of medication, then the court wouldn't enforce a contract whereby you agreed to sell all your possessions for $1,000 when they were worth much more.

The subject matter of the contract must be legal, as well. If you signed a contract to "invest" with a betting syndicate $100 a week for 1 year to make bets, the contract wouldn't be enforceable as this is an illegal activity (unless the state's laws change). If you agreed to lend $5,000 in return for a 20% share of your friend's current marijuana crop, then the courts wouldn't enforce your demand for payment when your friend said "Tough rocks."

The list of exclusions, rules, and definitions goes on and on when you're considering the area of contracts. Attorneys have many ways and arguments to challenge or uphold a contract ranging from mistake, fraud, mutual mistake, unforeseen difficulties, unfair bargaining power, a particular state statute, usury (the interest rate charged was too high)—you name it. One of the most important laws, however, is that certain contracts must be in writing. The general rule is to be sure all your agreements are in writing when possible.

Put All Agreements in Writing

The greatest failure by people is not putting ordinary transactions into some form of writing—the problem being that people forget over time what has been said. The judge or jury then needs to toss a coin to decide who's right when there's no evidence other than what each swears to be true, and some contracts can't be enforced by law when not in writing.

It doesn't matter if the agreement involves selling your car, lending money, hiring a roofer, or selling the equipment used in your business. Unfortunately, many disputes end in court without anything in writing since "it's easier" to trust the other party. It's better to have something in writing and signed, regardless how brief or handwritten, even when a lawyer hasn't done it.

Certain agreements must be in writing to prove that the contract exists and was intended. Contracts involving real property, guarantees of debt, promises that can't be performed in 1 year, and sales of goods priced $500 or more must be in writing to be enforceable. State statutes add a variety of other areas that more than likely will affect you.

The requirement that certain contracts must be in writing dates back to old English law before our country was founded. Even then, it was decided that there were times when an agreement had to be in writing simply to protect people from fraud. For example, it would be too easy for your next-door neighbor to say you had verbally agreed to sell your house at a low price and have it enforced. And these concepts have carried over to modern times.

Similarly, it was decided that if you promised to pay for another's debt, this should be in writing. It would be too easy for that used car salesman, when your son couldn't pay the installments, to scream you had promised to "make it good." If an agreement couldn't be performed at all within 1 year, then this situation was felt to be too far away to allow oral agreements. For example, if a business associate orally promised that your venture would continue for another 10 years, then it would be attacked on this ground.

This doesn't mean that the entire deal is invalid if there's no written contract covering all the details. The requirement for a written agreement doesn't apply when the agreement has been entirely performed. If you sold your house to a neighbor on a hand shake, then that deal couldn't be attacked for not being in writing if it had already taken place. The statute of frauds is more concerned with proving what the understanding was, and not that the contract is void by operation of law.

Important exceptions were further carved out. One states that substantial part performance by one party (for example, you agree to buy a car, pay a down payment, and take title) gives the necessary evidence as to what the understanding was, thus removing it from the requirement to be in writing.

Another is that you don't need a formal written contract that's signed by both parties. A note or memorandum is all that's required, provided that the parties to the contract, a brief description of the subject matter, the price, and the general terms of the understanding are stated. The brief writing generally needs to be signed only by the party being held responsible. However, with real estate the memorandum must leave little uncertainty, such as stating the property precisely so that a court can order that the agreement be upheld.

This doesn't mean that all contracts must be in writing to be legal. As long as an agreement doesn't fall within what your state's law says must be in writing, then oral contracts are enforceable. For example, low-priced contracts for the sale of goods under the Uniform Commercial Code don't have to be, although all should be (and see Chapter 11 for a further discussion).

The problem is that everyone forgets or doesn't fully remember over time what was verbally decided, and this leads to problems. How such contracts will be treated in court depends entirely on what the judge thinks. If the parties can't agree, then the judge doesn't have a clue either. When its only your word against another's, then you have a bigger problem.

The courts have carved out other exceptions, such as detrimental reliance by one party to where it would be unfair not to hold that there was an enforceable agreement. There have been numerous lawsuits deciding what falls within these categories or what constitutes an acceptable writing, in addition to what each state has enacted.

How Should Agreements Be Documented?

An agreement may be written on a check, cocktail napkin, chiseled on a rock, or put on anything provided the essential terms are readable and it's signed. The sale of an NFL football team was upheld when the essential terms were written down on a cocktail napkin and signed, even though the buyer later changed his mind. The sale of an NBA basketball team was upheld when the parties initialed a three-page handwritten memorandum, not reviewed before by their attorneys, as the important terms had been included.

However, these were major transactions, involving long, expensive lawsuits. Although they prove you don't need a long contract drawn up by an attorney to have an enforceable agreement, you don't want to have an expensive lawsuit either, especially if that could have been avoided.

All of the important details should be written down, as the courts understandably are reluctant to supply the missing terms. If you are lending money, for example, it's important to list who the parties are, the amount lent, the interest rate, terms of repayment and dates, and where payments are to be made, and to have it signed by the borrower. Missing any of these details creates problems, not to mention the danger of unenforceability. Without a written note, the judge can't tell if the transaction was a loan or a gift. When the note isn't sufficiently detailed, the attorneys need to step in, and the judge may not enforce it.

It's different with business contracts involving the sale of goods between merchants, as the law allows the court to imply certain important terms left out from the agreement. The terms that can be implied are the price, time for delivery, place and manner of delivery, and warranties, to name a few. Leaving out such terms can cause unintended and bad results, because if you can't agree over what those terms were, then the attorneys and judge will have that task.

Using forms is one way to document an agreement. Stationery stores (individual form contracts), bookstores (form books), and county law libraries (law book forms) are all good sources. Another way is to write or type your understanding and sign it. The fact that it's handwritten doesn't render the contract unenforceable; however, courts generally resolve ambiguities against the party who writes the agreement. The terms should be fair, as "unconscionable terms" (i.e., one party loses his or her house if a neighbor's loan isn't paid back) won't be enforced. You need to be careful, however, when dealing with contracts, as even attorneys have difficulties in understanding the various rules and laws.

Lending Money or Selling Your Car

There are a variety of situations when documenting the transaction legally doesn't mean you have to hire an attorney. If the situation doesn't involve an important, complex, or valuable transaction, then do it yourself. Even when it does, it is important to make an effort to put your understanding into writing, if just to prove the essential terms and that there was a contract. Two examples are presented below, one when you are lending money and the other when you are selling your car that show some of the considerations and when an attorney might be used.

Lending Money Let's say a friend is in financial trouble and asks for a loan. If a $1,000 loan is involved, then you don't need an attorney. However, if a $15,000 loan is desired and a truck is offered as security, then you should consider consulting one. This doesn't necessarily mean you would hire that lawyer to draft the agreement. You could buy a do-it-yourself book, prepare the documents, then consult an attorney over what was to be done. Or you could ask the lawyer first what was legally required and which problem areas to avoid and then do it yourself. It would be possible to follow the instructions in a book (provided it covered secured notes and transactions) and forget the attorney. There are several choices that can be made.

However, what's important is to document the transaction legally without undue expense, remembering that your time is also valuable. It could be that your time is better spent earning a living or being with your family. No matter how successful you are in business, reading law books at your local law library or a do-it-yourself book can be complicated. It could be better to negotiate the best fee and have someone else do it. For example, it might be worth spending a couple of hours talking by phone with attorneys and negotiating a $500 fee to document a complicated transaction (they already have it on a word processor), then spending your free time reading, learning, and creating it by yourself.

If you decide to do it yourself, then common sense still rules. Let's assume a friend of yours wants to borrow only $1,000, pay it off in monthly payments of $100, including interest at 10% per year. Write it down that way. What's important is that at least all the *business aspects* of your agreement be written down.

You could write down the following: "I, Carole Banning, borrowed $1,000 at 10% interest from Tom Brown on July 19, 1994. I promise to pay him $100 per month until it's all paid back." It is then signed and dated by Carole Banning. This indicates that it's a loan, not a gift, and sets down the repayment terms. However, there are still some important details missing. What happens if you aren't paid back in full? What if a payment is late or a check bounces? What happens if it costs you money to collect what's owing? Do you want security? These are the details that make the difference between a good agreement and a bad one, even when the business points have been included.

It would be better to use an up-to-date form that discusses your state's law, rather than writing the details down on a piece of paper or cocktail napkin. Using store-bought forms or form books has one advantage to writing the agreement down yourself or visiting the local law library—the blanks should tell you what information is needed. However, be careful that the form isn't out of date and what's being used is the correct one for your transaction.

If you used a form or an attorney, it could look like this:

PROMISSORY NOTE

"FOR VALUABLE CONSIDERATION, the receipt of which is acknowledged, the undersigned, Carole Banning, promises to pay to Tom Brown, or order, the principal sum of One Thousand Dollars ($1,000), together with interest on the unpaid principal balance from July 19, 1994, at the rate of ten percent (10%) interest payable: Equal installments of $100, or more, each month until paid in full. Should any payment be received later than the tenth (10th) of each month, then a $5.00 fee will be paid as a late payment penalty. Any check drawn on insufficient funds will incur a $10.00 fee.

All installments of principal and interest of this Note are payable in lawful money of the United States of America addressed to holder at 34 Fourth Street, Boulder, Colorado, or at such other place as the holder may designate in writing. The privilege is reserved by the maker to prepay without penalty any principal prior to the due date of same. All payments shall be first credited to accrued and unpaid interest and thereafter to reducing the principal. The maker hereby waives presentment, demand, protest, and notice of protest in case of a default.

Should interest not be so paid, it shall thereafter bear like interest as the principal, but such unpaid interest so compounded shall not exceed an amount equal to simple interest on the unpaid principal at the maximum rate permitted by law. The unpaid principal balance of this Note, together with any accrued and unpaid interest thereon, shall become due and payable at the option of the holder in the event the maker fails to pay any installment of principal and/or interest when due. In the event an action is commenced to enforce this Note or to collect any sums due hereunder, the prevailing party shall be entitled to receive attorneys' fees and costs as determined by the court.

Signed as July 19, 1994—Carole Banning, 12 First Street, Boulder, Colorado."

If the loan is paid off as agreed, then it makes no difference how this note was written or structured. But if not, and you had to sue in small claims court, then either one of these notes would suffice to prove you had made a loan and the details of repayment. What was important in the second form was that the note could be declared due if an installment was missed as well as the attorney fees provision, among other details. These added legal provisions become even more important as the transaction increases in complexity or importance.

If you were lending $15,000, or taking back security, the first approach wouldn't make sense, as there would be too much room for error. You would want to be more careful that everything was legal and set down correctly.

Selling Your Car Similarly, if you were selling your beat-up, old, second car for $2,000, there would be less need to document the transaction. You would transfer the registration to the new buyer upon receipt of a $2,000 cashiers check. If you were selling your 2-year-old BMW or 917 Porsche, however, then you would want to have the extra protection of an attorney's review or at least handle it with more care, especially if that car were prone to needing expensive repairs.

What if you agreed to accept a down payment and monthly payments on the balance? If you sign over the registration, then there's nothing to secure your note if the buyer defaults. You would need to sue the buyer on the amounts owed and then begin collection activities on any judgment. If you want the protection of security, then you would consider talking to an attorney about what to do. But there are even more details to consider.

Let's say that Steve Jones wants to buy your car for $9,000 and gives you a $500 deposit after you've told him how great the car has been. You accept the deposit and give him a receipt. You write down the following: "I, Sally McGuire, agree to sell my brown, 1990 Toyota (I. D. Number 357867896) to Steve Jones for $9,000, of which $500 has been received as a deposit. Steve agrees to pay the rest within 1 week in a cashier's check. I will then transfer ownership to him." Both of you sign and date it. You transfer the car registration to him when he brings a cashiers check for the remaining $8,500, filling in and signing a bill of sale you purchased in a stationery store. It read:

BILL OF SALE

"For good and valuable consideration, the receipt of which is hereby acknowledged, the undersigned, Sally McGuire ("Seller"), does hereby grant, bargain, sell, and convey to Steve Jones ("Buyer"), the assets of Seller described as follows: A certain brown, 1990 Toyota (I. D. Number 357867896) in return for a total payment of $9,000, all sums having been paid in full.

Seller represents and warrants she's the lawful owner of all the assets transferred hereunder, free and clear of any mortgages, liens, and/or encumbrances of any nature, and Seller will warrant and defend the Buyer against the claims and demands of any and all persons, firms or entities as to this.

Seller agrees she will, at any time upon written request, execute and deliver to Buyer, its successors and/or assigns, any new or confirmatory instruments and perform any further acts which Buyer may request to fully transfer and vest in Buyer title to these assets."

You sign and date this, giving it to Steve, and keeping a copy. Everything is fine until Steve calls up 6 months later, screaming that the car's transmission broke down and that this is the third time he's had to take the car into the shop for repairs. He says he's going to sue you for selling him a lemon. You calmly tell him that he had test driven the car and you had no problems when you owned it.

A few weeks later, you're sued by Steve Jones in Municipal Court (he's really mad and representing himself) for $15,000 representing the cost of the repairs, his out-of-pocket expenses for the car being out of commission, retrieval of his money, and punitive damages. You then discover, while talking with an attorney, that you may have a problem.

The form didn't provide for any disclaimers when selling the car. There was a lot of legal-looking language, and it looked good. But it was only a simple bill of sale that didn't provide for the buyer taking the car "as is," noting its condition, or disclaiming any representations. Now, you know there are specific forms to use when selling your car and are feeling bad until the attorney says another person had called that week with a similar problem.

Being Careful

Having something in writing is better than nothing when trying to prove an agreement exists or what the price, terms, and conditions are. However, a contract is still a legal document with legal rights. Be careful when using a fill-in-the-blanks form, and don't select the first form you think applies or the first book that appears to cover the subject, when doing it yourself. Take your time to be sure everything's done right. If you aren't comfortable with what you read or don't understand it, especially in a complex or high-dollar transaction, then talk to an attorney. Or talk with someone knowledgeable who has done it before.

For important transactions, at least list the significant details and ask an attorney to draw it up or advise you on what should be included. You can save costs by having the lawyer review what you've done by yourself, rather than having it drafted from scratch.

But Things Do Go Wrong

"The biggest mistake people make in agreements is not thinking about what could go wrong and what to do about it in the beginning. They center on the deal, such as how much money is paid, by when, and to whom. What they forget to do is to talk about what happens when all the money can't be paid or the other party doesn't do as agreed. Everyone is rosy about the deal going into it. What's needed is to talk about what happens when things go wrong, then write that down. Unfortunately, most people wait until after the contract is signed and the problems have occurred. By then, it's too late as they can't agree anyway," observed one experienced contract attorney.

"I go through all the aspects of the transaction before drafting the contract. For example, I'll go through when and how an agreement ends when the problems occur. I want them to think about how to unwind it now, not afterwards when they're probably in court. Sometimes a bad deal doesn't go through because one party finally sees the hidden problems. Talking about the problems in the beginning just makes sense," commented another attorney.

For example, you should ask when lending money what will happen if the borrower can't pay you back as agreed. If the person says he will give you something such as jewelry to hold until you are paid back, then ask if you could hold that now for safekeeping. If the car could have problems, then say what you'll do if repairs are needed within, let's say, the first 3 months. Or if the price being paid is low, then say and write down that the car is being bought in an "as is" condition, without any warranties, and the buyer pays for all later repairs.

It is difficult to talk at first about what to do when problems occur. Most people are interested in getting the agreement done, whether it's with a contractor or buying a computer for the business. You don't want to lose the deal. However, now's the time to talk about what to do if things go wrong. You can agree as to what's done by each party and weave this into your contract. Hiring attorneys to argue over what should be done later is an expensive penalty for not doing this.

There Are Various Areas

The number of areas where you should have something in writing is not, of course, limited to when you buy, lend, or sell something. For example, if you're planning to live together with someone, then it makes sense to sit down *before* you do this and decide who owns what. If you run into later difficulties, at least there shouldn't be an argument as to who owns that beautiful painting of the clipper ship hanging over the couch. These written "live-in" agreements (as distinct from premarital agreements governing property between married people) would mention who's primarily responsible for what bills and how you own property brought with you or aquired once you are living together. This shouldn't be left until after you've moved in, as it becomes more difficult to say who owns what by then.

Other important written documents are releases (see Chapter 7), your will and any trust agreements, premarital agreements, home repair and remodeling contracts, household help, and even child care. In short, you should try to have an agreement in any area where a misunderstanding could be costly.

What the Attorneys Add

The job of attorneys is to think about what could happen with the contract that the parties didn't consider. Usually this involves questions as to what could go wrong and what happens when it does. The problem is that they must anticipate whatever problems could occur, regardless as to how likely they are. Attorneys are concerned also with the applicability of state laws, what's called the boiler plate (the wording that doesn't change from deal to deal), and the details.

What Could Go Wrong

For example, when considering the sale of a house, attorneys should make provisions for what happens if the house burns down before title is transferred (allocation of loss), the roof leaks (seller warranties), the seller doesn't have complete title (title checks and title insurance), the buyer can't obtain financing (conditions to the sale), the buyer backs out (breach of contract provisions), and the status of the deposit (liquidated damage provisions). Over time, these provisions become tested in the courts as to what language holds up and what doesn't. They become part of any standard contract involving the sale of real estate in that state. The same process is applied whatever type of contract is involved—whether it's a bank loan, buying furniture on an installment plan, or an employment agreement.

State Requirements

Each state has developed its own case and statutory law on individual contracts, whether a consumer loan, promissory note, or sale of real property. These considerations must be in every contract of that type, and they depend on what the state has decided for that situation.

For example, the state's legislature might have passed a law requiring that certain warnings be given to any buyer of real property or products on the installment plan. This needs to be added to the language of the "standard" contract when that occurs in that state. Should a court have decided a case in favor of one party or another to a contract, then the lawyers will try to add wording so that their contract will be upheld.

Let's say that the state has passed a law on the rights a landlord has when the tenant doesn't pay the rent. Rather than referring to that statute as covering what happens, the attorneys might paraphrase that provision, even put in the entire language, so that the parties know what can happen.

Boiler Plate

Unfortunately, attorneys have argued in court whatever could bring about a favorable judgment for their clients. This has been over anything having to do with the facts and that agreement, ranging from what happens if there were more than one written understanding to whether one party was or was not properly notified as to a default. Over time, these technical loopholes were developed into what's called "boiler plate."

Attorneys add provisions routinely to every contract, regardless of subject matter, and usually at the end of the agreement. This language is designed to cover areas that apply to every contract. Examples of such clauses are:

✔ *Attorney fees* (stating who has the right to be awarded their attorney fees should a dispute occur);

✔ *Hold harmless* (requiring one party to guarantee that the other won't be held responsible for actions by the first, including any damages, attorney fees, and court costs);

✔ *Notices* (specifying who receives, the location, and type of notice required underneath the contract);

✔ *Alternative dispute resolution* (whether mediation, arbitration, or a form of dispute resolution, not involving litigation, is required);

✔ *Governing law* (which state's laws govern);

✔ *Definitions* (attorneys would argue that "he" in the agreement didn't mean "she" or that the words used in the contract didn't apply to their client. These provisions define the various words that are being used);

✔ *Waiver* (typically, if a party ignores one provision of the agreement, this doesn't affect the other provisions or that same provision in the future);

✔ *Headings* (that the heading of a paragraph or section doesn't define or mislead as to what's underneath it);

✔ *Survival of Terms* (that warranties and representations in the agreement survive the termination of that contract);

✔ *Severability* (that the invalidity of any one provision doesn't affect the remaining provisions of the agreement);

✔ *Entire Agreement* (that this agreement is the entire agreement between the parties);

✔ *Final Agreement* (that this agreement is the final and last agreement between the parties); and

✔ *Amendment* (that any other change to the agreement will have to be in the from of a written amendment signed by all the parties to the agreement).

This listing is only part of what has been developed over time. The boiler plate at the end of complex agreements can run 10 or more pages.

The Details

The details of a contract are most important, as a court can render any contract in your favor or not in the blink of an eye. You need to be sure that the contract is accurate. For example, it must be clear as to the terms of repayment on a note, the installments when selling your car, and what you're buying from a friend for $500.

You need to discuss and write down what happens if there's a default. If the contractor doesn't paint your house before the wedding, then what's the penalty? Put down what happens if your roof isn't repaired by the first rains.

The proper party to be held responsible for performing your agreement should at least sign it. For example, if you're lending money, then have the borrower sign it. If you simply sign it, there's nothing legally binding (although the note could be evidence in a lawsuit).

Be sure that the proper parties are named. If a contract involves a married person, then it's good practice to be sure both spouses sign the agreement, regardless of the fact that one had nothing to do with it. For example, any contract to buy or sell a house should be signed by both spouses; otherwise, it may be unenforceable. You should take care to specify who the proper party is to a contract, whether a corporation or partnership, and who's signing on its behalf. It's also good practice to have someone sign in both corporate and individual status—if something goes wrong, then you aren't blocked by the corporate shield but can go after the individual.

The contract should include the consideration (or what's valuable for both parties) that binds the contract. If both are promising to perform for the other (i.e., you'll paint the house for $500; the other will pay $500 upon completion), then state what both are going to do.

We have discussed trying to cover the point when the contract is considered to be at an end (the rights of termination). If you and your friend are going to invest money together for a minimum, but high-yielding account in a mutual fund, then what happens if he or she can't put up the agreed amount of money—is the contract over? You should discuss the time allowed to get the money together before this problem arises.

An important area is how the contract must be executed in order to be legal, and state laws vary widely over this. Assuming that the proper parties are signing, do these signatures need to be notarized or witnessed under your state law to be effective? For example, wills must be witnessed according to state law or they are invalid. Even bills of sale and assignments of income in some states need to be notarized or witnessed. If you are selling real estate, then the deed must be notarized, sometimes witnessed, and recorded with the proper county official, depending on your state's requirements. This is an important area to watch.

The Problem

When attorneys add the many provisions they do, whether they are required or boiler plate, a simple contract balloons in size. Hundreds of concepts and paragraphs bring about a mind-numbing inability to even comprehend what's involved. As if this weren't bad enough, the writing style of many attorneys can be worse. This style can be redundant, replete with "legalese," and use indecipherable words. For example:

> The party of the first part shall not be a party to this agreement, nor shall it be bound to inquire into, nor shall it be chargeable with notice of, any provisions hereof. Notwithstanding any provision of or in this agreement to the contrary, the signature of the party to whom all rights have been reserved by the terms of this agreement shall be full and sufficient authority to the party of the first part to take or permit any action in connection therewith. Payment or other performance by the party of the first part, in accordance with the terms of any of its agreements, shall completely discharge said party of the first part from all claims, suits, demands, controversies, and problems, including attorney fees and court costs, or demands of any and all persons, corporations, partnerships, entities, or organizations, wherever located or situated.

Lawyers can read this several times and still not know what it means. To be fair to the attorneys, it isn't all their fault. The form books used by attorneys (for example, at the local county law libraries) employ a lot of this language, including the "wherefores," "therefores," "whereases," and "now, let it be saids."

There is a fortunate break for all of us in that large corporations, including banks and other lenders, have asked their attorneys to draw more consumer-oriented contracts in understandable English. Home mortgages and car loans, for example, are more often being rewritten in language that's consumer friendly, using the informal word "you," and not convoluted paragraphs that wind up in court. A litigator observed "There have been somewhat fewer lawsuits over the preprinted, understandable contracts, as more people understand what they're getting into. I guess the attorneys are also understanding them."

The Preprinted Contracts

Whether you buy a home, insurance, a car, or even a refrigerator, a contract will be provided by the seller. If a loan is involved in the purchase (which it usually is), then this will involve a lender's agreement. Whether dealing with a bank, a realtor (with a preprinted lease or purchase contract), or even the buyer of your business (with long documents of sale), you need to understand what you're signing—even what's at the end of the contract. Sometimes attorneys stick important clauses at the end of the contract.

How to Handle the Long, Preprinted Contract

If the lender or seller doesn't send you a consumer-worded contract but supplies you instead with a long, "legalese" document with lots of "whereass", don't despair. There are still ways to handle this.

How Important Is It? It always depends on how important the deal is. For example, you should spend more time trying to understand the $195,000 sales offer on your house, rather than the $2,500 credit card limit on your gasoline card.

Look It over to See What's There Don't start reading it, line by line, at the start. Take your time and glance over the pages to see what's there. Usually they'll at least have headings so you can determine the general areas that are being covered. Once you have gained an idea as to what's there, then read the detail of the important areas.

Look for the Numbers and Business Details Don't lose sight of your basic understanding in the detail. There are business points that attracted you in the first place to this arrangement. If it's a loan, you should confirm what the amount borrowed is, the interest rate, the term for repayment, the points (or prepaid interest), the monthly payments, and the security. Be sure you check that all the numbers and business details in the printed contract are as you first agreed. After you've confirmed that the business aspects are as you were informed, then go back to the contract wording and details.

Read the Entire Contract Be sure to read the entire contract, including the boiler plate. Make a note of any areas you don't understand, whether it's the "legalese" or general areas.

If you just can't handle this line-by-line reading any more, or it doesn't make any sense, then pick up the phone and call the company you're dealing with. Ask them what certain things mean and where specifics are located in the contract.

The penalties can be severe when you don't know. One client observed, "The judge asked me basically one question 'Had I read the contract?' I hadn't, it was there, and I lost the case."

Ask Questions Never be embarrassed to ask questions. The contract is obligating you to its terms, and it's your right to understand ahead of time what you're signing. A smart friend can also be as helpful in answering your questions as the company or business entering into the agreement. One corporate counsel said with a shrug, "I always have neighborhood friends fairly quickly when I move to another place. Everyone has a legal question, now and then." People who have gone through this before (whether borrowing money or buying a house) can be just as helpful as the people whose business it is to explain what their contract means.

Know What Happens when You Can't Perform As previously mentioned, most people sign a contract believing there will be no problems later on, but jobs are lost and unforeseen problems do occur. You should understand what the other party's rights are should you not pay or do as you've agreed, and this should be done before you sign any contract.

Legal Review For important or complex deals, you should consider running the agreement past an experienced attorney. Remember that all attorneys are not alike—there are litigators, divorce specialists, even oil and gas specialists. You will need an attorney who's experienced in reviewing the type of transaction you're involved with. If it is the sale of your house, then go to an experienced real estate attorney. If it's the sale of your business, then go to an experienced business attorney who does such reviewing or drafting for a living. "You can pay me now or much more later," said an attorney who had seen the problems that developed later into court fights.

Don't forget to consult an accountant when you sell or buy an important or high-value asset. Taxes are a part of life also. Whether consulting an accountant or attorney, or both, be sure to set a fixed fee or receive an estimate as to what that review will cost.

Understanding Releases and Their Limitations

A release is commonly defined as being a discharge from an obligation or a relinquishment of a right or claim. Releases come in two different types—those that represent the agreement of the parties to release each other from something that has *already* happened (postinjury or "past" releases) and those that operate to release claims based on something that *might* happen in the future (prospective or "future" releases).

Judges look at all releases closely to ensure that the person relinquishing the rights understands what's being done, that the release is signed voluntarily, and that it is fair—all quite subjective criteria and involving questions of fact. Additionally, the person releasing the rights must receive something in return or a benefit in exchange for that release.

The law calls the benefit received in return a "consideration." This benefit is usually money but may be a nonmonetary benefit, such as performance of services (planting trees and landscaping to replace what was erroneously cut down or repairing a broken window) or being allowed to participate in a community bike race (in the case of a prospective or future release).

To be enforceable, a release must provide enough specific information so that a court can enforce its provisions, if necessary, as to the specific parties and the act covered by the release. Thus, it must specifically identify the parties, describe the reason for the release, and indicate the benefit received for that release. Additionally, a release usually needs to have legal language stating that it binds all people who could have a right to the waived claim (such as the spouse or heirs of that person) and that the release applies to all claims that could arise later from the released dispute.

The use of releases would seem to be fairly straightforward. However, questions are raised when one party appears to be in a superior bargaining position or the releasing party doesn't appear to understand fully what is being signed. For example, if a company's attorney induced an elderly widow to sign a release printed in small type for $200, the release giving up her rights to legal damages against a company when one of its trucks ran over her husband, it shouldn't be a surprise if the judge rules that this release wasn't fair and is unenforceable. Similarly, if a severely injured man receives $5,000, or even $10,000, for signing a release but cannot understand or read English, then the courts may very well rule the release to be invalid if he could have received substantially more money by filing a lawsuit.

Putting words in a release that the releasing party is signing voluntarily or that the agreement is fair will not bind the parties if in fact this isn't true—the voluntariness or fairness of any release may be decided by the court if a party complains later in the courtroom. The release must be actually and in fact fair to both parties.

An additional problem is that people signing releases usually don't think there will be any further damage from the forgiven act in the future. But later damages do and can occur. For example, a landowner executed a release and received $1,000 as compensation when trees on his property were cut down by mistake, expecting that there would be no more problems. However, a severe rainstorm caused a landslide that would have been preventable had the trees been there, and the owner sued. The court ruled that the signed release was invalid. When others have complained similarly, the courts also have tended to rule in their favor. States have also enacted statutes that provide that a general release doesn't extend to claims that weren't known at the time and would have materially affected the agreement.

Postinjury (Past) Releases

Postinjury or past releases can be of the form in which one party releases another (a general release) or in which both have claims and release each other at the same time (a *mutual* general release). Such releases are commonly used to evidence a settlement after an agreement has been reached.

The one-party release is employed when only one side has a claim. Let's say that a neighbor borrowed some of your tools to construct a home addition but a few didn't work after being returned. After discussing the matter, Jimmy Casey agreed to pay you the $275 it cost you to repair the broken tools. If you wanted, the understanding could be written down:

> I, Bob Jacobs, release my neighbor, Jimmy Casey, from all claims arising from his breaking my tools when he was working on his house. This release is given in return for his paying me today the $275 cost to repair those tools.

You would sign and date it, giving a copy to Jimmy.

A mutual general release is used when both parties feel they have claims against one another or enter into a mutual agreement that runs into later difficulties. For example, Walt and George agreed to start a part-time mail-order business, but George couldn't pay his entire share of the money after Walt paid for the products. If they agree to terminate their agreement (Walt keeping the products), releasing both from the obligation, then they would use a mutual release approach, signing and dating the following:

> We agreed to start a mail-order business, but George couldn't raise his share of the money. George agrees to let Walt keep the products bought with both

our money, and he can sell them as seen fit and keep the money. Both of us now release each other from any claims we have arising from this, and the business is considered terminated. Either of us can conduct this type of business separately at any other time.

Although preprinted, do-it-yourself forms are used frequently, understanding the "legalese" of such forms can be difficult, and some prefer to write down the agreement in their own words as shown above. Courts will go to lengths to uphold the intent of the parties with respect to their agreements, regardless that these understandings are handwritten. If the releases between private individuals contain the essential information identifying the parties, the facts and reasons behind the release, and the monies paid or services to be rendered, then they will be enforced, provided they are fair to both parties and have been entered into freely and voluntarily (although you have to be careful that your state's "boiler plate" laws have been met).

However, the problems subject to releases aren't necessarily clear cut. For example, Judy Smith's car is hit by her next-door neighbor, Andy, as he turns into his driveway. Andy tells her he will pay for the car to be repaired. They decide to write up a release. The release states:

> Andy Thomas drove into Judy Smith's Ford Thunderbird last Monday. Judy's Ford was parked in front of her home, and the door on the driver's side was dented. As Andy promises to repair Judy's car at his expense, including matching the paint correctly, Judy Smith releases Andy from any problems or claims against him for hitting her car.

It is signed by both the parties and dated.

However, Andy decides later that Judy's car was parked too close to his driveway and won't pay. Technically, the release may not be enforceable because it didn't have various protective language as required in some states. However, having this in writing would make it difficult for Andy to argue it wasn't his fault, if Judy sues him in small claims court for the cost to repair and paint the car door. For the small amount of damages in the accident, this approach is fine.

In matters where the amount of damage is low with no possibility of later problems, simply handwriting a release as discussed above, with both parties signing and dating the piece of paper, is sufficient. However, the form of the release becomes quite important, particularly with respect to a given state's requirements as the problem becomes more serious.

For example, if Andy had hit Judy's small child at the same time, the considerations would be different. If Baby Anthony didn't appear hurt, although he had been frightened at the time, Judy might have decided to accept Andy's offer of $100. If Andy talked Judy into signing such a release in return for the $100, then the release would already be in trouble. If it turned out later that Baby Anthony had suffered serious internal injuries, Andy would try to argue that he had already been released by Judy. The courts more than likely would strike down that release, stating that it wasn't fair, against public policy, Judy didn't have the authority, or in violation of the required statutory language—whatever the court needed to "hang its hat on." Judy made a mistake also, as she should have waited until a doctor had checked out Baby Anthony before she signed the release.

If Judy were married, then another consideration arises. A release should be signed by anyone who is injured or damaged by the act, including that person's spouse. This is required in community property states where one spouse's signature to a release won't bind the other as to community interests. However, the practice is always to obtain both signatures, whether in a community property state or not. The reason is simple—a spouse who hasn't so agreed is more likely to complain to an attorney, especially if marital difficulties arise later.

Before signing any release, you should be sure that what's being given up is clearly understood. This should be discussed with a friend, spouse, business associate, or your attorney while you determine what else could happen later due to an accident or event that is not anticipated now. For example, if you were hit by a speeding bicyclist while walking, then you better be sure that your back injuries have healed and will never appear again before signing a release. If you have any injuries, whether they have healed or not, talk to your doctor. Then, and if still in doubt, the rule is simple: call an attorney.

If the matter seems to you to be complex or not a minor problem, then a lawyer should be consulted if you're the one trying to get a release signed. It saves you money in the long run. Remember that it's usually cheaper for an attorney to tell you the validity of any do-it-yourself release over the phone, or to review the release after you have prepared it, than to have the lawyer draft it after meeting with you and going over all the facts in detail.

Prospective (Future) Releases

Prospective or future releases are found in many service and commercial agreements. Parking lot tickets, for example, generally contain small print on the back that basically provides: "In consideration of ABC company providing parking facilities for customer's car, owner and driver assume all risks of future damage or injury. ABC shall not be held liable for any act or omission, within or without its control, and owner and driver waive all such rights, including for any injury to person or property," among other phrases and provisions. Wording to that effect is found on admission stubs for theaters, amusement parks, and circuses; services such as home security, banks, and motels use language that states that the consumer assumes all risks of damage or injury from the use of that service, waives any future claims, and receives in return the right to use the company's services.

Courts and state statutes flatly find future releases invalid in the majority of commercial activities, don't favor them in most other areas, and construe all of them strictly. The law doesn't favor future releases under a basic legal doctrine that provides that any party to an agreement shouldn't be allowed to contract against the effects of that party's negligence or relieve itself contractually from liability. The only reason they aren't flatly declared invalid is that the law has a conflicting policy that favors the ability of parties to contract freely and as they desire.

This conflict has resulted in a number of areas and exceptions where the law doesn't uphold future releases, even when the basic activity and written language generally would be upheld. One such area carved out is that prospective releases will not be upheld when fraud, gross negligence, or intentional conduct is present—only simple negligence, or a small amount of "misconduct," will be tolerated for starters. For example, a burglar-alarm company prints up claim release language conspicuously on all its contracts. An alarm sounds at the company's headquarters, and the dispatcher immediately orders a patrol car to that house. Unfortunately, the car doesn't arrive in time to stop the thief from stealing a valuable painting. If the guards tried their best to arrive there in time but took a wrong turn, the court could overlook the conduct and review the release language. However, if the guards had been drinking and decided to forget that call, the court wouldn't even consider the release language, because this intentional conduct was more than just a simple mistake.

A second area is that future releases won't be upheld at all, regardless of the conduct, where an unequal bargaining power exists or the party does business with the general public. Thus, parking lots, garages, motels, storage businesses, moving vans, and the like have been held by the courts not to be able to contract against their own negligence. Museums, agricultural fairs, and associations sponsored by the state or county have run into similar problems. Exculpatory or future releases by medical clinics, hospitals, banks, escrow companies, common carriers, and public utilities also have not been enforced as a rule.

Another exception involves people who are in special relationships of trust with their clients (called "fiduciary" relationships by the law). Accordingly, professionals such as physicians, engineers, real estate agents, and lawyers will not be able to use future claim releases to avoid being held liable for their actions.

The exceptions go on, depending on what a court or legislature feels is fair or unfair in any given situation. The question then becomes why even use them? The reason is that they may discourage some attorneys from suing and in limited cases will be upheld. The general rule is that in cases where the public interest (which is how the court defines it) or an invalidating statute is not involved, then a party may contract to absolve itself from liability, given that these provisions will be strictly construed against the person relying on them.

The courts have created various rules during their strict review of future releases. Releases using small print, type that hides the release, or incomprehensible "legalese" will be struck down. The party waiving its rights in many cases must have actual notice of the clause, it must be clearly readable, be in at least 10-point boldface capital letters (according to several states), and clearly understandable to an uneducated layman with ordinary intelligence. The courts have played with the definition of actual notice, but it generally means that the customer must be made aware of that language before signing the agreement.

Future releases have been upheld in various states for recreational activities that involve a high degree of risk, such as sky diving, white-water rafting, dirt-bike racing, auto racing, scuba diving, mountain climbing, skiing, and even exercising in health clubs. Additionally, courts more frequently find in favor of exculpatory releases used by burglar- and fire-alarm companies, bank-night depository service centers, and pest control services; however, the language used in such releases is drafted quite carefully for the specific situations by lawyers and modified continually as interpreting court decisions are handed down.

Clearly, if your company is doing business in any of these areas, then future releases should be used and an attorney hired to draft one that's appropriate for you. The cost of drafting such a release is small when contrasted with the risk of a large, damaging lawsuit.

The great interest for the use in future releases, however, is in noncommercial or personal activities, such as babysitting for a neighbor, taking care of a friend's show dog, or having a neighbor trim your trees. These generally will be upheld by the courts, provided the wording is simple, understandable, in large print, has adequate "consideration," and the person understands the implications of the release when signing, among various conditions. The example presented below is for illustrative purposes only and isn't intended for use in any particular situation.

FUTURE RELEASE OF ALL CLAIMS
WAIVER OF LIABILITY
ASSUMPTION OF RISK

<Releasing Person's Name>, in consideration of **<State Person's Name Receiving the Release and the Service To Be Performed>**, without charge and to help out, AGREES to release **<Person's Name Receiving the Release>** from all future claims AND WAIVES ANY LIABILITY DUE TO: **<State What Possibly Can Go Wrong When Providing the Service>**. **<Releasing Person's Name>** agrees to assume these risks, including those not known now and/or which may occur later, as to such services to be performed. We both agree **<Person's Name Receiving the Release>** doesn't perform this service as a business for profit. Both of us intend that this Release and its waiver of any liability, future claims, or causes of actions, including attorney fees and court costs, in favor of **<Person's Name Receiving the Release>** shall also bind our spouses, heirs, estates, insurers, and assigns. This Release is agreed, understood, and signed on **<Date of Release>** between **<Name the Parties Signing>**.

_____   _____
(Service Providing Person's Signature)   (Releasing Person's Signature)
<Person's Name Providing Services   <Releasing Person's Name>
and Receiving the Release>   <Address>
<Address>

For example, suppose Edwin Tower agrees to take care of Jimmy Baldwin's prize show poodle, Alpha O, while the owner is on vacation. Although Jimmy lives next door to Edwin, the poodle doesn't adjust well when he leaves. Edwin would be well advised to have Jimmy sign:

Jimmy Baldwin, in consideration of Edwin Towers feeding and taking care of my dog, Alpha O, for 2 weeks beginning October 1, 1994, without charge and to help out, agrees to release Edwin from all future claims and waives all liability due to Alpha O becoming ill, sick, or dying while under Edwin's care. Jimmy agrees to assume these risks, including those not known now and/or which may occur later, as to such services to be performed. We both agree Edwin doesn't perform this service as a business for profit. Both of us intend that this Release and its waiver of any liability, future claims, or causes of actions, including attorney fees and court costs, in favor of Edwin, shall also bind our spouses, heirs, estates, insurers, and assigns. This

Release is agreed, understood, and signed on September 23, 1994, between Edwin Towers and Jimmy Baldwin.

This release can be modified even further. As long as the essential elements of the release are present, it can be written or modified in various ways. An alternative form follows:

> In consideration of Edwin Towers feeding, walking, and taking care of my pet poodle, Alpha O, at my home for free while I'm on vacation for 2 weeks, I waive, release all claims (whether I know about them now or not), and assume all risks of any injury or loss to Alpha O while he is in Edwin's care. I agree Edwin can take Alpha O to my veterinarian, Dr. Freiss, as he sees fit, and I agree to be responsible for all bills (including food and medication) owing to the care of my dog. This release of all claims I could have against Edwin for taking care of Alpha O includes all wives, heirs, estates, and assigns. September 23, 1994— Jimmy Baldwin and Edwin Tower.

Edwin could hand print this, and both parties would sign and date the release. It would be better if Jimmy wrote it all down in his own handwriting, then signed it, and even better if he wrote it himself without any help from Edwin. The wives of both should also sign.

This release would be generally upheld if something happened to Alpha O. However, this doesn't mean that Edwin would be able to take the dog and drop it from a window to see if it could fly. He still needs to use some element of care in watching over the dog. But it also means there's an understanding between the parties, regardless of its legal validity. It is a stated understanding with nothing left unsaid between them. Edwin will take care of the dog for free, and Jimmy will assume the risks if the dog becomes sick or dies during that time.

Any future release should: name the parties, including their addresses; the subject of the release, such as watching the dog or baby-sitting baby Anthony; the consideration, such as doing it for free in exchange for not being held liable for what happens (or receiving only $1 dollar); the specifics of the time and place for the activity, such as at Jimmy's home for the 2-week period; and what's being specifically assumed by the other, such as Alpha O becoming injured or dying.

All form releases and examples presented in this chapter, whether for future or for existing claims, should be reviewed first by an attorney before they are used or relied on. All states have varying legal requirements for a valid release, and one form might be fine for one state but invalid in another.

It may be uncomfortable to take releases like these to neighbors and tell them you won't watch the dog or baby-sit the child unless they agree to sign one. The best approach is to say you aren't sure you want to watch the dog or baby-sit, because you're worried over what to do if something goes wrong. They will respond "What could go wrong?" You should reply that the child could fall down the stairs or the dog get hit by a car. They'll quickly say, "Oh...I wouldn't hold you responsible" or something to that effect because they want you to help them. At that time, you'll say "Let's put it in writing. I'd feel better that way."

You could approach your neighbor and say sheepishly "My attorney told me to do this....I don't know. But that's what was said....Here's a form release to sign." Or say that your insurance agent is handing them out. Or that your husband (or wife) was handed one at a seminar.

It's different when someone is coming over to help you, rather than the other way around. For example, if a friend comes over to your house to help cut down the large trees in the back but is a "klutz" with power tools, it's better to use the "my attorney told me to use this form" approach rather than the "I'd feel better if you sign this" way. Try doing this over coffee, as you know your friends. Whatever works is fine—it's all in the approach. Or if your friend is really that inept, then graciously decline his offer.

As the value of the property or liability increases, then it becomes more important to secure a signed release. For example, if a friend wants you to watch her prized Arabian horse while she's gone, or to safeguard her valued stamp collection, then using a prospective release should be clearly considered. If friends are coming over to ride one of your nervous horses, or they are helping you with anything involving electricity, fire, or gas, then use a release.

Another "growth" area for attorneys involves recreational activities on private lands. Any number of situations occur—people take shortcuts; they want to fish, ride horses, or hike on your land; or children like to play in your garden. Then a problem occurs. A hunter shoots someone or falls into a ravine. A child slips and hits her head on a rock. What do the lawyers do? They simply sue the landowner and anyone else they can think of, then look around to collect from whomever has the deepest pockets or an insurance policy that can be found.

These are the times to use a release. A landowner could print up a land-use release, have everyone fill it out or leave, and use it as protection. An example, for illustrative purposes only, follows.

FUTURE RELEASE OF ALL CLAIMS
WAIVER OF LIABILITY
ASSUMPTION OF RISK

I, *<Name of Person Who Wants to Enter the Property ("Name of User")>*, in consideration of *<Name of Owner>* allowing me the right to *<State Use of Land, such as Hunting, Fishing, Walking, Bicycling, Jogging, Swimming, etc.>* on his or her property without charge on *<Specify the Date of Use>*, agree to assume all risks of any damage, injury, death, or illness while *<State Use of Land>* on this property. I agree to take all reasonable care while on this land, to not disturb the property in any way, and to pay immediately any damages caused by me. *<Name of Owner>* has informed me as to various risks on the property, such as *<State Specific Risks such as Ravines, Deep Holes, Fast Rivers, etc., and Their Location>* and other such risks. I agree to waive all future claims, release all liability, and accept all such risks, including attorney fees and court costs, whether known or unknown to me, disclosed or not disclosed, or occurring in the future. I agree to all provisions of this Release on behalf of myself, my spouse, heirs, personal representatives, insurers, and assigns in favor of *<Name of Owner>*. This is agreed, accepted, and understood on *<Date of Execution>* by *<Name of User>* and *<Name of Owner>*.

Please remember that as the severity of an injury increases (and more money is at stake), a plaintiff's attorney is more motivated to attack any release that is used. Any form exculpatory release(s) should be modified by your attorney, especially when your activities involve any work for a volunteer or nonprofit organization. If your organization is sponsoring any fund-raising events that involve a race or contest of any kind (whether skiing, bicycle racing, marathons, biathlons, or even the world pillow-fighting championships sponsored in tiny Kenwood, California), then these reviewed releases should be used as a condition for anyone to enter your contest, whether an entry fee is required or not.

As the public involvement increases, however, the likelihood that a court or state law will invalidate the wording also increases. For example, volunteering to work or being hired by a school district as a coach in wrestling, football, or baseball, for example, generally hasn't been protected by using future releases signed by the participants. Neither have organizations such as the Boy Scouts, Girl Scouts, Little League, Pop Warner Football, or even the Red Cross usually enjoyed court protection with future releases, especially when negligence has been proved.

You should know, whether using releases or not, that there is adequate insurance in place when you are doing volunteer work. Although there is a difference between helping a high school debate team and being a director for a fund-raising downhill bicycle race, you will need to exercise your best judgment. This doesn't mean you should stop volunteering, but it does mean investigating what lines of defense are in place should there be an injury or loss.

As a final note, remember that if your attorney advises that a future release might not be upheld if challenged, that doesn't mean the other party's lawyer necessarily will come to the same conclusion. You could make a business judgment to use it, knowing the limitations, and possibly catching an unsuspecting attorney off guard. The other lawyer might not want to go through the time and expense of the extra hearings, motions, and costs required to knock out the release. This only makes his or her task more difficult in close situations—which is only fair. But you will need to be sure that insurance and other lines of defense (such as a corporate form of organization) are also existing.

Watch Your Taxes

Nothing is more a fact of modern life than taxes. Taxes are assessed on your wages, income, gifts, purchases and sales, real property, and much more, both for you as an individual and when you own a business. Taxes are levied at the federal, state, and local levels.

The area of estate or transfer taxes (including gift taxes) is treated in Chapter 9, whereas some areas to watch out for in your business are addressed in Chapter 11. The area of federal income taxes is addressed in this chapter.

Over 125 million taxpayers file individual federal income tax returns, and it's rare that a person doesn't have some problem with the IRS over a lifetime. Unpaid income taxes are a personal liability for individuals, aren't dischargeable often in bankruptcy as are ordinary obligations, and have become a leading reason for personal asset seizures.

The matter is complicated further by four out of five states having enacted additionally a state income tax that usually mirrors the approach taken by the federal income tax authorities. If you have a problem with the IRS over taxes, then later you generally will receive a bill from the state demanding its additional share of what is owed.

This chapter will not address the massive numbers of income tax concepts, nor how to minimize federal income taxes. There are many sources of information on this, including IRS publications, tax-preparer guides, accountants, do-it-yourself books, and accounting treatises. We'll discuss what to do when there's a problem.

Problems easily occur simply because of the complexity and confusion of a tax code that is over 2,000 pages long. Special interests create their own loopholes, and the tax code changes each year as Congress fine-tunes what's confusing from the start. There is room for different interpretations of such complex laws, as you will discover if you are selected for an audit.

Although taxpayers can create their own difficulties by not filing income tax reports, failing to pay owed taxes, underreporting income, and making mistakes, the IRS always adds to the problem. This huge bureaucracy, created solely to collect revenues for the United States Government, isn't as interested in your personal finances as you are. What is a prime matter of concern for you is simply another day at the office for them. Delays, inefficiencies, and even flat misinterpretations of the tax code and laws by the IRS are commonplace.

Your responsibility begins with the annual filing date for federal income taxes on or before midnight of April 15th. The great majority of us file such forms regularly before the due date, either preparing them ourselves or hiring someone else. If we were born wealthy, then there would be no problems—our accountant would prepare the tax return from the documents kept by our business manager; our financial manager would cut the check, and all we would need to do would be to sign the check and return the form. However, 99% of us aren't in this category, and even country singer Willie Nelson discovered that this didn't work for him.

Why File a Return (Especially when There's No Money)?

Not filing a tax return when taxes are owed is a crime. However, if you file a tax return, but don't include any payment for your taxes, there's no criminal penalty (although you're subject to civil penalties and interest). People rarely go to jail for not filing a return, unless they are flagrantly protesting the tax system or not reporting substantial amounts of income.

There are a number of problems created when you don't file a return, regardless of whether you have the money or not. First, the IRS eventually catches up with you. Second, when they do, you have to use the tax returns and schedules for the years you missed—a task that can be difficult, not to mention the need to find out what the tax laws were then. Third, the IRS has the power to prepare and file tax returns for you if you don't do it. This is the last thing you want to happen, as the IRS is overly generous in determining your income. Fourth, the penalties for not filing, or filing late, are excessive.

Filing late when taxes are due causes a 5% penalty to be assessed *each month* up to a maximum 25% penalty, just for starters. Interest up to 1% per month is added to the owed amounts, the exact percentage changing each year depending on interest rates. The interest on unpaid taxes runs from the day you owe them (basically April 16th of the year in question) until the day they are paid, *compounded daily*. These penalties and interest create a liability over the years that can easily double, even triple, the amount of any taxes originally owed. And states have enacted their own penalty and interest provisions, many mimicking what the IRS provides. Filing late jeopardizes any refunds owed, and returns filed after 3 years from the due date aren't entitled to refunds, regardless of how much the IRS owes you.

The conclusion is inescapable, and as an accountant advised, "The biggest problem is failing to file a return. People get scared if they don't have the money to pay the taxes. This is wrong. Always file your income tax returns by the due date, if at all possible, paying what you can. This applies both to yourself and your company or business."

When in Doubt, Request an Extension to File

Most people file their tax return by April 15th because they are owed a refund. However, sometimes you don't have all the money to pay the taxes or can't file your return on time. Rather than filing late and being subject to the 5% per month late-filing penalty, you're better off requesting an extension to file your tax return.

> The first extension is automatically granted by filing before April 15th the proper form (currently Form 4868), entitled "Application for Automatic Extension of Time to File U.S. Individual Income Tax Return." You will be granted until August 15th to file the return and not be subject to late-filing penalties. This extension of the time doesn't extend the time for paying the taxes—you still will be charged interest on the taxes owed. Further, you'll need to pay 90% of the owed taxes to avoid being assessed at this time a monthly penalty of 1/2 of 1% on the amount paid beneath the 90% floor.

A second extension will be given, but subject to the discretion of the IRS, by filing Form 2688, "Application for Additional Extension of Time to File U.S. Individual Income Tax Return." You'll be granted until October 15th, provided the IRS agrees with your reasons, to file the return and not be subjected to the late-filing fees. You need to show good cause to be granted this second extension, such as illness (yourself or a family member) or not having sufficient information to make the return. The interest and late payment penalties still continue.

What to Do When You Don't Have the Money

Given the daily interest compounding that continues until the entire tax owed is paid, you should do what it takes to pay taxes off, even if you have to borrow the money. The collection powers of the IRS are extensive, despite tax reform efforts, and these powers are abused by IRS agents. This liability continues for life, even into your estate.

If you can't arrange the money, then remember that being unable to pay your taxes isn't a valid reason for an extension to file. It's possible to file Form 1127, "Application for Extension of Time for Payment of Tax," to request an extension of time without incurring an underpayment penalty. However, this approach is complicated, very difficult to receive, and is only mentioned in passing.

If you can't pay your taxes, then file your return on time and pay what you can. When sending a partial payment, be sure to write your social security number on the check and identify the tax year. Fill out and file Form 9465, "Installment Agreement Request," at the same time for the remaining taxes that are owed.

> Any time you're in a dispute with the IRS or can't pay everything, be especially careful when paying by check. Remember the IRS can use that account information (and does) to levy against that bank account later without warning. Using money orders or cashiers checks is one way to avoid the problem. As the IRS does keep a record of bank accounts from prior years, the information already may be available to them.
>
> When in doubt, set up another account to deposit your funds, using the old one to only pay the owed taxes. Remember that any account information required to be sent to the IRS (such as Form 1099 interest) will wind its way into the IRS's computers. Keeping money in a safe deposit box, under the mattress, or with a friend has also been used (but be careful of fraud, which is treated later).

The IRS implies that Form 9465 is only to be used for tax obligations of $10,000 or less. However, tax professionals and IRS agents recommend sending in the installment request form for amounts greater than $10,000 and regardless of what's owed. However, remember that the IRS generally files a lien automatically when the amounts in question are over $10,000, irrespective of your sending in an installment request. You will be requesting a monthly payment amount on this form. The IRS may or may not accept what you can afford, and it may ask for more information before making a decision (this is treated later in the chapter).

The importance in filing the Installment Agreement Request (or sending in a letter with the same information) is that the IRS usually stops doing anything more until the agency has looked at the request and made a decision. As an experienced accountant observed, "Even if you have no money, filing for the installment request can buy some time to accumulate the funds needed to pay the owed taxes." Another said "The IRS program for collecting delinquent taxes seems to run faster when you ignore them. The system appears to slow down instead when you send in Form 9465, negotiate, and then make payments now and then as can be afforded."

Filing Back and Amended Returns

It's always better to file back returns with owed taxes than to wait for the IRS to find and contact you. The IRS unofficially looks more kindly on voluntary compliance and is more likely to work with you. This doesn't mean they will waive the late filing fees, penalties, and interest, but it does mean your life could be made easier.

You must use the missing years' tax forms and schedules when filing skipped returns. These can be ordered from the IRS, if necessary, but it may be months before you receive the necessary information. If a large amount of money is involved, then you would be best advised to contact an accountant before filing any back returns.

A problem with back filings is the interest that is compounding and the penalties. The extent of these can be enormous if some time has elapsed since you last filed. Unless you've come into an unexpected amount of money, you'll need to work out a payment plan. However, be sure to identify specifically on the check the year and owed taxes that the payment is to be applied against. Accountants warn, as one explained, "The IRS loves to apply undesignated payments to what's best for them (and worst for you), such as the interest and penalties on the oldest debt, leaving the unpaid taxes to keep accruing more interest and penalties to keep running on the untouched, still-owed taxes."

You can change a tax return after filing. If you sell your home and don't reinvest the proceeds within the statutory 2 years from sale, an amended return must be filed. Whether you found out later what you did was wrong, or discovered that any information provided was erroneous, you would file Form 1040X, entitled "Amended U.S. Individual Income Tax Return."

You have until 3 years from when the first return was due to be filed in which to file an amended return. This date is extended to 7 years should you be claiming a refund based on a bad debt or worthless security. Amended returns can be complicated, and you should consult an accountant for assistance. If large amounts of money are involved, there should be no hesitation to secure the advice of a tax professional prior to contacting the IRS.

The Penalties

It's in the imposition of penalties and interest that the IRS earns its reputation. If you're late in paying *any* income taxes, a nondeductible monthly penalty of 0.5% (1/2 of 1%) can be imposed on the amount of taxes not paid, up to a maximum 25% in total. This is in addition to interest and any penalties for negligence or fraud, although this is included in the penalty for failing to file. The failure-to-pay penalty runs past the cut-off date on the failure-to-file penalty. You can have your bill increased nearly 50% by this tactic alone, not to mention what the state does.

The penalty will not apply if you're able to prove that the failure to pay was due to a reasonable cause and not willful neglect. It can double to 1% per month if you don't pay a deficiency notice after: (1) a demand that the IRS will levy upon your assets unless payment is made in full; or (2) immediate payment is demanded due to the IRS's belief that payment of the tax is in jeopardy.

If taxes are underpaid because of negligence (you should have known better), in addition to other reasons, a 20% penalty will be applied to the portion of the underpayment attributable to this. You may be subject to the 20% penalty simply by understating your tax liability currently by the greater of $5,000 or 10% of the correct tax. If the failure to file is deemed to be "fraudulent," then the monthly penalty is 15% per month to a maximum penalty of 75%.

These penalties can be assessed arbitrarily by the IRS. For example, the definition of "negligence" and proving that the failure to pay is due to "reasonable cause" and not "willful neglect" is a question of fact—not a very straightforward decision. But as you can see, these penalties and back interest can make the original nonpayment of any owed taxes pale by comparison. However, remember also that the IRS threatens negligence penalties more than they actually assess and collect them, and this also depends on the individual agent or examiner. Still you should take the IRS seriously in these matters.

> If you have assets to protect, then you need to take taxes seriously. If you don't, then the IRS can heap penalty on top of penalty, and it won't make much of a difference. He or she who has the least money has the best bargaining power with the IRS.
>
> A word of warning. Any time you receive a demand for payment, whether buried in the small print or not, stating that the IRS will levy upon your assets unless payment is made, it should be taken seriously. This is the only notice they may give, and it won't necessarily be a large notice in bold-face print. They can immediately start actions against your assets after that stated time period.

Domestics and Household Help—The "Employee" Tax Problem

Although not strictly a federal income tax problem, one troublesome area is whether a worker in your home is an employee or an independent contractor. Workers classified as employees, rather than independent contractors, create major but varying tax liabilities. You need to withhold monies from the wages of employees, but you don't when they're independent contractors. Babysitters, contractors, housecleaners, and even gardeners, as with many other household jobs, have one thing in common—it's possible to do the same job and be either an employee or independent contractor by what seem to be small differences in the work relationship.

Being held to be an employee by the IRS creates substantial responsibilities. Social Security payments must be withheld, matched, and paid to the IRS; W-2 forms need to be provided; federal unemployment tax withheld; federal and state minimum hourly wage and state overtime laws apply; federal and state income taxes need to be withheld (although you and the worker may agree otherwise if they're household help); and workers' compensation insurance may be required.

Most people don't follow these requirements when hiring a babysitter or housekeeper. In fact, the people hired prefer to be treated as independent contractors, promising they'll pay their own payroll taxes and accurately report income. More than likely, they won't.

Independent contractors basically (1) work free from direct supervision, setting their own hours, and being only responsible for the final result; (2) own the necessary equipment and tools for the job; and (3) operate independently, offering the same services to others. Factors, however, leaning toward employee status are: a continuing relationship; an hourly rate or salary paid under a routine established by the employer; the person's working usually for just one or two clients; and the employer's providing the instructions on how tasks are performed and what's done. Any ultimate decision by federal and state agencies employs up to 20 separate factors, weighing each, but always leans towards holding that the worker is an employee. The reason is simple—employees, not independent contractors, provide funding for Social Security and other government programs.

As homeowners generally set work duties, pay, hours, and conditions of employment, people who work on a regular basis for you are nearly always held to be employees. Unless they run an independent business, provide the necessary equipment and supplies, and service other clients, among other factors, they won't be treated as independent contractors. Your live-in nanny *is* an employee.

Many homeowners initially appear to escape the consequences of treating employees as independent contractors. That is, until they are audited and the examiner asks about those regular payments to the household help or until a worker retires, quits, is fired, or becomes injured. The penalties in this case can be severe.

Workers who quit or are fired quickly decide they've been employees all the time. They march down and file for unemployment compensation. If they are not covered by unemployment insurance and you are held to be their employer, you're financially responsible for those payments pursuant to state law.

What if your full-time housekeeper files later for Social Security? If nothing has been paid into the system, and that person proves the amount of wages, then the IRS will bill you retroactively for the withholdings, plus interest.

Worse yet, the "now" employee becomes injured on the job. It makes no difference whether that person is a sales clerk at your business or a gardener at home—the results are the same. You're liable for the medical expenses and lost wages of the worker (including penalties) when no worker's compensation insurance is in force. The only question is to what extent you're liable.

Unfortunately, federal and state laws tilt strongly to holding that "if it smells like an employee, then it is one." Given the penalties for making the wrong decision, domestic employers have limited options—you can pay now rather than later (treating "borderline" cases as employees), assume the risk, contract with an outside payroll service (avoiding paperwork hassles), or not hire and do the job yourself. Check with your accountant or the IRS first as to the rules before making your decision.

Now, They've Contacted You

Everything had been fine with you and the IRS for years. You mailed off your returns, paid your taxes, and never heard back from them. That's great. Then one day, you look at your mail and there's an envelope with an IRS District Office address printed as the return. Being contacted by any taxing authority, especially the IRS, only means headaches.

On opening the envelope, you determine that the IRS is planning to audit your tax return. Or it could be they're requesting information that would support, for example, head-of-household designation you took on your return. Or they are wondering about those deductions you were taking for child care and your in-house "nanny."

> The first and most important rule is *never* ignore the IRS. Never disregard any computerized piece of paper from any tax agency, no matter how off base or inane.

Don't throw away what you receive, thinking they won't follow up—they do, like a bulldog. An experienced tax pro said "If you bury your head in the sand, depending on the piece of paper, then you probably have 3 months before the IRS begins some type of collection activity. If you talk and write and send them information, or some dollars if you owe them already, then you can delay and stretch out this time while you try to solve the problem."

The IRS never goes away once they have sent you an examination audit. In fact, even if you die, they will continue the audit with your executor or surviving spouse. Look over the return or returns that are being questioned. If an audit isn't involved, then see if simply answering the questions meets what both the IRS and you want. When in doubt, call your accountant for advice. Talk to business associates or friends and see if they know someone who has gone through the same process and will talk to you about it.

If deadlines are set down, try your best to meet them. The IRS doesn't look well at tardy replies or to being ignored as if they didn't exist. They do—just take another look at the section on penalties. This doesn't mean you should be afraid of the IRS, as you do have your rights (discussed below). An accountant with 20 years experience put it this way, "Communicate with them and stand your ground, but don't try to mess with them. That's a mistake."

The IRS may be drawn to your return because of your profession, the types of transactions reported, or claimed deductions. Any one of the following will increase your chances of an audit:

✔ A prior audit occurred that resulted in increased taxes.

✔ Itemized deductions exceeded the IRS target.

✔ Net income from the business is lower than the IRS target.

✔ An amended return was filed.

✔ An informant's tip.

✔ The business has been audited.

✔ Complex transactions or write-offs of business losses are reported without clear explanations.

✔ The business or income earned is subject to cash payments, such as with a waiter, bartender, doctor, or attorney.

✔ A large uninsured casualty loss, bad debt, or worthless security is present, especially when involving a wholly owned company.

✔ The overall income looks like you couldn't have lived on what was reported to have been earned.

It Starts with the Audit

The odds that your return will be picked for an audit in any given year are low. IRS statistics indicate that less than 1% of all returns are picked for an audit. This risk increases, as expected, as your income does. For example, whereas individuals with less than $50,000 in income have less than a 1% chance to be audited in any given year, those with incomes greater than $100,000 have a 5% chance to be audited. If you look at these odds over your lifetime—let's say more than 40 years worth of tax returns—then the odds increase greatly to where it's likely you will be audited at least once.

What's important is to understand what the IRS is. It doesn't care about your health or welfare. It isn't in the business to be popular or to serve the people like other governmental agencies. It's sole function is to collect as much money as the law permits, including your money, so that the U.S. Government can meet its obligations. It *is* the tax collector.

Types of Audits

The audit process commences with the first correspondence. This letter identifies the type of examination you'll undergo; whether it will be at your business or the IRS office; the date and time of the examination, or the date by which you must return the necessary information; and a brief explanation of your rights.

The easiest process to endure is the correspondence audit. The IRS sends you a letter requesting additional information, such as a claimed deduction on your return. If they're satisfied with your answer, then you won't hear back from them. If not, then they'll call you in for an office examination. Correspondence audits also correct your tax returns for clerical mistakes, mathematical errors, and failures to report income (i.e., a bank or business reports 1099 income that you haven't).

Most individual return audits are conducted at an IRS office. Audits at your office are called field audits and usually are conducted for businesses and self-employed individuals. Roughly one-half of all audits are conducted in the IRS office with the remaining one-half split between correspondence and field audits. Overly complex transactions usually are field audited. It is rare that anyone has to endure a full audit on every aspect of his or her return—usually an audit is directed into specific, identified areas of designated returns.

The Taxpayer Bill of Rights

One response of Congress to the abuses of the IRS was enaction of the Taxpayers' Bill of Rights. Although it's amended or changed from year to year, these taxpayers' rights aren't known as well as they should be. If the IRS sends you a notice of deficiency or collection action, it must inform you as to your rights during an audit and an explanation of their collection and appeals procedures. You have the following rights, among others:

✔ To have a representative, such as a lawyer, CPA, or enrolled agent (a person who meets certain IRS requirements), handle your audit. If you've employed someone, then you don't have to appear in person. The representative can only appear for you if you have given that person your written power of attorney to do so.

✔ To stop an audit when you need to talk with that representative for advice.

✔ To not meet at a time or location that's inconvenient.

✔ To avoid the penalties, but not the tax or interest, if you can prove that you relied on erroneous, written IRS advice.

✔ To make an audio recording of the proceedings at your own expense. The IRS may do the same thing, but you must be given prior notice and can obtain a transcript by reimbursing them for the printing costs.

✔ To propose an installment payment plan should you not be able to pay all your taxes.

You have the right to sue the IRS if they have intentionally disregarded the law. However, it is *extremely rare* that a taxpayer has won when doing this. Typically, the taxpayer ends up paying the IRS's legal fees in such an action.

You must be given 30 days written notice of an IRS intent to levy on your property. This notice must clearly describe the levy procedures, your alternatives, and steps to redeem the property if seized. This time period is to allow you time to contest their action or to work out a deal.

All in all, these rights sound nice. However, in practice the IRS at times simply doesn't follow their rules. It depends at times on the agent you get—many are doing their job by trying to follow the rules, but some agents get their kicks by making life miserable for others.

Problems Resolution Program

The Problems Resolution Program (PRP) assists taxpayers when using the regular IRS channels doesn't work for a taxpayer—even the IRS recognized that its computers caused problems with erroneous levies on accounts, over-zealous tax collectors took arbitrary actions, and unreasonable delays occurred in receiving refunds. It is intended to be used when a taxpayer can't solve a problem but has tried.

Most taxpayers use the PRP when they can't get a refund. You are supposed to have first made at least two inquiries into where the refund is hiding before using PRP. But accountants recommend otherwise. Technically, you have to make two or three responses to the IRS's computerized demands when owing taxes; however, if your bank account was levied in error, most IRS agents won't hold you to this requirement either.

The PRP isn't to be used when you're under criminal investigation, disagree with tax policies, or don't like their answer (you have the normal rights of appeals, in any event). It doesn't send forms or give answers to tax questions—that's handled by different departments. Its main purpose is to accelerate the payment of refunds or to stop a consistent flow of erroneous, computerized notices. However, you must have tried to have the problem solved using normal channels.

The rule is simple: when in doubt, use the PRP. All IRS District Offices have a PRP person—call or visit your local office and ask where the nearest PRP is located. Once you have located it, call and explain your problem. Whether you call first or not, always send a written description of your problem, including copies of all documentation. The IRS never follows up on telephone calls—you need something that sits on someone's desk.

The Time Limits on Assessments

The time limit prohibiting the IRS from assessing more taxes against you depends on the status of your tax return. The limit changes, depending on whether it's been filed, amended, deemed fraudulent, or has not been filed at all.

The IRS is limited to 3 years after your return's due date (usually April 15th) to assess any additional taxes, provided you filed the return on time. If you filed your 1993 return on or before April 15, 1994, then the IRS would have until April 15, 1997, to assess any additional taxes for that year. If you filed an amended return showing more taxes owing just before the 3-year period is up, then the IRS has 60 days in which to assess the additional taxes, regardless of when the 3-year limit was due to expire.

Don't Just Pay Up

If you have received a computerized statement that more taxes are owed, then check your returns closely to be sure that the IRS's position is correct. Be aware that these statements may be in error. Surveys have indicated that the IRS is in error, one way or the other, as much as one out three times in such cases.

If you come to the conclusion that they're wrong (i.e., the deduction and amount was proper but in the wrong place), then send your written conclusions in reply. Try calling the listed telephone numbers for questions, although you may not get through, but always send a written answer.

However, the time limit is increased to 6 years when you failed to report more than 25% of your gross income on any return filed. There is *no* time limit on the IRS's ability to assess additional taxes when no return was filed or the return was false or fraudulent (filed with an intent to evade taxes). The problem is that whether a return is "fraudulent" or not is a question of fact and subject to argument. The IRS will use this as leverage to go back as long as they want when they *suspect* fraud.

The above limitations are general rules. Depending on the specific facts, it may be as much as 10 years, even an unlimited time, when a fraud tag is placed on your return. For the limitations in any specific situation involving your returns, consult experienced tax counsel or an accountant immediately.

Preparing for an Audit

The very first thing to do is to get your information and returns together for the year(s) in question and look over what's being questioned. Be sure to schedule the time for the examination sufficiently ahead so you can contact your accountant, if necessary, along with obtaining other documents and preparing your defense. If you are confused or the problem is complex, then consult an accountant.

Head to the local IRS office with your questions before the audit, but don't be argumentative or threatening. That won't help your case. If the problem doesn't involve something you knowingly "fudged" or did wrong, then listen to what they say. Otherwise, talk to an accountant.

The preparation for any audit will, of course, depend on whether it's a correspondence, IRS-office, or field-examination audit. If you should receive an IRS letter asking for additional information, such as documenting deductions or income, then be glad you weren't asked to participate in a broader office or field audit. Send in the requested information.

If the audit is more extensive, such as at the IRS office or your place of business, then the task becomes more extensive. Collect all your canceled checks, receipts, invoices, and supporting documentation. Review them and, if necessary, consult your accountant in advance.

An audit at your business is the most extensive. You should review any areas called for specifically in the audit letter, prepare the arguments supporting your position, and consult your accountant. Go over the files, separating out what the IRS wants to see from those that weren't called for. Go over all files in detail, so you aren't surprised by any contents when the IRS examiner reviews them.

The prime areas examiners look for are if all income has been reported and that the deductions were proper, not including any personal expenses. The business's deductions for travel, entertainment, meals, automobiles, insurance, and salaries, for example, are usual areas of interest. They more than likely will review your bank statements against what your books report as income.

Only records and documents *pertaining to what was in writing* should be organized. The rest should be put away. Don't bring or show any papers, documents, or returns that aren't directly related to the audit areas in question.

You want to be able to go quickly through your case, showing a carefully thought out and prepared position. Giving an unprepared or scattered image won't help. You have the right to ask that a field examination be held at your accountant's office (or that of your tax attorney, but they're usually more expensive) and not at your business or home. This should be considered carefully, especially if there are too many records at the business or its appearance would give the wrong impression.

Don't tell the whole world about your problems. Confine your discussions to your spouse or significant other—everyone else should be on a "need to know" basis. Information can always wind up in the wrong hands, such as with that disgruntled employee who turned you in to the IRS in the first place.

Preparation for the audit also includes seeing if you have a good offense. An accountant recommended: "Try to find things that are good for your side. A good offense is a good defense in the negotiations. Dig out those receipts and see if you have more deductions than you claimed. But be sure that you're right so that another hornet's nest isn't opened up."

When Should You Consult a Professional?

Many audits can be handled by you. You know the facts, have the papers, and understand what's happening. When you do it yourself, you're only using your time and money. However, you may make a mistake because you don't do this for a living. "You need to be aware of the rules before you talk with the IRS and not when you're there. If the case is important enough, then you should consult a professional to be sure you're on the right track," commented one accountant.

If the amount of money involved isn't large, then look for the necessary information by yourself (but with one exception that we'll discuss later). There are a number of books at bookstores, IRS publications, and tax guides (located in county libraries, law libraries, and federal agency libraries in major, metropolitan areas) that can be consulted. It's also possible (but there will be delays) to call the IRS toll-free tax information line (ask the "800" operator), to visit your local IRS office for needed information and pamphlets, and to order IRS publications.

It's easier to get the information from a professional, instead of researching it on your own. However, in determining whether they're worth the expense, there are three considerations. If you're staring at a large deficiency (remember the penalties and interest provisions), then it makes sense to choose a professional based on that person's experience, cost, availability, success rate, and how you get along. Similarly, complex transactions should usually involve a professional.

Don't consult an attorney who isn't a tax specialist. An accountant has had the training, but you will need to determine how much experience he or she has had with audits. Enrolled agents are accountants or tax preparers who have passed an enrolled agent's IRS exam or have had 5 or more years experience in front of the IRS. What you have to decide is whether you can afford one.

Leads to such professionals can be generated in many ways (see Chapter 5). Should you already have an accountant or tax preparer, then start with that person. He or she has a vested interest in your problem, from preparing your return. If you don't have one, then ask family, friends, and business associates. As a last resort, look in the yellow pages and interview several over the telephone.

You will want to determine the fee in advance, including the possibilities of a fixed fee (although usually difficult to obtain in such cases). If the fee seems high, then ask what can be done to lower it. As indicated in Chapter 12, ask for a written fee agreement, whether it involves an accountant or attorney.

The third reason (the "one" exception mentioned above) is when you've committed fraud and know it, or it looks that way. Then you will want to consult a tax attorney. Further, if heading into any appeal requiring court appearances, such as the Federal District Court, you should consult a tax attorney.

Once in the Audit

Audits aren't fun. If you go to the dentist, at least you're getting something fixed. "I couldn't sleep before the audit, was nervous throughout it, and was furious afterwards," commented one taxpayer. An attorney who ended up owing more money after one said "I knew I was in trouble just after sitting down. The recently hired IRS examiner started by saying he had been interviewed by a national magazine. He pulled it out and sure enough he had been. There was his name and picture in an article with others who had been interviewed for being able to live on less than $20,000. I knew I was dead from the beginning. And I was." Another audited person commented "The first thing the examiner said was to ask how I was. I couldn't answer...I was just speechless."

No matter how you feel, there are straightforward rules to guide you:

▓ *Only bring in what is requested.* You should bring to the examination only the records, documents, canceled checks, and papers that bear directly on the areas of examination stated in the audit letter. Anything else carried in can only open up other areas of inquiry. You want to keep the discussion just to those topics you were given notification over. Remember that the agent is interested in discovering whatever can be found out.

Only allow your originals to be copied by the IRS—don't allow them to keep them. Information becomes lost, and copies fade.

▓ *Be courteous, polite, but firm.* When first meeting the examiner, introduce yourself and warm up by commenting about the drive, the weather, or recent local news. The auditor is also a person, and don't begin with any hysterical rhetoric about how insane your audit is or the mess the government creates with your tax dollars. This all may be true, but making an enemy of the agent isn't good sense. Try to avoid personality clashes and keep the meeting on a professional level. But don't be afraid to stand up to any challenges made by the examiner.

▓ *Listen more than you talk.* You need to know what the IRS agent is looking for and is interested in. If you talk more than you should, then you won't know this and might give the IRS more to look into. A seasoned professional observed, "A big mistake is not listening to the examiner. The problem might not be as difficult as you first thought. Don't babble on about stuff that's not relevant to what they want. And you don't want to confuse them, because then the agent might think there's something else around that's more important."

▓ *Understand the game.* The examiner does this for a living and is trying to see whether you're honest, in addition to flushing out the areas where more assessments can be made. As part of this, the agent may make comments such as

"Where did you hide the money?" or "It has to be here, somewhere, doesn't it?" Don't rise to the bait with these comments—just give a laugh and shrug it off.

Some agents may become combative at times. It works for them in some situations. An aggressive approach should be countered by saying you'll terminate the meeting unless a more civil approach is used. Don't raise your voice but be firm.

▦ *Don't lie but also don't volunteer information.* If the auditor asks how you treated other years, and you don't know, then just say that. If asked why a deduction isn't fully documented, say "It should be" and leave it at that. Your answers should be short, to the point; then back off and don't say anything more.

Remember it's a crime to lie to the IRS—it isn't when you're evasive or don't provide information. You must be subtle in this. It's better to say "I'll check further," or "It should add up." Don't say "Forget it, Charley, I'm not giving you that information." It's all a game, and they've played it before.

▦ *Don't make it worse.* Don't back-date documents, perjure yourself, or phony up papers supporting your position. There's no need to arm-twist friends to write phony statements trying to help you out. It is too easy to be found out, and then you'll need to hire an expensive tax attorney who handles criminal defense work.

▦ *Don't admit to anything.* Stick to your guns. As bad as volunteering information or talking about your finances too much is saying "You're right. I blew it. I thought about it at the time and made a mistake." That type of comment only gets you in worse trouble.

A favorite trick of examiners is arguing that your deduction is denied because you don't have all the documentation. That's not correct. If the auditor is convinced you're telling the truth, then your word may be sufficient. Although that's not frequent, the extent of the documentation you need is simply another part of the negotiations. Substantial documentation, not all of it, is what's required.

▦ *Don't be afraid to challenge the unreasonable examiner.* If the auditor is hard-nosed, unreasonable, or continues to be insulting, then either request another auditor, a meeting with the agent's supervisor, or state that you're terminating the meeting. If that's refused (which is rare), then say you're leaving to consult your professional advisor. Stand up, shake hands, and leave. You have the right to leave an examination at any time to meet with your professional representative. Call up that agent after talking with a professional and inform the examiner you want to talk with the supervisor or another agent. Or have your representative do it.

▦ *Keep the agent in one place, if at your business.* If the audit occurs at your business, don't allow the agent to wander around the place. Provide an area, hopefully away from where business is conducted, just for the agent to work. You should instruct your employees not to talk about the business or its operations—that's your responsibility.

▦ *Understand that much is negotiable.* The IRS wants to settle every audit case as soon as possible. They don't want a lot of appeals and subsequent court battles. In fact, they would like to settle their cases at the first audit levels. Although this doesn't mean you'll get what you want, it does mean to be alert to what the examiner says.

Let's say you're discussing your deductions for nonreimbursed business expenses. Although the auditor states more receipts are needed, he also asks "Can you get them?" You might answer "That would take some time, but rather than that, why don't we just agree to take 15% off the amount. I probably could find them, but it would take a lot of time." If that's refused, then say "OK, I'll spend the time." As you are leaving, the auditor could say "I'm going to take 50% off if you can't find the additional documentation." You could say that's unacceptable and offer 25% instead.

When you're leaving the examination, try to discover what adjustments will be proposed and where your differences still are. What you are looking for are the areas of negotiation. If the agent replies that the deductions, for example, are going to be denied in full, then answer by saying that's entirely unacceptable and you'll take it to the supervisor, then to appeal. Show you won't hesitate to take the matters further up the line, then see what the next response is.

The Examination Report

You may need to send in additional information, even have another meeting before the agent prepares the Examination Report. This states the specific areas and computations showing the additional taxes that are owed. When you receive that report, you can either accept it, fight it further with that agent, request a meeting with the supervisor, or continue the process.

If you accept it, then you will sign Form 870, which assesses the deficiency, penalties, and interest. If you don't have the money, you can propose as part of the acceptance that a payment plan be established. Should you not agree with these findings, then the battle may have just begun.

The Appeal

If you don't agree to the proposed deficiency, then you normally will receive a 30-day letter after receiving the Examiner's Report. This notice states you haven't reached agreement and have 30 days in which to bring an appeal. An appeal over the Examination Report is made directly to the IRS Regional Appeals Office for your area.

The IRS doesn't necessarily have to send a 30-day letter, nor need it accept your request for an appeal. Although most cases are granted, the IRS simply isn't required to give an appeals hearing after an audit. The reason why it does almost routinely is because this is as cost effective for them as it is for the taxpayer.

The appeal process is started by filing a written protest under penalties of perjury, following the IRS Regulations stated in their *Publication 5*, all of which needs to be done within the stated time period. You need to state your specific

---

If you or your accountant feel there's a case, then use the appeal route. "It's surprising that more people don't use this, given the advantages," commented several tax professionals. Appealing doesn't need to cost anything because you represent yourself. Although the interest continues running on any unpaid taxes, you have the chance to whittle down enough from the Examiner's report to offset this. You may be able to reach an agreement simply by phone. The average appeal ends with some reduction from the Examiner's Report.

reasons in writing for not agreeing with the Examiner's Report. Your file will be shipped to the Appeals Office upon their receiving the notice of appeal.

The negotiations or appeal can be conducted even by telephone, since it is not an absolute requirement that formal hearings be held. This can be an advantage when you are located a distance from the Appeals Office. However, if your case can't be settled by telephone, then you'll need to have a formal appeals hearing. You can be represented by a professional, if you want, but that's also not a requirement.

The Notice of Deficiency and Other Alternatives

If you decide not to appeal or lose an appeal, then you will eventually receive a Notice of Deficiency, or as it's otherwise known, the 90-day letter. At this point, or if you have already settled, you have joined the rest of us. Over three-fourths of everyone audited ends up owing more money.

The 90-day letter notifies you that the IRS will assess the extra tax at the end of 90 days from the mailing of the letter. At this point, you have several options. Again, you can pay it (the interest and potential penalties are still mounting). Or there are three courts you can consider.

Within 90 days after the Notice of Deficiency's mailing date, you can file a petition with the Tax Court. Or you may pay the disputed tax, file a refund claim, and then sue (after it's denied) in a federal district court or the U.S. Claims Court. Or you may sue in a small case division of the Tax Court, if the amount of taxes and penalties in any year is $10,000 or less.

At this point, you should definitely consult a tax attorney for advice, if one hasn't been consulted yet, as to which alternative is best. Should the disputed tax be large, including the penalties, or if the problem is complex, then you should definitely consider retaining an experienced tax attorney for any courtroom battles. See Chapters 18 through 20 for recommendations in finding a litigation attorney and controlling legal costs.

The small tax case procedure in the Tax Court should be considered when your dispute is $10,000 or less. As part of the Tax Court petition, you need to specifically elect this procedure. Small tax cases are heard by special trial judges, and jury trials aren't permitted. It operates very similarly to small claims court proceedings with low filing fees, informal proceedings, and quick decisions. You need to be able to prove your case, including providing witnesses and notarized statements.

If you are over the $10,000 limit, you can still proceed but need to waive what's over this amount. For example, if the amount of disputed taxes is $13,750 (including interest and penalties), then you would contest $10,000 of the total amount. By waiving the contested difference of $3,750, you would be agreeing to pay that amount, regardless of what happened in the proceeding. You don't need to be represented by counsel, and, in fact, most claimants aren't. All decisions are final, as these cases by law can't be appealed.

If you bring a case in regular Tax Court, you don't necessarily need to be represented by counsel. Whether or not you do so will be decided by balancing the time you have to spend, the size of your dispute, and how versed you are in representing yourself—all against the expense of retaining experienced tax counsel.

You should, in any event, consult such counsel on a no-charge courtesy basis before making your decision. It is also true, as in most other litigation, that most cases in regular Tax Court settle before trial.

Cases brought in a Federal District Court or Court of Claims are large cases. The jurisdictional amount for federal courts in such cases is currently $50,000 or more in dispute. These cases must be handled with care, given the potential damages of an adverse judgment, not to mention the interest, penalties, and high cost of lawyers. Adverse judgments from a Tax Court (cases not in the $10,000 and under small claims tax court), federal district court, or Court of Claims case can be appealed to a U.S. Circuit Court of Appeals. The last stop would be the U.S. Supreme Court.

You need to be careful that your case isn't frivolous. "They get very upset over this," observed a tax attorney. If the court determines you brought an unreasonable case or unreasonably failed to discuss your position within the IRS's procedures, then the Tax Court may impose a penalty up to $25,000 against you. If an attorney abuses the Tax Court procedures, then you and/or the attorney may be required to pay the excess court costs or attorney fees made necessary by to the resulting delays.

If you believe the IRS took an unreasonable position, then you're entitled to sue for all or part of your legal fees and costs in a civil tax case, but there are limitations and conditions on this. To recover such costs, you need to "substantially prevail" on the key issues involved in the controversy.

You also can sue if an IRS agent recklessly or intentionally (which you must prove) disregarded the law when making a tax assessment or other collection activity. The suit must be brought in Federal District Court. There are limitations on the amounts of damage that can be collected, but you can be fined up to $10,000 if the lawsuit is determined by the court to be frivolous. A suit for damages also can be brought against the IRS for wrongfully refusing to release a lien on your property, the damages being the actual economic damages proved to have been sustained along with court costs and attorney fees.

Any person considering such courses of action should consult a second legal opinion before deciding on any such actions. You already are facing financial losses from the disputed taxes, including interest and penalties, and this is only adding another lawsuit to your problems. The likelihood of success is not as great as when you were at the IRS appeals or Tax Court level.

When You Owe the IRS

People or their companies owe the IRS because they didn't have the money to pay them, didn't file, were additionally assessed by audit, lost the appeal, and for other reasons. Let's say you lost the appeal, the government sent you the 90-day letter, and you owe more taxes (not to mention the odds of a state sending you a bill now, as well).

If you have the money now, then that settles the problem, although reluctantly and unhappily. If you don't have the money, you can try to work out an installment plan, play the game of delay (through working towards an installment plan) while trying to raise the money, reduce the liability through a compromise offer, or even consider bankruptcy (which doesn't discharge most amounts owed, depending on the facts, but stops their collection efforts), among other alternatives.

Playing the Game

The IRS relies on computers and insufficient personnel to assess and collect taxes. The same mistakes, delays, and headaches they create by erroneous billings, mistaken audits, and tardy refunds, can now work to your benefit when you don't have the money to pay what is owed. This also depends on whether you want to keep your house or prized thoroughbred horses, because if you don't have assets that matter to you, then you're always in a better negotiating position.

Let's assume that you do. The game is called delay, and the approach recommended by the tax pros is to answer every computer print-out that's sent to you. Take your time in answering the various requests, but send a written response to each one. Write that you don't have the money to pay the bill now and need another 60 to 90 days. If possible, try to include a small payment and do this with every piece of paper you receive. You may or may not receive an extension, and any extension may only be from 30 to 60 days. However, some anonymous IRS employee may punch a key on the computer, and it's possible that you'll get your delay. The IRS's inefficiencies may even result in delays in getting around to your responses.

But you need to be careful with this approach. The IRS is a beast that's neither consistent nor predictable. Anne never filed income tax forms for 6 years out of eight years; as a matter of fact, she only did file when there were refunds. Her source of income bounced up and down, depending on the economy. She had lost her house, although she'd delayed that for years by using a number of tactics, including bankruptcy (see Chapter 10 regarding creditors) in one bad downturn. She never responded to the IRS computerized printouts, because she didn't have any major assets to worry about (even her car was leased). Anne finally got around to calling the IRS because one notice stating that her income would be attached did get her attention. She cried over the telephone, saying that she was trying but her husband had left her with the children. It turned out the IRS person on the other line also was a struggling, single mother with children. She told Anne not to worry, because she would take care of it. She did. Anne didn't hear back from the IRS for years. Although difficult to believe, this actually happened. But *you* can't count on it.

On the other hand, Carol, a hard-working investment banker, lost her job because of cutbacks on Wall Street. At the same time she had lost her appeal on owing back taxes. Within 6 months after receiving the Notice of Deficiency, the IRS was seizing her assets in payment. Carol played "hard ball" with the IRS, refusing to accept the decision (but doing nothing else) or trying to work out a compromise. That doesn't work unless you have a case, the IRS's position is weak, or you don't have any assets. It's better to play the game.

If you are playing the game for delays, then remember you need to have an objective. Interest and penalties are mounting up daily, and these costs can increase dramatically even if you're being successful with your delaying tactics. The delays don't mean you won't have to pay the IRS down the road—you will, as it's only a question of time. *The objective should be more than just delaying, such as gaining the time to raise the money owed or arranging for installment payments.*

Installment Plans

We previously discussed installment requests, and the IRS usually doesn't ask for financial information with owed taxes of $10,000 or less when you are filing your return. You will need to know your assets, liabilities, income, and expenses for all other times before requesting an installment tax payment program. Be aware that the IRS may even offer an installment program to get to know your finances more in detail.

The question of financial disclosures then becomes tricky. You have to disclose records to gain the IRS's agreement (which is discretionary on their part) when they request them under an installment program request. However, showing your assets gives the IRS the ammunition to ask you to do other things before they agree. They may ask you to get a bank loan on your house (say you can't qualify, which is usually true by now), sell your assets (answer there's no market), or even demand you pay everything at once (say that's why you're there—you don't have the money). This doesn't mean that they will accept your answers.

After the interview concerning your ability to pay, you will need to prepare Form 433, "Collection Information Statement," which itemizes your financial status. You may be asked to submit additional documentation, such as past income tax returns, deeds, bank statements, and your debt.

> You will need to negotiate the amount of monthly payments and the time required to pay off the debt, including the running interest. Only agree to a monthly payment plan that can be met. If you can't meet it, then don't sign the agreement—if there's a default, you're back to where you started. Further, you'll usually not get another agreement, because you already broke the first one. They may even begin immediate collection activities.

Once it has been prepared, the agent may use that to demand again that you sell property, obtain loans, or even start collection efforts without granting you an installment program. The best protection is simply to be honest. Don't ask for an installment program unless you need one.

Whether an installment plan has been accepted or not, remember you've disclosed everything to the IRS, including where your bank accounts, cars, and property are located. Even if you haven't supplied them with your financial account information, they could have obtained it already from past filings, the 1099s sent in by your banks, or by investigating on their own. Change all bank accounts immediately, depositing only enough money into the old ones to make any required payments to the IRS. Everything else should be run through the new accounts. See the heading "Transferring Your Assets" later in this chapter.

Offers in Compromise

An offer in compromise makes it possible to eliminate your entire tax debt, including interest and penalties, and usually at a substantial discount. It's this aspect that makes it so attractive, but at the same time so difficult to receive. The IRS has limited motivation to let you off the hook entirely, unless the agent feels what you offer is the only money that will ever be seen by them.

The IRS must feel that it can't collect the taxes from you, now or in the future. Your income must be low with limited aspects to it improving over time. You won't be able to keep the equity in your property. Whatever equity you do have (the value left after subtracting what's owed) will have to be transferred to them as part of any accepted offer. There's no incentive for the IRS to give up all its rights if there are assets that can be seized in the future.

The agent has the discretion to either accept your offer in compromise or turn it down flatly. Remember that the IRS is interested in raising revenues, not in letting you off the hook because it's good for you. You will be negotiating not only over the assets you have and the downpayment, but also as to the amount of any monthly payments.

If an eventual offer in compromise is accepted, then you're one of the luckier ones. If it isn't, then the IRS may begin to actively collect on the assets you've identified. Again, the best protection is to be honest and to secure an offer in compromise when you have nothing further left to lose.

If you're trying to hide assets, then you will have big problems if the IRS discovers them. Not only may you be referred for criminal prosecution, but immediate collection efforts will be brought against the newly found assets, not to mention what you've already disclosed. However, people still try to do this.

The Collection Efforts

Meanwhile, the IRS hasn't been totally inactive during these times. They already may have been looking for your assets. You will need to be careful and gauge when such activities are being considered, processed, or being brought. The IRS is notorious for swooping in on bank accounts or property without warning. Although they're required to give such notice, you may have disregarded them. Or if you moved without a forwarding address, the notices were never received. Sometimes, the notices aren't processed by the IRS correctly (that's saying it nicely). You then receive a bank notice stating your account has been swept clean.

The IRS has a tax lien on your properties by law as soon as you owe any unpaid taxes. Should they file the notice of this lien, or a "Notice of Federal Tax Lien," then the public and any potential buyers of your property are put on notice as to its existence. Such notices, when recorded (for example, with your local county recorder's office) will be picked up by the title companies or examiners. When you go to sell such properties, the lien will need to be paid off before title can be transferred to the buyer. This lien notice, as distinct from the actual levy, normally won't find its way to warn a buyer of your car, furniture, antiques, or computer.

A problem with tax lien filings is that they're picked up by credit-reporting agencies. If you are trying to obtain a loan, the bank or financial institution may discover your problem. You will have to pay the IRS off to get the loan, if the bank is still interested in talking with you. A tax lien is a real problem on credit standings.

However, the tax lien is only the notice of the tax obligation. To collect the monies directly, the IRS must levy or seize your property, after notifying you of the intended activities. The notice of the levy will be either delivered to you in person or more normally sent to your last known mailing address.

By law, the "Notice of Intent to Levy" must give you 30-days' notice before the IRS can start these proceedings. However, the problem is that the 30-day period runs from the date of the notice, not when you receive it. You will lose time if there are any delays in receiving the notice. It's not difficult to see, regardless of what the law provides, why numbers of taxpayers first discover such proceeding when informed by the bank or at the time an agent hands them the papers seizing the assets.

Once at this stage, there are limited options. You can only pay off the taxes and interest or negotiate with the IRS to gain extra time to sell off your assets before the collection date. You can file or threaten bankruptcy, whether it's a Chapter 7 (liquidation of assets and debts), Chapter 11 (business reorganization), or Chapter 13 (reorganization or payment plan for individuals). Although such a filing will stop any immediate collection efforts by the IRS, it doesn't solve the problem of the unpaid taxes, most of which aren't discharged in the average case and are subject to complicated rules.

When property is seized by the IRS, it is typically sold later at an auction—the IRS isn't in the business to own property, just to collect revenues. The sales are to the highest bidder at public auctions with a minimum acceptable bid. Whether it's your car, boat, computer equipment, or house, you have the right to get your property back before the sale by paying off the taxes completely, including all interest and penalties. It's possible to negotiate with the IRS for an installment payment program (you might now accept their first offer), but don't count on this. It's better to work out an arrangement before anyof your property is seized.

If you don't buy your property back, then it's sold by the IRS. The net proceeds, after the costs of the sale and collection activities, will be applied against what is owed. Remember that any unpaid tax amounts still owed, after deducting the net sale proceeds, are still your responsibility. The IRS can and will still continue its efforts to collect what is needed to pay off the remaining balances (according to their records).

Transferring Your Assets

As the IRS becomes more efficient through modern management techniques and technology, using delay tactics or negotiating over time for payment terms becomes riskier. You should be making plans to move assets from where they can be seized before you receive a collection notice. Bank accounts should have already been transferred, keeping in mind the IRS knows people do this and have printed instructions as to what their agents should do in response.

The IRS already has information on your existing accounts, and if not from your discussions and past information, then by their own outside investigations. They will be searching for bank accounts when not able to find money by "tapping the till" at your old accounts.

When establishing new accounts, there are a few rules to observe. First, as the IRS is looking for them also, be sure there are a number of banks in your area. Or set up an account in another state. Second, consider putting your money in a non-interest-bearing account. Although banks and financial institutions don't alert the IRS when accounts are established, they will on large cash transactions of $10,000 or more, as well as report interest earned at the end of the year with the infamous 1099s. Third, to be totally safe you could give the money to a trusted family member to hold in safekeeping.

However, you need to be careful. Although people change bank accounts and sell cars and property as part of ordinary life and living, transferring or hiding assets to evade the tax collector specifically is illegal. There is a thin line between what can and can't be done. Before hiding or transferring property, consult an experienced tax attorney.

Real property must be sold before any "Notice of Tax Lien" is recorded. Waiting past this time is too late. As discussed before, the taxes must be paid off completely once the title company or examiner has knowledge of them. Otherwise, the lien follows the property into the hands of the unsuspecting buyer. Transferring real property to a family member, for insufficient cash or value, won't be accepted by the IRS nor allowed by law.

Selling homes, lots, and buildings *is* a common occurrence. If they're sold for market value and terms with escrows closing before the tax lien is filed and becomes public information, then cash has been freed from illiquid real estate. However, if there are gains on the sale, you might also have added another tax problem to deal with later.

Placing title to real property in the hands of family members, corporations, and trusts can delay or thwart the IRS's efforts, even after the tax lien has been filed. Although it makes a difference whether you simply give it away (it's easier for the IRS to unwind the transfer) or sell it for market price (the problem is who would buy it privately, knowing about the tax lien), such transfers do make their job more difficult. But not impossible.

A distinction is sometimes made by tax attorneys between transferring property after the tax lien has been filed and after you've received the IRS's 30-day notice to begin collection. The area can be "gray" if you haven't received the 30-day notice to levy. You are in the illegal area when transferring assets after the receipt of such a notice.

Typically, personal property is rarely affected, no matter what notice you've received. You can sell, transfer, or relocate your computer equipment, furniture, prized antiques, paintings, and car without anyone having notice of the tax dispute or the IRS having a *prior* legal claim to the proceeds as it does with real property after recording a tax lien. The IRS may, however, have a legal right to the proceeds, should they discover what's going on.

After converting property to cash, you have to do something with it to keep the monies away from the IRS. At some time the IRS may catch up with you, so all your efforts could have been wasted. Moreover, by doing this after receiving the required collection notice, you've definitely entered into criminal violations of the tax code (which isn't recommended).

It may make sense to rent property now rather than owning outright. Leasing your furniture, computer, car, and even renting a house can help you to avoid problems. You might want to move your prized stamp collection to a safer location. You don't need to keep your car stored in the garage all the time.

But it is imperative you consult experienced counsel prior to doing any transferring or hiding of assets, no matter what they are, when, or how. It is illegal to intentionally thwart the collection efforts of the IRS by property transfers that conceal or hide such property from them. It's true people do this with few criminal prosecutions, but there's no need for you to become one of the exceptions.

Filing Bankruptcy

Bankruptcy is a legal proceeding whereby you ask the bankruptcy court to help you either liquidate or re-arrange your debts. It's a complex area of varying rules and laws that affect you differently depending on your particular situation and the type of bankruptcy you file.

Whether to file bankruptcy can be a difficult choice, and people try to put this decision off. It is an anguishing feeling and a tough choice. However, taxes can be a different thing—if they are dischargeable. "It was an admission of failure," one bankrupt admitted. "I didn't like not being able to pay my creditors. But I didn't mind when my attorney informed me how I could knock off some of the old taxes. I didn't mind that a bit. Not with their approach."

Whether or not your tax debt will be discharged (or erased) by the bankruptcy depends on a number of varying, complex rules. For example, taxes owed due to fraudulent tax returns, unassessed taxes, and tax evasion won't be discharged, regardless of which bankruptcy proceeding is chosen. Moreover, late returns and taxes assessed within certain periods before the filing may not be discharged, depending on the facts.

Filing bankruptcy does operate the same, regardless of the proceeding or your tax position, in one important area—the IRS is treated as any other creditor and can't continue its collection efforts, including any levying, selling, or attaching of property. This prohibition, called a "stay," can be challenged in the bankruptcy court later by the creditors, including the IRS. However, the IRS usually doesn't.

If you are in a Chapter 7 liquidation proceeding, then only certain income taxes can be discharged. For example, obligations due at least 3 years before you filed for bankruptcy would be discharged, provided they weren't fraudulent, were assessed by the IRS at least 240 days before your bankruptcy filing, and the tax return had been filed at least 2 years before the bankruptcy filing, among other factors. As you can see, the discussion is complicated and requires a consultation with a bankruptcy specialist. However, the intent is that recent IRS tax liabilities and assessments won't be discharged under Chapter 7, and thus will remain individual liabilities.

You need to be careful with the 3-year rule. A CPA observed, "Pay close attention to the time when owing taxes can be extinguished. There are horror stories where people filed too soon and discovered that they missed by months the time for discharging their old tax obligations. Pay off the newer ones, when possible, and don't file when you have a short time to go in eliminating the taxes that can be discharged by a bankruptcy filing."

Chapter 11 (for businesses) and Chapter 13 (for individuals) are bankruptcy proceedings that don't involve liquidation. They are reorganization procedures whereby a payment plan to creditors over time (including the IRS) is agreed upon. In such reorganizations, the great majority of your debts and even some IRS liabilities may not need to be paid in full. Businesses also can be liquidated in

Chapter 7 proceedings, whether filed directly or converted from a Chapter 11 when a repayment plan isn't workable (but certain tax liabilities will still remain).

There are a few important differences between Chapter 7 liquidation and Chapter 13 reorganizations for individuals. Although generally interest and penalties stop when you file under Chapter 13 (but are included in the payment plan), they may be liquidated in a Chapter 7 filing (although this depends again on the rules). In Chapter 13, recent tax filings and assessments (those due within 3 years before your bankruptcy filing or assessed less than 240 days before the filing) must usually be paid first before the payment plan will be accepted. Again, it's a very complicated area requiring expert legal help, and even the IRS agents are confused about all the requirements.

The importance of Chapter 13 is that the IRS cannot negotiate a better payment plan that the bankruptcy court will approve. The IRS is simply another creditor in this regard.

> You don't, however, want to file bankruptcy for federal and state income tax reasons alone. Unpaid taxes, including the interest and penalties, should only be part of this decision. You'll need to consult experienced bankruptcy counsel before making a final decision. See Chapter 10 on surviving the tough times for additional information and remember that the above general rules are subject to specific limitations not possible to be gone into here.

Tax specialists are waiting for the IRS to allow taxpayers the right to use credit cards for taxes. With the taxes paid, the liability becomes what's owed to the credit card company. As one accountant observed "If the IRS allows you to pay income taxes by credit card without protecting legislation, then you could pay the nondischargeable taxes off, then have the credit card balances discharged through bankruptcy. We'll have to see what happens with this."

An Overview—Controlling the Problem

Having problems and losing money to the IRS and other taxing authorities is a fact of life. Those who earn the money will be contacted at some time by Uncle Sam to pay more.

Advanced tax planning, at least in the beginning and at the end of each tax year, can alert you to tax problems before they occur. Keep detailed records as long as possible, including documenting the existence of large deductions as well as you can, in case you receive an IRS audit letter.

By staying on top of all tax requests and demands, not ignoring them but following up and trying to solve them, you can avoid the surprise levy. *The IRS should be taken seriously.* Prepare in advance for all meetings, not just the beginning audit; understand the processes and rights of appeal; and don't make the problem worse by back-dating documents or committing perjury.

Consulting with an attorney and/or accountant before an extensive audit, especially if you've lied or intentionally reduced your taxes improperly, should be done before you meet with the IRS—not after you've received a notice of additional fraud or negligence penalties.

What you're trying to do is prevent or solve tax problems without needing expensive attorneys or accountants on a nearly, full-time basis to get you out of a big tax jam. You need to pay attention to your income taxes, especially given the way states follow the lead of the IRS in collecting revenues.

Plan for Your Estate and Old Age Now

Most people don't worry about estate planning. In fact two out of three Americans will die without having at least a valid will in place. It's easier not to concern ourselves with the difficult topic of death and what to do with the money or assets left over. The problem is that these considerations are put off to be thrashed out later by our heirs and the courts.

It is your money, and you can do with it whatever you want. A friend of mine said her definition of happiness was to die when she was 90 years old on the day she had spent her last dime. Spending all your money, even giving all of it to a yogi or a home for abandoned animals is your prerogative.

Most people try to save money for their retirement, investing it as well as possible to live off the income without jeopardizing the principal, if that's possible. If not, then they live off whatever was saved. Should they die before all their money was spent, then a will had better be in existence—otherwise, state law determines who gets the money and how much.

A will shouldn't be put off until you're old. It makes no difference whether you are young or old, with or without children, or even employed. Everyone should have a will in place, even though most people don't take the time to write one.

Why Have a Will?

There are several reasons why a valid will should be in effect:

▓ *To state who should receive your assets, how much, and in what manner.* A legally effective will ensures that your estate will be given to the people, organizations, or associations you want. You can include controls that otherwise wouldn't be available—for example, establishing a trust with a trustee that determines how much money your minor children receive and when.

If you don't have a will, then you're guaranteeing a fight between your heirs as to who gets what. If you promised your grown son that he would get that sentimental carving of a small elephant he played with when he was young, then he will be very disappointed when his sister also wants it. Your son won't be the only person disappointed. Should you die without a will (the legal term is to die "intestate"), then the laws of your state determine everything. And if you have no heirs, then all your assets go to the state when a will isn't in place.

Contrary to public opinion, a surviving spouse doesn't inherit everything owned when someone dies without a will. The surviving heirs have protected interests, and surviving heirs may include parents, brothers, sisters, children, or children of a deceased brother or sister. Depending on the laws of the particular state, a surviving spouse may only be entitled to from one-third to one-half of the estate. Property will go to people whom you don't want to receive a dime.

If you have minor children, dying intestate could mean the remaining parent would be restricted in the use of the minor children's inheritance. Even when there are limited assets, the surviving spouse would need to be selected by the court as the guardian of your children's property, then be bound by a slew of expensive, inflexible legal requirements.

If you die in a community property state, the intestacy statutes typically apply only to separate or noncommunity assets. The surviving spouse in such a state will receive all of what's considered to be community property—since by definition both spouses own one-half of the community property, the survivor keeps his or her one-half, then inherits the remaining one-half of the deceased spouse. This means that without a will the children could be left out unintentionally when there's only community property in a state recognizing this.

▓ *To select a guardian for your children.* Although the surviving spouse will usually be appointed the children's guardian, you still haven't addressed the question as to who raises the children should both parents die. Moreover, many states require the guardian (let's assume it's your surviving spouse) to post a bond, make at least an annual accounting, and pay more costs and fees. It's also possible that the state will appoint a guardian for the children's assets and another guardian for their person, all subject to varying laws, rules, regulations, and costs. This subject is treated later in the chapter.

▓ *To select who is responsible for your estate.* Should you die intestate, then the court appoints an administrator to handle and dispose of your estate. Although this can be someone who's part of the family, there's no guarantee that this will happen. Administrators must be bonded, are subject to varying laws, and must report formally to the court. It's also possible that a public administrator could distribute your assets. Court-appointed administrators charge fees to distribute your assets and incur more costs by needing court authorization for most tasks.

You can appoint your best friend, spouse, sister, or anyone of legal age who accepts to be the executor (the equivalent of an administrator where there is a will) of your estate. The executor provides primarily a financial function, as opposed to what a guardian does in raising minor children.

It's possible to direct in your will that the executor serves without needing to obtain an expensive bond (or the guarantee that a person will perform the services in good faith) and distributes your assets without court approval on all except for a few basic hearings and areas. You can change the executors in your will just as easily as a guardian.

▓ *To commence estate planning.* The presence of a will forces you into estate planning and consideration of the ways your property should be disposed. A common mistake made is to assume that since a surviving spouse who inherits all the property pays no estate taxes (that is, your estate pays no estate taxes), then no estate planning is required. The problem is that the assets become bunched up in the surviving spouse's estate, and, depending on its size, estate taxes that would have been entirely avoidable in the beginning may need to be paid later.

Property that passes outside the estate by contract does avoid probate (the court's administration of the deceased person's will and estate). For example, property held in joint tenancy (the property passes to the survivor), life insurance (provided there's a specific, designated beneficiary and your estate retains no rights over the proceeds), and pension benefits pass outside your will. However, although these aren't included for probate purposes, they will be included in the gross estate for federal estate tax purposes.

Drafting and executing a valid will does bring about control over your estate and by itself is an effective estate planning device—except for the fees and costs of probate. Unanticipated costs and legal fees, excessive delays, unwarranted guardianship appointments, and unintended inheritance fights can be avoided by taking the time to execute a valid will.

But What about a Living Trust?

The problem with using only a will to dispose of your estate is that the costs of probate are high and can require expensive lawyers. One of the great growth markets for attorneys in response to this has been advertising and recommending the use of revocable living trusts to avoid probate. There are widely available seminars promoting the advantages of such trusts, not to mention the flyers continually sent by mail telling you to disregard your will and use a trust instead. Although living trusts have advantages in avoiding probate fees (and these fees can be unreasonably excessive), revocable living trusts aren't the "cure all" for everyone. You need to be careful when deciding if a living trust is best for your situation.

To make this decision, it's necessary to understand a few terms and concepts. A *trust* is a legally enforceable relationship whereby one person or entity holds property for the use and benefit of another. The person who owned the property originally and established the trust is called the "*trustor*," "*grantor*," or any number of terms. The entity or individual receiving the title to the property for another is called the "*trustee*," and the person for whose benefit the property is being held is called the "*beneficiary*." The trustee can be any person of legal age or an institution, such as a bank or trust company.

This relationship is created when property is *transferred* by the owner to be held in benefit or trust for the beneficiary. For example, you deed over a house to Red Mountain Bank to hold in trust for the benefit of your daughter. Your brother Alvin could also be deeded the property to hold similarly in trust. The ownership by Red Mountain Bank or your brother isn't the same as when you owned it. Neither one can use the property as they see fit—the trustee only manages it for your daughter pursuant to the terms of the *trust agreement* (the legal document establishing the trust's terms and the trustee's rights and duties.

The bank or your brother owns the *legal title* to the property when in trust; your daughter owns what the law calls the "*beneficial or equitable*" title in the property. A trustee is held to the highest standard of conduct and good faith in its management of property for the beneficiary's benefit, and this standard is called a "*fiduciary*" relationship by the law. Trustees, guardians, executors, and administrators are all held accountable to this high standard of conduct.

Trusts can serve the function of a will as to the properties included. The trust instrument states what will happen to the property upon the death of the person who set up the trust (or upon some other event). The family car can still go to Aunt Edith, and the family residence can still be transferred to the kids—if included in the trust. These provisions can be as unique and different as in any will. However, a trust shouldn't be used as a substitute for a will, and this is discussed later.

Trusts can be *revocable* or *irrevocable*. This decides whether the trustor (the person originally owning the property) can later change or even rescind the trust after setting it up. You need to be careful when establishing a revocable trust. Although you want flexibility in changing the trust as new circumstances arise, this can cause estate tax complications. The property you hold in a revocable living trust is included in the valuation of your estate for estate tax purposes, whereas an irrevocable trust meeting federal estate tax regulations won't be so included.

A trust, whether revocable or not, can be established during your life or in your will. A trust set up while you're alive is called an "*inter vivos*" trust, whereas one that's established when you die by your will is called a "*testamentary*" trust.

Trusts can be either funded or not at the time of their creation. An inter vivos trust can be funded (when substantial assets are put into the trust) at times during your life, depending on your estate planning, or upon your death by a "pour over" provision in your will. When property is transferred into an existing trust by such a requirement in your will, then your assets pour over into that trust.

There can be estate tax and other benefits when using a testamentary trust to manage your assets for the benefit of your heirs. Property given this way to minor children, for example, generally isn't subject to estate taxation until the death of the children. Testamentary trusts allow you to retain complete control over your assets, then pour your assets upon your death into trusts for your children and spouse. These trusts can be administered by experienced investment trustees, such as banks and trust companies, who would manage the money and properties, thus taking the problems of this task away from your survivors.

There can be other advantages to using a testamentary trust, rather than a living trust, at times. The field of federal and state estate tax planning is an extremely complicated area, especially in the area of trusts and their relationship with wills. You should consult an estate tax specialist for assistance, especially when your estate is sizable (this is treated later). The costs of such a consultation are small when contrasted with the size of your estate and its proper handling.

The Pros and Cons of the Living Trust

The use of revocable living trusts has been made into an industry by attorneys and others. The selling of stock is more highly regulated than the claims made in this area. Be very careful before going along with the seminars and advertisements advocating that a particular revocable living trust is best for you.

Trusts are legally binding contracts. These documents have pages of intricate boiler plate and are confusing to many, including attorneys. You must know what's written, how it operates, and what happens under *your* state's inheritance, tax, and general laws. The "cookie-cutter" trusts sold to the general public are for straightforward situations, and, as one estate specialist said dryly, "Some will work fine for the first and only marriage with grown kids and no complications. They generally don't handle situations very well involving second marriages with the blending of stepchildren and children. They generally just give it to the children."

This doesn't mean that a low-cost trust isn't appropriate. But if you are in a second marriage, don't want your assets to go to your children equally, have a special situation (such as a disabled child), or some different circumstance, then be sure to consult an estate specialist before deciding on a standardized, living trust. Additionally, wanting to give conditional gifts (such as those to be received upon graduation from college), disinheriting, making a number of different bequests and situations—where your heirs have outstanding loans as well as others—dictate using care with the standardized trust approach. The same estate attorney observed, "Any client can buy an off-the-rack or more expensive, custom-made trust. The only question is how it's going to fit." Be careful, as it's your money, and be sure that what's in the documents covers your situation exactly and legally.

Once satisfied that a revocable living trust is best for you, then remember you must transfer your assets into the trust. Real property (your house, rental units, and buildings) must be transferred by a formally executed deed, complying with your state's laws, whereas personal property (your stocks, bonds, cars, boats, and antiques) must be transferred to the trust by a formal assignment or written transfer agreement.

You must notify any lenders before transferring property secured by such debt to gain their approval, being especially careful with real property. Lenders have what's called a *due-on-sale* clause allowing them to call your deed of trust or mortgage immediately due and payable if a transfer is made without their consent. Some estate practitioners avoid this problem by deeding the real property to the trustee but not recording it until needed (i.e., the death of the first spouse). This can create difficulties when refinancing, whether the deed is recorded or not, and you need to discuss this area before deciding on a particular living trust.

New bank accounts and separate financial accounting need to be arranged. All insurance, including the title insurance on your real property, should be changed to reflect the new ownership.

Any activities formerly done by simply signing your name now are done in the name of the trust. Whether the activity is investing stocks and bonds or building a room addition, the trust is the owner and not you, and these financial affairs must be kept separate from the property you still own individually. Financial institutions usually require copies of the trust instruments for their inspection, and borrowing monies on such assets can become more complicated.

Income that flowed directly to you before, now sits inside the trust and isn't available as before. Remember you have taken your assets and transferred them away, and some other entity now owns them. There are income and gift tax implications that must be reviewed by an accountant, and you may be required to file separate state and income tax returns (although not usually).

This isn't to say that revocable living trusts don't have advantages. They do, and some can be considerable. The probate process is lengthy, a matter of public record, confusing, and can be very expensive depending on the state. A living trust is quite suitable when a trustee is needed to make decisions that an elderly or disabled person can't. Being revocable, it is adaptable to changed circumstances, although this can jeopardize estate tax planning with large estates.

Living trusts can be used to separate assets from personal holdings when you are faced with asset-threatening risks, such as not being able to get necessary business or professional liability insurance. For example, attorneys recommend establishing living trusts to put another barrier between a potential judgment creditor and those assets. When faced with a substantial lawsuit, some people transfer assets away into living trusts, although this can be jeopardized by not establishing the trust before the lawsuit begins. Whether creditors can reach living trust assets depends entirely on your state's laws. Be advised that some states allow trust assets to be seized by judgment creditors, regardless of when they were established.

> The use of a living trust can be quite appropriate for many people, provided they obtain independent advice as to its use in their situation. Although trusts can minimize probate costs and delays, they do have some problems in funding and may not be the most effective estate planning device. Trusts can be very sophisticated and take many forms—generation skipping, insurance, minor children, credit shelter, charitable remainder, special child, stock redemption, qualified domestic, and so on. The advice of a specialized attorney should be gained before signing any trust instruments, especially when you're using a revocable living trust, and a will should be used with that trust.

The use of a trust doesn't mean that a will isn't needed. Quite to the contrary, a will should be in effect to dispose of what you've retained. Even when all your assets are transferred into a trust with provisions for their disposition, estate specialists still recommend keeping a valid will with a pour-over provision into the trust. You may acquire property afterwards, receive an inheritance, find property forgotten about or thought lost (i.e., your grandmother's jeweled pendant), some property that couldn't be transferred legally into the trust, win the lottery, or any number of situations requiring disposing of later-acquired assets.

The Need for Estate Planning

"It seems that the more money and assets a person has, the more resistance there is to estate planning. They procrastinate, believe they won't die until age 80, fear losing control, don't want a fight with their second spouse. You name it. And they need it the most," commented one estate specialist with multi-million dollar estate clients. Whatever the reason, the consequences of not planning an estate can be disastrous.

Unfortunately, people don't live as long as they think, whether because of an accident, sudden illness, or something unforeseen, and the need for estate planning isn't just limited to the wealthy. "People don't really know what they're worth, especially if they own appreciated real estate. Some have high amounts of insurance and with a high-income year, slip into needing estate planning," said another estate planner. "If you're single or married to the same spouse, have an estate under $600,000, both spouses are U.S. citizens (a non-U.S. citizen spouse is penalized under federal estate tax laws), have no children from other marriages, none of the children or spouses requires special care (such as with Down's syndrome or Alzheimer's), *and* there are no controversies over who gets what, then you probably don't need estate planning. Anyone not meeting this profile should consider it," observed another planner.

Estate planning is another area where investing legal dollars now pays high dividends later by avoiding unnecessary estate problems and taxes. It's a highly technical and complex area that can require the use of a specialist.

A Few Estate and Gift Tax Fundamentals

Although making a gift and planning your estate would seem to be different, these two activities are part of the same process and subject to taxes. If you transfer property to someone before you die, that transfer is called a gift and is subject to a gift tax. If your property is transferred after you die, this transfer is subject to an estate tax at the federal level (calculated on your estate) and/or an inheritance tax at the state level (calculated on the recipients) in many states. Federal gift and estate taxes are often called "unified" taxes, because the same rules, deductions, and rates of taxation generally apply to both, and any gifting and gift taxes paid affects the amount of estate taxes assessed.

Gifting

At this time, anyone may give up to $10,000 each year to someone else without incurring a gift tax. There's no limit on the number of such gifts that can be given, so long as no one person or entity receives more than $10,000 in total. You can give $10,000 every year to the same person without a gift tax liability, as this annual exclusion. If you're married, and provided other rules are met, your spouse can join you in a gift to the same person—the allowable transfer to any one person is increased in that case to $20,000 each year.

Thus, you can transfer property to your children, brothers and sisters, parents, even people not related to you, which isn't calculated as part of your estate and estate tax (provided you stay within the $10,000 annual limit). This can be a considerable reduction of any estate over time, as giving your daughter $10,000 per year amounts to $200,000 over 20 years. Gifting appreciating property ahead of time can be helpful in keeping such assets out of a large estate. However, most people don't enjoy such disposable amounts of money and assets and need everything instead for living expenses and then retirement.

A gift tax return, Form 709, needs to be filed each year when such gifts are made, regardless of the amount. Gifts between spouses usually don't require this form to be filed. Regardless of what is required, most people making gifts under $10,000 fail to report them anyway.

Gifts in excess of the magic $10,000 annual exclusion may result in a gift tax, as the excess over $10,000 correspondingly reduces the available unified credit equivalent. Before embarking on any gift program to reduce your estate, you need to understand that this is a very complex area requiring the services of an estate tax specialist.

Please keep in mind that you don't need any charitable intent to make gifts for estate planning purposes. It makes no difference why you gave that money or stocks to your daughter. However, if you donated a gift to a charity (i.e., United Way, your church or synagogue, or the Boy Scouts) that meets IRS requirements, then this donation qualifies for a federal income tax deduction. There's no effect on the unified credit allowance when making charitable gifts that qualify as proper deductions for federal income tax purposes.

The Unified Credit

Each person can reduce at this time the amount of transfers subject to taxation, whether by gift or will, by a one-time $600,000, unified credit equivalent. If your assets are less than $600,000, your estate won't pay any federal estate taxes because of this one exclusion alone. However, if any noncharitable gifts were made in excess of $10,000 per year to anyone, then to the extent of such excess, the $600,000 exclusion is reduced. Gifts that stay within the $10,000 limit don't count toward the $600,000 total of estate and lifetime gifts that can be transferred free of tax. Thus, appreciating assets such as real estate or stocks are targets for gifting if you have someone in mind.

If you alone gave $20,000 in stocks to your son for college for example, then your total unified credit would be reduced by the excess $10,000. If this was your first such transfer, then your unified credit now would be $590,000. Transferring only $10,000 to your son that year would result in no gift tax implications or change to the total unified credit.

As a highly simplified example, if you owned (with no other exclusions, deductions, or offsets under federal estate tax law) a total of $600,000 in net assets (after liabilities), then there would be no federal estate tax owing. However, if you had reduced that estate by giving $150,000 to your brother in any one year before your death, then the unified credit would be reduced by $140,000 ($150,000 less the $10,000 that's allowed). Thus, the reduction of the unified credit would allow $140,000 of your estate to become taxable should your estate become more valuable.

Your Estate and Estate Taxes

There are two major deductions enjoyed under federal estate tax computation—the unified credit and the marital deduction. The unified credit equivalent, set at $600,000 presently, basically eliminates the first $192,800 of federal estate tax otherwise payable. Additionally, any property transferred to your spouse after your death is deducted from the valuation of your gross estate, but anyone not legally married cannot use this deduction.

> The unmarried person must look at varying trust and gifting approaches, after consulting with an estate specialist, if their estate is greater than the $600,000 (or the amount if changed) unified credit equivalent. As important, if any spouse is not a U.S. citizen, then the restrictions on what are otherwise favorable rules (i.e., no unlimited marital deduction and restrictions on gifting, among other problems), mandate consulting a specialist.

Under the marital deduction, an unlimited amount of property may be given under your will to your spouse (if a U.S. citizen) without *your* estate paying any estate taxes. Thus, any remaining property after the unified credit equivalent can be given to your surviving spouse to avoid estate taxes. You can achieve the same result by giving the remaining property to your spouse in trust for life, then to your surviving children or even someone else after your spouse's death.

At first reading, you would say this is great. However, as with anything involving the federal government, there's no free lunch for taxpayers. First, property given away may be brought back into your estate if you retained too much control—for example, a revocable living trust. Second, property given away during your lifetime, assuming you didn't need it, can't be enjoyed by you after that. Third, the property stacked up in your surviving spouse's estate will all become taxable (subject, however, to the same protection of the credit) upon that person's death.

Your gross estate includes all property owned by you at your death, whether it's real or personal property. This would include all real estate, jewelry, stocks, bonds, boats, cars, furniture, and even copyrights—any interest you owned in property at your death is included. Business and partnership interests are included, as well as insurance proceeds received by your estate (or by anyone else if you owned the insurance policy and paid the premiums on it). Moreover, even property given away during your lifetime may be brought into your estate, if you retained a power or some right over it. For example, retaining the right to say who can receive the income on property, or the right to such income, can be sufficient reason to bring that asset back into your estate.

Although property held in joint tenancy avoids probate and passes directly to the survivor, the rule for estate tax purposes is different. The general rule is that the entire value of joint property is included in the estate of the first joint tenant to die. When the joint tenants are married, then the deceased's estate includes one-half of that valuation, unless some portion of the value was contributed by the survivor (i.e., an addition was made with that individual's own money). States recognizing community property treat that the same as joint tenancy for estate tax purposes—one-half is included in the estate of the first spouse to die.

These assets are then valued at their fair market value as of the date of death. The unified credit equivalent of $600,000 is deducted from that value, as lowered by gifts made in excess of $10,000 per person per year. Deductions are allowed for the expenses of the funeral, estate administration, and any claims against the estate. The property willed to your surviving spouse is deducted, as well as any charitable bequests and uninsured casualty losses. The amount of any debts or liabilities is subtracted in arriving at the adjusted gross estate value.

Before the federal estate tax is computed on the adjusted gross estate, an adjustment is entered for any gifts made on which a gift tax had been paid in the past. A gift tax is not paid on gifting until the value of the gifts (made in excess of the allowed $10,000 limit) exceeds the $600,000 unified credit equivalent. The value of such gifts when made is added back to the gross estate valuation with a credit given for any gift taxes paid. If the value of the estate is in a higher marginal rate, then you will be paying slightly more taxes based on the inclusion of the value of these gifts (as reduced by the credit for any gift taxes paid).

Estate planning is more than establishing a plan for the care of family members after a person's death or minimizing estate and inheritance taxes. As important is ensuring that your estate has enough liquidity to pay all debts, including estate taxes, the costs of administration, and creditors. There's nothing worse than having an estate plan without the cash to pay the bills and taxes. If your estate has appreciated real property or is heavy in other illiquid assets, then you should look into ways to have sufficient cash on hand. There are various alternatives used, such as arranging life insurance, mortgaging property, and selling portions of assets ahead of time. This is also part of the estate planning process.

The resulting estate tax, if any, is reduced by any state death taxes paid, among other credits. If your estate owes federal estate taxes, then it's likely a state inheritance tax (assessed on the beneficiaries' receipt of the property) will be due, as many states have a pick-up tax mirroring the federal tax assessment. Although not very likely, it is possible to be paying a state death, transfer, or inheritance tax, even though there's no federal estate tax liability. In this connection, any estate planning should include state inheritance tax considerations along with the federal estate tax planning.

Your executor doesn't file a federal estate tax return (Form 706) unless the gross value of your estate exceeds $600,000 (but there are some exceptions). If the net worth of your estate (assets less liabilities) is less than $600,000, then your estate will not have a federal estate tax liability no matter what you've done—provided you haven't made gifts in excess of the $10,000 limit per person per year prior to your death. If your estate is assessed a federal estate tax, the rate is graduated and ranges at this time from 37% to 55%.

However, it is possible that the $600,000 unified credit equivalent will be lowered at some time in the future. If it is so reduced, then pay particular attention to this change. Your estate already could be in taxable waters—any lowering of the unified credit simply adds taxes onto your estate if you aren't paying attention to this.

As your gross estate is reduced by the $600,000 equivalent (applicable to anyone, not including your spouse, to whom you leave property), the unlimited marital deduction on what's left to your spouse (but applies only to legally married, surviving spouses who are U.S. citizens), and the deductions for liabilities and charitable gifts, many Americans don't have a federal estate tax liability.

As can be seen from this short discussion, the concepts, rules, and regulations are very complex. It's worth consulting an experienced estate attorney to determine what's best for you. Unquestionably, if you don't have much in the way of assets, this won't be a concern. As the value of your estate increases, however, it makes sense to look into this more closely than you've done before.

Getting the Information Ready

Making a will requires getting the necessary facts together and making decisions. You need to write down your personal information, as well to make a financial inventory of your estate and finances. Decisions will need to be made on who inherits from you and the people who will serve as your trustee, executor, or guardian.

Personal Information

It's important to specifically identify the family members and others whom you'll be mentioning in your will. Family members should be identified by complete name, current address, date of birth, and social security numbers, wherever possible. You will need to identify specifically any previously married spouses, including their name, current address, and the date and place of the divorce. Similarly, any spouses who predeceased you should be identified by name, date of birth, and date and place of death. The more precise you are in identifying those who will inherit or won't under your will, the less likely you'll have ambiguities and disputes later.

Financial Information

A complete financial inventory should be taken with your assets listed in order along with their approximate current market valuations. This would include all the property you own, such as real estate, businesses, checking and savings accounts, investments (such as stocks, bonds, mutual funds, and notes), personal property (such as art, sculptures, jewelry, antiques, and silverware), life insurance policies, annuities, Keogh Plans, stock options, and anything of value. All of your assets need to be specifically identified, with their location, identifying facts, purchase price or cost, and approximate market valuations. Against each asset you should deduct the amount of any owed liabilities, including the financial institution, address, account number, original principal amount, current amount owed, and where important papers are located. Any nonsecured debt should be similarly identified.

These worksheets will be used in your deliberations, then stored with your will and other valuable papers. This information, safeguarded in one place, will make the administration of your estate that much easier. The more precise you are in identifying the assets you're bequeathing (transferring by will), the less problems there will be later in this regard. For example, simply saying, "I leave my savings account to my son, John, Jr.," isn't helpful if you have three such accounts. Mentioning instead "I leave my savings account at Sonoma Valley Bank, Sonoma, Colorado, Account No. 432–572, to my son, John, Jr., and my money market account at Valley State Bank, Fort Collins, Colorado, Account No. 778–332 to my daughter, Carole Anne," is preferable.

The Decisions

Dividing Up Your Estate

It's easy to say that the next step is deciding who gets what. That's always the hardest part to do, especially when you have an extended family, friends, a second marriage with stepchildren, and children of your own. You know, and correctly, that someone is bound to be disappointed.

It isn't just determining who gets your important possessions and amounts, or your prized gun or painting collection. You need to identify whether the estate pays for your debts, which ones are paid out of general bequeaths, and any specific property that carries that debt to its recipient.

There are a few approaches that can make this received easier after you die. When your will is being written up, think about including language that shows why you're doing something. For example, most wills say "I leave my book collection to my sister, Anne, my 1956 Corvette to my son, Kenny, and $50,000 in cash to my stepson, Timmy." It would be better to write, "My beloved daughter, Anne, with her great interest in books, shall receive my extensive book collection, being all the books that are owned or to be owned by me. My son, Kenny, who has always shown an ability to love and take care of cars, is to receive my prized, 1956 Corvette, registration number 14503982. As my children Anne and Kenny have been quite successful on their own, I am leaving $50,000 in cash to my stepson, Timmy, with the hope he will use it to start up a similar business venture of his own. I love all of you equally well."

Perhaps this won't make your children feel any better, but at least it's a step away from the cold, straight language that lawyers typically employ. Another idea is to videotape your reading of the will, explaining why you provided as you did. This can soothe hurt feelings and show the reasons behind your "madness." Estate specialists also recommend doing this when someone might contest the will, arguing you were senile or under the undue influence of someone else.

Your Business

As part of the estate-planning process, the owner of a small business needs to consider three areas—the continuation of the business in case of death, the valuation of the business, and the "cashing out" of that ownership interest.

One of the greater failings of entrepreneurs is not having a succession plan in case of untimely death. Children often don't have an interest in running the business, and the owners are usually unwilling to give sufficient options or enticements to retain key managers. Grown children, looking at the company as the prime source of their inheritance, enter management and can quickly ruin the business. Each business has its own requirements and needs, and owners should look closely at who should run the company when they can't.

A second problem is valuing the business for purposes of estate taxes and getting the equity out of the business. If the company is traded publicly on a stock market, then this problem isn't present. A company with this size and liquidity already has grappled with the problem of valuations and cashing out. There's a ready market for any shareholders of that company.

The problem is with closely-held companies that aren't traded on a stock exchange. Even when valid appraisals are secured, there still is no way for the owner(s) to realize that value, short of selling the company first.

If the business is run as a sole proprietorship, it's difficult to cash out except by selling to someone else. When it is owned as a general partnership or corporation with other "partners," then it's possible to obtain sizable life insurance on the key persons or owners of the company. The premiums are paid by the business with the proceeds earmarked to the company and used to buy back the shares or interests owned by the decedent. This life insurance funding is coupled with a stock or partnership buy-back agreement, signed by all the owners.

Another approach is to put a highly appreciated business into a charitable remainder trust. The income is received at a specified level for life, then deeded over to a charity upon death. No capital gains tax is paid on the transfer, and the owner can receive a charitable deduction based on the present value of the charitable gift.

There are a variety of buy-back concepts, funding techniques, trusts, and other approaches used to solve this problem. These estate techniques are complex, have sizable tax consequences, and must be worked out with an experienced accountant or tax attorney. However, a business owner should consider these issues now rather than wait until it's too late. One estate professional said "They really say they don't want to worry about doing any estate planning now. The problem is that the surviving spouse and children aren't too happy when they have to worry about it later. It's easier to plan for your estate now if you understand that you're providing for your family and children."

Choosing the Executor, Trustee, or Guardian

Selecting the people who'll be administering your estate and needs is as important as determining who receives what. Your situation may require having a will (appointing an executor), a living or testamentary trust (appointing a trustee), and appointing a guardian for your minor children (in case your surviving spouse dies or you're a single parent). Unfortunately, many people assign these roles to their spouse, favorite brother, or grown child without considering what's really important.

The *executor* locates and gathers up the assets, pays the bills, and distributes the property in accordance with your wishes. As the executor usually hires an attorney to answer any legal questions, it isn't important that the executor be a lawyer—but it is necessary that this person be honest, exercise good judgment, and be mature. It's also helpful if the executor has an administrative bent, given the different reports and court filings needing to be made. Although executors will be paid compensation for their services as fixed by statute and/or the court, a surviving spouse or close friend could waive this fee.

You're looking for the best person to do the job honestly, not the one you like best. Talk with whoever's being considered and ask that person questions about how he or she would handle this position. Another factor is whether the individual lives in your state. It can be a problem for an executor to live in one state but need to watch over an estate centered in another—select someone who lives in your area whenever possible.

As the diversity and size of your assets grow, the need to have an executor with more investment or business experience also increases. It may be worthwhile to hire a bank or bonded financial institution to be the executor or even coexecutor, of your estate. This will be expensive, because of the fees charged, but it will give protection in case you have some doubts about the financial abilities, for example, of your brother. List one or two successor executors in case your first choice decides not to assume the duties or dies. Be sure to gain the consent of any prospective executor before putting that person in your will.

The decision as to who should be the *trustee* depends also on what the person will be doing. If you're setting up a standard living trust where you're the trustee, then you've already hired the person. If the function is only to watch over a few assets, such as a house, truck, and furniture, then the job shouldn't be complicated.

However, if the trustee will be required to make complex financial decisions, such as overseeing a seven-figure "blind trust," then an experienced bank or investment institution should be retained. Talk to several institutions, comparing experience, fees, and the services offered. Remember that various trust income, tax, and financial statements need to be prepared, all of them distinct from your personal situation. These can be prepared by banks and trust companies as part of the services offered.

If you are married, then your surviving spouse usually will be the *guardian* and executor. However, you need to consider at least two alternate guardians and executors, should your spouse die in the same accident as you, and the first alternate decides not to accept. The risk is that any gaps are then filled by the court.

Naming a guardian can be the most vexing but important decision you make. Children are most important and this can be a difficult and personal decision, as both parents may not agree over whom they want. But it won't be as difficult as the expensive court fights between family members vying for guardianship, all arguing that they're the best choice.

You always can amend your will to change the designated guardian if you change your mind. Remember there's a difference between watching over the children's personal needs and their financial needs—one doesn't have to be the other. This allows a safeguard whereby one person doesn't have authority over both functions. For example you could name your married brother as the guardian over the "persons" (the children) but appoint your single sister, Jane, with the M.B.A.

It's useful to talk to those people whom you haven't named as a guardian or executor. You'll need to be as tactful as possible. But full disclosure when you're alive, although feelings can be hurt, is better than having bad feelings when you're not around to smooth things over. Do the same thing as to who gets what underneath your will.

to watch over their financial needs. It's also possible to put conditions in a will on that guardian, such as "I appoint my brother to be the guardian of my children, provided he's still married to his wife, Helen."

Should You Use an Attorney?

Once you have accumulated the necessary information and made the important decisions, you are in the position to make your will (including a trust, if necessary). There are any number of ways—hiring an attorney or a legal clinic to draft it; purchasing a self-help book and doing it yourself; buying a form from a stationary store and filling in the blanks (but be very careful with this); or even using a statutory will (state-preapproved forms with instructions), obtained in some states from a county or state bar association.

However, the preparation of the will should follow your estate planning, as it sets the stage for the distribution of your estate. Even if you don't have a large estate, taking the easy way out and buying a "fill-in-the-blank" form isn't always the best approach—especially if there are family heirlooms that need to be passed down. Although federal estate taxes won't be a problem, there's no telling what problems aren't addressed when you're using such forms.

Additionally, the formalities for executing a valid will differ from state to state. You need at least two witnesses signing to attest to the validity of your will, and in a few states there must be three. Any witness who attests to your will can't take property underneath that will, otherwise they lose that right and/or the will becomes invalid. Holistic wills, or those entirely in the handwriting of the deceased, are simply invalid in some states and subject to express conditions in others. And the rules go on and on.

It doesn't make sense to take the time to work on your estate, then jeopardize it by trying a form that could be ruled invalid by the court. Then, you're no different than if you die intestate—the probate court takes over jurisdiction and your estate is administered by the laws of intestacy and that state.

You should interview several attorneys or clinics, comparing their stated fees and experience. Simple wills without a trust shouldn't be expensive—depending on the state, they can cost $200 or less. Some attorneys will quote a lower fee just for the chance to be listed as the executor of the will, but unless you've known that attorney well and for years, don't go along with that.

If you want to save money, then shop around (wills are usually quoted on a fixed-fee basis) and select the best value. Consult Chapters 5 and 12 for further details on selecting and hiring the right attorney. As an alternative you can save costs by preparing the will yourself, then taking it to an attorney for review with all the information already set down.

Using do-it-yourself form books also is an alternative, but be sure that your state's laws are covered in such a book. Call up your local bar association and see if they have a recommended will form or format. But be very careful of blank forms bought in stores as they may not be up to date or include everything you need.

If you attend a living trust seminar or buy a living trust book for the information and forms, pass the filled-out trust documents by an experienced estate attorney for a quick review prior to execution, especially if you have valuable assets. Ask what needs to be done to get your assets legally into that trust. You might even make a checklist of what to do and have this reviewed, as well.

As your estate becomes more complex or larger, you'll need to retain a specialist. A living or testamentary trust may become desirable, along with a will, and you may consider a gifting strategy. As the drafting of trusts and their execution is more expensive than a will, you first should find out what the costs are. As with wills, shop around and compare fees and experience. Time spent carefully at first with your will, trust, and estate planning will save thousands of dollars and avoid costly battles later when you can't do anything about it.

Be Sure to Update Your Will or Trust

Wills, once executed, must be updated—this updating is formally called "*amending*" your will. The document with the necessary changes, called a "*codicil*," is then executed with all the formalities that your will first was in order to be valid under your state's laws.

You must be careful to update your will when circumstances change. For example, a friend of mine had lived with a man for nearly 12 years before they split up. Both of them had executed wills with testamentary trusts, leaving money to the other and appointing that person as the trustee of trusts to be established for the separate children of each by prior marriages.

Both parties married others within 1 year after moving apart. The man was nearly killed in a freak airplane accident but escaped unharmed. At that time, even though married to another woman, his will was still as it was when he was living years ago with his ex-girlfriend. He changed it 1 week later.

This was one of the more fortunate cases. It isn't rare for a divorced spouse to remarry, forget to change the will, then die. The second spouse has to go to court and fight for what would only be a three-sentence amendment. *Wills should be amended promptly to reflect new-born children, changes in feelings towards people and charitable institutions, divorce and/or re-marriage, permanent decreases or increases in the valuation of properties (i.e., that 30-year-old baseball card collection is now worth $150,000), and any event that affects the disposition of your property.*

Similarly, any trust instruments should be reviewed as conditions change. If you retained the right to modify the trust, then this should be done as soon as practicable. Revocable living trusts should be changed as soon as you would your will.

Health and Illness Considerations

We don't stay healthy or live forever. Moreover, the best estate plans have been wrecked by uninsured, unforeseen lengthy illnesses and nursing home costs, regardless of Medicare and Medicaid. Unexpected illnesses and disabling health problems make it difficult, if not impossible, to sell homes, change investments, or make decisions, when not planned for in advance. If no one is authorized to make everyday decisions when you can't, then bills aren't paid, liens are placed on property, and heirs may not inherit as you desire.

There are ways to handle these problems. A power of attorney can be used to allow someone else to make decisions when you can't, even acting in fact as your alter ego in financial decisions. A living will, as distinct from a living trust, can be used to cut off unwanted medical treatment and costs when such treatment would be against your wishes. Obtaining information as to what Medicare and Medicaid do or do not cover for older individuals, along with reviewing your existing health insurance and/or nursing home insurance, must be done as part of your estate planning and to guard against the costs of a major, long-term illness. As one estate lawyer reflected "If a client is serious about estate planning for the children or heirs, then the effect of major illnesses and incapacities on the estate must be considered as part of this process. It's difficult, because no one likes to consider what to do when you become senile or die from a major illness. But it's done and people find a way to deal with it."

Power of Attorney

A power of attorney is an agreement whereby you grant another person the right to act on your behalf when you're unable to or are disabled. If you are married, then each spouse can grant the other the power of attorney to act on his or her behalf. If you are traveling overseas on an extended vacation, then execute a power of attorney to a trusted family member to make decisions in your absence. It is especially appropriate when there's a danger of senility.

A power of attorney can be used to access checking and savings accounts, to pay bills, sign deeds, close sales of property, sign income tax filings, and even operate a business. An older women shared a savings account with her sister that required two signatures. She thought about having a power of attorney drawn up but never got around to it. Her sister unexpectedly became ill and fell into a coma. The aunt was never able to access the accounts to pay those bills. She had to file a guardianship procedure, which was time-consuming and expensive.

These occurrences are real. A power of attorney can be as specific or as general as you want. If single, whether with a "significant other" or not, you should consider giving a power of attorney to a *trusted* friend or family member in case you are disabled.

A power of attorney should be considered separately from that of a living trust—they do different things. Also, as a power of attorney expires upon your death and doesn't meet the required formalities, it cannot operate as a will.

The laws affecting a power of attorney can differ from state to state, although various states have enacted a durable (or lasting) power of attorney form by statute. This power of attorney concerns the power over your financial affairs, as distinct from a medical power of attorney, or living will, that concerns the power to make decisions over extraordinary health care considerations.

You can pick up a "fill-in-the-blank" power of attorney from a legal stationary store to save money—but be careful. Be sure it's the most current one and valid in your state. In some states, there are limits as to whom the power of attorney can be in favor of (i.e., close family members), whereas in other states you need to record it with the county recorder's office. This needs to be known. Alternatively, buy a good do-it-yourself book, research the matter at your county law library, contact your local bar association, or talk to an attorney.

The use of a power of attorney is like anything else. If there are no problems, then you don't have a need for it. Not having one is simply another risk that's being assumed. However, the need for one becomes greater as you grow older. It should be definitely be considered if you're getting on in years.

An interim step is to add a trusted person as an additional signature on your bank accounts. However, this doesn't let someone sell, exchange, or buy property on your behalf as you might have wanted. You should only appoint someone you've known and trusted for years—usually this will be a close family member, your spouse, or a significant other. Otherwise, an expensive guardianship proceeding will be necessary when you're unable to sign your name to necessary documents.

Living Wills

Living wills are used when you want to avoid extraordinary medical care or life-saving measures. The need for living wills was created by the rapid technological development of costly medical treatments that prolong life, although not necessarily without pain, inconvenience, and continuing huge, uninsured medical bills. The stories of accident victims and the elderly who have been kept alive for months, although not conscious or in considerable pain and agony, are known. The best estate plans are irrelevant when the assets become exhausted by extraordinary medical expenses. "It is difficult for people to come to grips with their mortality," reflected one estate specialist. "It's easier when they think about what happens to their loved ones if they don't."

The living will, or durable power of attorney for health care, was developed to answer this problem. You are able to decide now what should be done or not done should you become seriously ill or disabled. Hospitals, medical clinics, physicians, and state medical associations have or can direct you to finding the living will appropriate in your state. If you have questions about this, ask your doctor. If he or she can't answer you, consult an attorney.

You will need to be specific in what you do or don't want done. State that you don't want your life continued by artificial means if you have been diagnosed as being brain-dead. If you have been unconscious for, let's say, a month or more, state what you think should be done. Consult with your doctor as to what should be considered, given your history and medical background.

Although the living will is viewed as preserving your right to say what *won't* be done, it also can be used to state what you *do* want done. Although this is presumed to mean doing everything possible, it doesn't necessarily mean your loved ones would want that. The living will is used to specify what you want.

The living will usually combines these directives with the appointment of another person who makes the medical decisions on your behalf when you're incapacitated. In some states, you might need to execute and/or record a power of attorney with that medical appointment. This person should be appointed only after considerable thought and care, and it should be someone who's concerned entirely for your welfare, not governed by thoughts of preserving the estate.

You might consider appointing one person for your living will and another for the power of attorney concerning your financial affairs—they don't necessarily have to be the same person. If one has more financial expertise than another, then this person could be appointed, for example, over your spouse. This assumes that your spouse wouldn't be upset if you appointed your brother or sister with power over your finances or health-care decisions.

Medicare, Medicaid, and Nursing Home Insurance

Currently, the expense of long-term, uninsured catastrophic medical and nursing home care is a fact of life, and this risk needs to be weighed when you are reviewing your overall estate plan. Medicare and Medicaid, two quite different programs, were enacted by the U.S. government in response to this problem. However, they only cover part of the risk. Medicare is a program for nearly anyone over 65 without regard to need, income, or assets—but it doesn't cover you if you're under 65. In that case, you must look at your own health insurance program, should you have one.

People are entitled to Medicare coverage because of their Social Security contributions and payments of premiums. Medicare is a federal program, and the rules presently are the same regardless of state. Medicare provides basic hospital

At the time of this writing, it's not known how the current health care initiative by President Clinton ultimately will be enacted into law and affect the following discussion. However, to the extent that existing programs are changed, any remaining risk of extraordinary medical bills still needs to be factored into your overall estate planning.

coverage for inpatient hospital stays (Part A), posthospital nursing care, and posthospital home care. There are deductibles for Part A.

Part B of Medicare pays 80% of what it finds are the "reasonable charges" for doctors, lab work, medical equipment and supplies, outpatient work, therapy, and other costs not related to hospitalization.

Nearly one-half of all people over 65 buy private health insurance to cover the gaps in the Medicare coverage. One problem with "Medi-gap" insurance is that they pay for the 20% not covered on Part B, but only as to the "reasonable charges" set by the government—it doesn't reimburse for the difference between what the physician charges and what's decided to be a "reasonable charge." The private insurance company Medi-gap programs also vary widely as to coverage and premium costs.

The other half of the population either is at risk or has gone on Medicaid. This program is only for low-income and disabled people such as the blind and permanently disabled. Medicaid is a federal/state program with laws and regulations that vary dramatically from state to state. This program will pay for a number of services and costs Medicare doesn't cover, such as dental care, eyeglasses, and prescription drugs. It also can pay for the Medicare deductibles under Plan A and the 20% differential (similar to Medi-gap) that Medicare doesn't cover under Plan B.

The problem centers on the cost of catastrophic health care. If you are under 65, then unless you have your own health insurance (including supplemental coverage when those limits run out), you will lose your estate in the event of a long-term, disabling illness or accident.

If you are over 65, then unless you can afford good Medi-gap insurance, your estate has a sizable risk. With the costs and charges of physicians these days, 20% of the "reasonable costs" (including the difference between what the Government says is reasonable and what's charged by doctors) can be a considerable amount. It would take no time to wipe out $50,000 or more.

Even if you can afford Medi-gap insurance, the cost of nursing home coverage is only covered when the nursing home stay is due to and required after hospitalization for treatment of a specific medical condition. It *doesn't cover* any time in a nursing home or a similar facility because that person needs help in dressing, feeding, or simply living. Neither does Medicare.

These expenses can be extraordinarily high and range from $2,000 to $3,000 or more per month, depending on the state, area, and type of facility. A few years at this level of expense and your estate has been chewed up.

But wait, you might say, there's still Medicaid. Medicaid, depending on the state, will cover nursing home costs not due to prior hospitalization. The problem is to qualify you have to be of low income with a negligible estate. In other words, you need to have depleted your estate down to next to nothing before you qualify.

Your private health insurance normally doesn't cover private nursing home stays. In its place, the industry has created nursing home insurance. This insurance is controversial, with critics claiming the expense isn't worth the coverage.

Some states have passed laws establishing insurance plans enabling the elderly to receive nursing home care without first having to spend their estate. These programs, which vary from state to state, allow the elderly to shelter assets in their estate by an insurance policy that pays for the initial years of nursing care—thus, they aren't required to "spend down" their estate before qualifying. This insurance first pays with a combination of private and public funds, then Medicaid takes over. These laws aren't widespread, are controversial, and some are in the process of amendment. However, be sure to determine if one is in effect in your state.

The coverage of Medicare, Medicaid, privately offered Medi-gap policies, state laws, and private nursing home coverage need to be reviewed as we grow older, especially as substantial changes are made by Congress and the individual states. It can be confusing, and it's easier not to deal with the subject of nursing homes, illnesses, and senility. Unfortunately, this is another fact of life that has to be addressed, and it's no different than needing to decide who gets what upon our death. In this case without sufficient planning, you could lose parts or all of your estate that should have gone to your heirs.

Proper handling of illnesses and nursing home needs is part of the overall estate-planning process. It is this process that allows assets to pass down as you desire without being unnecessarily eaten up by estate taxes, court fights, and medical bills.

When Times Get Tough

Even with good planning and living within your means, things happen out of your control. You lose your job unexpectedly, the bread winner is injured, or there's an uninsured fire or flood. Times suddenly are tough. You have no cash reserves, or whatever cash is left won't last long. The bill collectors will start contacting you at any time.

There's incredible stress. "If your house burns down, you're still probably employed. When you're not working, and had all your life, then that's stress," said one who had gone through this. Now's the time to take immediate action—don't think optimistically that you'll find another job quickly or win the state lottery. The question is: what to do next?

The Financial Inventory

When your income suddenly comes to an end, you need to take an immediate financial inventory. List your household expenses in order of importance. Be sure to put in a contingency for unexpected expenses such as that new suit for job interviews or school fees for the kids. Then, you need to think about other sources of income. If you're lucky, there will be some savings, unused credit cards, or even severance payments from the last job. Financial survival turns not only on finding additional sources of cash, but also on cutting expenses quickly to the bone.

Cutting Expenses

You'll need to decide how important your various living expenses are. That shouldn't be too difficult, because the first-line, important expenses are what you need to live—these are the basics such as shelter, food, and utilities (gas, water, telephone, electricity, and/or heating fuel).

If the mortgage or rent can't be paid, then head to your local law library or a bookstore to determine your rights. Contact an attorney to assess this, especially if there's equity in your home. Consider moving to a less-expensive place, including putting your home on the market if the payments are too high. Although you love your privacy, renting out rooms also helps pay the bills.

If you don't have enough money for food, then contact local aid agencies, including welfare and unemployment—it's tough, but survival is also. Contact the utility companies and see what their policies are for low-income (you're now there) or nonpayers. Talk to them before you begin missing payments.

Owning a car is the next line of importance. The problem isn't just the monthly payments—it takes money to pay for gas, oil, parts, and repairs, not to mention the high cost of insurance. Although not having a car can be a very serious inconvenience, there are still bicycles, motorcycles, mopeds, buses, friends, and mass transit. If you can arrange alternate transportation, then sell your car before the finance company repossesses it, using the cash for your essentials. Or use the cash to buy a paid-in-full, used car.

Another difficult area is insurance. There are medical, homeowners or renters, life, even umbrella and supplemental medical insurance policies (if you're a senior citizen). A friend who went through this said simply, "Insurance is the first thing to go." However, she was healthy, and if you have medical problems, keeping such coverage could be critical.

You, of course, will choose paying for food and shelter over your ex-spouse or the IRS. But that involves problems with the IRS, and your ex-spouse doesn't care about your current problems. Be careful with child support, since if this is not handled right, you could be facing a contempt-of-court hearing or worse.

An automobile loan is secured by the bought vehicle—if you don't make the payments, then the car is repossessed. Other items are handled similarly. Computers, televisions, stereos, furniture, and even refrigerators could have been used as the security for repayment. That is, the company lending you the money to buy it also looks at that item as the security for being paid back completely. If you don't make the payments, then they have the right to take it back. Having someone knocking on your door to repossess your TV isn't a good experience—you don't have to let them in, unless the Marshall is with them, but who needs this?

If you don't care about the item, then you won't worry over missing payments. There is the risk you could be held liable for the deficiency between what's owed and what's received when the company sells the repossessed item (that's treated later). However, if you want your computer equipment, then you'll either keep the payments up or worry about it while keeping your house locked and letting no one in (unless it's the Marshall with a court order to seize it).

If a creditor has already sued you, then the question becomes whether a judgment has been obtained or not. If the judgment has been secured, then the judgment creditor has an array of rights, ranging from creditor examinations (asking where your assets are) to garnishing wages and seizing assets. That's treated later in this chapter, but at a minimum you'll need to negotiate over this.

The next level is what you owe that's not secured. If you've used your credit cards to pay for purchases, then at least those purchases aren't subject to being repossessed. Credit cards are unsecured—that is, the monies weren't borrowed from the store that sold you the furniture or computer, or the lender didn't take the item as security for repaying the debt. Credit cards, doctor and dentist bills, gasoline card charges, department store charges (provided it's a revolving charge and not a secured loan), and newspaper subscriptions, for example, are unsecured debts. So are your legal and accounting bills, or any other professional expenses such as an engineer, surveyor, accountant, or consultant.

These expenses can be slipped. However, everyone still can sue you, obtain a judgment, and exercise their judgment rights ranging from seizure of assets to the garnishing of your wages (when you finally get work). A distinction should be made between what you owe professionals (such as attorneys and doctors) and what you owe your contractor or babysitter—they have different rights. For example, a contractor can lien (place a claim) against your house and sue to enforce that right to payment, including foreclosing on your house. Your babysitter might march down to the local labor commissioner or wage enforcement agency and have them sue you directly for those wages—she has no legal costs and the enforcement powers of these agencies can be considerable.

Sources of Cash

Friends and family are the usual sources for loans and money. Otherwise, you'll need to get part-time and temporary jobs; there are a variety of books on the market in this regard. Selling your house or car is another alternative; however, in bad markets you can wait forever for an offer. This might be the time to sell that coin collection or whatever else you think is valuable.

What's left on your credit cards can be used for just about anything, including buying food at supermarkets. It is this pre-approved credit that's so valuable when you're in financial trouble. By now, you were wishing those new credit cards appearing in the mail had been accepted (but only if you didn't use them up). Borrowing against life insurance policies, tax refunds, suing someone to whom you lent money (and won't pay you back), and whatever else peculiar to your situation should be done.

Another source involves finance companies and home equity loans, if you own your own home, but there's a limit on how much can be borrowed. Lenders appraise the market value of a home conservatively—which means if they err, it's by accepting a lower appraised value on a home. One appraiser explained "We almost always end up with a lower value than what the homeowner thinks. The sales of comparable properties are lower, and the market is usually not as good as the owner believes." The lender only loans up to a certain percentage of this appraised value (from under 50% to even 80%), then deducts what else is owed on the home.

For example, if your home was appraised at $150,000 (this isn't its market value, which is usually higher) and the lender would finance up to 75% of this valuation, then the total lending amount would be $112,500 (75% of $150,000). If the amount of your first mortgage were $82,500, then they would only lend $30,000 (the difference between what loans the property would support and what was already in place). You wouldn't receive the entire $30,000, as there would be fees and expenses deducted from this.

After you have made this calculation, be sure you add in all your expenses, including paying off the past debt. This then becomes your financial budget or

However, be careful when considering this, as you must be able to meet the higher monthly payments—otherwise, you'll lose the remaining home equity. You will need to calculate how many months you can "buy" before you need a job.

Let's say the net proceeds from the second home equity loan were $30,000, your monthly living expenses (including the first mortgage and an allowance for past bills) is $2,100 per month, and the cost of the second mortgage is $400 per month. You'll have 12 months ($400 plus $2,100 equals $2,500 per month; $30,000 divided by $2,500 equals 12 months) before you need to pay the $2,500 monthly expenses from other sources. This also doesn't make any allowance for completely paying off past bills, property taxes, or any increases in your living costs.

forecast. People will go for the home equity loan they can qualify for, however, without regard to terms or how much time they can buy—if they'll lose their house anyway to foreclosure because they can't meet the currently existing monthly payments.

Never write a bad check, no matter how down or desperate. Go on welfare before doing this. It makes no difference that you're paying for medical services or your telephone bill. You more than likely will be prosecuted, and you don't need these additional headaches along with everything else.

Talking to Your Creditors

It's always better to talk to your creditors, as soon as problems develop. Don't wait for them to hand your debt over to a bill collector after ignoring their demand letters. Bill collectors are much less understanding and will try to collect what you owe by any legal means, as they aren't paid anything until collecting some money from you (they generally receive a percentage of the amount recovered).

Creditors, like the IRS, hate being ignored. The problem is that people try to avoid them and this simply fuels the fires. A well-experienced bankruptcy attorney said: "The biggest mistake people make is waiting too long to talk with their creditors. People who owe money become frightened...Downright scared. They will wait, hoping that the creditors will forget, but they don't. If you have a dragon in your life, then you had better deal with it now. If you wait and delay, then you only burn yourself."

It's also generally easier to work out something with the original creditor than a collection agency assigned to collect your debt. Department stores and merchandisers typically are more concerned with their good will and reputation—they want you as a customer. The original creditor knows that it's better to receive something than nothing at all. This doesn't mean that creditors are pushovers. Far from it. But they are in business to make money and business considerations prevail.

Creditors know they'll lose anywhere from 25% to 50% of the account value when it's assigned to a collection agency—that's the commission the bill collector charges. Any payments received after that, even if you pay the creditor directly, will be subject to that agreement. If they send it to an attorney, then the collection efforts cost them expensive legal fees, and debtors rarely are able to reimburse such costs (even when awarded by the court). If they send it to an in-house collection agency, this costs them the department's time and overhead. It's possible to receive discounts for cash payments—given severe financial problems and a convincing story—of one-quarter, one-third, even one-half and more from the original balance. So talk to them, and the sooner, the better.

If you have some money, don't simply pay a lower amount, writing "paid in full" on the check and sending it in a letter. This doesn't always work. You're better off talking with the creditor, explaining your poor financial position, then in conclusion saying you'll contact them later. One or 2 months later, contact the same person at the company and offer less than the amount in full payment or ask for extended terms, whichever you want or can afford.

Creditors will discount amounts, waive interest and penalties, and extend the payment terms. One principle does govern—cost versus terms. They will accept less principal, if it is if paid now. If you want terms, then they will want more cash paid over time. For example, you owe $1,000 to a store. Let's say they'll accept $750, given a convincing story that you're paying more to them than their competitor, and that's all you have. But they generally won't accept $750 paid over time. They might accept $800 or $850 over time, and whether interest also is paid will be negotiable.

If you don't like talking with creditors, then find out what's legal in your state *before* sending in less than what's owed as full payment, marking on the check "payment in full." In a number of states, the creditor can simply cross out that notation, cash the check, and still hold you responsible for the difference.

You need to have an overall plan as to what everyone will be offered. What you're trying to do is establish an informal creditor arrangement. If you're able to work out deals with all your important creditors, then this is nothing more than a bankruptcy arrangement would provide.

If you don't have enough money, then center on the essential accounts. Start by identifying why you can't pay and be honest—whether it's because you lost your job, have too much debt, or became severely ill. Then, tell them if there's any hope for the future. If you can send a small amount of money, then do so—such payments show good faith and can keep the collector off your back.

Bargain hard, but stick to your bottom line. Threaten bankruptcy if they threaten you with a lawsuit or the bill collector. The worst that can happen is that they'll sue you. There are no debtor prisons in the United States (A few states have enacted antiquated laws that provide for jail in isolated situations, but these are hardly ever enforced). It's possible to be jailed for not paying child support and intentionally defrauding the IRS, among other situations, but be careful here.

It will, of course, make a difference whether you have assets to protect in any negotiations with creditors. If you do, then your bargaining position may be less, regardless as to the amount of income loss. If you don't, then it makes little difference when you're sued. The best player is the one who has assets but acts as if there are none and actually believes it. Above all, don't fill out financial state-

If the creditor is agreeable to taking a smaller amount to settle the account or payments over a period of time, then be sure you can meet your end of the bargain. Nothing brings a lawsuit faster than a broken deal or a bad check. For important debts, try to send partial payments on a regular basis, no matter how small.

But always stay in contact with your creditors. All letters from a creditor should be answered by at least a telephone call, and writing back is preferred. You may not like talking with or answering them, but it makes a difference by keeping the bill collectors and attorneys out of the picture longer.

Be sure to set up a different checking account when sending in partial payments. Creditors will note the account information from the checks. Use the old account only for paying off your creditors, setting up a new one at another bank for your other needs.

---

ments, give updated information as to your assets, or anything else that could be used against you should the negotiations fail.

If possible, follow everything up in writing. If there's an honest dispute over a debt (such as an unauthorized charge or mistake made by them), then stick to your guns and don't waive your rights to contesting that debt. Be sure to specify that any payment sent on a contested bill doesn't amount to a waiver as to the amounts still in controversy.

Some Have More Rights

It does make a difference if you're trying to work out a payment schedule with the lender on your home, car, or even with your landlord. They have more rights than unsecured lenders, such as the credit card company or your local drug store. Pursuant to state law, the lender on your home can file a notice of default, wait a number of days (usually 60–120 days) as established by state law, then foreclose and evict you.

Home lenders may accept a reduced payment plan for several months, but it depends on their policies. In any event, they usually don't waive the amounts owed, including the penalties and late payment fees. When your house is at risk, contact an attorney if you can't work out an acceptable payment plan or if you have sufficient equity in the house that needs protecting.

Landlords have strong rights as well. Depending on local law, they must serve you with a "Notice to Pay Rent or Quit" within a certain time period (generally a short period of 3–5 days). If you don't pay what's owed, then they can sue you with an unlawful detainer action (eviction proceeding), and evict you after receiving the judgment. This can gain time while the landlord's in court, but finding another place to rent when you have no money and a bad reference can be a problem. If you convince an attorney or legal aid clinic to take your case, you'll gain another month or two (even more), depending on their tactics.

Utility companies usually give a month or two grace period, but you should talk to them first. They're at times bound by state laws as to what they can do with low-income or financially troubled customers. Don't ignore them, otherwise they will shut you off after you receive the notice.

Secured creditors know they can get their collateral (the possessions you secured), so they're in a somewhat stronger position. It's possible to give them back the property in exchange for a complete release from the debt. However, this doesn't happen often, as by now the property is less valuable due to wear and tear. "TVs, stereos, and furniture don't hold their value very well and get beaten up from use," said one bankruptcy specialist. "However, you can do this with cars and houses, given some equity still being present. That is, if you want to do this."

Be careful when talking with secured creditors, given the fine line between gaining their confidence and giving out too much information. There's no need to tell where specific assets are located or where your car is parked (this is treated later).

The Barrage of Letters

The first contact is the polite one, saying something to the effect that your account is now due, but if payment has already been made, then please disregard the notice. Most people do—they throw it away. If you haven't already talked with that creditor (or did and it didn't work), then you should start talking with him from the first letter on. Ask for more time, and say that you will pay when you do have the money.

The second letter will be a little more to the point. For example, "We have not received your payment and would appreciate it being made now. Please call us should you have any questions." If you answered the first letter and still received the second, then call again and tell that person how severe your problems are. Send them a token payment, when at all possible.

The letters increase in severity and tone. For example, "If we don't receive immediate payment from you, the matter will be immediately turned over to an attorney for collection. Your delinquency in payment will be reported to all credit-reporting agencies." Or you'll receive one that warns "Your account has been turned over for payment to a collection agency who will use all appropriate legal means to collect the owing amounts." At this point, it's best to write a short letter saying you are broke.

If you're still receiving letters after having made a token payment, at least you haven't been sued yet. What you're trying to do is stall for time. Each month the creditor is kept from filing a lawsuit becomes another 30 days in which to find work or cash.

Creditors sometimes send dunning letters that look like they're from a collection agency—a computer printout letter with the name of a company not related to the original creditor. There's no reason to change your bargaining position. You only have so much money.

If you do reach an agreement, then ask that creditor to help you improve your credit rating if possible. When a creditor doesn't reach an agreement after several letters and months have expired, then the letters stop. Your account has either been written off or sent to an agency or attorney for collection.

What Are Your Legal Rights?

At some point in time, you'll be contacted by a collection agency. You have legal rights that regulate what bill collectors can or can't do. The Fair Debt Collection Practices Act ("FDCPA") took effect in 1978, and it brought under control many of the abusive, intimidating acts of debt collectors. Although there still are abuses, this law has helped curb those problems.

The FDCPA applies to collection agencies, bill collectors, and any creditor who uses a name other than its own when trying to collect its debts. An original creditor who collects debts under its own name isn't subject to the federal FDCPA. Some states have their own statutes regulating these creditors; other states don't. Most states do have laws regulating collection agencies and bill collectors, in addition to the federal FDCPA, and these laws govern when stricter. The FDCPA allows a collector to make a reasonable effort to talk with you about the debt, but it's *not* reasonable or permitted for a collector to contact you:

- ✔ at an inconvenient or unusual time with the hours between 8 a.m. and 9 p.m. deemed to be convenient;
- ✔ at an inconvenient place;
- ✔ at your place of employment if it's known that the employer doesn't allow such contact; or
- ✔ if an attorney is known to represent the debtor;

Contact may not be made if you notify the collector in writing of your refusal to pay the debt or object to the original sale. The collector is allowed to contact you in that case for the sole reason of explaining the possible consequences to you.

A bill collector may only contact a third party to discover or verify your address or location. When doing this, the bill collector must identify him or herself, limiting any questions to confirm or correct your whereabouts. The following *can't* be done by a collector when talking or contacting someone else:

- ✔ reveal that you owe a debt;
- ✔ communicate again with that person unless there's a reasonable purpose. For example, the collector could call your sister back if believing that her original response was wrong or incomplete and that she had more accurate information;
- ✔ send a post card; or
- ✔ do anything to indicate debt collection activities, such as putting words or symbols on the outside of an envelope.

The FDCPA further *prohibits* collection agencies and collectors from: using threats of violence or harm in any way; advertising your debts, such as in a list of deadbeats; charging you for collect calls or telegram fees; repeatedly using the telephone to annoy you or anyone else; using obscene or profane language; implying that they are an attorney or work for the government; stating that you've committed a crime or under investigation to get you to pay; or lying about the amount of the debt or saying that you'll be arrested for not paying.

In short, the law is designed to keep bill collectors from using abusive, intimidating, or misleading ways to get information about you, either from yourself or others. However, they will try to do this. Should you believe there's been a violation, then contact the Federal Trade Commission, which oversees the FDCPA. Also, contact your state Consumer Affairs or Consumer Protection agency for their help. But remember it will be the bill collector's word against your's, unless you have outside proof, such as another person overhearing what was said.

Negotiating with Bill Collectors

By law, bill collectors must within 5 days of the first contact, by phone or letter, tell you: the amount of the debt; the original creditor's name; that you have 30 days within which to dispute the bill's validity; and that if you do so dispute the debt, that the collector will send you verification of what's owed.

> *Remember that bill collectors only are interested in getting money from you.* As one said, "My job is to get people who don't have much money to pay what I'm collecting. Some can be intimidated and some will do it because I convince them it's right...or they feel guilty if they don't after I talk to them. And there are a bunch who just don't give a damn." They will say anything to do this, because that's the way they get paid. They'll work on your sense of ethics, morality, duty to God and country, if not outright intimidation by threats of lawsuits, costs, and a destroyed credit—even if they "follow" FDCPA or your state's laws.

You can negotiate with a collection agency just as you would with the original creditor. However, you'll need to recognize that the collector has no loss unless a lot of time is put in and there's no or little payment. Collectors will threaten you with a lawsuit, then a judgment, then the garnishing of your wages or attaching your property. Tell them simply, you'll file bankruptcy first. Or that the law prohibits what they're talking about. You're only negotiating—but only agree to pay *if* you have the money to meet your end of the bargain. If you don't, then politely tell them you're broke and will file bankruptcy, leaving it there.

Practically, bill collectors aren't going to sue when the amount of money is small—it isn't cost effective, and they lose money. The computerized, collection

> If you can pay something, then say you'll make one offer and *only* one offer. Tell them it will be the best offer you can make. Do it and stick to your guns—don't change it, no matter what they say. The smell of payment to a bill collector is like the smell of blood to a piranha. It is a waste of time and energy to keep negotiating or be polite. Tell them to either accept or reject the offer within, let's say, 1 week. You don't want any more telephone calls from them, and cut off any further discussions if they don't accept it. But make it your best offer, just in case you're sued later.

complaint generated by law firms, however, is the same form with only a few minor changes from one lawsuit to another. This isn't a very expensive process. The bill collector appears in court; the attorney is retained only in the larger, disputed cases.

"You'll be safe when owing less than $200, and it can be much more than that, depending on the agency," observed a bankruptcy attorney. Understandably, as the amount owed becomes larger, a bill collector will spend more and more time on your account, even bringing a lawsuit more quickly when it is believed there's money around. They'll agree to lump-sum payments and installment plans, as well, but you won't get as good a deal for installment plans as for up-front cash. Remember they don't want to wait for their commissions to dribble in over the years as you make payments. If you have the money, deals can be made; if you don't,

When Should You Hire an Attorney?

You don't need an attorney to negotiate with creditors, unless there's a legal offset, statute of limitation (the creditor has waited a long time before suing you), or unauthorized charge problems *and* the debt is large. With the number of self-help books available, including those on bankruptcy, it's entirely possible even to file bankruptcy by yourself when you have limited assets and little home equity.

It could help if you've retained a bankruptcy attorney (but get a fixed fee, if possible) to write a standard letter to your important creditors, outlining why you're in difficulties, the prospects for the future, and your proposal. Just the attorney's letterhead can help. However, it's certainly not necessary.

Once you've been sued, the decision becomes complex. It depends on whether you own assets requiring protection, intend to file bankruptcy, and the size of the lawsuit(s). If you have important assets to protect, then you should consult an attorney, whether bankruptcy will be filed or not. For example, a number of states allow you to file an exemption with the county recorder's office that lists certain real property that can't be attached by creditors. Usually the important asset to be protected is your home equity. *Filing a homestead exemption can bar creditors from attaching this equity. The amount, coverage, and provisions vary from state to state. They can be minimal to over $100,000, depending on the state.*

Should you have problems with owing child support, alimony, federal income taxes (see Chapter 8), and other complicated areas, then consulting a lawyer can be a cost-effective move, provided you cover everything in that meeting. Pay the attorney in small increments, as well.

When assets are small and you're planning to file bankruptcy, an attorney isn't needed to defend you against lawsuits, but you should consult a bankruptcy attorney on whether you qualify for bankruptcy and what will happen when you do file. An attorney should always be consulted, but not necessarily retained, when you are sued for large amounts or damages. Ask if it would be discharged in bankruptcy. *If you plan to file and it is dischargeable, then you could forget about defending it and save the money for the bankruptcy filing.*

then the problems continue. However, sending in payments in small drips and drops appears to stall lawsuits, although this depends on the agency or creditor.

Talking to All Your Creditors

If you have some money or assets to pay your creditors, then it's possible to talk to all of them and work out an arrangement. In effect you'll be working out a bankruptcy plan without filing for it. However, this does depend on a few factors. "First, you need some assets or money—otherwise it doesn't work. Then, it depends on the amount of debt and how old it is. My experience has been that new debt isn't resolved that quickly. Middle-aged debt and old debt are easier to work out. When you work out an arrangement with all your creditors, then the basic effect is as if you had filed bankruptcy. In fact, working out an arrangement with most of your creditors saves you money, should you have to file bankruptcy later," observed one bankruptcy specialist.

Creditors are more open to working out something with businesses, especially when times become tough in a given region. It makes sense to try and structure something that the creditors will accept, whether it's some payment or even a share in the company's profits or stock. Again, working out some plan with the creditors ahead of time, even if the business should be forced into formal bankruptcy proceedings later, will save a lot of money in legal fees—you've made the arrangements and not the attorney. "If creditors feel their interests will be protected and that they'll be paid in good time, then they will work with a debtor," said another bankrupcy attorney.

If You Own a Home

Creditors and collectors are quick to argue that they can get a judgment and attach your home equity. Or that you should sell your home to pay them off. An argument used by bankruptcy lawyers when confronted by this is that there won't be anything left to be attached after the sale of the home. You might think there's good equity in your home. However, selling in a bad or slow market, coupled with the expenses of sale, federal and any state income taxes on the capital gains, and the state exemption protecting home equity can reduce this to a minimum.

For example, let's say you own a $200,000 home with a $100,000 mortgage. If you assume that the expenses of a sale (real estate commissions and closing costs) are $15,000, the state and federal taxes to be paid are $50,000 (you had owned a previous home and switched in the gains), and your state exempts $35,000 of equity from attachment, then the creditors can't get anything after you pay off the mortgage. (This argument assumes you're already protected by a bankruptcy filing). This also assumes you can sell the house for $200,000 in what's presumably a bad market.

Prior to talking with your creditors, you could consult a bankruptcy attorney over whether you should file and what arguments are best to use with your creditors. Then, do it yourself or retain the attorney to work out a payment plan with your creditors. If that doesn't work, you can always file for bankruptcy as you first said you would.

When Talking Doesn't Work

There's a difference when debt involves property. If the claim doesn't involve your purchase of property (provided you didn't sign a security agreement), then the creditor only has the right to sue you over what is owed. When property is involved (such as your house, car, or furniture), then there are other rights.

If Property Is Involved

If property is involved, then you must determine whether what's owed is secured by the bought property. If you used a credit card to purchase a stereo from Tom's Electronics, then what's owed isn't secured by the stereo. However, if you signed a contract with Tom stating what's owed is secured by the stereo and they can take it back if you don't pay, then that debt is called a secured debt. Whether a debt is secured or not depends on what the contract provides and your state law.

As we've discussed, the lender can take back the property when the loan is secured by it, even without a notice or lawsuit. It does make a difference whether the item in question is something moveable (such as your car, RV, computer, video recorder, or couch) or not. You can't move a house, so there are different rights should you default on your mortgage or deed of trust. The lender must give you notice of the default and any proceedings to take back your house when you haven't made the payments.

If the property can be moved, then the creditor can take it back (repossess it) without suing you or giving any notice. Although this does depend on what the agreement says and your state law, the creditor has more rights when property is secured. Although they usually don't repossess property when you miss the first payment or sometimes the second (they would rather have the money than the property), you must be careful when talking with secured creditors.

For example, cars are repossessed just as you see in the movies. Repo artists can legally do nearly anything to get your car back, including hot wiring and duplicating keys. They can't break into a locked car or garage, however, although some do this anyway. They can't throw you bodily out of your car while you're driving it, so most repossessions of motor vehicles become a cat-and-mouse game—you're trying to keep it hidden in a locked place (which is breaking some laws), and they're trying to find it. If you use your car a lot, then the odds are more in their favor. The repo person (women do it as well) simply looks around the area by your home or follows you back after an errand, and the car is gone the next night. If you can't make the car payments, you're better off selling it and buying a used one with no payments. But many people, unfortunately, don't want to do that.

Other types of property, whether furniture, stereos, refrigerators, or even computers, are subject to the same right of repossession. However, these usually will be safe—provided you keep the house securely locked and refuse to let creditors into your house (which is your right). Also, these articles don't have the resale value that cars do. This doesn't mean they won't try to repossess these items (some do), but the odds are low that they will. More likely, such creditors will sue you over what you owe.

A creditor, even after repossessing property such as your car or stereo, can often hold you responsible for the deficiency. Some states do allow the creditor to take back the property without going to court, sell it at an auction (either private or public), then still hold you liable for the difference between the net proceeds (what's received less the expenses of collection and sale) and what you owe (including late payment penalties and interest). They don't even need to sue you over the difference and can continue after you. You do have rights (which vary among the states) when in this process: redeeming the property (getting it back by paying what you owe, including interest and costs) after the sale; receiving notice as to the right to redeem (including the right to reinstate the contract before the sale); and reasonable assurance that the sale price at the auction will be fair under the circumstances. As auction property sells at large discounts, usually less than one-half of what was originally paid, the likelihood is you still will be owing something.

The good news is that states allowing deficiency judgments on personal property (some states allow it on real estate, as well) typically exempt lower cost articles. This exemption is from $1,000 to $2,000, depending on the state. If a stereo originally cost $800, and your state prohibits deficiencies for items bought less than $1,000, then you're not liable. If creditors are required to sue for the difference in court by your state, then they can collect a personal judgment for the difference, including their attorney fees and court costs. This judgment is called a deficiency judgment. If you're planning to file bankruptcy, then this deficiency liability won't normally be a concern. And given the expense of courts and attorneys, if you didn't have the money to pay them in the first place, most creditors reason, then why should they spend more money over what is still owed.

Remember also that secured creditors aren't limited to taking back the security. Whether the state provides for deficiencies or not, they always can sue you directly over what's owed. If they do elect to sue you, many states provide that they can't repossess the property after obtaining a judgment. This is called an *election of remedies* by the creditor. You will need to ask an attorney, go to a legal aid clinic, or research it at your county law library to see what rights secured creditors have. There are self-help books on this subject, but be sure your state's laws are covered.

If your house is being sold at foreclosure, then you need to consult an attorney immediately. Although many states prohibit a deficiency judgment, there are states that allow the lender to sue you for the difference between the net proceeds and the debt. As houses are substantially more valuable than cars, this liability can be a problem, especially when other assets are owned. Even more important, there may be ways to delay the lender from the foreclosure proceedings, thus buying needed time to refinance or sell the home. If you're planning to file bankruptcy, then you would consult a bankruptcy attorney in this regard.

Judgment Creditor Rights

Any creditor can sue you if there's no agreement on the debt repayment terms. Lawsuits can be brought in small claims court or higher courts such as municipal or superior courts. See Chapters 14 through 22 for a further discussion on what to do when planning to sue or if you've been sued.

In contrast to the rights secured creditors enjoy as to their collateral, unsecured creditors don't have a legally enforceable right to your property or income (unless your state allows a prejudgment attachment order that attorneys usually don't ask for) until they receive a judgment. There's no right until that judgment is entered against you. If the creditor wins in court, then he's called the *judgment creditor* and you're called the *judgment debtor*.

Judgment creditors have years to collect on a judgment, no matter where you live. If you move to another state, there's a procedure by which the judgment creditor can have that judgment recognized in the new state, then proceed against any assets that can be found underneath that state's laws.

The judgment creditor usually records a copy of the judgment in the counties of states where you reside or own property, and this recording gives notice as to the existence of the judgment and that it needs to be paid off (such as to subsequent purchasers of your property). It then becomes a lien, or charge, against property in that county (whether it's real or personal property). The judgment creditor either can wait until you sell or refinance real property (then it has to be paid off) or begin procedures to force the property to be sold. In the latter case, should there be sufficient equity (after the expenses of the sale, your homestead exemption, unpaid liens, and prior secured loans are paid) in the house, then the judgment creditor could be paid off in full. Then, if there are taxes owed on this sale (which are assessed the following year), you could wind up with no money to pay for them. So be careful here.

Judgment creditors can seize your personal property, such as bank accounts, your stamp collection, or even car, by levying against that property. But first they have to find it. After identifying and locating the property, they can apply to the court for an order allowing them to levy on it (which is usually called a *writ of execution*). The Marshall or Sheriff is given the court-approved writ and then seizes the identified asset. In the case of a bank account, the writ or order is delivered to the bank which must set aside the specified amount of funds up to what is available in the account.

You don't have to allow the Marshall to come into your home, unless the order allows such entry. Given that or your permission, the Marshall seizes that specifically identified asset and puts it into storage. It's then sold with the net proceeds (after the costs of collection, storage, and sale) applied against what's owed. As discussed before, you can still be liable for the difference (depending on your state law), and the judgment creditor can apply for another writ as other nonexempt property is discovered.

The judgment creditor, pursuant to your state law, can attach wages and apply for orders to attach property that hasn't yet come into your hands, such as tax refunds, bonuses, and other payments. It's easy to see that if the creditor doesn't know where something is, then the creditor can't get at it.

Various states allow a judgment creditor to question you in a hearing about your finances—what you own, where it's located, the debt against it, and your

Each state has exemptions that limit what creditors can levy against and that vary extensively from state to state. These exemptions can cover furniture, the tools used in your trade or business, your car, pensions, insurance, jewelry, and other articles as provided—but these exemptions are limited by type and amount. These amounts can be as low as $100 or range upward to several thousands of dollars, even exempting all of that particular property. Most states prohibit furniture, clothing, and public retirement benefits, for example, from being taken by a creditor—check your state law for its specific requirements.

Disability, unemployment, social security, and welfare benefits are prohibited by federal law from being garnished or attached. If you've finally secured another job, federal law currently exempts 75% of all net earnings per workweek or 30 times the minimum hourly rate, whichever is greater, from garnishment. Most states have accepted this level; however, others have a higher exclusion (which is allowable under federal law). The creditor is only entitled to the amounts over these limits, no matter how much the judgment. These state and federal exemptions (but not necessarily the federal level as we've seen) generally apply in bankruptcy proceedings.

income, among other areas. Other states allow these questions to be sent to you in writing, asking for the same information.

Regardless of the approach taken, you must use care when filling out such forms or appearing for questioning. The written questions about your finances must be signed under penalties of perjury; if you don't show up for the hearing, the judge may declare you in contempt of court and order your arrest. Each state has its own way of enforcing the examination of a debtor.

What Should You Do when You Are Sued?

The approach depends upon your personal situation. If deciding to file bankruptcy, then there's no need to fight the lawsuit unless it's not dischargeable (it's still valid even after the bankruptcy). It would be better to save that money to use for your living expenses and the bankruptcy proceeding. If the only reason for not paying the claim is no money, then why fight it? You're only wasting more time and money.

When there's a good reason for defending—for example, an erroneous charge, the finance charges were usurious (the interest and penalties were excessive under state law), or an unauthorized charge—then fight it. But being honest is important, so don't conjure up reasons to not pay, if in fact, you owe the money.

If a lawsuit is allowed to go unopposed to judgment, that doesn't mean all negotiations end. All that a judgment means is that the creditor has reduced to one amount what you owe at that time. That creditor still has to legally enforce your payment through collection efforts. And all of this is still negotiable.

If under state law, you have limited assets or little over what's held to be exempt from collection, then you're *"judgment proof."* This means that creditors can sue you from one side of court to the other and not be able to levy on your assets.

It also means you don't have much to protect either. Self-help books on your state law, the local law library, legal aid clinics, consulting attorneys, or debt counselors may be contacted as to what your state law provides in your case.

Other fortunate facts of life to a judgment debtor, but discouraging to a judgment creditor, are the steps that need to be taken to collect on a judgment. These steps take time and cost money, whether by the creditor or a lawyer. Assets must be discovered, then levied against, and this isn't all that easy. It's usually worth a discount from the judgment for the creditor not to go through this process.

The Continuing Discussions

If a creditor sues, even takes a judgment, some debtors continue talking with that creditor. Although this might be looked upon as a waste of time, it's always possible that something can be worked out, especially when the creditor gets tired of paying legal fees. "They say they won't settle, but they will. Talk to them, even if you don't have the money. Talk to them, even if they sue and take a default judgment, even after putting a lien on your property," said one person who ran into financial problems and worked out arrangements with a number of creditors. However, this approach depends on the creditor, how much in assets you have, and whether you even want to keep up these discussions.

Other Ways

Some people who owe money try to hide bank accounts and assets from being levied upon. Please consult Chapter 8 for a discussion of the dos and don'ts with respect to taxes. Renting post office boxes and filing change-of-address forms to the post office box is one technique. People order a new, unlisted telephone number for privacy. Checking and saving accounts are changed to a different bank, with any address, telephone numbers, and other identifying information deleted from the new checks. Living trusts are looked into to see if creditor liens can be avoided (many states don't, but check your state's laws). However, taking pains that the living trust's name isn't the same as yours can frustrate those trying to find the asset in that trust.

It is important to sell or transfer assets before there are judgments and any postjudgment proceedings to find your assets. As these proceedings are under penalties of perjury or contempt of court, a false answer can subject you to penalties. Although being broke means difficulties in affording any legal advice, try to work out some arrangement and talk to a lawyer. A 30-minute conversation may be all that's necessary to keep you from getting into more trouble.

Bankruptcy

The decision to file for bankruptcy is a difficult one, but it can be a definite improvement over what's being experienced. "It was upsetting to file bankruptcy,

> If you have several lawsuits at once, then you should consider bankruptcy. Having to appear in court or answer creditor examinations, duck levies, and endure sleepless nights has its limits. You should think about filing bankruptcy when you're spending too much time with the creditors—you would be better off spending this time earning a livelihood. If the creditor, you're better off to determine first if the debtor can or even would pay off an award (or file bankruptcy instead) before spending the legal dollars to obtain a judgment.

even after the discharge. But it was a relief not to have the phone always ringing with calls from the bill collectors," said one who filed.

Chapter 7 filings are used for liquidating assets and liabilities, whether by an individual, farmer, or business. When it's possible to work out a repayment plan, then most businesses use Chapter 11 reorganization, farmers employ Chapter 12, and individuals file under Chapter 13.

Contrary to what most people believe, bankruptcy isn't a straightforward discharge or rollback of all debts and liabilities. Before making any decision, you need to consider whether your debts are dischargeable and whether there are assets needing to be preserved.

Dischargeable Debts

A debt is discharged when it's eliminated or erased by the bankruptcy court. This discharge, however, is granted by the court at different times depending on the type of proceeding. The discharge of debts in a Chapter 7 liquidation, whether by a business or individual, is granted immediately after the time has expired for a creditor to file a complaint objecting to that discharge. This is normally 90 days after the bankruptcy has been filed.

The technical discharge in Chapter 11 business reorganizations occurs at the time the plan of reorganization is confirmed. This can be anywhere from 6 months after the filing to years later in the case of major corporate reorganizations. However, once the plan is in operation, the business must make the payments as agreed and honor the plan. If not, then the creditors can force the company back into Chapter 11 or even a Chapter 7 liquidation.

The discharge in a Chapter 13 wage-earner bankruptcy is granted upon the completion of the payments under the terms of the plan. The plan usually provides for payments over at least a 3-year period. In certain hardship cases, it's possible for the discharge to be granted even though the payments weren't completed, but you shouldn't count on this.

Nondischargeable Debts

Congress, when deciding the bankruptcy codes, determined that certain types of debts shouldn't be dischargeable. Otherwise, people could use the process to discharge debts and liabilities that should be kept as responsibilities. Nondischargeable debts remain as obligations and to be paid by the debtor, even when granted a discharge in bankruptcy. The following basic liabilities were decided to be *nondischargeable* in Chapter 7 and 13 bankruptcies (and there are others):

- ✔ Child support and alimony;
- ✔ Recently incurred student loans;
- ✔ Any federal, state, and local taxes (but see Chapter 8);
- ✔ Certain consumer credit debts incurred shortly before the bankruptcy proceeding, such as that last trip you took to Las Vegas on your credit cards;
- ✔ Liability for damages caused by willful and malicious acts, such as drunk driving, assault and battery, or fines and penalties due to criminal conduct (ranging from speeding tickets to victim restitution); and
- ✔ Fraud (under Chapter 7).

Special mentions must be made of fraud. For example, proper debts and liabilities that you forgot to list when filing your bankruptcy papers are *nondischargeable* under both Chapters 7 and 11. Debts incurred by fraud (for example, lying about your income or a false financial statement) aren't permitted to be discharged in Chapter 7, but Chapter 13 does allow for the discharge of debts incurred by fraud because the creditor is paid off eventually.

> Fraud can be either hiding or concealing assets from creditors (which can block the entire bankruptcy proceeding) or in the obtaining of credit for certain debts. Experienced bankruptcy attorneys are always concerned over the existence of fraud in any debt, because if the lawyers for the creditor can prove this, then the debt is still owed even after the bankruptcy. As one said, "You want a total discharge in a Chapter 7 liquidation. A problem here and you've still got that debt after the bankruptcy. Or the other attorney makes you cut a deal on payment that you don't want." Be careful with this one.

Unsecured debts not involving any of the above may be discharged in bankruptcy. This means that they will be liquidated completely under a Chapter 7 or accepted in the payment plan (even partially liquidated) in a Chapter 13 plan. Examples of *dischargeable* debts are:

- ✔ Medical bills from doctors, surgeons, hospitals, therapists, and prescriptions;
- ✔ Professional bills from lawyers, accountants, engineers, and consultants;
- ✔ Credit and charge cards;
- ✔ Retail, drug, and department store charges;
- ✔ Past rent;
- ✔ Deficiency judgments and liabilities;
- ✔ Court judgments;
- ✔ Utility, gasoline, car repairs, subscriptions;

✔ Bank notes and loans; and

✔ Guarantees of loans.

Dischargeable court judgments include matters involving the above, breach of contract, and damage awards not involving intentional conduct. Dischargeable claims also don't have to be in the form of a lawsuit. If they can be sufficiently identified and are dischargeable, then they can be listed and erased by the bankruptcy. The advice often given by bankruptcy attorneys is to wait as long as you can before filing to "sop up" all the potential claims.

Secured debts are treated differently, as you would guess from the preceding discussions. Although bankruptcy eliminates your personal liability under secured debt, it doesn't mean you can keep the property without further payment. If in a Chapter 7, you'll either have to give the security back to the creditor or pay the current value, or amount of debt, whichever is less. If in a Chapter 11 or 13, any payment plans must be acceptable to the court in order for you to keep the property.

Nondischargeable Conduct

There is certain conduct that means you won't be discharged from bankruptcy, even if you filed—it is as if you'd never filed in the first place. Such prohibited conduct occurs if the debtor:

✔ Defrauded creditors, within 1 year or during the bankruptcy, by concealing, wrongfully hiding, or transferring property;

✔ Destroyed, mutilated, or falsified records, unless proved as being justified under the circumstances; or

✔ Presented false claims or committed perjury during the proceedings.

Be wary, as these can defeat the very purpose for filing a bankruptcy.

The Pros and Cons of Bankruptcy

If you are deep in debt and hounded by creditors and lawyers, then bankruptcy may be the best thing. The worst possibility would be to speed down to the courthouse, file bankruptcy, and then discover that a major debt is nondischargeable. However, given that your important debts are dischargeable, then there are a few other negatives to consider.

Bankruptcy may be expensive, should you retain an attorney, and it can take time to make it through the system. Should you decide to do it yourself and save the money, this approach can be time-consuming, confusing, and leave you open to making a bad mistake. Bankruptcy is a matter of public record, and your finances are available for anyone to see by simply going down to the bankruptcy court and inspecting the records.

Filing for bankruptcy does stay on your credit report for 10 years, destroying much of your credit. You need to determine how valuable this is to you, although what has happened to date already has impaired your credit. It's possible to reconstruct credit cards and credit—consult a credit counselor in this regard whenever possible. An alternative used after bankruptcy is to agree with a bank to deposit funds into a "frozen" savings account. They in turn agree to grant you a credit card, and the credit limit depends on the amounts deposited, with that account securing the repayment of any credit advances.

The advantages are that filing for bankruptcy places an immediate freeze on any collection activities, examinations, lawsuits, or actions against you at the time of the filing. Creditors are prohibited from contacting you to demand repayment, making any garnishments, and continuing or starting collection actions against you. Creditors can't drain your bank account, attach your wages, or throw you out on the streets—at least for the moment. The silence of the telephone by itself may be a good enough reason.

This freeze is called the "*automatic stay*" in bankruptcy court. The stay stops the proceedings to collect child support, evict you, foreclose on your mortgage, or shut off your utilities. However, this freeze doesn't stay in place forever. The creditors can make an application in court to lift the stay later, thus allowing their proceedings to continue.

> If you have assets to preserve and are under a barrage of creditor claims, then bankruptcy should be considered when those claims are dischargeable. When you have the ability to pay back those claims in a 3-to 5-year period, then you should consider Chapter 13 (personal) and Chapter 11 (business) filings. If there are negligible assets with dischargeable claims, then a Chapter 7 liquidation is appropriate. Be sure to consult an experienced bankruptcy attorney before making your final decision.

For example, a home lender will argue that the stay is jeopardizing the property's security and that the house will lose its value, if the freeze is left in place. Given a favorable court judgment, lenders can foreclose, the landlord evict you, and the utility company shut off the electricity or water. The responsibility for making child support and alimony payments soon resumes, and these obligations must be kept current. You'll need to contact an attorney as to what your local law requires.

The Decision

Bankruptcy has become less of a social stigma, especially after the highly debt-ridden times of the 1980s and 1990s. Actress Kim Basinger, facing a $7.4 million judgment for failing to act in the film "Boxing Helena," filed a Chapter 11 bankruptcy. Basinger's attorney said during the trial that her assets were approximately $5 million at the time, while she said she was earning as much as $3 million a movie. The court directed her to post a $12.1 million bond or else face having her assets seized for the judgment. Her attorney was quoted as saying that the bankruptcy filing was done to avoid paying for the bond. The action also placed pressures on the judgment creditor, Main Line Pictures, to negotiate some form of settlement on the court award.

Actors, actresses, movie producers, and even Government officials use bankruptcy when their debts have gotten out of line. Even a well-known bankruptcy attorney, who owned a chain of bankruptcy offices, was forced to file a Chapter 7 liquidation bankruptcy in the wake of a large, uninsured malpractice claim.

Filing bankruptcy does involve emotions. "For some it's a business decision, and there's little feeling, at least on the outside. Most people are troubled by it, worrying about their future credit, the neighbors, their reputation, and paying the bills, all at the same time. They've become battered by the stress of not having any money," said one bankruptcy attorney. "Small business owners are always worrying about the effect on their customers and suppliers if they file. Usually by then, they're already on COD and the customers are complaining," said another.

Once the decision has been made (ideally after consultation with a bankruptcy attorney), you should make decisions about debts, cash, and property. People are tempted to hide property with friends, relatives, or associates. As seen above, the consequences can be disastrous when this is discovered—any discharge from bankruptcy can be denied. Rather than continuing to pay off creditors, you should stop any payments and keep the cash for your living expenses and the costs of bankruptcy. Try to hold off filing bankruptcy as long as possible, especially if there are still-to-be-received medical bills or expenses such as your children's tuition and large car repairs. This doesn't mean stiffing creditors; it's just that if you file too soon, then some claims will be made as services rendered during the bankruptcy. These bills can be designated as administrative claims, which must be paid off from the first available cash.

Chapter 7

A court-appointed trustee assumes control of all nonexempt property (what the law says the creditors can't get their hands on) under a Chapter 7 liquidation. The trustee sells that property and uses the proceeds to pay off the expenses of administration, the trustee's fee (usually a percentage of the property regained for the benefit of the creditors), other expenses pursuant to law, and the remainder is then allocated among the creditors. All your dischargeable debts are extinguished, and you keep a small allowance of exempt property, with all other assets liquidated.

Chapter 7 is ideal for a high-income-earning person who has accumulated debt without much in the way of assets. The previous "roaring" times had many professionals borrowing beyond their means to live well without putting any money away. When the crunch times appeared, they were left high and dry. Chapter 7, provided the debts were dischargeable (for example, student loans usually aren't), allowed them to erase these debts and continue on with a fresh start. Let's say a surgeon was earning $350,000 per year but because of poor decisions ended up with defaulted loans and lawsuits. To eliminate these personal liabilities, the surgeon could wipe out the claims in Chapter 7 and might be permitted (although there's no guarantee) by the bankruptcy court to continue spending the $350,000 income as desired.

The same reasoning applies to a family whose wage earner lost her job and ran up debts just trying to live. Upon finding a job, she could consider a Chapter 7 to stop any wage garnishments (although at least 75% of wages are exempt, depending on the particular state, the 25% at risk and hassles could make a difference). However, if she still owned the family home and were able to pay the debts off in a 3- to 5-year-period, then she could consider filing Chapter 13, all after consulting an attorney as to which action was best for her.

You can't file for a Chapter 7 liquidation if you received such a discharge within the past 6 years, as measured from when you filed for that bankruptcy, not from when you were discharged. These proceedings are relatively fast, as opposed to Chapter 11 and 13, and usually are completed in a matter of months.

Chapter 13

The key difference between Chapter 7 and 13 is that you keep your property under Chapter 13. In return for keeping your property, you agree to a plan that pays off your creditors over a 3- to 5-year period. A trustee in a Chapter 13 bankruptcy also normally doesn't take control or possession of your business or assets as is done in a Chapter 7 liquidation. An individual also may continue to operate his or her business during a Chapter 13 bankruptcy.

Chapter 13 is a bankruptcy plan available to individuals and often referred to as a *consumer* bankruptcy—the total secured debt can't exceed $350,000 or unsecured debt exceed $100,000 in order to use this plan, and this is strictly enforced by the courts. The debtor must have sufficient income to make the regular payments, and a creditor can't force an individual into this filing. Individuals not meeting these limitations can file a Chapter 7 liquidation or, if they own a business, can file under Chapter 11.

A major advantage of Chapter 13 is its broad discharge provisions. Debts not dischargeable under a Chapter 7 or 11 bankruptcy can be discharged under 13. For example, certain income taxes, debts incurred by fraud, using a false financial statement, embezzlement, or causing a willful injury are dischargeable under Chapter 13; and even though debts such as income taxes and already owed child support aren't dischargeable, they may be included as part of a repayment program. The reason is that the creditor receives payment for such obligations under the approved plan, the complete discharge being received only after all of the agreed payments have been made.

A hybrid of such filings is called a "*Chapter 20*" proceeding. To take advantage of the broad discharge provisions of Chapter 13, a debtor can file for a Chapter 7 liquidation to discharge most debts. This is followed quickly by a Chapter 13 filing to partially pay and discharge the debts that survived Chapter 7, such as those incurred by fraud.

The proceedings begin by filing a form listing all your property, debts, income, and expenses. At this point, the dealings are quite similar to a Chapter 7. However, along with the filing, you are expected (yourself or your attorney) to file a reasonable plan outlining your ability to pay off your debts within at least 3 years based on your expected, disposable monthly income. This usually means that most creditors must be shown as being paid back at least the value of your nonexempt property over a 3-year period. If you want more time to pay off debt, up to 5 years can be granted, provided a larger percentage of the debt is paid off.

The proposed repayment plan is presented to the bankruptcy trustee and then the court. If the plan is approved by the court, then a meeting of the creditors to approve the plan is scheduled. Unsecured creditors generally accept the plan as long as they receive as much under it as they would if all the property were liquidated.

The court may also reduce the amount of debt to be repaid. These unpaid amounts can be discharged, but for secured and non-dischargeable debts. The bankruptcy court has the power to let you modify your plan, given that problems occur, even discharge the remainder of your debts on a hardship basis. However, this is a discretionary power. If you can't meet the scheduled payments, and the court doesn't modify the plan or grant a hardship basis, then your Chapter 13 bankruptcy may wind up as a Chapter 7 liquidation.

The advantage of a Chapter 13 plan is that it lets you keep your property during the time that the repayment plan is in effect. Any liquidation of assets may not be necessary, and the bankruptcy court can even approve reduced payments on secured debts. This filing allows you to discharge debts not dischargeable under Chapter 7. Debtors who receive a Chapter 13 discharge don't lose their right to file for a Chapter 7 liquidation in the future. In fact, when a repayment plan isn't possible or breaks down, then it will be converted to a Chapter 7 liquidation (and most Chapter 13 filings do).

When You Own a Business

What to do when you own a business depends on whether it's viable or not. If the business is mortally wounded, then it would be sold or liquidated under a Chapter 7 proceeding. If the basic, underlying business is viable, regardless of its financial difficulties, then a reorganization filing would be made—either under Chapter 13 (assuming it is owned individually and that the debt limitations were met) or Chapter 11 (if not).

A Chapter 11 election allows you to continue operating, and the provisions are similar to those in Chapter 13. This election is by larger companies, usually triggered when a secured party begins foreclosure on property. The business is allowed to reduce its debts, paying the remainder over a 3- to 5-year period.

The business continues to operate while in bankruptcy, and the debtor usually controls the company during the proceedings. If the creditors can prove, however, that management is incapable or is stealing from the company, then a trustee will be appointed by the court to run the business.

The company must propose a reasonable business plan that indicates it can pay off its restructured debts over the repayment period. The concept is the same as in a Chapter 11—the plan must show that the creditors will receive at least the same or more from the plan than they could from the liquidation of the company. If the repayment plan isn't feasible, then the company will be forced to liquidate under Chapter 7. In fact, the great majority of companies, although optimistically electing a reorganization under Chapter 11, are forced ultimately to convert to Chapter 7 and liquidate.

It's about Income and Expenses

The mistake that most individuals and companies admit, once having gone through this process, was having been too optimistic when income or revenues first fell. If they had cut expenses to the bone, immediately tried to work out an informal plan with their creditors, and done whatever was legally possible to survive financially, then their times could have become easier. One small-business owner said ruefully "I would have still had my business if I had reacted quicker and laid off people and cut back sooner than I did. But I just didn't believe the business downturn would last as long as it did. It was too late by the time I began cutting costs."

People should look at their personal assets and life as they do their work requirements—unfortunately, this is neglected by many to the detriment of their personal finances. Save for the rainy days that all of us have or will experience in our lifetime. If disaster strikes, then don't be optimistic that you'll find work quickly—slash expenses to the bone and follow the other suggestions to survive through tough times.

You and Your Business

The areas of personal asset protection, liability, and controlling legal expenses with a business depend upon whether you're an employee or the owner. If you work for a company, then the prime concern is nearly always the company's financial success. Provided you're doing your job, problems usually only come about when the company can't meet its bills, and you may be laid off. Although this chapter primarily addresses the problems faced when owning a business, there are legal areas that you, as an employee, should understand.

When You Work for a Business

The prime areas to be aware of when you are working for a company involve situations in which you:

✔ Drive your car on company business;

✔ Sign or are responsible for the checks;

✔ Do something outside the scope of the business;

✔ Do something indicating ownership; or

✔ Act as an officer or member of the board of directors.

Driving Your Car

Whether you're on business or not, an accident caused by you is your personal responsibility. The company becomes liable only in turn due to a legal concept that states an employer is responsible for the actions of its employees who are performing services for the company within the scope of their duties. Injured parties always go after the entity with the deepest pockets, and the business is usually this target. However, if you work for a small business that doesn't have the required, nonowned automobile insurance coverage, then the injured party could look to you to pay the damages (especially since the business is uninsured for this accident).

Even when you're covered by personal automobile insurance, the carrier may not accept coverage if you were doing this for business reasons. For example, you drove your car on sales calls (with the business reimbursing you for your out-of-pocket costs) or dropped the mail off at the post office each night. "It's not clear what insurance companies do as a rule in these cases, although if the damage is great, they'll probably deny coverage," said one agent. Just be sure your business driving is covered by specific insurance, whether it's yours or the company's.

Being Responsible for the Checks

Payroll taxes include federal income taxes and FICA contributions (for example, Social Security and Medicare) withheld from employee paychecks. FICA withholdings must be matched by the employer, and the entire amount of the payroll taxes remitted to the IRS through a depository bank. Many states also require payroll taxes (i.e., state income and unemployment taxes) to be withheld similarly with varying penalties for noncompliance.

Businesses that don't pass withheld payroll taxes on to the government create a real liability for owners and employees alike. "Responsible persons" for such nonpayment are held equally and personally liable by the IRS for the unpaid taxes, including late-payment penalties and interest. This is called the "*100% payroll tax penalty.*" The IRS makes nearly 75,000 100% payroll tax penalty assessments each year, averaging $25,000 in assessments per each responsible person.

Bookkeepers, officers, and owners alike need to be careful, given the strong enforcement of these personal penalties, to fund payroll taxes before paying their suppliers or even the landlord. It makes sense to consult a tax attorney immediately when this situation develops.

An all-too-typical story is continually replayed by businesses struggling to pay their bills. A company has run into cash-flow problems. The owner decides to pay the suppliers to keep the doors open and not to pay the payroll taxes for that quarter. Following the owner's instructions, the financial officer tells the bookkeeper who prepares and signs the checks. The business barely continues to keep operating, and the IRS demands payment of the taxes owed. It makes no difference if the company continues operating, goes bankrupt, or is shut down by the IRS for the nonpayment—the "responsible" individuals will be assessed the 100% penalty.

This IRS penalty, separate from the owed payroll taxes, is equal to 100% of the withheld but unpaid employee deductions. A "responsible person" is anyone who signs the checks, makes the financial decisions, or has the duty under the law to make payroll tax payments. The IRS looks particularly at the owners, officers, and employees with check-signing authority.

In this case, the owner, bookkeeper, and financial officer would all meet the test. Each person would be assessed the 100% penalty. If the owner disappears, and the financial officer is broke, the bookkeeper could be held responsible for paying the entire penalty.

The 100% penalty is not discharged by bankruptcy, is "joint and several" (each person is responsible for the entire amount, regardless of relative fault), and can be assessed against innocent, nonmanagerial employees who meet the test. IRS agents pursue these unpaid taxes fiercely even over delinquent income taxes, maintaining that unpaid payroll taxes are held in trust for the employees with nonpayment ranking near embezzlement.

If you're forced to pay the entire penalty, it's possible to sue the other responsible parties for contribution. However, they may be broke. An attorney should be retained when you are considering these options. But the simplest step is to avoid the problem by being sure that these taxes are paid in the first place.

Doing Something Outside the Scope of the Business

Although a company is responsible for the actions of its employees, what isn't known is that employees are also personally responsible (the company can't be liable if the employee wasn't first at fault). Since companies have the deepest pockets and largest insurance coverage, they will be targeted with the employee looked at secondarily. In order for the business to become liable, the employee must have been working within what's called the scope of the employment.

For example, if an employee drives a personal car without insurance to meet with a company client, then the business would have liability for an accident caused by that employee (as well as that person individually). However, if the worker decided to drive to the supermarket first, then this wouldn't be generally held to be within the scope of the employment, and the employer wouldn't ordinarily be found liable.

Additionally, intentional torts (committing a wrongful act) may or may not bring about company liability, but they will cause personal liability for the *tortfeasor* (another legal word—the person causing the problem). For example, a bouncer at a bar beats up a patron outside after hours. Clearly the bouncer will be personally liable for the patron's injuries; however, attorneys for the injured person would try to hold the bar owner liable (there are more assets), arguing negligent hiring and anything else to pin the damages on the owner. If this happened while the bar was open, then the lawyers would be closer to pinning responsibility on the owner as well.

Individuals, whether working within the scope of their employment or not, incur personal liability for any intentional torts committed such as assault, battery, slander, libel, and even trespass. If your job involves activities that could involve liability when performed as an individual, then be sure that the company (or its insurance) will defend you and pay for any damages.

Sexual harassment deserves special mention. Although any conduct injuring another person shouldn't be done, including sexual harassment, this tort involves personal liability for the guilty employee as well as the company. Although the overwhelming majority of employees, both men and women, don't have any problem with these laws, all need to understand that simply working for a company doesn't mean there won't be some sort of personal liability.

Doing Something Indicating Ownership

If you sign a business contract with your name, without indicating that it's on behalf of the company, it's possible to be held individually responsible for that contract. Although owners always are advised to sign contracts clearly showing that it's done in their capacity with the company (and not as an individual), the same advice is given to employees who are managers or officers.

There is a risk in small companies for employees who own stock but aren't majority owners. It's not always true that a corporation totally protects the shareholders when there are unpaid bills or a lawsuit. A little-known law is aptly called "*piercing the corporate veil.*" If the corporate veil (the corporate shield against individual liability) is pierced, then all shareholders can be held personally liable for the operations of the business. This happens when the business is substantially undercapitalized or not handled as a corporation, among other factors, and when it would be "in the interests of justice" (as determined by the court) to hold the shareholders responsible. Most creditors, however, don't consider this action when trying to get their bills paid—it's expensive litigation. But nothing puts more pressure to settle than suing the individual shareholders along with the company when it's appropriate.

Lenders generally want the owners of a small business to co-sign loans individually, as well as to have the company be responsible for the repayment. This is usually a condition of the loan, and it's a common occurrence when loans are made to small companies. If you own only a small percentage of the stock, then try not to be so included. If you are, then be sure to know what you're signing and that the company has the ability to make the payments.

Being an Officer or on the Board of Directors

Corporate directors and officers are subject to high legal standards. They are charged with running the company for the benefit of the shareholders and must maintain a high standard of good faith and due care. Shareholders can sue officers and directors for damages sustained by the company for a variety of reasons—self-dealing with corporate assets, misuse of corporate funds, illegal pay-offs, excessive compensation, personal gains at the company's expense, and other conflict-of-interest or personal gain situations.

All conflicts of interest must be disclosed to the shareholders and directors in advance of any proposed action, and an interested officer or director can't vote on proposals that involve such a conflict of interest. The potential conflict of interest, when so authorized by the board of directors and/or shareholders, must be documented in the corporate minutes. However, even if the potential conflict of action has been authorized, it still can be challenged by a dissenting board member or shareholder when the action isn't in the company's best interest.

Officers and directors can be sued by suppliers and vendors for fraud and misrepresentations. For example, the officer states the company's "very solvent" when in fact it will declare bankruptcy the next month.

Federal and state statutes can impose even more liability on officers and directors. We have discussed the liability for unpaid payroll taxes when one is held to be a "responsible party." Likewise, a director or officer can be held liable to third parties for hazardous waste problems, security law violations, issuance of "watered-down stock" (stock issued for less than its fair value), discrimination violations, and other matters.

Over the last decades, minority shareholders, public interest groups, and government regulators (such as with the savings and loan scandal) have caused dramatic increases in the numbers of lawsuits filed against officers and directors of privately held and publicly traded companies. If a minority shareholder believes that the value of stock is considerably less valuable now, then a lawsuit against the officers and directors will be considered. The failures to prevent bribery of foreign and governmental officials, illegal campaign contributions, and other activities also result in civil and criminal proceedings.

This doesn't mean you shouldn't serve as an officer or director of your company—there's no gain without risk, but you should be aware that risk exists. Many companies provide for the *indemnification* (an agreement to protect another) of their officers and directors in such situations, in addition to carrying specific liability insurance for this. For example, the board of directors will pass a resolution requiring the company to pay any damages and the legal defense of officers and board members who are sued when acting in good faith in their capacities. The extent of this protection and insurance coverage is limited by state law, as well as by the insurers. This insurance is expensive, may not be available, and may not cover a particular situation. Again, you shouldn't worry needlessly about these problems, but be aware of them, ask questions, and decide what can be done.

When You Own the Business

As the owner, you feel responsible for your business and the law accordingly attaches personal liability in different situations. The clearest case is owning an unincorporated business as a sole proprietorship or as a general partner. The liabilities of that business, whether for debts or operations, are personal liabilities. Claims involving the business do result in a liability on personal assets. If you own an unincorporated business, then you should consult an attorney as to whether it should be incorporated.

Should You Incorporate?

Business organizations basically can take the form of a sole proprietorship, limited partnership, general partnership, joint venture, or corporation. You should determine with your attorney whether the proper form of organization is being used, given the nature of your company's business.

A *sole proprietorship* has maximum flexibility and no operational formalities such as needing to keep minutes, but there's *no* limit on personal liability, no corporate tax benefits (but check further with your accountant), and others can't be involved in sharing ownership. The *joint venture* is treated in many ways as a general partnership. The *general partnership* has few operational formalities and does involve others in the company's ownership, but there's still no limit on personal liability. The *limited partnership* has more formalities than a general partnership with limited liability for the limited partners and is typically used as an investment vehicle in real estate and research and development businesses.

Courts historically have upheld the principle that a corporation is separate from its shareholders, officers, and directors. Shareholders risked their capital investment, but their personal assets were beyond the reach of business-related creditors and lawsuits. Provided the company was sufficiently capitalized and treated as a separate entity, personal assets were shielded from attacks on the corporation (but there are exceptions that are treated later).

The *corporation* has limited liability (given proper operation and the meeting of corporate formalities) with centralized management. It's easier to raise financing, but there are increased formalities (such as keeping proper minutes), paperwork, costs of incorporation, and double taxation on dividends. You'll need to check an accountant to determine the tax implications for whichever form of organization that you choose.

The incorporation decision, versus continuing with a sole proprietorship or general partnership, can turn on whether adequate insurance covering product liabilities is obtainable. If affordable product liability insurance is available, then you may decide not to incorporate. If the company manufactures deep sea diving helmets, for example, then this insurance probably isn't obtainable or is too expensive—incorporating would be a good decision.

The availability of affordable insurance affects the decision of many companies as to the form of organization chosen. For example, large accounting and law firms have organized mini-corporations in the states where they do business, replacing their former partnerships. This is in response to the threat that a large malpractice judgment against one individual partner might become a liability of the remaining partners.

> The incorporation decision depends on factors other than simply minimizing personal liability. There are tax consequences, such as double taxation (corporate profits are taxed, then any dividends passed through to the shareholders are taxed individually) and the extent to which certain deductions can be made. This can be avoided by making a Subchapter S election, provided you meet the requirements, and any decision to incorporate should be made only after discussing all the pros and cons with your accountant.

Should you decide to incorporate, it's important to "act as a corporation" by holding regular board of director meetings; keeping individual assets out of the corporation; signing all contracts in the name of the corporation; keeping separate books and records; and maintaining proper corporate resolutions and minutes. In some states, the presence or absence of adequate corporate minutes is a factor considered when determining whether to "pierce the corporate veil."

The keeping of proper books, records, and minutes is also needed for the IRS. They're especially interested when a company is not being run as a company—the tax penalties when income and assets are allocated back into personal income tax returns can be substantial.

Meeting these requirements can shield personal assets from corporate creditors and in many business liability situations. However, shareholders of closely held corporations (where only a few people own the stock) are beginning to face personal liabilities for federally mandated environmental cleanups, unfunded pension liabilities, and unpaid union dues. We have seen that personal liability attaches for unpaid payroll taxes and with "piercing the corporate veil" attacks. Where shareholders also manage their business, courts are treating shareholder liability as a matter of "fairness" (which is how the court decides).

Even with these attacks, experienced business attorneys still recommend incorporating for personal liability reasons, provided there are no adverse tax consequences. This does make it more difficult for attorneys to attack your personal assets, regardless as to the theory being used. The general principal that personal assets are normally shielded from attacks on the incorporated business still applies, even with the exceptions being carved out in every state.

Your Areas of Liability—Even when Incorporated

Incorporation of your business usually protects your individual assets from lawsuits when you've run into financial problems. It should protect you individually from product liability lawsuits against the company (given no facts allowing a "piercing the corporate veil" argument).

However, even when your business is incorporated, pockets of personal liability are still present. You still incur the liability areas explained above for employees, as you're more than likely also an employee, officer, and director of the company. Of course, when you sign a loan individually, or guarantee anything personally, you're putting personal assets at risk.

This doesn't mean you should worry needlessly about these areas—only know about them, so that they can be dealt with. Being in business involves change and risks for profit, especially when you're on the firing line making the decisions.

The Malpractice and Product Liability Problem

Professionals and other service providers do have a unique problem with malpractice concerns, and this exposure has increased extensively these days. Whether you're an attorney, doctor, veterinarian, beautician, or even a dog groomer, you'll be held responsible for your mistakes. This liability is a personal one, regardless of the existence of a professional corporation—especially in the case of doctors, lawyers, and accountants.

Although this is only fair, professional malpractice now is being alleged even when there hasn't been a mistake—injured parties don't know the difference, feeling they've been victimized, and the malpractice attorney is always looking for business. The basic problem is that the alleged injuries or financial loss can occur years after the service was performed. Although it depends on your viewpoint—whether you're the consumer with a problem or the professional earning a living—each patient or client has the potential to claim later that there's been a problem.

Professionals have three clear approaches to this problem: be selective when taking on new clients, be careful in all aspects of the work, and obtain malpractice insurance (which is expensive and can be hard to obtain). Or find another way to earn a living. As you would expect, the cost of the "sue or be sued" problem and malpractice insurance premiums are usually passed on to the consumer.

The equivalence to professional malpractice for a manufacturing company is product liability. Product liability insurance is at times unobtainable, usually expensive, and has numerous exceptions. Although incorporating can protect your individual assets, it doesn't mean your company couldn't be put out of business by such a lawsuit.

Again, the cost of liability insurance is passed onto the consumer (when such insurance is available), provided the company still wants to be in that business with its litigation risks. As one example, there's hardly any manufacturing of small private planes (two- to four-seat private planes) now because of the liability suits brought and prohibitive cost of product liability insurance. United States companies built over 14,000 single-engine, piston-powered airplanes in 1978, but only 600 in 1990. With plane-crash judgments in excess of $100 million and a successful defense costing upward of $200,000, it is a very lucrative business for the lawyers. The plaintiffs' bar argue strongly that they were protecting the public's interest. They did it so well that U.S. manufacturers are virtually no longer in the business. That's just one example.

Trial lawyers network to determine where the latest product liability actions are being taken in finding more growth areas for their business. Whether it is the manufacture of computers, software, bicycles, mopeds, or automatic door openers, no one's safe. This is a lucrative business for attorneys, and the liability isn't limited to product liability. You name an area of business activity, whether it be manufacturing or service, collections, finance, or employees, and you'll find a litigation specialty for the attorneys. However, you can take preventive actions to cut down the potential of these lawsuits or to have a better case if you are sued.

An Ounce of Prevention

Given the litigation-oriented society we live in, the question becomes what should a business person do? Litigation and its "damage control" create costs over and above the expensive legal fees and settlements. The downtime involved in lawsuits takes time away from marketing and running the business. It disrupts your operations and is bad publicity. There's the risk that confidential company information will become public during the legal process. Litigation is expensive, negative, and costs valuable time.

Working with any attorney over time, you'll discover how risk-oriented that lawyer is. Most business lawyers are conservative, as they don't get sued when a transaction *isn't* made. It's when an executed agreement runs into problems that the attorney receives a call from an unhappy client. You will need to factor in this conservatism when making your decisions.

You don't have to consult an attorney every time there's a legal problem. However, you will need to factor in the legal risks of business decisions when making them. For example, a supplier says he'll sue you if the bill isn't paid. Consulting a lawyer isn't necessary, but you should give your best offer under the circumstances, accepting that a lawsuit is no worse if the offer is turned down.

The best use of the company's legal dollar is the "five-minute phone call" to your attorney asking if there are any legal problems in a proposed company action *before* it's implemented. Whether involving a decision to terminate an employee for off-the-job conduct, a customer's complaint, or a new advertising campaign, preventive law is the most cost-effective use of your legal dollar. It makes sense to consult the lawyer before signing a contract rather than to retain expensive counsel to defend you later over it.

This doesn't mean you won't be sued—lawsuits can be brought for any reason and not necessarily for good ones. Attorneys are always looking for the right case, and "right" many times means they can receive a substantial settlement in lieu of your incurring even higher legal defense costs. However, not being at fault means you don't ante up as much money should you be sued, and the odds of winning become that much greater.

The Unsolved Business Problem

Litigation indicates an unsolved business problem. It's a red flag indicating that something is wrong with your business. For example, an increase in breach of warranty disputes and lawsuits is signaling that your products aren't performing as advertised. Dealing with such disputes by rationalizing that the company is in a lawsuit-happy business isn't the answer. You need to determine *why* the disputes are occurring.

Litigation with an ex-employee isn't always the result of the worker being disgruntled and trying to get back at the company. It could result from poor management policies, subtle prejudices by your managers, or not having an escape valve in place for your employees to air their grievances. It's necessary to look for the business reasons behind your disputes and then solve the underlying business problems.

Preventing Disputes

Preventing disputes in the first place is a cost-efficient strategy in controlling your legal costs. It's better to run your company in a way that can avoid the *unnecessary* disputes and problems that end up in lawsuits. This isn't to say that risks shouldn't be taken when making business decisions, as a company can't grow without taking aggressive moves. However, there are ways to lessen the risks of wasteful lawsuits, and these can simply be a matter of common sense.

The Areas

There are various places to center your attention in getting a handle on this. The prime legal-related areas are: those matters related to the business organization; the way business is done by the shareholders, officers and directors; product liability considerations; how the company handles its contracts; employee management; dealing with the company's lenders and investors; protecting trade secrets

172

and confidential information; establishing credit and collection policies; and managing taxes. These are discussed in turn.

Business Organization

The general area of business organization involves more than how the business is first structured, including also whether the company has secured the necessary permits and licenses. This means maintaining your corporate formalities, acting in good faith in any dealings as an officer, and signing all contracts in your corporate capacity—all previously discussed. Paying attention to these details can make your business life less complicated.

The Required Licenses and Permits

If you're in the environmental or hazardous waste business, then you already know the complications that can arise when the necessary licenses haven't been obtained (including getting them in the first place). Further, in many states the lack of a proper license or permit prohibits your business from suing for services rendered or even defending against lawsuits. For example, not having a proper contractor's license when it is required can stop your ability to sue over a contract in many states even if you did all the work and the monies are still owed you. The need to check whether your business has all the required licenses needed for operating includes more than business activities—a federal tax I.D. number, state sales tax permit (if a retailer), fictitious business name statement, and more may be required.

The Proper Form of Organization

Having the right form of business organization in the beginning was important enough that we discussed it already. Unnecessary problems can be avoided by paying attention to this area.

Restrictions on Stock Transfers

If your business is a privately held company, then be sure adequate restrictions are in place on the ability of the shareholders to dispose of their stock. Otherwise, they will be free to sell or transfer their stock to people you don't want in your business. For example, a shareholder in a small company could sell shares to a competitor or someone who's trying to take over your business. The way to avoid this is by the company having a "*first right of refusal*" to purchase all stock back in the event of any transfer including divorce, termination of employment, or death. If the company decided not to buy the stock under this right, then the shareholder would be free to sell the shares as designated. An attorney should be consulted as to whether a shareholder's agreement (providing for this and other matters such as valuation) should be in place before any stock is issued.

Shareholders, Officers, and Directors

If you represent the majority shareholder group, then don't pay excessive salaries to yourself and other key executives. Don't sell assets in "deals" to majority shareholders, officers, and directors for inadequate compensation, or self-deal in business activities to the detriment of the minority shareholders. This only ends up in litigation. The majority shareholders have a duty to act in good faith to protect the minority shareholders' financial interests. Use the golden rule in dealing with all shareholders.

Not taking advantage of partners and minority shareholders is the only way to conduct a business profitably over the long-term. This isn't a lesson in morality. Just think what you would do if you were taken advantage of similarly—you would also use private investigators, retain "pit bull" attorneys, and wage all-out war.

Match Investors with Your Business

Be selective when accepting any investor in your business. The argument is heard frequently that "I need the cash now; I'll worry about what they want later." Later always comes sooner than expected. The investor's expectations should be matched with whether the company and its operations can meet those expectations. If the investor is conservative and wants current income, then don't tell the investor that your start-up venture will do this. The costs of attorneys, lawsuits, and court costs will outweigh the use of the investor's capital.

Product Liability

Product liability law suits have been increasing faster than most other areas of litigation. Companies are being forced to trim product lines and products simply to avoid bearing the brunt of excessive damage awards. The litigation explosion has eliminated or damaged entire industries ranging from the manufacture of small private planes to breast implants, tampons, heart implants, asbestos products, and others. Although it's constantly debated how much of the litigation was socially responsible, the waves of lawsuits have affected other companies and industries not at fault.

The Bad News

In just a few decades the law changed from "buyer beware" to "let the seller beware." The negligence of the consumer in most cases isn't a bar to liability. The legal theories used in product liability cases involve negligence (failure to use reasonable care), breach of warranty (both on the expressed and implied promises made as to the use of the product), failure to warn, and strict liability (that the resulting damage or injury occurred is evidence enough). These theories apply whether a service or a product is involved.

A defendant can be held liable for an injury if there's a failure to warn of the risks in using the product, even if the product isn't negligently manufactured or designed. A manufacturer or even a distributor has a duty to warn when it knows about a particular danger or if the product could become hazardous when being reasonably used. Any warning must be adequate to identify the danger, the ways to avoid that risk, and the extent of the risk if these steps aren't taken.

The Good News

The following are all advisable positive steps to take: reviewing customer complaints and changing the product or manufacturing process; consulting governmental agencies as to the specific warnings that should be on your products before there's a lawsuit; purchasing product liability insurance (when available and affordable); putting into place a system to manage product claims and complaints (i.e., a company ombudsman to handle such complaints, rather than ignoring them) as a safety valve; and always "warning when in doubt."

If your business has a sufficient product liability exposure, consider retaining an attorney and a product expert before there's a substantial claim. It would make sense, if you can afford it, to conduct a review as to your product and manufacturing processes from product liability standards. The expert could analyze your product and manufacturing process, along with reviewing consumer complaints, and give practical advice on what should be changed. Your attorney could take this information and change the warnings, express warranties (stating that the facts or representations made are true), and implied warranties *before* you end up in a "bet your company" lawsuit.

Let's say you're manufacturing a new line of children's furniture and begin receiving complaints that the pieces fall apart under certain conditions. Such complaints are more than potential legal problems, as they also involve your losing business and customer goodwill. You would at this point consider redesigning the product and its production, at the same time creating warnings as to when certain uses wouldn't be appropriate. You would be reviewing your product brochures, as well.

The extent to which such work is privileged should be decided by counsel prior to performing a legal audit. In various states, the extent to which a problem was identified and/or written recommendations weren't followed can be used as evidence that the company knew about the product defects and failed to take proper action.

Business Contracts

You and your managers need a basic understanding of contract principles if you are spending any time with significant contracts, whether involving suppliers or customers. In fact, business contract disputes are the largest single category of lawsuits filed in federal courts. See Chapter 6 for a further treatment of contracts.

Contract Basics

To form a valid business contract, you need basically an offer, acceptance, consideration or value, and enforceability. Contracts based on fraud (your salesman tells your customer the product is waterproof and it isn't), mutual mistake (both of you thought it was waterproof), and "unconscionable terms" (the finance charge in your finance contract is 5% per month), for example, are unenforceable contracts. Any acceptance that modifies the original offer with new or different terms becomes usually a counteroffer, and that must be accepted by the first-offering party without change in order to have a valid contract (but the Uniform Commercial Code (UCC), as discussed below, can bring about different results in commercial transactions).

An offer may be oral (subject to limitations) or in writing and should be restricted specifically to what's being contracted for. What's written in a letter, an advertisement, or on a slip of paper can end up as an enforceable contract against your company. An acceptance can be either oral or by written acceptance, by performance of the action requested, or by the other party's conduct, which indicates an acceptance. You can rescind an offer before it's accepted, but not afterwards.

As can be seen from this very abbreviated discussion, problems can unintentionally occur, as you're negotiating back and forth on an important deal. A simple telephone conversation with your attorney over what's different or unique, before signing, can help prevent costly lawsuits. You could put into place a rule, for example, that any contract over an assumed value, let's say of $10,000, is discussed with your attorney unless clearly covered by your standard sales contract.

What you do depends on your type of business. If the company owned a chain of retail ice cream stores, only vendor contracts would be centered on. If your company manufactured heavy equipment or electric transformers, every sales contract and most vendor contracts would be discussed in advance with your attorney. This isn't designed to give business to your company attorney—it's to take more business away from your defense attorney.

Never Do Oral Contracts

All contracts should be in writing to avoid misunderstandings, enforceability problems, and the operation of the Statute of Frauds (see Chapter 6). No matter how clear one's memory is, everyone forgets details over time and this leads to problems.

The Uniform Commercial Code

The Uniform Commercial Code (UCC), enacted by all the states except Louisiana (this state omits certain provisions, and its format is different) has substantially modified general contract law when commercial transactions are involved, ranging from the enforceability of business transactions to product liability considerations due to a seller's warranties and representations. Each state has made its own changes or adaptations to the UCC, but what's important is to recognize that a different set of laws affects business transactions.

For example, contracts involving the sale of goods between merchants (those who normally deal in such goods for a living) with a price of $500 or more aren't enforceable unless there's some writing sufficient to indicate that a contract has been made. This can be the same as when individuals have agreed to a private sale (i.e., your friend agrees to sell you her car). However, all the important terms don't need to be included to have an enforceable agreement between merchants, and the writing doesn't need to be signed by the party being held responsible. Given the practice of making deals by telephone, then sending a written confirmation, the UCC allows for a *valid confirmation even when it is not signed* by the party being held responsible. This is contrary to ordinary contract law and the laws governing transactions between private parties.

You need to be careful with business contracts and the UCC. Since business contracts over $500 don't need all the essential terms in writing to be enforced, such as the price or time for performance, a court is permitted to determine what those omitted "details" are. Be sure to include all the essential terms in your business dealings, as you don't want the court to imply them (or even be in court). The essential terms that can be read into your agreement, if absent, are the price, time for delivery, the place and manner of delivery, the buyer's right of inspection, the seller's right to cure nonconforming products, the duty of the buyer on rejected goods, the right of the seller in the event of the buyer's insolvency, the allocation of the risk of loss to the product, and warranties. This is quite a list—so be sure everything's in writing with all the areas covered.

Business transactions are treated differently, because there's usually a background of previous dealings that indicate the price, time for performance, and other essentials. If a used car is sold between private parties, then ordinary contract law applies, because you don't have such a history of prior dealings. If the same car is sold by a used car salesman, then the UCC applies. Different rules for commercial transactions under the UCC also exist when rendering services, selling securities, or lending or borrowing money.

Product Warranties

A product when sold is subject to express and implied warranties. Express warranties are what the seller explicitly states to the buyer. Additionally, every product sold includes other warranties that are implied by law, such as the implied warranties of merchantability (setting certain minimum standards of performance and acceptability) and fitness (that it's adequate for a particular purpose). If your business sells goods or services, then you'll want to limit the effectiveness of these warranties. If your company is the purchaser, then you'll want these warranties to be as broad and strong as possible.

Express warranties can be limited by reducing what's said or written about the product or service in your sales brochures. Implied warranties can be limited by allowing the buyer a full inspection before purchase or a trial use with an "as is" sale, among other solutions. Your attorney should research the applicable law to determine what's most advantageous for your business. The state of present market conditions and competition may govern what you do in this area, but you should be aware of it.

The "Battle of the Forms"

Business agreements are usually written down on preprinted order or sales forms. One company sends its form sales agreement to a customer, but the customer sends back its acceptance on its own form. As both forms have different provisions protecting each, the question is always whose form controls. Generally, under the UCC, the one who sends the first form wins.

However, the UCC has a different rule for transactions between merchants, whereby new terms added in the acceptance become part of the contract, unless that new term materially alters the contract, the other party objects, or the first sent form expressly limits the acceptance to the terms of its offer. Each transaction needs to be looked at differently, given the different facts in each. You might set up a minimum contract dollar limit for your employees before any consultation with an attorney is allowed over the "battle of the forms."

The "We Can't Perform" Problem

A seller is generally not liable when it can't perform a contract because of unforeseen problems that occurred after the signing. For example, a storm wrecks the plant, and the products can't be manufactured. However, just because a contract is more difficult to perform doesn't allow the company to say "we can't perform." If the company entered into a bad contract, the courts will not let the company out of it just because it will lose money. Be watchful, as your employees or managers might say anything in order to get out of a bad contract that they had negotiated.

An installment contract requires that goods or services be delivered in specific amounts over time (such as rebuilding your plant) or in separate lots (those shipments of electronic components) that are to be accepted one by one. A manager who has entered into a bad deal may be tempted to repudiate the entire contract if one lot or installment is bad. The general rule is a customer may reject any lot that doesn't conform to the agreement *only* if the defect substantially impairs that lot. However, if the supplier gives adequate assurances that the defect in that lot will be cured as to the remaining orders, then the customer can't reject the ones that follow. Thus, the company can't use the first bad lot to get out of a contract it doesn't like (for example, if it finds a cheaper supplier). The company will have to buy out that contract, renegotiate it, or make a business decision to break it *after* knowing what the law and contract damages could be.

If the seller says "I won't do it," then the buyer has certain rights. The company may pursue its legal remedies (i.e., sue for specific performance of the contract or for damages), take steps to find another seller, or wait for a "commercially reasonable time" for the seller to perform. Under the UCC the buyer doesn't usually have to mitigate (or reduce) its potential damages by finding a substituted product or vendor (as opposed to general contract law), but it's a good idea.

A judgment for damages is the usual award. It's rare for a company to want the other party to perform as agreed, since there already were problems. Most sue for their delays, the problems, and the difference between the contract cost and substituted costs. However, specific products that can't be obtained from other suppliers, such as designer jeans and real estate, still will be wanted and can be specifically enforced. Service and employment contracts (such as with actors, actresses, designers, or your vice-president of finance) won't be enforced to force them to work for you, if they don't want to. However, if they steal customer lists or engage in unfair competition, many courts will enjoin (or stop) them from working for others. An unjustified refusal to follow the terms of such a contract, moreover, may subject the employee or person to considerable monetary damages.

Develop an Understanding

It's helpful to develop an understanding of basic business contract law if you deal with it every day. Your time is valuable, being spent usually in putting out the daily fires that happen. However, knowing when to let a deal go through as it is and when to call an attorney for a quick, telephone conference is an art. At least do this for the important, infrequent, or complex problems.

Employee Management

Employment litigation has become very troublesome for businesses and companies, rivaling product liability and contractual litigation. For example, discrimination cases can be filed under state law and/or with federal and state administrative agencies; these actions have accelerated in the past years with three out of every four discrimination cases filed alleging discrimination in firing. However, there are a number of preventive rules that can be adopted to mitigate this.

Use Specific, Objective, Job-Related Standards in Hiring

When an employee leaves or is terminated, potential legal problems are created that relate back to the personnel practices used when *hiring* that individual. Promises that "your job is secure" could form the basis for litigation alleging an implied employment contract, and employee policy manuals should be reviewed to eliminate any wording that could imply such a contract.

Employees may be hired only when using objective and "lawful" criteria—unintentional discrimination with "protected classes" will cause headaches. Clear job-related standards when hiring must be present to prevent a disgruntled employee from using unclear or "cloudy" hiring practices as additional proof that discrimination was the reason for being fired. These standards cannot have the effect of precluding any class, including the handicapped under the Americans with Disabilities Act (ADA), from performing a job that in fact could be performed by that class.

Any hiring and testing criteria must be specifically related to the tasks that need to be completed by the applicant. Only ask for "necessary" information on job application sheets, information that is reasonably related to the job tasks needing to be performed. Test only for the job completion essentials, and don't test for anything you don't need. Avoid general knowledge and IQ tests when at all possible. If information is needed for administrative reasons, such as for medical insurance and benefits, ask for it after the hiring.

What this means is that you need to determine exactly what job-related skills are important for an applicant to have. For example, if you are hiring a word-processing operator, then the strength and even weight of that person might not be as important as when you're hiring for a warehouse position.

Applicants that aren't hired should be treated with courtesy. Be specific about the reason(s) for not hiring, so the applicant doesn't draw the conclusion that discrimination was the reason. For example, tell the applicant that the typing test results failed to meet your criteria or that the employee didn't have the required job experience. Don't say "There was no opening," when in fact there was.

Use Written Warnings

A written, reasonable policy should be adopted stating what an employee can or cannot do when on the job. Be specific that drinking, using drugs, sexually harassing, passing confidential information, and unsatisfactory work performance won't be tolerated. Use a written system of warnings, probation, suspension, and then termination, for unsatisfactory job performance and prohibited on-the-job conduct. Any discipline taken should be written down, along with any notes made by you or your managers, then placed immediately into the employee's file.

The more proper written evidence of a worker's problems and noncooperation, the better and easier it is to defend a lawsuit. You don't want to be in the uncomfortable position before a jury where it's only your word against that of an unemployed, broke ex-employee.

Keep Good Written Files

You should conduct periodic evaluations of all employees and retain good records, whether an employee leaves in good standing or is terminated. Experienced litigators maintain that the presence or absence of an extensive, written file is the critical difference between who wins or loses. Employers frequently argue that they warned an employee on various occasions that their job performance wasn't to company standards, placed that person on probation, and then terminated only after these procedures. The employee argues the firing was illegal because it was motivated by discrimination—the employee's age, sex, race, or some prohibited classification—or whatever it takes to win. The party that wins is the one who has the best documentation and can prove its case.

Use "Escape Valves"

A formal grievance system and/or complaint system should be established for confidential use by all employees. Reasonable suggestions and complaints can be listened to, then addressed, before there's a lawsuit. Employee meetings and even the appointment of an "ombudsman" who acts as an employee counselor can be used as listening posts. It's necessary to establish a system to hear grievances and correct mistakes made by supervisors and managers before an attorney files a lawsuit for an employee who quit because no one was listening.

Your Employees Are an Asset

In a day and age of layoffs and contract workers (short-term workers who have no benefits), owners can lose sight of the fact that employees are human assets of the business. Treat and manage employees as you would like to be treated if working there. Managers should be instructed to be consistent and fair in their handling of employee problems. Workers should be given a second chance if they've "screwed up." An employee, unless guilty of blatant dishonesty or misconduct, should receive a written warning first, be counseled on ways to improve, then given a second chance. Although the law encourages these good faith reactions by a company, it also makes sense to work with someone who's known.

Show courtesy when firing an employee—there's no need to create further ill will by rubbing the worker's face in it. However, be sure you and your managers document *every* finding, warning, and discipline that's been given. All warnings should be in writing, and keep all employee files current.

Your business should keep up communications with your workers, not just by the annual summer picnic. Employees should be kept current as to your business' progress and developments. Information concerning important changes should come to the attention of your work force as soon as possible, because change (such as new shifts, cutbacks, new products, or a new location) causes anxiety and distrust when not explained properly and in time.

Line supervisors should be supported in their decisions and also kept informed on what management is doing. They should be properly trained in the handling of employee problems. Competitive wage and salary structures should be in place for employees, along with a motivational system of raises and bonuses. A consistent evaluation system should be in place allowing feedback to all workers on what needs to done for improvement.

Use Good Cause When Firing

The old law of being able to terminate at will for any reason is dead, extensively eroded by the many exceptions to where a "fair and honest reason" or "good cause" (having a legitimate business reason) is becoming the law in many states for all intents and purposes. The company always has the right to terminate or lay off workers when it has financial problems, needs to cut back overhead, or trim production (however, federal law requires notice to be given in various situations). Off-the-job conduct generally isn't considered to be adequate reason for termination

But Don't Hesitate to Fire the Troublemaker

There's an implied covenant of good faith and fair dealing in all contracts, including those involving employment and personnel matters—but don't hesitate to fire the troublemaker. Despite the risk of problems and lawsuits from unhappy workers, fire them immediately. Retaining a disgruntled employee only causes dissension and problems with your work force, as others will wonder why the company's letting that person "get away with it." Terminate those who don't do their part, but be sure you've documented the file.

unless the employee deals with the public. State laws differ, so consult an attorney before terminating any employee for such conduct.

There are several strategies to consider when laying off workers—out counseling, avoiding favorable recommendations (when a lawsuit is suspected), requiring a release for any severance pay (but this can't be done for wages that are already owing for service rendered), and requiring in your employment manual that all disputes be mediated first (see Chapter 16). Even when fired, if workers believe they are being treated as human beings, lawsuits can be headed off before the attorneys begin knocking on your door.

Have a Written Personnel Policy in Place

A stated policy on all personnel matters must be in writing, and these policies can run from 20 or more to over 100 pages for large corporations. Specific prohibitions should be listed for conduct deemed unacceptable, such as sexual harassment, unsatisfactory job performance, the use of drugs and alcohol on company time, along with other prohibited conduct. It should discuss the company's grievance system and early warning devices, along with reasonable discipline for violations that lead to termination. Benefits, pay, vacation scheduling, leaves, absences, holidays, and the work week, among many other provisions, should be listed.

Employees have a right to know the conditions of their employment and what can or can't be done, as well as the received benefits. This written policy forms the defense that any discipline or termination of a worker was consistently applied against known and fair employment policies. It can form the contract and provisions that the worker accepts when deciding to work for the company.

An expensive attorney isn't needed to create a personnel policy from scratch—contact your local Chamber of Commerce, friends who also own their business, a manufacturer's or trade association, or even a nearby book store (buy a personnel book with forms). Be sure that all provisions are up to date, and comply with your state's laws before any use. If there are doubts, then send it to an attorney for review, but be sure to receive a not-to-exceed estimate.

As state and federal laws change frequently in this area, your personnel manual needs to be updated by an annual review or as laws are changed. Seminars are given by local business and trade associations. These meetings are not only usually cheap, but also distribute materials that can be duplicated and placed into personnel binders. Several business owners also can decide to share an attorney's review of one personnel policy and then copy the changes.

Wages and Hours

All federal and state requirements covering minimum wages, when overtime is payable, and rules regulating work conditions need to be known. The penalties and problems when state agencies (who always seem to favor the employee) get wind of violations are well in excess of the cost of a phone call or the time required for a manager to stay current.

A Word about Sexual Harassment

Workers greatly underreport sexual harassment problems. A senior executive who had experienced sexual harassment in her career explained, "You think no one will believe you, and there's the fear that your career will be set back. Some women I've talked to pass it off, saying the harasser was just a jerk—it's easier that way. But if you lose your job, then you think about it again." As employees are subjected to this, their opinions of managers, jobs, and companies decline greatly. Such cases also present one of the great growth areas for lawyers.

Federal and various state statutes prohibit sexual harassment, and there are two types—first, when any term of working is conditioned on the employee's giving in to another's demands for sexual favors (i.e., a manager demands sex from a subordinate for a promotion); second, when unwelcomed conduct unreasonably interferes with the worker's job performance or creates a hostile or offensive workplace (i.e., exposure to sexual jokes, slurs, or showing pictures of sexual activity).

Sexual conduct is "unwelcomed" when the employee hasn't invited the conduct and regards it as undesirable or offensive. The courts consider whether the wrongdoing was seen or could be proved by others, invited by the harassed worker's sexually-oriented conduct, and followed by a complaint at the same time as the unwelcomed conduct. This means that you have to consider all the facts to determine if sexual harassment was present. That won't be easy, especially when it's only one person's word against another's.

Unwelcomed sexual conduct is "hostile" if the effect alters the conditions of employment and creates an abusive working environment. In determining if the conduct was hostile, courts weigh: if the harasser was a supervisor; others joined in the activities; the harassment was directed at more than one person; and whether the type of conduct was verbal, visual, physical, or all three.

An employer can minimize sexual harassment claims by: preparing and distributing a written, reasonable policy against sexual harassment; following that written policy; confidentially informing the involved employees about the results of an investigation; and disciplining the harassing employee, the severity proportional to the severity of the sexually harassing conduct. The written policy should: state that sexual harassment is prohibited; identify at least two employees in the company to whom to direct complaints; assure everyone that the employer won't penalize anyone who complains about harassment; and state that the employer will

Both the employer and employee are liable for sexual harassment. The employer under federal law is strictly liable in such cases when the employer knew or should have known about the sexually harassing conduct. State laws differ widely, but they will govern if there's a stricter standard. Substantial punitive damages, from $50,000 to $300,000, lost wages, benefits, and attorney fees will be assessed when such conduct is proven.

promptly, thoroughly, and confidentially investigate all sexual harassment claims, promptly resolving them with appropriate administrative action.

Companies that diligently enforce such programs get results, even more than putting legal protection in place. A female career manager with a large manufacturing company observed "The men have certainly changed since that [antiharassment] policy. They're very, very careful about what they say. It's easier to fire people these days over sexual harassment than for any other reason." A fine balance, however, should be maintained between the accuser and the accused to be sure that you're being fair and not taking the easy way out.

The problem isn't that your workers always try to sexually harass others (some people get upset, no matter what happens or is done), but it's also that they have sexual affairs that don't work out and involve boss-subordinate roles. When they breakup, subordinates now feel uneasy about their work relationship. The explosion hits when that worker is laid off or fired, regardless of reason, and complains all too frequently that the layoff or firing is due to what has now become sexually harassing conduct by the ex-lover. The contingent-fee lawyer is now happy to argue about the boss's sleazy conduct when it was only in fact caused by a broken relationship.

The easy rule is to prohibit or discourage office romances. But they'll continue over time, as long as opposites attract one another. This isn't just a male problem, given the numbers of women entering managerial positions and reported cases involving female supervisors. When an office romance comes to your attention, then tactfully warn both about the consequences. Write down your observations, putting a copy in the file of both, then make a fast call to your attorney.

Lenders and Investors

A business should cultivate its banking relationship and obtain lines of credit before it needs the money, making a clear, documented request with accurate financials in all proposals. The temptation to hide damaging facts when looking for financing does create greater problems down the road. It's easier than people think, especially after the savings and loan scandal, to look behind the numbers and proposals—when things quickly continue down hill, there can be no question about the committed fraud. When a lender brings a lawsuit for payment and damages based on fraud, it usually includes suing the company officials and directors who were involved, and this liability is personal.

A lender can proceed separately against individual guarantees, as well as the corporate promise to pay. All loan documents should be reviewed prior to signing; retain your attorney if they are unnecessarily complex or complicated. This can save a lot of grief later.

Don't *ever* make a guarantee to any investor on any return of investment or when the money will be returned. All material facts should be disclosed in writing, and reasonable care taken to select an investor who's compatible with the company's goals and personalities. This also minimizes later disputes.

Remember that federal and state security laws apply every time you arrange investor financing. Every security (whether it's a note, stock, limited partnership interest, or option) must be registered with the SEC and/or the appropriate state regulatory agency unless there's an exemption to such registration. Should you issue such securities, then the failure to comply with these regulations automatically subjects you to liability, regardless of fault. An attorney specializing in this area should be consulted prior to soliciting any investments in your business.

Protecting Your Secrets

Protecting and preserving a company's trade secrets and confidential information can be best summarized by "a good defense is the best offense." It doesn't help to bring a lawsuit to preserve your trade secrets when those secrets and confidences are already out.

Preserving Your Trade Secrets

You and your managers should know what's in your files and how important these documents are. The most sensitive documents—customer lists, operating secrets, names of suppliers, trade secrets, and what you don't want your competition to know—should be kept in separate files, marked "Confidential and Privileged. Don't Copy or Remove." These files should be kept in secured, locked file cabinets.

Confidential materials shouldn't be mixed with the company's everyday files. This indication of intent, establishing what's confidential to your company, can persuade a court to not allow a competitor access into what are your most important files via a lawsuit.

Written procedures should regulate who has access to these files and when—everyone else should stay away. Of course, confidential files shouldn't be circulated generally, and you do want confidential files to be shredded or destroyed, not simply tossed out by the janitor. Confidential information should be made available only on a "need to know" basis.

Violations should be grounds for discipline, suspension, or termination, depending on the severity of the infraction. For example, a worker who is handing over sensitive documents to the competition, after the company has taken all steps to recover what has been lost, should be summarily dismissed and possibly sued. Preserving the confidences of trade secrets and confidential information should be made a covenant in all your employment agreements.

Patents and Copyrights

It isn't always advisable to incur the expense and time needed to patent an invention. There's the danger information will be disclosed simply by the patent application. Patent reviews can take time (two years or more), are expensive, and require the use of a patent lawyer, not to mention the filing fees.

If the market for a product is small, the cost/benefit ratio may not be favorable to patent it. However, if you already have secured patent rights, then you need a system that monitors the company's licensing or patent agreements, pointing out the deadlines when patent fees need to be paid. All goods should be appropriately marked with the patent logo. Consult an experienced patent attorney before charging to the courthouse to sue a defendant who apparently infringed on your patent rights (such rights and the law can be ambiguous).

A copyright is secured at the time the work is created. The author owns the copyright unless it was a work for hire or agreed otherwise. A copyright is lost unless the work has been reduced to something tangible (you can read, see, or touch it) and the proper copyright notice (©, author's name, and year of first publication) has been printed on all works and products. Copyrighting by using the proper copyright notice on all products and registering your copyright with the U.S. Library of Congress in Washington, D.C., will protect your tangible ideas. This registration isn't a condition to obtaining a copyright, although it does make your claim a public record, among other advantages.

Credit and Collection

It does make a difference whether you're trying to avoid payment or trying to get it. Checking credit references, obtaining personal guarantees, setting proper limits on the credit available to any customer, and providing for the debtor to pay the legal costs when you are collecting outstanding balances are techniques frequently employed. A company should be careful not to hound a debtor or adopt abusive collection efforts that are prohibited by law. A construction or building trade business should always use mechanic lien rights (charges against the property allowing foreclosure) when available under state law.

More businesses these days are viewing the collection of an owing receivable as a joint problem between the company and its debtor (as we have seen, the legal system can be of little help when the customer can't pay). If the debtor says it doesn't have the money, then say you'll work with that customer. One idea is to tell such customers that you'll collect *their* problem receivables. In return, you get all of the proceeds to service your delinquent account until it is paid in full.

Taxes

There are a number of considerations on federal and state taxes for companies that are beyond the scope of this book. However, be sure all federal payroll taxes (income tax withholdings, FICA, and FUTA) and the equivalent state payroll taxes are paid, before you pay any suppliers, the landlord, or even your attorney.

In many states, the failure to file corporate income tax forms and/or to pay owing taxes allows the state to void or suspend the corporation's status. This means your company can't file a lawsuit or defend against one. One experienced litigator, with an exceptionally good plaintiff's case, asked the company's owner if all of the required taxes had been paid. The owner said "yes" when the answer should have been "no." At the beginning of the proceedings, the defense showed the surprised attorney and judge that the state had suspended the company's charter (incorporation) for not paying the owing state taxes. In this particular state, such a corporation was treated as if it didn't exist. The unhappy attorney was forced to listen to 5 days of testimony by the defense, not being allowed to present any evidence in return. The verdict was quickly returned against the company, including an award of substantial attorney fees.

Controlling Legal Expenses

The Legal Function Isn't that Different

Another prong in the attack is simply controlling your company's legal expense when an attorney's time is required. Business owners, whether they employ in-house counsel or not, seem to view attorneys and their use as being somehow different from other management decisions. The law is looked upon as having a capital "L." It is this attitude that results in escalating legal expenses and unfortunate "bet your company" problems.

The legal function of any company must be treated the same way as you decide to fund research and development or hire an advertising firm for a new, untried campaign. The legal function *is* subject to managerial planning and control, not the other way around. The process of the attorneys telling you what the law is and what to do for a win must be changed. Owners, managers, and even in-house counsel must assume responsibility for the proper management of the company's legal functions–just as is done with marketing, financing, production, and cost control. The steps to be taken with attorneys are the same as with any service vendor, whether an advertising agency, consultant, or a bank.

First, You Identify the Problem Let's say, for example, that your company's sales are going down. The employees and managers are giving various reasons, but you know the general reasons. It could be that problems are happening with your products, competitive pressures, the marketing, or some combination of these factors. As you look closely into the problem, you decide better advertising and lower supplier costs are needed.

It's the same with the legal function. If you're spending too much time with attorneys and the legal costs are out of control, then you'll change attorneys, how you do business, or some combination of the two.

Second, You Determine with Whom to Talk To shape up and solve your identified problems, you'll first consider the recommendations of managers and employees, then interview several advertising agencies and suppliers. You want the best service at the lowest cost, and changes will be made. The same should be done with your attorneys. Given the numbers of law firms and lawyers looking for work in a price-competitive market, your company should be securing names, interviewing them, and determining the best mix of cost, service, and experience. See Chapter 5 for further details on finding and selecting the right attorney. Chapter 18 can be consulted as to finding the right attorney when you've been sued.

Third, You Enter into a Contract for What's Required After interviewing the suppliers and/or advertising agencies, you may call back two or three for a final presentation. After that feedback, the company enters into written contracts that specifically outline what services are to be provided, at what cost, by when, by whom, and with a specific budget that won't be exceeded without company approval. Why not do the same with your lawyers?

Attorneys, even state bar associations, provide standardized fee agreements. As a matter of fact, the legal profession is now informing its members that value billing (fixed fees, for example) needs to be considered by law firms in pricing their services in a cost-competitive market. The problem is that many companies haven't used the market power they do have.

Fourth, You Monitor Performance You or your managers will monitor the performances and costs of the selected vendors or agencies. The company *tells* them how their services compare against the goals and objectives of the contracts. You meet with them to work out changes. They should also know that the contract or scope of the work can't be changed without your consent.

The same should be done with attorneys. Large companies not only are requiring very detailed and extensive litigation plans and budgets in advance of any work being performed, but they're requiring the law firms to bid even for litigation work on a discounted or fixed-fee basis. Bidding contests, called "beauty contests" by the not-too-happy law firms who are doing this, are used by large- and medium-sized companies to control their legal costs.

Fifth, You Change What's Not Working When monitoring a vendor's work and costs, decisions are made as to whether to continue working with that vendor or what changes need to be made. If a vendor isn't working out, you hire one whose work meets your specifications, bring the work to be done inside the company, or modify the way you do business. For example, you change the design of your product or its manufacturing process so it can be produced more cheaply. The same approach applies with attorneys.

An advertising agency isn't allowed to get away with saying it had no idea the campaign would cost so much. Why should attorneys be any different? Although lawyers can't guarantee success (nor can advertising agencies), they can quantify their services and be held accountable for their work and the costs. The legal function is your responsibility to control, not the attorney's, and it *is* your business.

Several Rules

There are concepts and rules to follow in managing your company's overall legal expenses.

Educating Your Managers Is Cost Effective Your managers, officers, and employees are key in meeting your company's goals and objectives. It's not possible for any one person, or a few senior executives, to achieve the company's goals by themselves—this involves the focus of all your employees. The more understanding you and your managers have about the company's legal exposure and problems, the costs, and ways to keep them under control, the easier it is to attain this control. For example, consider holding company seminars to discuss the common legal problems, what to do about them, and how to hold the expenses down. Invite your attorneys so that they can comment on what can be done.

Start with Your Existing Attorneys Your present attorneys have some knowledge about your company and its legal problems. Whether you're dissatisfied or not with their performance or bills, the existing attorneys should be interviewed first regarding their suggestions as to how you can cut your legal costs and stick to a legal cost-control budget. Be straightforward with your approach—you're looking for the attorneys who will work with you, and they get your continued business in return.

Working with the Right Attorney as a Team Is a Necessity Controlling your legal expenses isn't an adversarial proceeding with your attorneys. It requires that law firm's understanding of your business goals and objectives and a joint commitment to reducing legal expenses in a long-term relationship. Your law firm's cooperation is as important as your participating directly in the legal decisions that the law firm makes concerning your business.

Law Firms Are Accepting (although Reluctantly) Alternative Billing Approaches It was common years ago for a company to farm out all its legal work to one large, reputable firm that would bill the company by the hour with hazy or no explanations as to what generated that bill. No more. Companies today are writing specific, detailed scope and descriptions of the legal tasks to be completed, sending the work out for bid, demanding budgets and even fixed fees. Today's cost-conscious environment demands that controls be placed on the legal function.

Rather than being hit with unpleasant surprises by the open-ended, hourly rate of partners, associates, and paralegals at a law firm's basic rates, clients are demanding alternative billing measures from law firms, especially during the last several years. Discounts can be negotiated from the firm's stated rate. Additionally, fixed fees, blended rates, modified contingent fees, and other billing approaches are being used (see Chapter 12). Convince your attorneys to use value billing instead or find another attorney. This is the clear trend these days.

Value Isn't Necessarily What's Cheapest Remember what's most cost-effective at the moment doesn't necessarily mean it's the cheapest over time, especially in important matters. For example, hiring a young, inexperienced attorney to draft and complete cheap business contracts on important deals could be disastrous. You would be better off marking up a form, taking it to a more expensive but experienced attorney for review, then entering the modified document into your word processor for subsequent contracts, all for a flat fee.

If you retained an attorney to defend your company for a fee of $25,000, some $25,000 under what a more experienced law firm quoted, then lost a judgment $125,000 higher than anticipated—there's no question you lost money on that decision. Focus on value and not just on the lowest costs.

Specific Billing, Budgeting, and Monitoring Techniques Are Available

Budgeting, detailed billing, and variance or monitoring systems can be implemented for every project worked on by your outside attorneys. These approaches are being accepted by law firms, although reluctantly as with all these changes, in their need to compete for the business. Your attorneys should be sending detailed monthly bills to the company that make it crystal clear where charges and time are being incurred (see Chapters 12, 18, and 19). Continually monitoring your legal budget against the bills received is part of this overall strategy.

Attorneys Are Like Anyone Else Arguing, employing, and negotiating with attorneys is no different than with any other process or profession. Attorneys come in many sizes, shapes, and personalities. They are not as fearsome, argumentative, smart, or aggressive as you or the public might think. Discard any anxieties or preconceptions you might have as to attorneys. Treat them as you would anyone else.

Look into Bringing Work in House The surplus of attorneys means you can look closely, if you already haven't, at employing your own counsel at an affordable cost. "If you're established," commented one senior litigator, "then you'll probably not work for your clients or other companies. However, if you're tired of practicing straight law or continually searching for business, then this can look attractive."

Simply review how much your outside attorneys are costing, then compare this to the cost of obtaining comparable experience (including benefits, secretary, bar fees, computer equipment and your usual allocation of fixed overhead expenses). Using standard management analysis, determine how much legal work can be shifted inside to create or expand your in-house legal department.

Even without an in-house legal department, your company can begin to lower its costs by employing a paralegal (an experienced person, trained to do legal work as allowed under state law) or a trained employee to do routine legal matters (but subject to review by your outside counsel). Deeds, leases, loans, standard contracts, personnel forms, and others can be entered into a computer and continually used (after your attorney has reviewed the first cut of that "form" document). See "Shifting the Work Inside" later in this chapter.

It's Possible to Avoid the Courts when Settling Disputes Avoiding unnecessary problems starts with your solving business problems before they land in the lap of an attorney. Defective products, unreasonable employee policies, and poor managers are all within your control.

The early settlement of claims and use of alternative dispute resolutions (ADRs) should be adopted as your business policy (see Chapter 16). The use of arbitration and mediation is more cost efficient and is a less time-consuming strategy than the traditional lawyering that's done. However, if an opponent wants to attack at any cost, don't hesitate to use a "scorched earth" reply, provided your law firm has agreed to your cost-control approaches.

Computers Do Make Your Life Easier The cost savings from producing your forms in-house or by your attorneys on a repetitive, computerized basis cannot be over-emphasized. Computers are used by attorneys and companies for every-thing—from tracking court dates and legal research to preparing commercial agreements and legal complaints.

Old files can be researched quickly, as well as organizing and managing the documents required for discovery (or fact-finding) in lawsuits, whether done by you or the attorney. Choosing knowledgeable lawyers with efficient word processing facilities translates into cost savings.

Preventing Legal Problems May only Take Common Sense Costly dis-putes can be prevented in advance by employee and manager education as to what can or can't be done, understanding where the problems typically occur within your company, and by consulting your attorney about concerns before there's a problem. Establish "escape valves" for grievances carried by customers, suppliers, and employees, alike. It is as easy as writing down what can be done on two sheets of paper and giving it to your managers.

Know Your Liability Insurance Coverage As discussed in Chapter 4, business liability coverage includes the duty to defend, as well as paying your damages on covered events. It makes good business sense to know what your liability policies do or don't cover. Be sure to contact your attorney when you feel there's coverage but the insurer says there isn't. Bring all policies to your first meeting with your attorney, especially when you've been sued.

Shifting the Work Inside

At the same time cost-saving procedures are being discussed with your outside attorneys, the legal areas that can be performed internally should be reviewed. The cost savings in doing such work in house can be significant. The trend in shifting legal work inside companies has accelerated, given both the lower costs and control over the work. There are several common strategies available to any business.

Identify the Routine Documents and Draft Them

Routine work and repetitive transactions are the easiest areas to shift inside your company. Transactional or non-litigation work form the bulk of these areas. Fully 80% of the terms and conditions in business agreements are standard and generally remain the same. Why pay your attorney to word-process 80% of the company's documents at law firm rates? Additionally, savings are present by eliminating the time spent with the attorney in discussing the facts behind the transaction prior to such drafting.

This process should be discussed first with your present attorneys. Point out that the monies saved by you can be put into the more complex case or into solving the unexpected problem. If you have an on-going relationship with that attorney, ask to be supplied with the form that the office uses. If necessary, offer to buy the form from the attorney and see what's offered in return. Forms can be obtained either from your attorney or a form book (available at your book store). You'll word-process them, fill in the blanks, and send them to the attorney for final review. Having compatible word-processing equipment with that of the law office will make your life easier—if that's not the case, then look into using conversion kits to handle the different software. The attorney or paralegal can then input the changes on your disk, print out the agreement, note the changes on the print out, then send everything back for your direct use. All other similar transactions can be handled by you from there.

You should establish a procedure whereby the attorney notifies you as to the important changes in the law or reviews the forms at least annually. The attorney gets the work (avoiding the initial drafting), and you get a much smaller bill. If the attorney wants too much or balks, then go somewhere else.

The areas most commonly identified for this procedure involve corporate formalities, employment matters, business ventures, business contracts, real estate matters, and other similar, repetitive areas.

Corporate Minutes and Formalities Preparing corporate minutes is a routine but recurring procedure, needing to be done at least quarterly or as you have meetings. Check lists and forms used for preparing minutes are available from your attorney or book stores. As you know your business best and the important decisions and events, why spend time passing this information onto the attorney, who dictates it to a secretary or paralegal, then transmits the minutes back for final review? The process is easily reversed. You prepare the minutes and send them to the attorney for final review. Once you understand what's needed, prepare these completely and send them only for an annual review by your attorney and accountant.

Agendas, notices for meetings, waivers of notice and consent, consents to action without a meeting, unanimous written consents, proxies, and others can be word-processed into your computer and handled similarly. However, don't wait until several years have passed before deciding you need accurate minutes. This is an expensive headache, especially if you need them at the last moment for an IRS audit or when you're selling the company.

Employment Matters Form contracts for hiring independent contractors, consultants, sales representatives, and employees, along with confidentiality and noncompetition agreements can be drafted first by the attorney and then entered into the company's word processor for repetitive use. A less costly alternative is to take a form from a form book, word-process it with the necessary changes, then give it to your attorney for review. Be careful when using form books, because your state laws may differ or require a different approach for your company and its operations.

Application rejection letters, preemployment checks, reference requests, employment letters, evaluations, warnings, terminations, and resignations can similarly be handled. Expense account statements, warnings, and even contract labor agreements can be so processed, reviewed once by your lawyer, then used as needed. However, it's recommended that any termination letters, given the expense and risk of unlawful termination litigation, should always be reviewed by the attorney (even if just the 5-minute phone call) before being given or sent to the employee about to be fired or laid off.

Business Ventures If you anticipate entering into more than one partnership or venture each year, put the form in the company's computer and send the draft to the attorney after the business negotiations. The attorney would be responsible for the legal points (whether the other party has an attorney or not) and you for the business points. Insist that the attorney stay out of the business negotiations.

One word of caution: be careful of fill-in-the-blank forms for general partnerships, limited partnerships, or even joint ventures. It's nearly impossible to draft a form that would include all the points important for your deal. For example, the owner of a travel agency used an old, fill-in-the-blank form when creating a partnership to allow additional owners. The partners had major differences later. It subsequently turned out that the form didn't provide for several major areas that were in dispute, including how the the partners would value the business when one or the other wanted a buy-out. They were in court for 3 years before that issue was decided.

Business Contracts Purchase orders, invoices, consignments, shipment notices, notices for returned goods, claims, cancellation orders, security agreements, assignments, bills of sale, credit applications, receipts, releases, guarantees—all and more are subject to this process. After the initial legal review, create them yourself. Or buy a "forms" disk and forget the attorney if your requirements are simple and understandable.

Real Estate Matters Businesses have a variety of real estate needs that require documentation ranging from subleasing office space to purchasing land and building a facility. Leases, offers on property, and even letters of intent can be involved. Be advised that real estate matters are subject to specific state laws and regulations, even more than business agreements, which have a more uniform approach from state to state. You should retain a lawyer to review any real estate forms before their first use to be sure that they are in accordance with your state's laws.

Other Areas As your business becomes efficient in the processing of form agreements, it can create any number of them, sending them to the attorney for an initial review, and continuing the process as in the other areas. Amendments to vendor contracts, settlement of customer complaints, account settlements, compromises, promissory notes, default letters, equipment leases, guarantees, and so on are all possible.

But Be Sure to Consult when There's a Problem The problem with the use of forms is that filling in the blanks takes precedence over what you should be doing about the underlying business or legal problems. Be sure to use the "5-minute" telephone call when the problem is complex or could involve litigation. For example, processing a letter of termination, a partnership agreement, or a promissory note involving a large sum of money distracts you from considering any potential future problems—you're trying to do something efficiently and quickly without creating a bigger, legally expensive headache down the road. There are accounting considerations to be looked into as well. Take the time to contact these professionals when the deal or problem is greater than what you would normally see in your business.

Who Should Draft the Documents? If the company has in-house counsel, then this is that person's responsibility. If you don't have in-house counsel, then it's your responsibility. However, your time spent as an owner might be more valuable in areas other than working with form agreements on a computer. It could be more cost effective to hire an attorney to do this on a fixed fee, or to train an employee (even have the attorney do the training). Such an employee should be intelligent and skilled in word processing and typing. At some time you might consider hiring a paralegal. Paralegals are trained employees, even certified in various states, who by law assist attorneys by drafting documents and court filings in addition to assisting in many administrative areas. In fact, they not only draft and prepare documents, pleadings, and motions, they also file them after they have been signed by the attorney (who may or may not have reviewed them).

By hiring a paralegal, you avoid the time of the attorney and paralegal working together and the markup on the paralegal's time by the attorney. Companies are increasingly using contract paralegals (who work for you on an "as needed" basis), whether or not they employ in-house counsel. Most states, because of the lobbying by the legal profession, have regulated this area extensively (including requiring that a paralegal can only work under an attorney's supervision). However, it's worth looking into this possibility and assessing it for yourself.

The paralegal's responsibilities could include monitoring and analyzing your law firm's budgeted and actual costs. Whether an employee or paralegal is hired, full- or part-time, will be determined by the amount of work that can be shifted into the company cost effectively.

Let's assume the cost of this person's salary and benefits (including the lease of a computer, allocation of fixed overhead, and other cost factors) would be $36,000 per annum or $3,000 per month. Let's be generous and say that the attorney's rate is $150 per hour, but that his or her law office's effective rate (making an allowance for the time billed by the law office's paralegal at a much lower rate, say $50 per hour) is $100 per hour. Three thousand dollars per month divided by $100 per hour indicates that a total of 30 hours per month needs to be worked on inside the company (but now done by your outside lawyer) in order for you to break even on the costs of your paralegal. Hiring the employee on a 50% part-time basis would mean that only 15 hours would be needed each month to break even on that employee (assuming someone else could use the computer at other times). Computing a higher attorney's hourly rate would drive this number even lower. This same analysis, using higher numbers, would be used to determine when you should hire your own in-house attorney.

Hiring In-House Legal Counsel

Given the high costs of outside attorneys and the cost efficiencies in performing legal work inside, companies look forward to growing to where they can hire in-house counsel who would arbitrate internal company disputes, oversee the outside attorneys, assist the business in meeting its goals with legal input, formulate legal strategy, anticipate legal problems at early stages of corporate planning and conduct preventive law audits. Paying for younger associates' education and salaries in larger law firms has accelerated this trend. In-house counsel usually are generalists for day-to-day problem solving and simple litigation, with outside attorneys retained for specialized or more complex litigation and financial transactions.

Making the Decision Let's say that the total salary and benefit cost for such an attorney is $100,000. The first year's budget* could be:

General Counsel's compensation:	$100,000
Secretary's compensation:	$30,000
Legal periodicals, supplies, bar memberships, etc.	$10,000
Computer equipment lease	$5,000
Miscellaneous	$5,000
Total:	$150,000

If the company's past 12 months of outside legal costs were $125,000, then it would cost $25,000 more to establish such in-house counsel. We will assume that the candidate could handle everything completed by your outside attorneys; otherwise, this difference would need to be factored into your decision. It's reasonable to assume that the next 12 months' costs would increase (everything else being equal) and this could offset that difference—unless your outside legal expenses resulted from a large litigated or contractual matter that wasn't anticipated to happen again. Also, your new general counsel would do legal work previously not sent to your outside lawyers because of cost or availability factors.

---

*No allocation of fixed overhead for the costs of the firm's facilities, utilities, and other fixed costs (as allocated by a cost accountant) is made in this example. If there are alternative uses available for the office space, then fixed overhead can be allocated as customary in your business. This example further assumes that office space is available at the company; if not, then the extra cost of leasing space needs to be added.

These cost savings can be stated another way. Assume that your in-house attorney will work a normal 40-hour work week for 50 weeks each year, which equals 2,000 hours. If 2,000 hours are worked on company business each year, then the cost of the in-house attorney is $75 per hour ($150,000 divided by 2,000 hours).

This hourly rate cost compares very favorably with any outside attorney's rate, even when the expected legal time is trimmed down. The experience of most companies is that the actual out-of-pocket cost for an in-house attorney is less than one-half what's paid for outside work similarly performed.

There are other considerations that indicate you should hire in-house counsel when this is affordable. The attorney doesn't have to work every week just on solving the firm's legal problems to be cost effective. Use the attorney in your planning sessions for legal input. If the attorney is a problem solver, use that person for business problems as a fact finder, consultant, or other management aid. Additionally, in-house counsel typically functions as the corporate secretary with responsibilities for preparing agendas, notices, and the minutes of meetings.

An Alternative If your company is still too small to hire in-house counsel on a full-time basis, then consider retaining a young attorney at a set salary or "retainer" for less then full-time employment. For example, a growing greeting card company needed more work than it was willing to pay its existing law firm to do. They agreed with an attorney, who was establishing his practice, to pay $3,000 per month in return for the attorney guaranteeing one-half of his time. This attorney prepared routine documents and conducted depositions in trials led by the lead law firm. The company reviewed its legal costs 1 year later; it discovered that it had saved $2,500 per month or $30,000 per year.

Keep Track of What Was Done Before

Various disputes, regulatory agency problems, and business transactions will recur with your business on a regular basis. If good files are retained reflecting past work done, the company can save money by sending this information to the new attorneys or even starting to compile and complete it in-house (provided some outside review is performed). Why pay additional legal dollars to re-invent the wheel?

If your company is facing an environmental agency problem, send the environmental report prepared last year by your consultant to your attorney. Even if the lawyer can't use the report specifically, reading it may save time in bringing that attorney up to speed. And saving time means saving money with attorneys.

Use Consultants Whenever Possible

Hazardous waste and environmental matters, for example, may be handled more cost efficiently by experienced consultants when you are making governmental applications, reviews, and appeals. Use your employees first to fill out the necessary forms, referring questions to the company's consultant. When all else fails, call your attorney. In the field of environmental compliance, determine if an environmental consulting firm would be more cost effective for handling the problem. Use the law firm only when complex legal problems are discovered.

Factual assessments, applications, and permitting procedures are more cost effective when handled by some combination of company personnel and/or your consultant. Immigration paperwork, employment tests, and product liability studies are best done by consultants at a lower overall cost.

Internal Fact Findings

Investigations and the discovery of facts required for governmental permits, applications, and even discovery requests should be accomplished by your staff. Outside lawyers can advise what information is necessary, its form, and any final review—but your own staff should find it.

There's no need for the law firm and its staff, at the company's expense, to dig through files, ask questions, and try to locate subpoenaed documents. If your company does not have to work around the law firm's availability, it has greater control over work scheduling when it does the fact finding.

Use Your Own Facilities

If you do your own locating and finding of facts, it's a quick step to decide that documents can be duplicated on the company's copy equipment at a fraction of the cost charged by outside law firms. Your business is the logical place to create exhibits. Be creative—whatever function is being provided by your outside law firm, see if you can do it more cheaply instead.

The Fee Agreement with Your Attorney

Using an attorney to discuss lending money to your brother or the adequacy of insurance coverage isn't the same thing as hiring someone to defend an IRS criminal investigation or to handle a "bet your house" lawsuit. A written fee agreement, establishing what the attorney is hired to do, the billing arrangements, and expected costs, needs to be entered into with the lawyers you hire.

It makes no sense not to have a written agreement with lawyers, just as you do with contractors, landlords, and the mortgage lender on your house. Various states have enacted laws requiring written fee agreements to avoid the disputes and miscommunications that arise between attorneys and clients over the fees and services to be rendered. State bar associations have even created standard fee agreements to be used by attorneys with their clients.

If there isn't a standard form available in your state, the attorney should send a letter agreement regarding the points discussed for that firm's retention. Hiring an attorney for a specific project should be no different than hiring a contractor to remodel your kitchen, although lawyers can be more expensive.

Bargaining Power

You have more bargaining power than you may realize when you're looking for a reasonable fixed fee or a reduced hourly rate. The factors revolve around the market conditions, the number of law firms contacted, the number of specialists in your area, the continuing nature of your legal needs, salesmanship, and the competition.

Although a large company has great bargaining power with the volume of its legal requirements and a recognizable name, a surplus of attorneys looking for work can only make your legal life easier, regardless of whether you're starting up a business or buying a home. Although each law firm or attorney has its own requirements dictating what fees need to be charged, the sheer numbers of attorneys seeking to earn a living, the competitive forces at work, and the growing sophistication of clients are working to lower these sometimes unreasonable fees.

If you live away from a major metropolitan area, the number of attorneys specializing in what's needed may determine how much bargaining power you have. For example, if there are only two tax attorneys in your town, then there's less room for bargaining (and they may be charging the same rate). However, this doesn't mean you can't retain a law firm outside your area, utilizing fax and telephone to conduct the business after your initial meetings.

The more law firms contacted, the better the chances are of finding the legal vendor you can afford. If more than one law firm is used, depending on what is needed, it's possible to use this to your advantage (unless they provide entirely different services). If you'll need continuing help on other problems, it's more likely you'll get a discount from the "normal" hourly rate based on the future work requirements.

Your salesmanship also can gain cost concessions from law firms. For example, if you own your own business, emphasize its strengths, such as being a stable company with ongoing needs. If your present volume is small, then center on what the business might need as it grows, saying that any considerations given now will be remembered in the future.

The best approach is to say that the attorneys down the street said they would do the work for $X and $Y, respectively, after having talked with them. Then tell the law firm that you'd like to use them, but you need a very competitive fee. If you can't get the best price, then ask if the bill can be paid over several months. If they bring up the subject of interest, then ask for a lower hourly rate. Everything is negotiable, and you should start negotiating at the outset.

What They Were Used To

Law firms used to bill once a year, but they began moving to quarterly and sometimes monthly billing in the late 1970s. The current practice is to bill on a monthly basis. Law firms, given the current environment and competition, would bill weekly if they could get away with it.

The fee most commonly employed then was the open-ended hourly rate, and the fixed fee or "not to exceed" estimate was used rarely. Knowing that each hour expended was an hour that was going to be paid was a very appealing way to earn a living. Although lawyers now are being forced more frequently to use value billing as fixed fees and modified contingency agreements, they are still more used to the hourly rate, retainer, and contingency fee agreement. That's easy to understand— these are very profitable.

The Hourly Rate

Attorneys believe charging an open-ended hourly rate each month is fair because they believe their time is valuable. However, everyone's time is valuable.

A lawyer's or law firm's inventory is the nonbilled time already expended for clients, and the accounts receivable are the billed time yet to be paid. It's easier for law firms to bill for their services on an hourly rate basis, but this billing approach bears little connection to a client's idea of value.

> Generally, hourly rates are higher in cities than in more remote areas, lower for generalists than specialists, higher for larger law firms, and higher for partners than associates. Even with the use of estimates and confidence in your attorney, the danger of the straight hourly rate is the client's lack of control over the bill and inability to determine how well time is spent. It's too easy for an attorney to round up time or simply estimate it, even when using detailed time sheets.

The Retainer

A typical retainer fee is used in two ways. One is when the attorney agrees to handle a determined set of requests or matters each month (usually for a business) in return for a set monthly or retainer fee. This doesn't generally include litigation or business agreements that are separately billed, but it does ensure that the attorney is available for your telephone calls and conferences. Although used by attorneys in the past, it's not as common as the second type of retainer fee.

The retainer fee today usually is an advanced payment that the attorney requires before commencing work and then charges against. For example, an advanced deposit of $5,000 is required before the attorney takes on a case. Attorneys try to require that the retainer amount be kept at the initially agreed level each month during the engagement period, that amount being returned less deductions for the last bill when all work has been completed. The retainer fee is basically used as a security deposit analogous to the security deposit required on signing real estate leases with the difference being that costs are charged against the retainer fee.

Retainers are used with new clients and generally for litigation, but whether you pay one is always negotiable. Retainers usually aren't required in long-standing relationships where the law firm has had good experience in being paid on time.

Contingency Fee

An attorney under a contingency fee agreement is paid on a sliding percentage basis that is dependent upon a successful conclusion of the case. If the case isn't awarded any damages or a settlement concluded, then the attorney receives nothing for his time. The client typically pays for the out-of-pocket costs incurred with the case.

Contingency fee agreements are used when the expectation of receiving a large damage settlement is high. Personal injury, wrongful termination, product liability, sexual harassment, and employee discrimination cases are usually handled on a contingent fee basis for the plaintiff. The defense of such matters is always on a straight open-ended hourly rate basis, although large companies are receiving fixed-price quotes for their legal defense work, and this trend is filtering down to smaller businesses. Collection work is generally on a contingency basis, as it wouldn't be cost effective for any client in the world to pay an hourly rate to collect monies owing from deadbeats.

Litigation over contracts and agreements, whether business or personal, is rarely handled on a contingency fee basis—there's no prospect of a large award to motivate the attorney. Although contingency fee arrangements can be used in litigated business and nonpersonal injury matters, plaintiff attorneys don't agree to them unless there's a good likelihood of receiving high damages to make it worthwhile for them to gamble with their time. Thus, litigating less "juicy" cases will involve both sides being billed as time is expended by their attorneys.

The percentage paid depends generally on the stage at which the recovery is received. A contingency fee usually increases depending on the stage of the proceeding, but this depends on the particular state and its laws. A common percentage approach used (although these vary from state to state) is:

Stage of Proceeding	Contingency Fee
Before filing the complaint	25%
After the complaint but before the trial	33%
Once the trial has commenced	50%
If an appeal is made	60%

If the case settles before the complaint is filed, the attorney usually receives one-quarter of the settlement, but it can be slightly less or more. If a settlement is agreed in the middle of the trial, the law firm usually receives one-half (but this depends on your state's law). You will need to pay particular attention to the specific definition of these "kicker dates," or at what stage of the proceeding a higher percentage fee kicks in. A higher fee can be charged solely on one additional procedure taking place. Using a contingent fee can result in substantial fees for the lawyer–if a seriously injured client receives $1,000,000 in a settlement, then the attorney takes home $500,000 under the usual arrangement (given that a trial has started).

In response to the inequity of this approach, various states have enacted laws that limit the contingent fee to a straight percentage, no matter what, and this can be as low as 15% (Indiana). Such an approach motivates the attorneys to settle as soon as possible and save their time. Other states such as California and New York have established for certain situations a decreasing percentage as the amounts received increase. For example when health care providers are sued in California, the following applies:

Amount Received	% Contingency Fee
First $50,000 recovered	40%
Next $50,000 recovered	33½%
Next $500,000 recovered	25%
Amounts over $600,000	15%

In states where limitations have been placed on both the amounts awarded and when the settlement is reached, the contingency fees are further limited. Ask what your state limits are (even check with your local bar association) before agreeing to go with any attorney. Even when limited by state law, contingency fee percentages are always negotiable. At least, they will be if you talk to enough attorneys and your locality is large enough.

You would handle this in the same manner as before by talking with several lawyers to determine the quoted range of the contingent fees. Select your prime attorneys, interview them, then negotiate and select the final one using the approach in Chapter 5.

The fee in attractive cases is negotiable, even when the lawyers seem to be quoting the same percentage fee. An attractive case is one where the injury is extensive, as well as the damages. Although damages are not nearly awarded as high or as often as the media reports, attorneys love contingent fees in high-damage cases. Even business attorneys cut referral deals to work with a personal injury specialist when a good case comes along. For example, a nonspecializing attorney could receive 15% as a referral fee, or what was negotiated, from the fees earned by the referred lawyer. High-damage cases are also referred to in the trade as "retirement cases" (for the attorneys).

Because of state law and convention, all attorneys must use written agreements in contingency fee matters as opposed to working on wills, loans, and other contractual matters. Before signing a contingent fee contract, you should look at least at the computation of the contingent fee, the treatment of out-of-pocket expenses, and the handling of counterclaims.

Fee Computation The stated contingency fee percentages should be stated as you agreed. You might want to check with your local bar association or county law library to be sure that the percentages are in accordance with your state law. How the contingent fee is computed should be looked over, as well. Are the out-of-pocket costs being deducted from the recovery before the percentage is applied? This can make a substantial difference in the net amount that you receive.

Let's say there was a $500,000 recovery, a 50% contingent fee, and $100,000 in out-of-pocket costs in Hurt Bob's case. Hurt Bob would receive $200,000 if these out-of-pocket costs were deducted first from the award before applying the percentage and $150,000 if not. Depending on the wording of the contract, the 50% compensation for the attorney either would be applied first against the full $500,000 (50% times $500,000 equals $250,000, then subtract $100,000, or $150,000 remaining for him) or $400,000 (50% times the amount after out-of-pocket costs are deducted, or $200,000 to Hurt Bob). This amounts to a cool $50,000 difference, based solely on one sentence in the agreement.

As part of this computation, you should determine whether the costs of medical care or the attorney's overhead costs are deductible underneath the agreement. These are never proper deductions in computing a contingent fee. Further, the attorney should always bear the cost of the firm's office overhead— never the client. The client does bear the cost of the medical bills after receiving the settlement, either reimbursing the attorney for advancing these costs or paying them directly.

Out-of-Pocket Expenses What expenses are assumed by the attorney or client, whether these will be advanced when the client can't pay them, and what happens with these costs if there's no recovery should also be discussed. The client typically is responsible for the out-of-pocket costs, such as consultants and expert witness fees, filing fees, transcripts, court-reporter fees, travel costs, long-distance telephone calls, court costs, and copying.

The attorney may advance these costs when the client is unable to pay for them, intending to recover them from the award. Whether the client pays for out-of-pocket fees in a losing case depends upon what has been agreed and whether the client has any money. In losing cases, attorneys must often bear any costs advanced because by then the client is broke or not happy about losing. Often, the lawyers usually don't sue to collect such costs, deciding that a malpractice claim isn't needed (what's usually claimed by the client's new attorney) on top of having lost the original case.

Counterclaims Look to see if the agreement requires your attorney to defend you under the same contingency arrangement when there's a counterclaim. Unfortunately, attorneys do try to establish an open-ended hourly rate when defending against counterclaims filed after suing the defendant.

Let's say that you sued for damages alleging your car crashed because oil leaked from the defendant's warehouse and caused a slick on the highway. The defendant answers with a counterclaim saying you were speeding and caused damage to their warehouse, and demands you pay up. The costs of defending these claims on an open, hourly rate basis could drive your costs up unexpectedly and excessively.

The Alternatives

A recent poll of California attorneys indicated that three-fourths of the lawyers responding believed that billing by the hour gave attorneys a financial incentive to "pad" a client's bill, the implication being that hourly billing benefited poor lawyers. That same poll indicated that nearly one-half of those polled had used fixed fees in their billing with one-quarter having used caps on total fees, at one time or another, and one-quarter having used "value billing."

The increased competition among attorneys and demands by clients across the country have ended up with the hourly rate form of billing coming under severe attack. Although this started with large companies and corporate work, the trend against straight hourly rate billing has worked its way into all areas of the law and the smallest of clients. Law firms are accordingly moving into value billing alternatives, whether they like it or not, and bar associations are increasingly recommending the use of this instead of the hourly rate. Attorneys are realizing it just makes good business sense to price services differently when the market has become saturated with lawyers.

Value billing is based on how the client perceives the value of the rendered services, not on how the lawyer believes the services should be paid. Value billing is used in place of the straight hourly rate or contingency fee, taking the form of fixed fees and other consumer-oriented approaches. It was only a matter of time before this happened.

When hiring a contractor to remodel a home, most homeowners would turn down a time and materials offer to do the work (which is how lawyers try to bill).

The contractor's incentive is to take his or her time on a "T & M" basis and do a perfect job, there being no limit to what the job theoretically could cost. You would insist on a cap as to the total cost, or a fixed-price contract (or at least you should), with a well-defined description as to what services are included in that cost. This approach should be insisted on with any attorney, as well, and this is what clients are doing.

Lawyers have argued back that their services are unique, too dependent on the other side's actions, and too intangible. Well, the larger clients weren't listening. And when the bar associations began recommending in their private meetings that attorneys begin using value billing to be competitive, the lawyers began to listen, or at least some of them did.

Contract matters (including wills, trusts, estate planning, and employment matters), repetitive work (such as a series of lease or sale transactions), and litigation problems with the same requirements (such as collection, simple divorce, eviction, small-claim personal injury defense, noncomplex litigation, and the like) have been and are excellent candidates as value billing alternatives with even complex matters. As these trends continue, value billing eventually will be brought into all areas in which attorneys practice law. Value billing primarily takes the form of hourly rate discounts, blended rates, fixed fees, bidding, volume discounts, modified contingency fees, and other creative consumer-oriented approaches.

Hourly Rate Discounts

Law firms sometimes discount from their "normal" hourly rates to induce clients to bring their work into the firm. Market rate discounts are brought about depending on how eager that law firm is for your work. A good response to the law firm's quote as to its standard rates is "I don't think I can afford that rate for this work. I would like to use you, so what if I paid you $X per hour (stating the discounted rate)?" You can't lose by trying and shopping around.

Blended Rates

Clients usually pay a higher hourly rate for the work of senior attorneys and a lower one for junior attorneys. The blended rate charges one hourly rate for both, no matter who performs the work. For example, a firm charges $250 per hour for partners and $150 for senior associates but agrees to charge $200 per hour, regardless of who does the work. The firm has the responsibility to assign the proper mix of lawyers who'll work on your case in the most professional and efficient manner, thus maximizing their profit. One advantage of the blended rate is that it encourages the efficient staffing of cases. Senior partners don't do inappropriate legal tasks, as the partner doesn't receive any more compensation for doing work that an associate should be handling.

Flat or Fixed Fees

Under a fixed-fee billing, the law firm handles the matter for a set, predetermined price, regardless as to the number of hours required to complete the work. The services are priced on their value to the client and not in terms of the hours spent on the project, whether lower or greater than anticipated.

This system is used most often at this time for repetitive word-processed problems such as contracts, documents, and other routine matters where the firm knows the amount of time involved in completing the task. They are often quoted for wills, trusts, simple divorces, bankruptcies, unlawful detainers (eviction of tenants), name changes, and other standardized matters.

Fixed fees generally aren't used when the opposing attorney has the ability, as in complex litigation, to run up hours by countless motions, hearings, and demanding unnecessary depositions unless the client has the corporate clout of a General Motors. They are usually quoted in business matters for transactional or document work, although routine litigation work is also being so quoted. Corporate minutes, dissolution of corporations and partnerships, and routine business contracts and forms such as leases, equipment purchases, purchase orders, work proposals, and standardized contracts are subject to being quoted on a fixed-fee basis.

Fixed fees force a law firm to become more efficient in the use of its computer systems and procedures, but look at who's doing the work. If most is being done by a paralegal or junior associate, even if subject to the final review of a partner, then it may be better to pay a slightly higher amount for everything to be drafted by a business specialist.

Fixed fees are definitely being quoted in more areas than before. Try to secure fixed fees for any work you need. Just ask around—you only lose if you don't try. If doctors get paid the same, even when complications are discovered in the surgery being performed, then attorneys shouldn't be treated any differently.

Bidding

Bidding usually comes into play when a large business invites several law firms to bid on its legal work, including strategy, staffing plans, and fees. Although it would be rare for an individual to use the "beauty contest" approach, if an extensive personal injury or high damage case is involved, you might consider using it.

Volume Discounts

If you have repetitive work, whether as a business or individually, then let the attorneys know you're talking to others and ask for a volume discount. This value billing concept is used primarily in commercial settings, although it has been used by wealthy individuals with various legal requirements. The only reason it isn't done more by individuals is that they don't have as many repetitive needs.

Typically a company agrees to refer all of a specific kind of work to one law firm in exchange for discounted fees. For example, all its leases or deals are sent to one firm and charged at lower rates. The law firm enjoys the assurance of the work in return for the price concessions. This is no different than what companies obtain from a major supplier in return for continued receipt of their business.

Modified Contingency Fees

This approach bases only a portion of the law firm's fee on its success in the case. The client is billed at reduced hourly rates *plus* a percentage of the amount saved the client or the increase in value if the client wins. The client gains a lower contingent fee in return for paying a guaranteed lower hourly rate.

Let's say that in place of the typical contingent fee, you had agree to pay $100 per hour (in place of the usual $150 to $250 pyramid rates used by this well-known law firm) along with a straight 10% contingency. If the law firm expended 2,000 hours on a personal injury case, then you win depending on the damages. If the case was settled as trial began for $1,000,000, instead of receiving $500,000 (50% of 1 million), the law firm would receive $300,000 (10% plus 2,000 hours at $100 per hour). You received an extra $200,000, and the law firm didn't risk all its chips on whether there was a win or loss. You will need to factor in your facts and state's laws similarly.

Other

It is possible to be quite creative if the lawyer wants your work. For example, companies have taken the concept of progress payments from the construction industry into a new application in the law. They require their law firms to estimate the cost of each phase of the case or project. The payment to the law firms then is based on the percentage of each phase's completion, not on the hours expended. This approach can be used when the law firm understands the hours required for the successful completion of the project (such as contracts, estate planning and drafting wills, and simple litigation), but it is applicable to anything depending on your negotiating power.

The application of the progress payment concept is being applied to litigation as well. A fixed fee is negotiated for the entire case, then allocated to each phase of a simple, routine case, such as pleadings and motions, settlement negotiations, discovery, and trial. The problem is that the law firm could spend more time than first thought, run through the phases into discovery, then be motivated for an early settlement when the monies have been eaten up. This would be no different than a contractor taking most of the construction money earmarked for a 10-story building, but using it all up by the 7th floor. Clients do have a check on this, however, as there's no settlement without their agreement.

The modified or straight contingent fee can even be replaced by a higher open-ended hourly rate, depending on your assessment of the case. For example, a less than 50% owner of a small corporation had been locked out from his company by the majority shareholder. No dividends were declared, the hapless shareholder was fired, and he had no say in the company's operations. A number of lawyers quoted contingent fees ranging from one-third to one-half of the total recovery. The owner felt these fees were so outrageous that he considered taking the low buy-out offer made by the other shareholder.

One law firm took a different approach, offering to charge two and one-half times its normal hourly rate for services up to trial, but a one-third contingency (against the hours expended) if the case went to trial. The client didn't feel the case would go to trial and accepted the deal. A negotiated settlement was obtained twice as high as the original offer but before trial. The law firm received $55,000 on the $1.6 million dollar settlement. It was happy receiving a guaranteed fee two and one-half times its normal rate; the client was happy receiving more than $500,000 over the usual contingent fee.

The Opportunities

In many of these cases the fee concepts aren't new, although the applications and increased use of them are. Attorneys are attending seminars, buying books, and receiving pamphlets put out by bar associations—all detailing these billing strategies as alternatives to use in a competitive market. Large businesses are utilizing all of these concepts. Sole practitioners and law firms already are used to quoting fixed fees for divorces, wills, trusts, and in other civil areas. Business contracts are increasingly being drafted on a fixed-fee basis. The time is now for their application in other areas—whether in defending a lawsuit or in suing to collect a large loan.

Most law firms don't have an optimum billing strategy. They undercharge, typically, for unique services and overcharge on common services—the law firm determines what mix of services to offer. Today's economy and legal market now dictate that the firm be flexible in its approach, and you can come out ahead.

Trading services or products for legal services is increasingly being done, whether you're a barber, doctor, or you manufacture clothing. Unless these transactions are being reported as required by the IRS, be careful until you know your law firm better—the IRS has an interest in monitoring these transactions when attorneys are involved. However, given that all IRS regulations are being met, then both parties can win. The attorney is being paid, and you're saving valuable cash, not to mention trading services or products at your retail price. It also may be a good way to trim your excess inventory.

Additional Areas to Review

There are other areas to watch for in the fee agreement. Such areas involve the soft costs, travel and other out-of-pocket expenses, the scope of the work to be performed, staffing levels, rate changes, and the hourly break-downs.

Soft Costs

A study done a few years ago of law firms in major cities determined that nearly two-thirds of all firms charged their clients 20¢ a page or less for photocopying. However, more than a third charged 25¢ a page or more. To send a fax, two-thirds said they billed their clients $1 a page or less. But one out of seven said they charged between $1 and $4 per page. These types of variations mean you must discuss copy, fax, postage, and other soft-cost charges before signing any fee agreement.

Review the standard rates employed in the firm's standard fee agreement, or if these are not available, ask about them. Negotiate the individual rates down for soft costs or establish a limit that no more than 3%, for example, of the total bill can be charged for soft costs, regardless of the standard billing rates for such items. The fee agreement should state "only reasonable and actual out-of-pocket expenses will be reimbursed, but not secretarial, stenographic, word processing, or other overhead costs that are normally reflected in the law firm's hourly rates."

You will need to monitor all soft costs continually as billings are received. A large law firm with over 600 attorneys was held by the court to be guilty of such excessive markups. Fireman's Fund sued the firm in court over the excessive fees and out-of-pocket expenses, including a costly swordfish dinner charged to the company's account. The law firm settled, paying Fireman's Fund $1.5 million, then soon announced a new disbursements policy that cut deeply into the charges made for copying, faxes, and other such expenses. The firm, in a letter to its clients, promised not to "bonus bill" (charging more for a good result) without prior consent, never to add profit onto any client-reimbursable charges, and to travel coach class only. The law firm also established lower copying and outgoing fax charges.

Travel Expenses

Travel expenses are not only the out-of-pocket expenses paid, but also include the time charged by the lawyer when traveling. The first question is whether the client should pay for the attorney to fly first class. It should be agreed ahead of time that no one does this without prior authorization. Attorneys, like all people, also have varying tastes when traveling. Some like to travel and stay at luxury hotels and restaurants. Others are more budget conscious. You need to set a per-diem rate for lodging and food, assuming that the attorney isn't staying with friends.

> Be careful of one, tricky item. Junior associates and even partners, given their monthly billing quotas, can be motivated to double-charge different clients for the same flight. The attorney spends 50% of the time for each client but bills both at 100%. Who's to know the difference? This isn't to say that all attorneys do this, but you need to be aware of the problem. Ask if all the time billed was spent on your legal business and decide for yourself if it took too much time to do the work.

The method and rate an attorney charges when traveling on your behalf also need to be agreed in the fee agreement. How the attorney charges time when traveling to another lawyer's office for a deposition or conference, for court appearances, or for flying to another city also must be known in advance. It's customary to pay for the travel time of the lawyer to fly to another city and return, including a per diem rate for the days spent on your affairs; however, long stays in cities should be compensated based on the amount of time the attorney actually spends on your business. Remember, this is all negotiable.

The Scope of the Work

It's necessary to define closely and accurately the scope of the work the law firm is to perform, especially if you have a fixed-fee agreement. Otherwise, if the scope is worded too loosely, the attorney will bill you separately for work not defined as being included, even if you thought it was to be. Or the firm can argue that the reason for not meeting an original estimate was because of the extra work required beyond what the estimate included. Let's say you wanted a divorce. Unless it's been made clear that suing a lender to force it to accept an agreed swap of assets with your ex-spouse is included, you will be charged extra for that legal action.

Staffing

Establish in the beginning who'll be the attorneys doing your work and what happens when the designated attorney(s) aren't available. This can be important if you agreed on hiring a law firm based on the partner you interviewed, and then that partner suddenly isn't available.

Further, what happens if a lawyer leaves the firm and the firm must spend time educating the new attorney assigned to your case? The answer is you will be billed for this unless the matter has been covered in the fee agreement or discussed before you receive the bill. At best you'll wind up negotiating the amount of the bill back toward where it should have been in the first place.

Rate Changes

The law firm should agree they will notify you in advance of any hourly rate changes and that such increases will not go into effect for a stated time period after they have begun work on your behalf. For example, when litigating a complex lawsuit for you, the attorneys would agree to prior notification and to not post any increases in hourly rates for 1 year after beginning your work.

Hourly Breakdowns

Law firms bill in fractions of an hour. Some bill in quarter-hour increments (0.25), although it's more standard for firms to bill in tenths of an hour (0.10) or twentieths (0.05). For example, rather than billing in increments of 0.25, 0.50, 0.75, the firm will bill at 0.25, 0.30, 0.35, 0.40 hour, etc., and based on the time actually expended. This can result in a significant difference over time.

If the firm rounds to the nearest quarter-hour (0.25 hour) rather than the nearest twentieth (0.05 hour), an average difference in their favor of 0.1 per hour billed in the billing cycle brings about dramatic results. If 1000 hours were billed, then this would translate into another 100 hours in their favor. If their billing rate is $200 per hour, then there's an additional $20,000 owed simply due to this practice.

The Estimate

The law firm must estimate its fees and state this in the agreement. Attorneys understand how quickly such estimates can be exceeded, and they cover themselves by stating the assumptions behind the estimate, that results will change as do the assumptions, and that there's no guarantee that the estimate won't be exceeded. They are attorneys, after all.

The use of the estimate is your back-up if the law firm is unwilling to enter into a fixed fee or a "not to exceed" limit on legal expenses. Estimates should be made whether the work involves contractual or litigated matters. See Chapters 19 and 20 for a discussion of estimates and budgets on litigated matters.

The Detailed Bill

A survey of the largest corporations concluded that law firm billings seemed to be based on what charges they could get the clients to accept and pay. No firm out of 40 of the largest law firms in two major cities required their attorneys to use a clock to determine the actual number of hours spent on a case in determining their charges.

This is typical. Review the monthly billing format and a form billing statement (or an actual one with any client references eliminated) prior to engaging that law firm. The statement should be sufficiently detailed to allow you to monitor the expenses as contained in the firm's billing statement against any budgets being used.

The billing statement should indicate, on a separate project-by-project basis, each hourly component of the bill by the date of the time performed, the amount of the time, the attorney performing the service, and an adequate description of the work performed on that date. For example:

Date	Time Expended	Attorney	Description of Services Provided
6–13–94	1.05 hr	JLC	Initial review of TLC contract
6–17–94	0.65 hr	TMP	Legal research re usurious interest
6–25–94	1.25 hr	JLC	Negotiation attorney Lee on contract

A sufficient breakdown of the costs expended for copying, faxing, travel, and phone expenses should be included, along with any other out-of-pocket expenses. Don't hire any attorney who won't give you the breakdown you need. The computer technology for breaking out costs has been in existence for years and you need to see the costs to ensure that you receive what you've contracted for.

Discuss Cost Control

Before hiring any law firm you must determine whether the attorneys will work with you on controlling your costs. If you have more than one problem to solve, sell them on the concept that savings in one area can be used for other problems. Tell them you're interested in working with them when you have other needs.

If you own a business, now's the time to discuss their assisting you in doing work in house such as minutes, contracts, and agreements in return for the final reviews of this work. Document production, if at all possible, can be accomplished by your people. In any event, you want to be contacted before the law firm or attorney does any work not authorized in advance.

The Resistance

If the law firm is entrenched in using the hourly rate concept, it very well may resist your approach, especially if your needs are small (at least to them). This resistance results primarily from two reasons.

First, it is always easier and more profitable to conduct business as in the past, even given the current trends. Although downsized law firms are saying that "smallness is better," the large firms are still wedded into the concept of leveraging. As computer manufacturers increase profits by leveraging the labor of lower-cost employees in manufacturing, so do the larger law firms with their use of inexperienced associates, although this practice isn't as beneficial for their clients.

Second, many attorneys and law partners still have unrealistic income expectations. They became used to high salaries and bonuses in the "good old days." These expectations and beliefs will have to be lowered if billings are to be set at value-oriented levels. The competitive market trends in place already are dictating the realities of the marketplace to these lawyers. You would think that simply surviving would be a strong enough motivation, but it takes time for this concept to set in.

Only Agree to Pay What You Can Afford

No matter what type of billing arrangement is ultimately agreed upon, you should only agree to pay what can be afforded each month. For example, if the attorney quotes a fixed fee for your divorce of $20,000 (it's high due to the assets involved), then you need to discuss when and how this is to be paid. If only $500 per month can be afforded, then tell that to the lawyer. Even if your savings could cover this, you still should try to obtain a payment plan, as there's no need to run your savings down to uncomfortable levels so your attorney will be paid as first wanted.

When that happens, simply talk to other law firms and attorneys. What you end up accepting for a fee arrangement is basically dependent on how many attorneys you contact and the time you spend doing this.

In numbers of cases, it is impossible for clients to pay non-contingent fee arrangements (whether a fixed fee has been worked out) in lump sums, and regardless of the amount negotiated—the lawyer knows this. In fact, any attorney who has been in practice for any amount of time has or is now being paid by clients over time on an installment basis. *The amount of the payments, any interest, whether some months can be skipped, and even if security for what's owed should be given are always negotiable.* Whether that lawyer will work with what you can afford is always an important consideration in your hiring decision.

Drafting the Fee Agreement

It is the law firm's responsibility to provide to you at no charge their standard fee agreement, but customized to cover the areas discussed and negotiated. If they don't have one, then they should send a simple letter agreement in understandable language covering all the areas. These are not complex or difficult to prepare.

  If you're the first client asking for this (which is doubtful), you are doing the firm a favor, as you will certainly not be the last. A law firm that says "We've never had any reason for such an agreement," shouldn't be hired. Go somewhere else.

  It is possible you may need more than one agreement. If the same law firm is working on a contract for you as well as bringing a lawsuit on your behalf on a contingent-fee basis, then you will need two separate fee agreements. It's no different than employing two different law firms to handle two different problems. Each agreement must stand on its own, regardless of the fact that it's with the same firm.

13

Managing Your Attorney and Legal Costs

Managing your attorneys means working with them. It's necessary to give them *all* the documents and facts, including the ones where you don't look very good. The attorney isn't there to judge you, but to determine the legal aspects of your problem. Let him or her determine what's important or not. Organizing the data before any meeting will make the attorney's job more effective and decrease your costs as well. Ask what can be done to make the attorney's job more effective, and you'll save money.

Set Up Case Files

It will be necessary to set up case files for each legal project separate from those of the law firm. These files will contain any applicable fee agreements, legal bills, your control sheets, any budgets, letters to the attorney, documents, and memos, even if many are duplicates of the lawyer's files. Copies of complaints, answers, motions, and other litigation matters will be inserted into this file.

   The file will be used when you meet to discuss the case with your attorney and to monitor the costs. Be sure to file all notes of all conversations and meetings. A "to do" list should be used showing what must be done, by whom, and by when for each matter. Don't rely on your attorneys to do this. They forget, become overworked, and need vacations just as anyone else does.

Keep Up with the Case

Tell your attorney to keep you advised as to any developments. Copies of anything filed with the court, sent to a third party, or connected with the case must be sent to you as well. This includes all letters, pleadings, notices, motions, and even contract drafts—anything in writing.

> Keep the attorney immediately advised of any developments as facts come to your attention. Demand that the attorney in turn keep you advised immediately of any developments pertaining to your case.

A big complaint of clients is that they didn't know what the attorney was doing and weren't kept up-to-date. Attorneys complain that the client didn't give them all the information they needed until the last minute (or not at all). Keeping the attorney advised from your end enables both of you to stay in touch. Establish a periodic visitation schedule to discuss the progress of all cases and projects on a regular basis (but use the telephone when possible to save costs).

Cost and Variance Analysis

Detailed Bills

As discussed in Chapter 12, it is necessary to have sufficiently detailed bills to control your costs when a fixed fee hasn't been agreed upon. A sufficiently detailed bill will be your guide for asking the necessary questions to discover how effectively your attorneys are spending their time. The amount and types of soft costs, whether proper staffing is in place, and the billable time patterns that can occur only can be found by such bills. The detailed bills should be questioned as received, then against what has been billed previously and any estimates.

The Control Sheet

Whether you have one attorney working on one problem or several (when you own a business), a control sheet should be established for each project and law firm. This control sheet will be used for your cost and variance analyses. The sheet would spread out the actual expense, budget, revised estimate, percentage completion (how far you've gone), and variance information by month. You spread out the bills as received and work with them on one sheet.

Although these can be strange concepts, they're necessary to stay on top of the costs. If you've ever had a budget for your household or business, you know you estimate what your expenses will be, try to keep them in line, then compare them afterwards. The difference between the actual and budgeted information is your variance, or the difference between the two. If you feel that your first budget didn't make it, then you'll make a new or revised one.

The same concept is used when adding on a room addition. Let's say you didn't get a fixed-price bid, and the contractor only gave an estimate. If, as you proceed, it turns out the expenses are going higher than originally expected, you would ask the contractor to make a revised budget (if you still want to use that person). You would keep the original budget to see how far everything's off. But you would use the revised estimate to be sure there is enough money to pay all the bills.

Now let's suppose you want to know how you're doing at this moment in meeting these estimates. If the contractor said the work was 50% done, then you know that if the costs were $20,000 at the time, the total costs at the end should be around $40,000. You would divide the costs-to-date by the percentage of completion. If your lawyer said your project was half completed and the costs were $30,000 then $30,000 divided by .50 would equal the projected final cost of $60,000. You would be arguing or trying to pin down that number.

Let's say you were sued by Black Bart when you sold your home. He was unhappy afterwards and felt you had misled him about the property (you didn't). Your attorney believed that $50,000 was "the most" that this litigation would cost but wouldn't enter into a fixed-price contract. You had answered the complaint, and been talked into a few procedural motions to kill the lawsuit (but they didn't work), and the depositions (informal questioning of witnesses) had begun.

By this time, you had incurred $35,000 of bills. After receiving the last bill, your lawyer said that you were "halfway through" the problem. (Note: if the attorney says it's impossible to tell what the eventual costs will be at the end, that's not acceptable—you can't give the attorney a blank check. You have the right to know what the eventual costs can be. We're talking about a lot of money here.) Your control sheet could look as follows:

Law Firm of T, B & T—Black Bart Lawsuit ($000's)

Month	Actual Expense		Budget %		Project	
	For Month	Total	Initial	Revised	Completed	Variance
May, '94	5	25	50	50	50%	–0
June, '94	10	35	50	70	50%	–20

You had taken the most recent bill of $10,000 for June, added it to the last one with a total of $25,000 since the start, and ended up with the $35,000 total. After spreading out the information, you aren't a happy camper. The $35,000 spent so far, when divided by 50% ("you're halfway through"), equals $70,000 (the revised budget), and this is $20,000 over the initial estimate of $50,000. That's a shock and you want to know why there was a bill for $10,000 with no further progress. The lawyer replied there had been unbilled time for previous months (which you would question) that ended on the June bill, and Black Bart's attorney hadn't responded to the last procedural motion.

Let's say your attorney didn't know what it would cost to finish the problem and was sorry it had been underestimated in the beginning (which is typical). He said the costs would be "higher than first thought," and you replied that was already known. This is when you must talk immediately about the overall costs and have the attorney be more specific, even bargaining for a not-too-exceed number. You wouldn't negotiate for $70,000 as the limit, however, but, rather, at holding the costs to the initial estimate of $50,000. If it seems that in all honesty, the number should be higher because there will be more court hearings than anticipated, then you'll have to set it higher. But this will be the time to negotiate hard for a fixed fee, especially if what was first told you is no longer the case.

When your attorney says that the "ballpark cost" is $X, then use that number for your budget if you can't get a better one (and try to get the number in writing). If the attorney says that you're about "a third through," then use one-third. For example, if the estimate for your business contract is $5,000 with no fixed price, then being one-third through on a $2,000 bill means you're already $1,000 over the estimate ($2,000 divided by 1/3rd equals $6,000).

The percentage completion on legal work is easier to determine when you are dealing with subjects such as wills, simple litigated matters, divorces, contracts, and the like. For example, the attorney should know about how much time is required to prepare a living trust or complete an uncomplicated divorce. Attorneys quickly argue you can't budget litigation, because it isn't known what the other party will do—will they be hard-headed, use a "search and destroy" approach, or settle at the last moment? All that is true but misses the point.

Cost increases are flagged quickly even when you are in litigation, and you can deal with them at the first sign of trouble. Advertising, real estate developers, and research companies all deal with the unknown, and they're able to come up with an answer. Fixed prices already have been asked for and gained in a number of situations, including simple litigation where there are such unknowns. The procedure is straightforward: you budget what you do; what the other party does is extra (see Chapters 19 and 20).

The point is you need a way to see where costs are going, then take action before it's too late. You might want to settle at a lower amount or not take that extra deposition. Or you could decide not to go first class. As important, the attorney must deal with your cost concerns now, not later with the last bill.

Review the Bill

As important as curtailing projected costs were the areas spotted in your review of the detailed billing submitted in June. For example, part of the bill for $10,000 submitted in June included a number of line items:

Law Firm of T, B & T—Black Bart Lawsuit: June 1994 Bill

Date	Expended	Attorney	Services provided
6–12–94	6.00 Hr.	RTL	Review case and motion to dismiss
6–13–94	8.00 Hr.	ADN	Legal research re seller's defense to fraud
6–14–94	6.50 Hr.	RTL	Negotiation attorney Bates on case
6–18–94	4.50 Hr.	RTL	Meeting RTL with ADN on case
6–18–94	4.50 Hr.	ADN	Meeting ADN with RTL on case

You questioned why the senior partner ("RTL") had to spend 6 hours on June 12th reviewing the case and the motion to dismiss, especially since the junior associate ("ADN") had prepared and argued it. You wondered what possibly could have been added, given the work previously done by ADN and the fact that the judge denied the motion. The partner said it did seem high and would check on it.

You next questioned the extensive time spent by ADN in researching the problem of a seller's defense to fraud—it seemed to you that some of this should have been known. You didn't even know why this was a problem in the case. RTL then explained to you why it was a particularly troublesome problem in this situation.

When you had asked RTL about how the negotiations had gone on June 14th, you had been informed they were "moving in the right direction" and you had been given the details. Finally, you wondered why it took 4.50 hours for the two attorneys to discuss the case on June 18th. This cost you $1,800 alone, given ADN's billing rate of $100 per hour and RTL's billing rate of $300 per hour. He replied there were considerable cost savings in using ADN for the basic "nuts and bolts of the case," but added that ADN needed guidance as to "a few of the finer points." He said he would get back to you.

When he called back 1 week later, RTL said he had good news. The law firm's accounting office had posted time to the wrong accounts on the June 12th charge: "You know how those bean counters love to count but don't know the difference between a red bean and a white one," he said with a chuckle. A credit of 3.0 hours was being given for the June 18th work "just because you're a good client." A correction would be on the next bill, RTL promised.

Somehow you know that the credit for 3 hours won't be reflected on the July bill and that the matter will need to be followed up again. After all, it took 2 months for a correction to appear the last time this happened. However, as one attorney said, "If I've made a mistake or the bill seems excessive after later review, then I'll reduce it. But if I don't hear from the client, then I assume it's fine." Although other lawyers may not be as reasonable, it's your responsibility to question the billing and know what's going on. For dealing with the unreasonable attorney, see Chapter 21.

This control process is an art, as legal matters aren't easily reduced to numbers in complex cases. However, the process by itself makes the lawyer cost conscious (or should). And since it forces both of you to make tough decisions, rather than the attorney simply mailing out bills, the process is as important as the actual numbers. Remember, every thing is negotiable—even after you are billed.

Other Areas

Don't forget to look at the expense side of the bill with its travel, copying, fax, telephone, postage, and other expenses. Are the retention of experts as agreed and as estimated? Is too much time being charged for "consultations" with consultants where you're being charged double (both attorney and consultant are billing you for that time)?

If you retained a larger law firm, then be sure the agreed staffing is happening and whether you're paying for associates just to talk with one another. Is there any person you don't know who's working on the case? Are there perhaps too many meetings between lead partners and associates on your case?

Determine if the agreed lawyer is working on the case and if there seems to be too much repetitive work. Are large clumps of time being billed that are hard to believe? This could indicate accounting errors or worse. Or are various fractions of time being billed? This could indicate someone is working on your project as a break or "filler" in between other cases. Both indicate something's not right.

Ask if you are receiving copies of the work that's being billed. If statements are received for several drafts of the same agreement, then you should review the drafts to see what has been changed.

Discussing the Bill

You need to discuss all questions and problems on reviewed bills with the lawyer before receiving the next bill. Treat the attorney, although respectfully and directly, as you would any other vendor. You have strong rights in the event of a disagreement, so exercise them, but do this in a courteous way. There's no need to create unnecessary hostilities, even if the charges seem to be outrageous, but stand firm.

Computerization

It's no secret that the efficient use of computers makes work easier. Computerizing any variance analysis allows quicker results, accuracy, and efficient management. The programs in place for analyzing the costs of your household, or that of your vendors with your business, could be used when reviewing the costs of lawyers.

The Billing Signature

Some businesses and individuals have begun to insist that the attorney or lead counsel sign each billing as a certification that the statement has been reviewed and is reasonable in amount. This approach forces the attorney to look over any billings before sending them out. It also gives you the argument: "These were looked over first, right?" Eventually, this can result in less hassles over bills.

Continue the Process

New work or projects won't be covered by the first fee agreement unless the first one envisioned repetitive work. It will be necessary to define the scope of the work, the applicable fee, and the budget for each new project. New budgets, control sheets, and monitoring need to be established on each project.

What if You Don't Get Results?

Discuss the problem with your attorneys and ask what needs to be changed so that realistic budgets and cost controls can be implemented. If billings greater than budget continue and you still don't feel you're receiving value, write the attorney that you're not happy and are contacting other law firms to handle the business. Negotiate what's been billed by simply saying what you believe is excessive, why, and what you are prepared to pay. Give them 60 days to remedy the problems to your satisfaction.

At the same time, talk to other attorneys about moving the work. Contact any backup firms and determine their availability. You shouldn't be overly critical about the previous law firm when talking to a new attorney. Lawyers will get nervous if they feel you're a problem client who shops attorneys, is hard to get along with, or doesn't pay the bills. But remember it's expensive to move work, especially during litigation, to a new law firm in the middle of the problem—it takes the new attorney time to be brought up to speed, and you'll be paying for this. The costs of the new attorney need to be negotiated and controlled, just as with those of the first one.

Many attorneys and law firms will try harder when receiving such a letter from a disgruntled client. Attorneys know the rights a client has in the event of a dispute over fees and the handling of a case. They know the cost and downtime when there's a dispute with a client.

But if you haven't received results after the grace period, then don't hesitate to change law firms. Arrange for the old firm to send its files over immediately. Negotiate hard with the previous law firm over the question of excessive fees or offsets for shoddy work. Don't pay the bill if you have good reason, and your new attorney should be consulted for any evidence of malpractice. See Chapter 21 for further details.

But What if You Aren't General Motors?

These concepts are applicable whether you're a large or small company or an individual. They only depend on how much effort you take to shop around, find the attorney who will work with you, and stay on top of your case and the billings.

Shop around for a fixed fee. The poorest of people are able to secure a fixed fee for handling their divorces, bankruptcy filings, or even cheap wills. The same can be accomplished for your needs. In time, most work by attorneys will be done by fixed fees (except for contingent-fee cases). It will take persistence, work, and ingenuity, but all you have to do is to find the right attorney. Spend time on your search for an attorny—it eliminates unnecessary headaches down the road.

If you aren't able to obtain a fixed fee, then be sure to secure estimates for each legal project, including any litigated matters. Search for law firms who want your business, and don't settle for less.

Nonlitigation Cost-Control Tips

There are a number of ways you can control the amounts of your nonlitigation costs when you are unable to obtain a fixed fee (litigation cost-control tips are discussed in Chapters 19 and 20).

1 Finding and working with the right attorney as a team are necessities. The process starts with the attorney. If you have one who is inexperienced, inept, or only wants to be paid the "old way," then you're going to have problems with out-of-control legal expenses and a bad result.

2 Always strive for a fixed fee as law firms are accepting (although reluctantly) alternative billing approaches. But remember, value is not necessarily what's cheapest. In complex or "bet the house," matters retain the partner or specialist who understands the area rather than the junior associate or generalist who doesn't. Cheapest does not necessarily mean the best value.

3 Determine ahead of time if a "first class" or "coach" job (and bill) is desired. Don't be afraid to make cost trade-offs against the importance of the work or the agreement. Determine the legal risks you're willing to take and save the "first class" approach for a "bet the house" problem, or other major lawsuits.

4 If legal research is needed, ask if the attorney has done similar research for another client in the same area. Law firms can't give a copy of what was prepared for another client, but they can use that for your work and not "reinvent the wheel." Then ask if the fee can be lowered.

5 Use the telephone instead of meetings, avoid "legal opinion" papering, and discuss more than one problem at a meeting or over the telephone to save money. If you don't have more than one problem, definitely try to discuss it over the telephone—decisions are made faster. Discussing matters in bulk rather than on a piecemeal basis saves money.

6 Attorneys feel they need to send letters protecting their position while charging you for that time. It covers their malpractice problem. Tell them when you want something in writing, you'll ask them for it; otherwise, they do it at their own expense. (They do always have the option of calling you.) However, if you're not sure about the attorney's advice or think it's wrong, then get it in writing (proof of malpractice).

Specific billing, budgeting, and monitoring techniques are available and should be used.

7 Maintain your own files apart from the attorney, including copies of all originals, as well as all papers and correspondence received. You can't control your expenses if you don't have the information.

8 Keep up with your project and quickly give the attorney any new information. This avoids the lawyer wasting time on old information at your expense.

9 Be aware of "bonus" or "win" billing where the firm rewards itself for a job "well done." Some law firms are tempted to bill a bonus if they do a particularly good job. As they get paid even for poor performances, they shouldn't receive more for doing what's expected.

10 Attorneys shouldn't charge for bill review discussions, whether in person or on the telephone. You should determine this, however, before you spend the time. Hold them to the fee agreement and your understanding.

11 Evaluate your attorneys periodically, giving them a chance to correct problems, but don't hesitate to fire anyone who's not performing as they should.

12 Consider doing it yourself, but always retain the attorney for the final review in complicated or high-value situations.

Check Your Attorney's Work

You need to have your attorney send you copies of everything filed or prepared on your behalf for two reasons. First, it allows you to keep track, along with the fee statements, of what work your attorney is charging you for. Second, and as important, is you need to check the work that the attorney is doing.

You are the best source for all facts. The attorney takes what facts you give, then puts them into a legal format. It's also your responsibility to be another check of the work that's being done. Take nothing for granted, because attorneys do make mistakes, some more than others.

In one case, an attorney actually named the wrong parties in a lawsuit, and the client failed to read the complaint. The statute of limitations (the limits on the time within which you must sue) ran out for the parties who actually were at fault and barred the injured party from suing for damages. It turned out that the attorney making the error didn't have either malpractice insurance or assets. That client lost out entirely.

Another client did check the bankruptcy papers filed on her behalf. Her check turned up the fact that the attorney hadn't properly excluded exempt assets from the bankruptcy filing, such as her car and certain valuable equipment used in her work. That oversight could have created a significant problem.

The stories regarding attorney mistakes and malpractice go on and on. Lawyers make mistakes as to the correct calendaring of dates and appearances. They also may go ahead with motions and procedural challenges that you didn't authorize or aren't needed.

You can't allow any attorney to be given carte blanche authority on any work or to do whatever he or she thinks desirable without first consulting you. It may be that you need to file a declaration under penalties of perjury (a criminal liability should you lie or misrepresent the facts) that attests to the accuracy of the statements prepared by the attorney from what you've said. In this case, it's your responsibility to check the correctness of the statements you're signing, as well as everything else that's being done on your behalf.

What to Do when There's a Dispute

How you handle a problem in the beginning determines what happens later. It is at the outset of a dispute that care must be taken so the problem doesn't worsen when it could have been solved. As one litigator said, "There are clients in the first meeting who are so angry, or so convinced they're right, that you know it will be handled by the courts or take a long time to settle."

Keep Your Cool

It's easy to say you should stay calm and not overreact. It's hard not to become upset when involved in a lawsuit. If your dog was hit by your neighbor or your daughter by a playmate, the first reaction is either to get even or be compensated for the damage. You come home from vacation and discover that your neighbor has cut down the trees by your fence. Or perhaps you were the one who hit the dog with a stick while defending yourself, or you cut down the trees impinging on your property.

This is the time *not* to overreact. It's more important to wait until your feelings have cooled down, than to jump into a heated argument. If a neighbor runs over and blames you, then try, if at all possible, to listen and not punch out the person. It's when the problem becomes worse, by screaming at one another or throwing temper tantrums, that small problems escalate into the hands of the attorneys.

Getting mad destroys objectivity, makes the problem worse, and doesn't solve anything. There are not many problems worth losing sleep over, night in and night out.

Find Out the Facts

The facts from both sides should be looked at first. For example, if your dog was hit by your neighbor, then listen to what's said. Let's say you're upset because your German shepherd limped back and your 8-year-old daughter said your neighbor had hit it with a broom. Your daughter's crying because the dog's been hurt, and you rush over to your neighbor's house.

Your neighbor says your dog was loose and attacked her small poodle. To save her poodle, she hit your bigger dog with the broom to keep it from killing her pet. It then lunged at her. You don't know whom to believe.

This isn't the time to get upset. Come back later and listen calmly before calling up an attorney to sue over this. It will cost you more for the attorney than it will for your dog's vet bills, and there's always small claims court.

Let's say that someone falls into a hole in your yard at one of your parties. Giving aid to the person should be more important than blaming "that drunk." You might call up later, ask what happened and how the person is feeling. If the injured party is covered by medical insurance, then the matter could end there. Showing a genuine concern could help retain a friend.

Attorneys comment that small problems become big problems because their client thinks the other's a jerk or the issue is over the "principle of the matter." This usually happens because people become emotional instead of staying calm and looking into what actually happened.

Your Subsequent Actions

Everything you do from the time a problem occurs becomes part of the court record should you end up in court. If you ran up to the person injured at your party and said "I'm so sorry. That was my fault," then you made an admission that can be used against you in court. Spend your time instead attending to the person's injury.

> Never admit that something was your fault, if the dispute is important or involves damages. That is a legal conclusion to be arrived at by a judge after reviewing the law and the facts. Everything you do or say that pertains to the matter can be asked about in a later deposition (the informal questioning of witnesses under penalties of perjury) and used as evidence in a trial. This is why you read or hear that, upon the advice of counsel, a party to a lawsuit has declined to give any further information or comments.

That doesn't mean you shouldn't offer to pay medical bills or car repairs should you feel it was your fault. Nor should you avoid filling in the pothole in your yard that a guest fell into. You should take steps to repair or offer to settle problems. The general rule is that such offers of settlement or repairs can't be offered into evidence. However, if the case is large enough or with a greater exposure, then you should consult an attorney quickly over what to do.

How Important Is It?

Some people become upset over the smallest issues—to them, every problem is a big deal. However, you need to find out how many dollars really are involved. If you've already been sued, then you know what the other side feels it's worth. Or at least is trying to get.

If a lawsuit hasn't been started, ask the person who was injured what the costs have been. You wouldn't say, "It's my fault—how much do I owe you?" But you might say "How much do you think all of this has cost you?" Although it makes a difference whether the answer is $100 or "My attorney told me it's in the six figures," you should have an idea as to the amount's importance to the other side. You can then decide what you think is fair.

The importance of any lawsuit depends on what exposure you have and the assets you own. If you own a house with equity and cash in the bank, then being sued over $2,000 may be a headache, but you won't lose your house over it. If you have no assets and are sued for $300,000 (discovering this is dischargeable in bankruptcy), it's not as important as if you owned a house with $300,000 in equity. If you're sued for $300,000 and possess at least that in assets, but have insurance covering the entire matter, then the lawsuit shouldn't be viewed as earth shattering (although it will be negative and time-consuming). On the other hand, let's say someone owes you $50,000, can't pay it, and you can pay only one-half what the attorney quotes you as the legal fees—that would be important. But you still need to put this into the perspective of what's really important in your life—you might say to yourself that things just have a way of working out for the best and go from there.

The importance of a case also involves other considerations. If a creditor sued you erroneously over $10,000, and you wanted impeccable credit, then this would be important. If that stepmother seems to be chipping away unfairly at your father's estate, even though you're well-off, you might think about a lawsuit and attorneys. If the case doesn't seem important to you, then you probably won't talk to an attorney. However, even if it is, then there are a few more things to do before consulting one.

Your Insurance Agent

Most insurance policies have a time limitation by when you must report a claim to the carrier or lose the coverage for that claim (see Chapter 4), so you should talk to your insurance agent as soon as possible. Your agent can advise you on what to do from there. An experienced litigator emphasized "Be sure and tender your claim or defense to every insurance company having *any* possible connection to your case."

Find Out the Law

You don't have to talk immediately to an attorney to find out the law. There are a variety of self-help and do-it-yourself books on the market that delve into subjects ranging from suing in municipal court to collecting on court judgments and dog law. There are books on tenant's rights, car "lemon laws," money problems, social security, Medicare problems, contracts, and even patents. There are even books available in federal buildings or county law libraries that tell you how to do legal research to discover what the law is. Browse through a book store or your library to see what's available.

Aside from self-help and do-it-yourself books, you could look for the answer at your county law library. Interestingly enough, you might discover that some of the do-it-yourself books are being used by lawyers as a reference aid. They happen to be more understandable than what's usually found at law libraries.

Should You Call or See an Attorney First?

Another alternative is to call up attorneys and ask them about your case, whether the case seems to be important to you or not. This doesn't mean you'll hire a particular lawyer, but talking to an attorney on the first phone call about your case isn't charged. (But be sure of this if you have a long conversation.) An attorney needs to determine if he or she even wants your case and in the process of deciding may assess the relative merits of your case for you.

Ask the lawyer whether you have a problem and if he or she would be interested in taking it. After you have talked to a few attorneys (found from the yellow pages, referrals from friends or business associates, or even newspaper advertising), you should be getting an idea as to how important the case is and your exposure or potential damages. If a lawyer wants to see you in person, then be sure that this initial meeting is at no charge.

The question is often posed by the self-help books: "Why see an attorney?" If the meeting will be at no charge to you, then why not? Whether you're leaning toward doing it yourself or not, legal advice can be helpful when you are deciding what to do. If there's a charge for the initial meeting, or you come back, then you have to decide whether this is affordable.

A Number of Outcomes Are Possible

Plaintiffs and defendants, along with their attorneys, come in many sizes and types. Some fight for the principal involved, regardless of expense, and others closely watch the bottom line. People and companies initially see a case as being very important, then change their minds later. Businesses can at first be conservative in their tactics towards disputes, then become aggressive with changes in management.

Some view litigation simply as another way to obtain what's wanted, but this time by using a lawsuit—the legal costs are seen simply as just another cost of life or of doing business. Others become greatly disturbed.

Suing or being sued doesn't at all mean that the judge will rule on the final outcome. In fact, this doesn't occur that often. The defendant may not answer, especially if there's no money, allowing the plaintiff to take a default judgment. The plaintiff may quit prosecuting the case at some point and drop it entirely. The parties may settle the case, hopefully sooner than later. The case may proceed to trial, and a settlement may occur even during trial.

Even obtaining a judgment doesn't mean that the dispute is over. It still has to be collected. The loser may not have any assets or may try to hide them from the winning party. The loser might file bankruptcy, or even appeal an adverse judgment to a higher court.

The great majority of all cases, whether expected to or not, settle before trial. The delays and high expense of the attorneys and court costs force the parties to put an end to their differences. What's too bad is that both parties, after deducting their legal costs, usually are financially worse off than they would have been had their accepted whatever was first offered at the beginning—unless it's a contingent-fee matter, and all the plaintiff has to do is endure the operation of the legal system.

The parties, either through their attorneys or not, eventually reach an agreement. Settlements can be reached through a third party, such as a mediator or an arbitrator. Although this is discussed in detail in Chapter 16, what's important is knowing there are a number of ways that lawsuits wind up and that the court-imposed solution is only one of them.

Before Hiring an Attorney

You can do it by yourself, whether it's a will, contract, or lawsuit—there are enough books on the market giving advice on how something should be done. However, many people don't have the time or the desire to do it alone. The law can be confusing, and no book is entirely applicable to what goes on or is legal in your state. In complex or "bet your house" types of lawsuits, representing yourself isn't wise—judges can be unsympathetic, there are a myriad of technicalities and procedural rules, and you more than likely will make a serious mistake.

The high cost of attorneys means looking into doing it yourself. Use the free consultations whenever possible to find out about the case and potential legal fees. However, be careful when any lawyer says you're entitled to have your legal fees paid by the other party under your state's laws. Until the other party pays them, you are the one legally responsible for the fees. After all, you're the one hiring that attorney.

You'll be paying these fees until they are paid by the other party, as this right to legal fees is only a technical right of reimbursement. The judge or attorneys much later must agree you're entitled to be reimbursed for these costs; the other party then has to agree and find the money to pay up. Until then, it's your responsibility, and what later happens with your case after you retain the attorney isn't what you might first think.

When you've been injured and an attorney agrees to a contingency agreement, the system swings heavily to your side. If you have a "juicy" personal injury case (which to an attorney means the worse your injuries, the better), then that attorney may even advance the costs of the case should you be broke. These costs can be extensive, involving the costs of expert witnesses, depositions, filing and jury fees, transcripts (the written summary of the proceedings), and other such costs. They also will be deducted from the winnings. The attorney is gambling that the return on expended time will be greater by "going contingent." For example, if there's a $200,000 settlement before trial, and the attorney is entitled to one-half, then $100,000 goes a long way.

The system works against defendants, and plaintiff trial attorneys count on this. It can cost you upwards of $50,000 (and more) to defend a lawsuit in a superior court setting. In this country, each party bears his or her own legal expenses unless a statute or prior contractual agreement between the parties provides otherwise. Since the great majority of lawsuits settle before trial, each party bears the cost of their expensive attorneys, unless the agreed settlement provides differently (which sometimes happens).

Thus, plaintiff attorneys in contingent-fee lawsuits can bring legal blackmail to bear against a defendant, regardless of the merits of the case. Many cases settle out of court entirely because of the high potential cost of the legal defense, and plaintiffs count on this. Let's say that the cost of a legal defense is estimated to be $50,000. If you don't have that, then paying $20,000 just for the problem to go away may be considered, regardless of whether the plaintiff has a case.

Insurance companies do this all the time—another fact that contingent fee lawyers count on. If they can just hang in there long enough, they'll be paid. Which is what this is all about—it's not about justice and social goals. This is about money—and the more, the better. Although plaintiff bar associations say they're motivated by protecting society from bad products and representing the downtrodden when injured, only a few would be doing this if the rewards weren't so extraordinarily high.

There's little motivation to settle a contingent-fee case in the beginning. These are usually settled at the time when the plaintiff's attorney doesn't feel there's a good case or doesn't see any further return from putting in more time. It's this understanding that motivates defense attorneys to fight to the last, hoping that all their motions, depositions, and trial procedures will tire out the plaintiff's attorney. It also balloons the cost of the proceedings for the defendant. You can see why the trial attorneys fight against this system being changed—it's very lucrative for them, irrespective of what happens to everyone else in the process.

In cases where the parties are on a more equal footing (i.e., both parties are responsible for their attorney fees), this cost should be assessed at the very beginning. Unfortunately, it usually isn't. It isn't until a number of bills are received that clients decide the case isn't that important after all.

Let's say you finally sued an ex-friend over the $20,000 you loaned him several years ago to start up a restaurant. He also owes you interest (a nice legal rate of 15%), and the entire amount owed by now is $30,000. When sued, he offered to pay you $15,000, with $5,000 down and $500 per month until a total of $15,000 was paid. That was all he had, his attorney told you.

You turned this offer down (your legal costs then were only $1,000), because he owed you $30,000 and you thought he "might" have more money. Your attorney stated you could get a judgment in 1 year at a cost of $10,000 and that the attorney fees would be reimbursed to you (your friend had signed a note providing for legal fees incurred in collection). As a net $30,000 could be received, you decided to go forward.

It may turn out you could get a judgment for $30,000, but after the collection efforts, your legal costs are $15,000. If the only money the defendant has is $15,000, then you could get nothing (you better believe that attorneys get paid first). If your attorney fees ballooned just to $10,000, then you would lose because this is less than what had first been offered (the $15,000 settlement over time with $1,000 in legal fees), given that's all he has. Also, you would have actually received money, not have had to wait years before being paid.

If it turns out later that your friend has no money, then you have totally lost, and your attorney is the only winner. If your friend has some money, then you'd better settle before the legal fees eat everything up. You would be well recommended to make an asset check (an investigator determines how much the other party owns and where it is located) in the beginning.

> What's important to focus on in the beginning is, if you're a plaintiff, you have already lost by having to sue. It's not likely that you'll be getting all your money back, regardless of how good the case. It's now a question as to the net amount that will be ultimately received, *after* the legal and court costs. Fighting for all owing compensation, interest, and legal fees to be paid back only means your attorney makes more money in most cases.

If you're the defendant and feel there's an exposure, then the best settlement offer should be made in the beginning. Let the other side know that this is your best offer, and there's no other money. Let's say you owe the $30,000 but have assets to protect. Rather than selling your home and moving out of state (if found, you still could have to pay), you've decided to do the honorable thing—negotiate the best deal possible.

The $5,000 down and $500 per month, to a total of $15,000, is proposed and turned down. If you are battling on all sorts of legal points (attorneys find a way to defend the most tarnished of people and situations), then you incur high attorney fees additionally, as well as the potential liability for the legal bills of your ex-friend who loaned you the money. This is on top of what you owe in the first place.

Let's assume that both attorneys charge $10,000 for their representation, and you agree to pay $20,000 in cash. If $20,000 was available in the beginning, then it should have been paid at that time. By waiting as long as you did, the settlement cost you $30,000 (the cash payment plus your attorney fees). The victor only received $10,000 (the cash payment less legal fees), but both attorneys did very well.

This discussion has been based on actual cases, and the rule remains the same, regardless of which side you're on. Make the best settlement offer in the beginning and tell the opposing party that it is your best one. If it's rejected, factor in the potential legal fees once again, and see what your best offer really is.

Keep Your Alternatives

Try not to make an enemy of the other party in your discussions before hiring the attorney. Once one has been retained, then inform the other party you're allowing 15 days, let's say, to work out a settlement before the matter is turned over to the lawyer.

If the deadline passes without a deal, then don't give up. Try to keep up communications, even while you're going through the legal process. You might be able to say "Look, you and I are paying a lot of money to try to settle something only we can decide. Let's save costs." It's always better to keep communication channels open, although this is discouraged by attorneys.

State bar ethics prohibit attorneys from contacting the other party when that party is represented by a lawyer, and some states discourage any contact between clients. If your attorney is the only one who can communicate to the other side, and then only through the opposing lawyer, your legal expenses will continue to climb—lawyers are notorious for not being able to reach agreements, especially when their clients are at each other's throats. Keep up communications, whenever possible.

The "Nonlegal" Solutions

The legal system focuses on solving a problem one way—but using attorneys and judges—but it is the problem that needs solving, one way or another. Even if the dispute centers around money, settling the problem doesn't necessarily involve how much is paid in cash and by when.

Look at what's important to the other side that may not be as important to yours. Settlements are made when one side appears to have more "give" than the other, primarily as a result of seing how important other considerations are.

For example, settlements in defamation cases are tailored around written apologies and the payment of some portion of the "winner's" attorney fees. Principles are important, but if a retraction is necessary for the settlement, then it's better to make it now than later. Arguments frequently take place over visitation schedules. If one spouse can only take the children on certain days because of work schedules, then try to settle within that framework and don't resist just to make it more difficult for the other.

If your trees were cut down in error by a tree-trimming company, then ask a nursery how much damage occurred. If not much occurred, then work out a deal with the company to clean-up, replant, and maintain replacement trees, rather than engage in a full-blown lawsuit over questionable damages.

What's important is to look for nonlegal solutions to the dispute. Using the courts isn't the best way to solve most problems.

Think about Nonmonetary Solutions

Thinking about nonmonetary alternatives is part of finding nonlegal solutions. Businesses are fortunate in having this flexibility when there's a dispute. They can work a settlement to take back bad goods and replace them with better ones. If there's a continuing relationship, a credit can be given for an account. Products and services can be supplied at cost over an agreed period of time.

Individuals have less versatility, but keep in mind that there can also be similar nonmonetary solutions. If you owe a friend money, and have little left with which to pay, then try to work the amount off. For example, agree to repair the other's roof or car. If you own a service business, then agree instead to provide free lawn work, dental care, or vet services in trade. If it takes a written apology to help settle the problem, then swallow your pride and consider doing this. This is the time to be creative.

Think if there's something of value that could be taken back in trade. If you own a tractor or some vehicle that's not needed, see if the other side will take that back in satisfaction of what's owed. Try to work out problems with the other party, regardless of how emotional the issue, as though these were next-door neighbors who had lived next to you for years.

Consider Mediation

There are other ways to settle disputes that don't involve the straight legal approach and are much less expensive and less time-consuming. Although this is discussed in detail in Chapter 16, using alternative ways to solve a disagreement start in the very beginning. Look for the telephone numbers of those attorneys and others who perform such services under the heading of "mediation" in the Yellow Pages. They can tell you whether the dispute is solvable without going through the courts. Always talk to mediators before calling the litigators.

Disputes Do Come to an End

Whether by agreement, one party or the other quitting, or by the judge's decision, all cases end sooner or later. Parties tire out from the time, expense, and negativity of the process. There are better things to do in life.

Although it's not known how any dispute or lawsuit will end, your approach in the beginning can determine whether the dispute will be solved in a quick and cost-effective manner. One client said "I thought it would never stop, and all I wanted was to get my money back. It took time, and I got less than I deserved. But I didn't end up in court, which would have been nasty and expensive. It was a relief to put it all behind me for once." The process will come to an end.

Is There a Case?

Previously we discussed the various outcomes that can occur in any litigated case, ranging from either party giving up, to settlement, and even trial. It's extremely important to spend time in the beginning to understand the case in legal terms, not at the end after the attorneys have been paid the great bulk of any monies that could have been used to settle the problem at first.

It's an unfortunate fact, but most people and even businesses typically listen to the attorney from the first as to what must be done. They are angry and would rather "give the money to the attorney than to that S.O.B." It's only later, after the costs have skyrocketed, with the whole process becoming wearisome, that logical decisions finally are made to end the case.

The lawyer who wins is popular with the client; the one who doesn't is not. The lawyer, therefore, has only one rule—to do everything that's possible to win, regardless as to cost. It's your task to decide at the beginning, not during or after a trial, what are the risks of the litigation, its cost or benefit, and tell that to your attorney. Although each case must be analyzed and decided by its own facts and law, there are two basic considerations that apply, regardless of the case.

The Basic Considerations

Each case has two simple equations that are easy in concept, but extremely difficult to apply when you're deciding the likelihood of a win or loss and the value or cost of that outcome. The likelihood of winning or losing any case depends on the extent to which the facts of the case and applicable law are on your side. That expected liability is then viewed against the likelihood of being awarded or assessed damages in determining the value of your case.

Let's say you lent money to a friend without executing a note. If the friend was a business supplier, and nothing else, then the facts are somewhat in your

The Facts and the Law

An old legal maxim provides: "When the facts are against you, then argue the law. When the law's against you, then argue the facts. When both are against you, then settle."

Any case involves deciding to what extent the facts are in your favor and your ability to prove these facts. Then, the extent to which the law is on your side must be determined. You must prove both sides of the equation for a win.

favor—more than likely it was a loan and not a gift (it would be better to have written a note). However, if you gave money to your boyfriend or girlfriend, then later broke up, it's up for grabs as to whether the money was a loan or a gift. It will then be one person's word against another, and both positions will be difficult to prove, whichever way it goes.

People look at the same event and come away with different opinions as to what happened. If you were driving around a corner and hit the plaintiff's car that was approaching from an alley, then a court would look at the police report, skid marks, and other evidence as to who was at fault. If witnesses were present, then their testimony would be important. If bystanders said you were traveling safely, then your case becomes much better. However, if one said you were going too fast and the other that you were driving safely under the circumstances, then your case becomes less easy. You have a big problem if both say that you were traveling too fast. *What's important is that what you think happened is not as important as what you can prove and the law holds.*

If the other driver was proven to be driving drunk at the time, then as a matter of law in most states, that driver could be held responsible for the accident. This would be regardless that one or both witnesses said you were traveling too fast. In this case, the other driver would be responsible, although courts could prorate the damages, depending on the relative fault assessed to each.

In the example of the unpaid loan, let's say you were able to prove it was a loan to your ex-lover. If the other party was able to prove that the interest on the loan was usurious (in excess of what was permitted under state law), then you would have a problem. Usurious loans, as a matter of law, are void in many states and create a liability to the lender, based upon the statutory penalties applied for charging such interest. Other states uphold the payback of the principal but with no allowance for any interest.

There is no such thing as a clear-cut case. Wins and losses depend on what can simply be a flip of the coin. If the facts totally support one position, but the law is against that position, then the law wins. Lawyers, when the law is against them, argue that the facts of the case are different and that the law doesn't apply. Whoever argues best wins, not who has the best, fairest, or clearest case.

This application of the facts and law to your case is applied continually in determining the assessment of liability, regardless of whether you're a plaintiff or defendant. This process is applied as well to the question of damages.

Liability and Damages

The second adage states you must prove liability (a responsibility or obligation to do something), in addition to damages in order to prevail. It's equally true that the likelihood of winning doesn't matter unless there's also the likelihood of damages being awarded. Even in the best of liability cases, if there are no damages, then the case shouldn't be taken further. No damages, even with liability, equates into a win for the defendant.

Liability Let's say you were jogging past a neighbor's house. You and the neighbor had never gotten along, and the neighbor's dog always barked at you when you ran past. It had been a bad day at the office, and the dog's barking had now gotten on your nerves. You stopped and banged on the picket fence, telling the dog to shut up. Then the dog bit you.

Proving liability means proving that someone else was at fault or failed to exercise some responsibility in a reasonable way. It would be tough to prove the neighbor was responsible for failing to exercise due care, if you were the one banging on the fence, putting your hand inside, and getting the dog so upset.

However, let's say you were running past, but the dog had escaped from the fence and bit you unexpectedly. The liability of the neighbor is greater now, as you weren't at fault or a cause of what happened. If you could prove that the neighbor knew that the dog habitually got free and menaced people, then that person's liability would be clear-cut. This liability would be greater if the neighbor could easily have put a board up where the dog kept escaping. Your neighbor owed the obligation to take such steps and keep that dog under control (and state laws can go even further).

Liability also can be under breach of contract, such as not paying back a note or performing agreed services. If you had agreed to paint your neighbor's house for $400 and didn't do it, or failed to return the tools borrowed from a friend, then you might have a liability for failing to do as agreed. If you sold your house and the buyer now feels you lied about its condition, then a lawsuit could be filed over the misrepresentations. In all cases, it must be proven that the defendant owed a responsibility to the plaintiff, contractual or otherwise, and failed to perform.

But the question of liability is never clear-cut. If you argued that the neighbor told you to forget about painting the house (and you had agreed), that would prove the contract no longer existed and present no liability on your part. Proving that your friend agreed to let you take the tools for your working on his house would eliminate your responsibility in giving the tools back. If it could be proven that your words about the house to the buyer reflected seller's pride, and the buyer had a contractor inspect all aspects of the house, then your liability over this might not be present.

Strict Liability Liability is based on wrongful conduct by a party, whether contractual or not, where a duty is owed to someone else. There are situations where the injured party doesn't need to prove the negligence or wrongful conduct of the defendant. Under common law, this resulted from the type of dangerous activity that the defendant was undertaking. For example, injuries caused by dangerous or trespassing animals, blasting operations, or fires can be compensable without proving negligence, fault, or liability (although state statutes have added to this list).

Strict liability is used in product liability cases when any seller or manufacturer of a product sells a product in an "unreasonably dangerous" defective condition. This is usually a question of fact, but if a product could be proven unreasonably dangerous, then the buyers only need to prove their damages. You're entitled to damages, whether it's your iron, lawnmower, vacuum cleaner, or hair dryer that malfunctions and you become injured. This doctrine has been extended to the manufacture of "defective" homes, airplanes, and many other products.

You should consult an attorney to determine the extent to which strict liability applies in your state. When it does, then you only need to prove what your damages are.

Damages Once the issue of liability is settled, then the question of damages needs to be reviewed. Legal damages are what the judge or jury decides to be proper compensation resulting from the wrongful conduct of the breaching or negligent party. Damages can include nominal, compensatory (or general), consequential (or special), and punitive damages.

A rule of law provides that for every wrong there's a remedy, no matter how slight. If there's liability, but no compensable loss, then the party would receive *nominal* damages. This is the terrible $1, $5, or $10 award. For example, if your neighbor said you were a drunk in front of your friends at a party (and you weren't), then unless you could prove you lost business as a result or this had put you in a position of being ridiculed in the community, you would most likely be awarded only nominal damages in your lawsuit for slander.

Compensatory damages are designed to make a person whole after the other party's wrongful conduct. In personal injury cases, actual damages are what's necessary to compensate you for your out-of-pocket expenses. Medical costs, treatments, medications, hospital stays, surgery, therapy, and medically related costs are part of such reimbursed costs. Lost wages and living expenses over what you normally would require (such as a nurse or household assistance) also are reimbursable. Actual damages include more than this, but generally they are what you can prove were due to the defendant's actions and caused you an out-of-pocket loss.

Nonpersonal injury matters involve compensatory or general damages as you would normally expect. If a loan isn't paid back, then the damages will be the principal amount, unpaid interest, and attorney fees (if provided for in the note ot by statute). As we have discussed, this doesn't necessarily mean you will recover these damages. You certainly could sue if a drunk broke your treasured vase, but unless it was a valuable antique (as supported by evidence as to sales on the open market), then you'd only receive the cost of the object (as depreciated over time). Sentimental value—that it was your only remembrance of your childhood—won't generally be awarded by the court.

If the defendant broke your stereo, then you'd be awarded what it costs to repair the stereo, not what you paid to buy a new one. If the stereo was ruined beyond repair, then generally you would receive compensation as to what it originally cost (not its replacement value), less a deduction for the wear and tear or age.

There are *special* damages that are over and above any reimbursement for your actual out-of-pocket expenses. These must be proved specifically. Pain and suffering and loss of companionship (when a spouse has been injured) are special damages awarded in personal injury cases, subject to proof. Pain and suffering, for example, is difficult to prove, as it's a subjective observation. What's painful to one person may not be as bad for another. A court will look at how the injury occurred and how long pain was sustained (a skinned knee versus a broken back) in determining the extent of an award for pain and suffering.

Special damages in contract disputes include those that were reasonably foreseeable to the defendant at the time of the breach. If your supplier failed to deliver a needed component for your product, and you weren't able to meet a sales deadline as a result (thus losing the contract), then these special damages would be part of your lawsuit. However, you would need to prove that the supplier knew about this (or it had been stated specifically in the contract).

A fourth element of damages includes *punitive* damages, or those damages awarded to one party in punishing another's conduct, as well as to deter others from engaging in such conduct in the future. Punitive damages are more commonly awarded in personal injury cases, although they are at times given in other civil cases (such as breach of contract) where the contract beach in itself is a tort (i.e., a product liability lawsuit involving injury with an alleged breach of the manufacturer's warranty) or owing to malicious conduct.

How Serious Is It? If the medical bills were quite small (one trip to the doctor who said your injury was "nothing"), then the dog bite wasn't serious—and neither are your damages. If you were just upset about it, had not even bothered to see a doctor, then there isn't much involved. Having pain for an hour won't get you much in the way of damages. However, if you had to see a doctor, missed several week's of work, and required continual treatment for deep wounds, then the case is legally much stronger. It will now interest the personal injury attorney, because pain and suffering, even punitive damages, are possible. The more damage or injury, then the better the case for the attorney (although you may rather just be better).

Of course, the greater the value of a contract, then the more serious the case and damages. An attorney isn't needed to collect on a $100 note (not a serious problem), but he or she would be quick to help you collect on a $50,000 note (a serious one).

It is easy to equate the seriousness of a case with the amount of out-of-pocket loss. For example, either the amounts loaned (breach of contract actions) or the medical bills and extent of injuries (personal injury actions). However, the law with the current victim's mentality in this country has evolved to where it's common that hurt feelings are argued by attorneys as an element of damages (although in a number of situations they aren't supposed to be). A good lawyer uses the anguish of the client as indicating that punitive damages should be awarded—that the hurt feelings were intended to be caused by the defendant. This in turns feeds on a victim's mentality, since if a person's feelings were hurt enough, then the feeling is that he or she really was damaged or injured.

> Hurt feelings aren't intended, by themselves, to be an element of damages. There normally must be some compensable loss upon which a monetary value can be placed. But where people a few decades ago were less likely to sue over hurt feelings, it's a fact of life now, whether over angry words, being upset, or crying. This doesn't mean that they have a greater chance to win.

An attorney, while listening to your case, is assessing both the liability of the defendant, the ability to prove it, and the amount of damages. If these are present with what the attorney *thinks* are sufficient damages, then your case usually will be taken, provided that the defendant has insurance, money, or assets with which to pay both you and the attorney.

Punitive Damages Punitive damages are always talked about, and attorneys love to sue when they feel such damages can be argued. The reason is these are extra monies awarded by the court (of which the attorney receives part), which don't go to pay for bills.

Punitive damages are damages assessed by the court or jury that are meant to punish defendants for their conduct and to deter future wrongdoing. Courts, including the Supreme Court of the United States, vary widely as to how much in punitive damages should be permitted in any given case. It's been established there must be *some* amount of actual damages in order to support an award for punitive damages. The ratio between actual damages and punitive damages isn't set by law, but determined by the court, based on the facts of the case before it.

This ratio can be much less than the actual damages to even a substantial multiplier on the actual damages. For example, Georgia's Supreme Court upheld a $1.3 million punitive award in a medical malpractice case where the actual or compensatory damages were only $5,000, a 260-to-1 ratio. The West Virginia Supreme Court upheld a $10 million award in a land-title dispute involving compensatory damages of only $19,000. General Motors was ordered to pay $105 million to the parents of a boy who was killed in a fiery, pickup-truck crash, of which $101 million was attributed to punitive damages (this is still being fought in the courts).

Now, this is something to think about, you say. You read all the time about large punitive damage awards and think your neighbor now will receive a well-deserved "come uppance." However, punitive damages aren't awarded every time. In fact, they are usually *not* awarded by a court.

Although sometimes the distinction is made between whether the defendant was just very dumb and very mean, large punitive damages such as the ones cited above are very rare. In fact, on appeal the amount of punitive damages can be and often are reduced because the appellate judges feel that there was no way such damages could be reasonable. For example, a Texas state court of appeals substantially reduced a $15 million punitive award in an insurance-fraud case to $760,000. Plaintiffs will accept lower amounts from what was initially awarded just to avoid the risk of being tied up in years of appeals with the risk of a large punitive damage award being substantially reduced.

The bottom line is that punitive damages usually aren't awarded by courts. Such damages aren't awarded in cases where the defendant was only negligent or simply at fault, because an element of intentional wrongdoing needs to be proved. Second, such damages are meant to deter plaintiffs from such conduct in the future, and many judges reason that being sued and losing a large damage verdict is bad enough. Third, most awards don't come close to multiplying actual damages, when actually given. Fourth, receiving a large punitive damage award can have the odds of winning a $1,000,000 lotto. Fifth, getting your feelings hurt doesn't necessarily mean that you're entitled to punitive damages.

Experienced attorneys counsel that you don't bring an action based on the likelihood of receiving punitive damages. Although they're used as leverage in settlement discussions, the average lawsuit and party will never see them. The awards you read about in the paper are just that—they do happen to someone else. If you want to sue over punitive damages, when your actual damages are low, then talk to an attorney about it before going any farther.

You Have to Prove Your Case

Despite what you read in the newspaper, people who sue over injuries aren't winning most of the cases. In fact, most studies indicate that slightly more than one-half of all suits filed on account of personal injury or product liability reasons are lost. Experienced litigators will tell you that suing is a crap shoot, no matter what type of action is filed. As you can discover in Las Vegas, you have to try it and lose before deciding it's not the best way to spend your time. Even winning a lawsuit doesn't mean it will have been a good experience.

What's forgotten when reading about the huge damage awards is that you *need to prove* that the other party was negligent or at fault, that the negligent act caused your damage, and that the amount of your damages was substantial. Having hurt feelings alone isn't the right reason to bring a lawsuit—that must be measured by other factors, whether it's a personal injury case or not, although statutes can provide to the contrary (e.g., sexual harassment cases).

Nor does proving your case mean that you're in the right—whichever side wins is the one that best proves its position to the judge or jury. Justice is whether you win or lose.

The judge, even though you're right, can choose to disregard your testimony or that of a key witness' in favor of different testimony. If there's no other evidence, the case of your word against that of another means only one person can be believed. For example, let's say that you went to a hair salon. After the treatment, your hair fell out and you sued the hairdresser.

Each plaintiff has the burden of proof in a civil matter to prove its case by what's called a *preponderance of the evidence* (that it's more likely to have happened the way you see it). If you don't have an expert in hair treatment who can testify, "Yes, that type of treatment will cause hair to fall out, and they should have warned the plaintiff," then it's your word against theirs. In this case, a tie doesn't go to the runner—plaintiff loses unless the judge clearly believes you. Even with an expert witness, if the judge doesn't believe your expert, then you still can lose.

If you once lent money to that now ex-lover without something in writing, then you're in trouble. Your ex-lover might have agreed to pay it back, but when there's a breakup, people remember different things. Unless you can prove it was a loan, then the judge might simply not believe your side of the story, holding that the act was a gift. You would get nothing.

It's more important to have favorable neutral witnesses, something in writing, and other outside evidence, then merely to be in the right. Remember we aren't talking about justice; we are discussing what can be proved and how.

Attorneys often give the reason for losing as being "They didn't believe my client." That's the real world. You need to spend time assessing whether you can prove your case better than the other party.

It Isn't Just What You See

An unfortunate fact of life is that people lie, cheat, change stories, and look at things differently than you do. A well-known artist owned a 50-acre piece of property in a beautiful, Eastern resort city, high in the hills. His lover, not as well known but still a gifted writer, invested money with him to help build an expensive house, all on the understanding they would share in the profits upon its resale. Nothing was set down in writing.

When they eventually split up, the artist denied ever making that agreement, arguing the monies were only a loan since the property was by now quite valuable (it's interesting how positions change). In a procedural argument, the witnesses counted on by the writer all changed their testimony—one by one. Where they had said before "You should sue the creep," once in court they changed their minds. Or at least the artist had changed them. He had put pressure on them, through his attorney and personally, calling in the favors owed over the years. Although the writer did get her money back with interest, she never recovered her cost of the legal fees and lost profits, which were in the six figures.

You must be clinical with a slight pessimism when considering any lawsuit to be undertaken as a plaintiff. You bear the burden of proof and must prove your case. Don't take anything for granted when deciding you can prove your case. People do change their minds as to what happened, and when they do, your case becomes more difficult. But your attorney still gets paid (unless it's a contingent fee).

"People don't tell the truth. They change their minds and just plain lie. It's a problem with any case," said one litigator. "I can't remember one case when the parties saw everything the same way, even when the conversation took only a few minutes. But that's to be expected because that's why they're in court," observed another.

The Law Has the Same Problems

Whatever the importance of the case, the law isn't a fixed set of rules and is as uncertain, at times, as proving the facts can be. There are vast amounts of statutes, regulations, precedents, rules, and arguments, many in conflict with one another for any given case. The applicable law is subject to varying interpretations, depending on the lawyer's viewpoint, ability, and even mood, just as with the judge and jury.

Attorneys always have different views as to how the law applies, and there is a large gap between the law and its argument or practice. A law can be straightforward, but the judge doesn't have to believe in it or its applicability. Laws aren't clear cut, as they deal with individual conduct, and people have different views as to what is right or wrong. Juries have to be educated in the law and how it applies in any case, and they are able to switch their positions in minutes.

Decisions are made by juries, even judges, that totally surprise the attorneys. There is no clear-cut case, whether you are being sued or are suing. It is just as likely that you will win or lose once you're headed down the courtroom path.

Especially If This Is Your First Time

If this is your first venture into the game of suing and the law, then take your time to be sure you have a case. Talk to several attorneys, if possible, and get the recommendations of each.

One person with experience in the courts and with numerous attorneys said "Attorneys come in various types. Most are hard-working, honest people just trying to earn a living in a difficult business. However, some are drunks, and you don't know it. Some are just plain stupid, and you don't know it. Some don't even give a damn, and you probably don't know it. It all depends on whom you meet and end up hiring, as well as how good's your case."

Commented one lawyer:

> There's never just one remedy or solution for a case, whether you're suing or defending, and attorneys will say different things. Let's say you owe some money and you're going to be sued. If it's a litigation attorney, you'll hear, "Let's go to court." The transactional lawyer will say "Let's try giving them a deed of trust and see if they'll accept that." A bankruptcy attorney might say "I think we can negotiate that." You need to educate yourself. Talk to several attorneys and look at all the alternatives before making a decision.

Get as much advice as possible as to whether you have a case. Take your time to evaluate its strengths and weaknesses, including any attorneys who are interested in taking on the case. Justice can be how good your attorney is, but remember that good attorneys are expensive.

It Can Take a Long Time to Play

The expense of litigation by itself is a turn-off. However, suing also takes a long time before you can receive a judgment. Attorneys like to argue that this doesn't

have to be the case. They're right when talking about an early se
going before the judge, but this depends on the attorneys involve

If they say there's a "fast track" statute in effect, then don'
fast track statute supposedly establishes short time periods
discovery completed and be into trial. For example, the state coul
case be completely ready for trial within 270 days of filing the ans
good but don't buy it—not all cases are handled the same. In one st
requirement, the parties are still waiting 3 years later. In anothe
waiting for 4 years.

> Attorneys have many more cases than just yours. They go on v
> to enjoy life just as anyone else does. They have family emerge
> difficulties, and too much to do. Your case will drag on, wh
> settlement possibilities or not.

You May Have to Sue to Get There

The process of winning or losing is simply convincing the other side that your
position is better in court, hoping you don't spend much time there. Some people
don't take your threats seriously or have dealt with the court system enough to
know how it can be used. People with a lot of money or no money benefit from this
system. If you have nothing to lose, then why worry about a lawsuit? If you have
money to throw at the other party in expensive attorneys, then you might even invite
one. For the rest of us, it's a problem, and we have to be careful with our legal
decisions.

It's possible to authorize the attorney to start the process, but not to go
further. For example, you would have the complaint prepared and served on the
party, then see what happens from there. But you must be careful with this
approach, considering how the other side will react.

If the other person's astute, he or she may direct his attorney to file a
standard answer to the complaint (which usually costs less then the complaint) and
do nothing further. You could then direct your attorney to take the first deposition,
then do nothing further. The other party could direct its attorney to file the first
motions with the court, then do nothing further. And on it goes until both of you
have spent your money on the attorneys with nothing left for the case.

The moral is simple: use the court system to pry out monies from a defendant
or to successfully defend yourself, but don't go broke in the process.

One seasoned litigator explained:

> I tell my clients that if I get a judgment, the loser might file bankruptcy. I
> ask them if the other person is the type who would file for bankruptcy. How
> far will they go to stiff us if we get a judgment? It makes a big difference. I
> tell them that there's no assurance that they'll make money on their case. I
> try to talk people out of litigation and give them that option—that sounds
> weird doesn't it? But I don't want them to come back to me and say I paid
> you all this money and got nothing for it."

Be Sure You Can Collect (and That There's No Bankruptcy)

If suing someone, then be sure to determine that you can collect if you get a judgment. Suing someone over a principle makes no sense if you're paying a lot of money for attorneys and the person being sued is broke. You might even consider doing an asset check first (the assets and their location are discovered by an investigator for a fee).

Having assets is only part of the problem. You need to assess whether the other party will declare bankruptcy—at the beginning and before you start running up expenses. As discussed previously, bankruptcy can either eliminate the entire judgment or cause any payments to be stretched out over a long period of time. And you are still responsible for your legal fees and costs.

The other side of the coin also applies. If you don't have a real defense or if you have a weak case, then you might talk to a bankruptcy lawyer rather than a defense attorney. As one specialist observed

> People get mad and fight, but you have to have something to defend. If you don't have any defenses, then don't spend $30,000 to fight it, lose, then 2 years later have to file bankruptcy. All you've done has been to feed a system that is imperfect. You're better off using the threat of a bankruptcy filing to prompt a resolution to the problem now. But you have to step back and honestly determine whether you're right or wrong in doing this.

Determine the Importance of the Case

It's necessary to discuss first with any attorney these general concepts before going further. You need to assess the chances of winning or losing and at the same time decide how much time and money will be thrown at the problem.

If you're suing, you need to determine whether there's a case. If sued, then you need to decide what your exposure is, in addition to the likelihood of the other side prevailing. The same general principles apply as to the facts, laws, liability, damages, and proving your case. What happens next depends on the size of your case and how important it is to you.

Small Cases

Small cases, of course, are handled differently from larger ones. Your initial decision will be whether you drop the matter, sue in small claims court (see Chapter 17), or hire an attorney. If you have been sued, then you need to establish how vulnerable you are, whether to settle, and how much money to give the attorney in defending it. When retaining any attorney in a small case, you must remember that a lawyer charging by the minute can build a bill faster than solving that problem might be worth.

You can save the money by doing it by yourself, even saving more in legal fees than the amount of an adverse judgment. Be careful that you don't become liable for the other party's legal fees, however, if the other side has hired legal counsel.

Parties use small claims court even when the amount involved is greater than that court's award limitations. Let's say you're owed $5,000. If the damage limitation in your state's small claims court is $4,000, you could decide to waive the $1,000 that's over the statutory limit. Since an attorney easily could charge you more than that to handle the case, then you are still ahead.

If sued for $5,000 (or what you consider to be a small amount), another way to defend would be buying a do-it-yourself book and handle the case on your own. When you come to areas not understood or known, you could call your attorney on a prearranged basis with those questions. It's standard practice for attorneys to give advice to clients on what to do when involved in small claims court. This doesn't mean you have to consult an attorney—it's only another alternative.

A strategy employed by defendants in small cases is to file a simple answer, then discuss settlement, or wait and see what develops. Or see if the lawyer's paralegal could handle the case at paralegal rates, rather than at standard lawyer rates. Another way is to only authorize your attorney to ask for and receive a written extension to delay filing an answer while settlement talks take place.

Larger Cases

Larger cases, whether you are the plaintiff or defendant, should receive estimates, including discussion of a litigation plan and budget (see Chapter 19) when there's no fixed fee and the open-ended, hourly rate is in effect. This approach forces both you and the attorney to consider where the case is going and how much it will cost. Additional cost control tips are contained at Chapter 20.

If you don't have the money to hire an attorney (or unable to find a contingent fee, if a plaintiff), then there are still some options. If you want to sue, you can treat the matter as a small claims court action and waive the extra amounts. You can try it yourself, even drop it. If you've already been sued, then all the options explained in small case matters are still applicable. But be sure you've talked to enough lawyers—at some time, a lawyer should show some interest even if you don't have much money.

Another alternative is to hire a lawyer who'll charge only for the time required to "coach" you or review what you're doing. You would prepare the court filings which would be reviewed by that attorney. After the lawyer's review, you would make the changes, do the word processing, all copying, and the filings of those papers with the court. Or you could split the work, making an arrangement to pay the attorney for doing certain services with you being responsible for the rest. Lawyers these days are willing to take on less work, even with the lower fees, as having a lower fee is better than earning nothing at all.

Important Relationships

When friends are involved, you may very well want to handle the case differently. Different approaches also are used when you own a business, and an important supplier or vendor relationship is involved. Consider contacting the other party directly before turning the problem over to the attorneys—even if you're the one who has been sued. Early settlements are more likely when the attorneys aren't involved.

See about working out your differences, even when an attorney has been retained. However, do use care in any discussions with the other side. We have seen that conciliatory but adverse comments can be introduced later in the courtroom or settlement discussions as an admission of liability.

The "Bet the House" Lawsuit

If the lawsuit threatens your financial integrity, then decide how much money can be used in defending or bringing the lawsuit. Be very careful in determining how good the case is in the beginning, as this will decide your settlement approach, whether to defend or prosecute at all costs, or some combination. Be sure that this is a true "bet the house" lawsuit, as many lawsuits sound more threatening at first than they do after time has passed. You should be able to get a good handle on this by talking to several attorneys in the consultative meetings.

You'll be more interested in retaining the experienced, although more expensive, legal specialist for these cases. Whom you choose will be a function of how much money you can afford, of course, to give the attorneys. If you're broke, then reading do-it-yourself books (and hopefully talking with attorney friends) may be the best you can do, although it's not recommended. Talk to legal aid to see if you qualify and whether they'll handle the case. However, it's rare that you do and they can.

If not, your salesmanship in attracting an attorney to represent you becomes even more important. Some clients promise what they can to get the attorney to work on their case, then try to pay what they can, even though they owe money. See if it's possible to work out a stretched-out installment payment plan on any legal fees, if it looks as though the fees aren't affordable.

Some clients also talk attorneys into taking their case, giving a small retainer, then don't worry about it when they can't pay the owed fees. One real estate developer "sweet-talked" a sole practitioner into expending over $125,000 in legal time and charges, then walked away. A business owner did the same thing for over $1,000,000, stiffed the attorneys, and they are still in court fighting over the matter. This isn't a recommendation of these practices, but nonpayment of owed legal fees isn't considered a crime either. Yet, I still remember what one seasoned litigator said about a client he took to court over unpaid fees, "I stiffed a few creditors on behalf of my client as part of the services rendered, and then he tried to stiff me. I couldn't take that, if anything for the principle of it all."

Attorneys who have been burned by this process know that they are becoming lenders. They may even ask for a security interest before taking on the case. If they do ask for security, such as a second deed of trust on your home, you

If you won't feel uncomfortable owing an attorney money over time, then as long as you're honest, sell the attorney on your case and obtain the representation. Even if you run into problems, there isn't an attorney in private practice for any length of time who hasn't written off client receivables. Attorneys sometimes don't do anything more, simply because the client was honest throughout but ended up not being able to pay them. Some understand the difficulties, even better than you, when trying to get someone to pay up who doesn't have the money.

have the right to be advised by another attorney due to the conflict of interest (but do you really need this?).

You could decide to do it yourself. The problem is that the court process is time-consuming, complex, and emotional. Although there are substantial cost savings, most people aren't successful, nor find the litigation experience to be particularly enjoyable. In important cases, do it yourself only when that's the only choice left.

Do You Litigate or Mediate?

More than 90% of all litigated cases settle before trial—many long after the high expenses of discovery and pretrial proceedings have been incurred.

The Vast Majority Settle

It may be a surprise to learn that the vast majority of cases settle before trial, one way or the other. In fact, 90% of all lawsuits settle before then. Your goal is to control your litigation costs while knowing the dispute will more than likely settle before it reaches the courthouse doors. It is true litigation costs are driven up excessively when an opposing lawyer believes in the scorched earth approach or when it's a "bet your house" dispute. However, by understanding what happens in litigation, you can gain the tools to help control these costs.

The Process and Some Terms

The filing of a *complaint* with the proper court by one party (called the "plaintiff") along with the appropriate filing fees, whether in federal or state court, commences the lawsuit. This complaint or pleading states the plaintiff's case, its story, what reasons and theories the lawsuit is based upon, and what damages the plaintiff wants in compensation. No one, including the judge, looks at the complaint at this stage to see if it's valid. Sometimes the complaint is filed along with a temporary injunction or *restraining order* for immediate relief.

A *summons* notifying the sued party (called the "defendant") that a lawsuit's been filed is issued by the clerk of the court. The summons, along with a copy of the complaint, is served on the defendant(s). The *service* of a complaint and summons must be delivered to the proper parties and in a timely and legally correct manner. Once the defendant is served with these papers, the defendant has a limited amount of time in which to respond. This is most important as not responding by the stated time with an answer (or some legal response, such as a motion to dismiss), will give the plaintiff a *default judgment*. Although a default judgment may be overturned for excusable neglect, fraud, and other reasons, after a certain time period (for example, 6 months), an uncontested judgment will have the same effect as one decided by the judge after a trial.

This time period for the answer or motion to dismiss to be answered depends on the particular court's rules of procedures and will be relatively short (anywhere from a few days to 15 days or more, depending on the state and what needs to be answered), so pay particular attention to this time period. The *rules of procedure* for a particular court govern the time by when answers or motions are to be filed, what must be included with the filings, what must be presented for a successful motion or procedure to be ruled favorably on, among other extensive and complex matters.

A *motion to dismiss*, typically based upon the failure of the plaintiff to state a claim against the defendant, is usually difficult for a defendant to win, and, even when it is granted, the judge typically allows the plaintiff adequate time in which to amend the complaint to remedy any defects. These motions can be a waste of time and effort and should be looked at closely prior to being filed.

Given no motion to dismiss being filed or granted with time to amend, the defendant must *answer* the complaint (or after an amended complaint has been filed) or face the danger that the plaintiff will move for a default judgment. The answer is used by the defendant to admit or deny each claim of the plaintiff, state any counterclaims (the actions or complaints by the defendant against the plaintiff that arise out of the same subject matter), and to state any crossclaims (actions or complaints by the defendant against third parties that arise out of the same subject matter).

Once the answer has been filed, the parties enter the *discovery* or fact-finding stage. Discovery involves interrogatories, depositions, and motions involving the production of documents, among others. Motions can be made with the court for any number of discovery matters, ranging from compelling discovery to motions for relief or for sanctions against opposing counsel. A *motion* is a written request, supported by quoting applicable statutes or cases, that's filed by an attorney with the court and asks for the requested relief. This request will be granted or denied by a judge in a later hearing.

Interrogatories are written questions filed with the court, served by one party on the other, which require a written response to the questions asked by the party who receives them. *Interrogatories* are much lower in cost than depositions, but they usually fail to result in the disclosure of major facts, since most attorneys counsel their clients to be evasive in the responses.

Depositions are taken, either by the cooperation of the attorneys or action of the court, whereby a person is asked questions and examined under oath. The statements of the deposed person and the questioning attorneys are written down by a court reporter who then prepares a book, or transcript, of the proceedings and witness's statements. Depositions are relatively costly, not only involving the hourly rate of two attorneys at a minimum for the time spent, but also the cost of the court reporter (whose charges average about one-third of an attorney's daily charge). The cost of the court reporter and transcript of the proceedings is usually paid for by the party requesting the deposition (although subject to being awarded to the winning party by the judge, if the case proceeds that far). The time for a deposition by a party's attorney also includes the time spent preparing that witness for the deposition, as well as the interviewing time at first, all of which can amount to a tidy sum.

Motions for document production, examination of persons or things, and requests for admissions also can be filed with the court. Motions for document production involve requesting the right to inspect documents pertaining to the lawsuit. Motions for the examination of persons or things are made in product liability cases, for example, asking for the right to sample, test, inspect, and copy whatever's described. Requests for admissions involve one party serving on the other a request to admit to the truth of the matters set down in the statements made. These matters may involve facts, the application of law to fact, opinions, and even the authenticity of documents. Requests are used to determine facts that aren't in dispute with the likelihood that the parties would agree with them.

If the discovery process has determined facts that clearly establish what happened, the attorney may make a *motion for summary judgment.* This motion states that there's no real dispute or significant disagreement over the facts *and* law, and the court can decide completely for the party in whose favor the facts and law rest. This ends the case then and there. As such a motion takes the case from the hands of the jury or judge in trying the case, judges are very reluctant to rule favorably on summary judgment motions.

As the case comes closer to trial, the attorneys usually will be scheduled to appear before the judge for a *pretrial conference.* Depending on the attorneys and judge, this conference can be either a waste of time or lead to a settlement. Judges are motivated to settle the case at the pretrial conference level, although the attorneys may have different feelings.

As the trial date looms closer (assuming it isn't postponed because of the judge's calendar or other cases that the attorneys have), a *pretrial memorandum* may need to be prepared by each attorney, even served on the other party. This will depend on the rules of the court, whether the case is being tried in federal or a particular state court. Preparing this extensive document is expensive and time consuming. It states the agreed facts and stipulations, the factual arguments that are to be proved, a list of the witnesses to be called and a summary of the testimony, the exhibits, and the questions to be asked prospective jurors, among other prescribed areas.

A *mandatory settlement conference* usually follows and is used strongly by the judge to move the attorneys into settling the case. The clients, or someone with settlement authority, must be in attendance and wait outside the judge's chambers as their case is discussed. Some judges nudge the parties toward a settlement by hinting how they're leaning toward ruling in the case.

Meanwhile, the case is becoming more and more expensive. Motions for sanctions against attorneys and their clients for not cooperating in the discovery process, motions to limit proof, additional discovery, and other expensive procedures may have occurred. Although both sides are learning more about the other side's case and how good it is, the expenses are mounting up with the parties becoming worn down by the process. Last-minute settlements before trial are due as much to these incredible, unanticipated expenses and the negativity of litigation, than as to the relative merits of any settlement offers. "I couldn't believe how expensive it got to be. Then it became a matter of cutting my losses," said one party in a case settled just before trial. "Who did win? I'll have to think about that one," said the other in whose favor the settlement went in that case.

Meanwhile the preparation for the trial continues. Witnesses are brought in and prepared. Exhibits, graphs, videos, and other elaborate presentations for the judge or jury are being created. It can indeed be a grand production but also a rather expensive one.

It's possible for a particular case to be decided by *arbitration*. An arbitration proceeding is the hearing and deciding of a dispute by a person (or a panel of arbitrators) agreed to between the parties in a more informal setting and procedures than found in the typical trial. Depending on the court's rules, however, an adverse decision by the arbitrator can be disregarded by the losing party with the matter then set directly for trial. When nonbinding arbitration is a prerequisite prior to litigating a case, some attorneys use this to feel out the other side's position, then go into trial (asking for a *trial de novo*) after an adverse decision with the additional information gained. However, arbitration can be binding, particularly when agreed to between the parties or as provided for in the agreement under dispute.

The first days of a *trial* involve the *voir dire* of the jury. The attorneys and judge ask questions at this stage of all prospective jurors to remove those who may have a bias. The lawyers try to find those more favorable to their position. Picking a jury can take days, even weeks, depending on the complexity of the case. As people change their minds, depending on what's been heard or seen, and keep their innermost feelings to themselves, it's nearly impossible to determine how any juror ultimately will decide.

The *trial* involves the examination and cross-examination of witnesses, along with introducing into evidence the prepared graphs, videos, and other exhibits. This is when the attorneys prove their case or not, arguing whether evidence should be admitted based upon debates that facts are misleading, irrelevant, hearsay, immaterial, not corroborated, argumentative, or other reasons.

The introduction of evidence in any case is totally dependent on the attorneys' arguments and the judge's interpretation of that state's *rules of evidence* as applied to the case. Trials usually take days and can last weeks. It is true that cases are won or lost by the attorneys; it is also true cases are decided because that was the way the judge or jury decided that particular day. The problem with jury trials is the expense and time needed to educate the jurors on your case and position so they'll vote in your favor without any certainty of a favorable result.

The jury's *verdict* either can be a decision on who wins and how much or it can be "yes" or "no" answers to a series of questions as instructed by the judge. There are also cases when the judge rules alone without a jury. Even if you lose or win a verdict, the process isn't over by a long shot.

Motions can be made during and after trial, such as motions for nonsuit after a party has presented its evidence, asking the court to rule as a matter of law that it has won. A judge typically will take the motion under advisement, not wanting to take the decision away from the jury, then rule on it after the verdict has been reached. Motions can be made for any number of reasons, including reducing the amount of awarded damages and overruling a jury's verdict.

An *appeal* can be taken immediately and within strict time periods to a higher court. The *appellate brief* will list the arguments and reasons why the court's verdict should be overturned. Appeals take a long time, ranging from many months to years. The appealing party usually must post a bond to file an appeal; the bond guarantees that the other party will be paid its damages in the event the appeal isn't upheld. Appeals aren't taken often from adverse judgments, as judgments usually are sustained on appeal, given the reluctance of appellate court to rule differently on the facts decided by the jury or judge. Remember that winning on appeal may mean you try the case over a second time with another set of costs and lost time. Appeals can also be made from adverse decisions or motions and rulings made before the trial.

Even after the appeal period has elapsed, *enforcing the judgment* has yet to be accomplished. Winning in the courts doesn't mean you get your money—it only means you have the legal right to collect it through another process.

Enforcing or collecting on the judgment can only be commenced when you have discovered nonexempt assets that can be seized (see Chapter 10). Compelling a debtor to attend a *creditor's exam* or answer written questions is a start. Although perjury (lying under oath) is punishable by jail and fines if it's proved that assets were concealed, more debtors get away with lying about their assets than have problems later. Debtors also can use the time gained during the lawsuit to hide assets beyond the reach of the judgment creditors.

If the judgment debtor hasn't spent all the money or given it away by the time a judgment's obtained, the debtor has the option to file for *bankruptcy*. Many types of judgments and debts are discharged when an individual files for a Chapter 7 (liquidation) or Chapter 13 (work out) bankruptcy.

It's true that defendants with "deep pockets" always are sought after—the opposing attorneys like to be paid. At best, this process is a long, expensive paper chase, requiring years to get into court, and you may not win. However, collecting the money in the event of a win can be as troublesome as getting the judgment in the first place. It's all a major headache. Unless, of course, you don't have any money, in which case none of this may make a difference.

An Overview

As one person who went through court observed, "It all depends on how good your attorney is, how good the other lawyer is, and how the judge feels. Then, the process is long, expensive, and never conforms to your schedule." Another one said "The attorney looks at life differently. What's an expense to me is income to that lawyer. Success is winning the case for the lawyer whereby I might become broke in the process." And another: "Best way to throw away money I have ever seen, even better than Las Vegas." A judge with years of experience noted "Many plaintiffs are broken financially by pursuing expensive litigation when possible returns are minimal. The case must be evaluated closely in the beginning before the attorney takes it any further."

One person who settled before trial reflected, "What I learned about the judicial system in my experience was enough to last a lifetime. Most people don't have any experience in the law. It's like a disease. You don't know what it's like until you have it. Try to learn something about it before going into the system with your eyes closed." And the observations go on and on.

The vast majority of cases settle after the major costs have been incurred, and these are expensive. Then, consider the long delays before reaching the judge or jury, the potential bad results, stress, and the negativism of litigation. Consider further your downtime and possible bad publicity; companies should think about the destruction of a long-standing supplier or customer relationship. Unresolved litigation can affect negatively your ability to borrow, whether you own a business or not, and you don't even know if you'll win or lose.

A few attorneys realized decades ago that litigation was a terribly ineffective way to solve disputes and wanted to do something about it by establishing alternatives. Rather than operating on a scorched earth approach, these alternatives rely on opening up communications and trying to establish a trust between the two warring parties so that the problem can be solved without court.

Alternative Dispute Resolution (ADRs)

The alternative dispute resolution (ADRs) techniques most commonly used are mediation, arbitration, private judging, summary jury trials, management trials ("mini-trials"), and negotiation and settlement. These are very effective alternatives to litigation whereby the parties, not the court or powers of the state, decide who owes what and what happens next.

> ADRs have seen an explosive growth simply because they're much less expensive and quicker than the one-shot-fits-all approach of litigation, despite the opposition of trial lawyers who see more of their lucrative business being taken away. As you've seen by now, litigation is a poor way to solve disputes and ends up gracing attorneys with substantial income at your expense. For example, a straightforward personal injury lawsuit in a county court may require a 2-week trial costing up to $100,000 for both parties, whereas an arbitration or mediation of the same dispute sometimes can be done in less than a day for $2,000.

More and more, ADRs are being used in individual disputes ranging from divorce and landlord/tenant problems to personal injury matters. A great increase has been seen in their use by businesses, now fed up with the high expenses and long delays when trial lawyers are used to settle what are basically business problems. They're used by construction companies, stockbrokers, banks, and even HMOs (medical service providers). The only people who lose when arbitration or mediation is used are the attorneys—the plaintiff lawyers who live for huge, damage awards and fees, and the defense attorneys who earn $200 to $300 per hour, particularly in the discovery and trial process.

The prime ADRs used today are arbitration and mediation. Arbitration involves an impartial third party or arbitrator who conducts an informal hearing and renders a decision that's usually binding. In mediation, the parties work together toward a solution through the assistance of a neutral intermediary or mediator.

A Brief History

The predecessor organizations to the American Arbitration Association (AAA), the dominant force in the alternative dispute field for decades, was established in the 1920s in response to the complaints by businesses and lawyers about court delays and escalating litigation costs (yes, even then). The AAA experienced success from its inception with nearly 40 offices located across the country and more than 70,000 cases now filed with them each year for resolution. Most of the cases the AAA handles involve arbitrated matters, although more cases are using mediation as their clients become more aware of this alternative.

For years, AAA was the only organized form of alternative dispute resolution. In the early 1980s, its dominance began to be chipped away by other firms seeing the opportunities. Arbitration had become expensive, as well, and sometimes laden down with rules from the attorneys and their continuing lawsuits. Mediation became a well-received alternative with very few rules that encouraged an even faster and less expensive way to solve disputes.

The largest private ADR firm, the Judicial Arbitration & Mediation Services (JAMS), was established in 1979 by a former California state court judge. It has been the most successful of the private firms presently with a case load in excess of 15,000 per year. Early on JAMS saw the opportunities for mediation, and the organization currently employs over 200 former judges in 20 offices located across the country as mediators. Other firms lined up quickly to provide both mediation and arbitration services.

In 1982, an attorney and a law professor started Endispute, JAMS's primary competitor and now the third-largest player in the ADR market, with nearly 7,000 cases handled per year. Together these firms and other smaller ones handle over 40,000 mediation and arbitration cases per year, although the use of mediation is emphasized. When AAA's caseloads are added, then well over 100,000 cases per year are handled by ADRs, and this figure doesn't include the vast amount of cases handled by nonaffiliated, private mediators and arbitrators.

One development has been the increasing competition for ADR business, especially as the major players expand into different states and regions. For example, a large ADR firm began widespread advertising of per party fees in personal injury cases with an estimated value of $50,000 or less as follows: $450 for a half-day mediation, $350 for binding arbitration with an opinion, or $450 for a half-day settlement conference. A number of services were included in each fee, including all research time, filing fees, a guaranteed hearing date within 60 days, and a 10-day cancellation policy. This can only benefit the public.

The savings for companies and individuals alike by using ADRs overall have been substantial. The Center for Public Resources, a nonprofit entity encouraging the use of ADRs by businesses and providing such services, tracked 406 companies and estimated they saved more than $150 million in legal fees and expert witness costs in a 3-year study. Over $5 billion of claims were involved in these disputes.

Other studies show even higher overall savings, including some indicating that mediation alone has realized cost savings per year in excess of $500 million. These are substantial numbers for an industry still in its infancy.

And There's More

There are additional advantages to using ADRs, over and above the large cost and time savings. Such techniques are particularly useful when there's a continuing relationship that someone wants to protect—such as with the child in a divorce case, a dispute between a landlord and tenant, or a customer relationship. Avoiding adverse publicity and ensuring confidentiality by not "washing your dirty laundry in public" are also significant benefits. ADRs can be employed at any time—they can be used before, during, or even after the case has ended. The parties can schedule this at their mutual convenience and not be dependent on the whims of a court calendar.

The ADRs are particularly appropriate when the facts and/or the law are not in agreement. Experience has shown that ADRs lose effectiveness when the facts are relatively clear or one party enjoys a stronger negotiating position. Additionally, ADRs lose their effectiveness when one party strongly believes it has the right to punitive or extra damages that can only be set by the court.

A particular strength of ADRs is that solutions can be tailored by the parties themselves based on their circumstances. As both sides have the ability to negotiate either directly or through the impartial facilitator (or mediator), they have the opportunity to form their own solutions (except in arbitration where the arbitrator makes the decision). Rather than the court deciding visitation rights, for example, the parties themselves can decide what's best for the child. Landlords and tenants can decide what needs to be fixed and how much rent is to be paid during the repair period, all under the watchful eye of the facilitator.

Mediation is especially suitable for disputes involving your company. Rather than suing over a shipment of defective goods, you could reach an agreement whereby the supplier replaces them, even giving a partial credit towards future purchases to compensate you for any damages. Two joint-venture partners, disagreeing on the required capital contributions, could agree to restructuring the venture and changing the funding requirements. Tailoring business solutions to business problems is well beyond the ability of attorneys who are still arguing over which one is the evil empire.

The problem solvers in ADRs can be any neutral person the parties agree on—whether an experienced judge, business person, or some third party—typically selected for having expertise in the matter. They don't have to be judges or attorneys with a limited knowledge in the technical or business aspects of the dispute. These processes focus energies on solving the problem, not on continued lawyering and posturing in seemingly endless court hearings and depositions.

But Be Ready for the Resistance

Arbitration generally is favored most by attorneys, especially since it's mandated by various states in certain disputes. States have encouraged the use of judicial arbitration in less-expensive cases, and this process is typically handled by attorneys. Lawyers also take arbitration courses in law school and usually conduct more arbitrations in a career than full-blown trials. Arbitration is also a more formalized and binding resolution approach (as opposed to other ADRs), thus more closely resembling litigation.

> The other forms of ADRs generally are ignored by attorneys, as they have very limited experience with them. Although mediation is the wave of the future and the most consumer-oriented of all dispute resolution techniques, convincing litigation attorneys to use them has been a problem. Fear always exists with the unknown, especially when lawyers lose business and make less money.

Unfortunately, ADRs Aren't always Appropriate

Notwithstanding the immense benefits of ADRs, they shouldn't be used in every case. There may be times when you'll have no choice except to continue prolonged litigation at great expense, especially when you have assets. If your opponent isn't flexible and wants to wage war, then you have no choice except to follow. Mediation can only work if the other party agrees to using it, although fully 80% of all mediations in study after study eventually result in an agreeable solution to the parties.

Companies resist using ADRs when settling a particular case would encourage similar claims. The tobacco companies would never use an ADR solution in place of litigation. When a vital corporate policy is at stake (i.e., the terms of a franchising agreement as applied to all franchisees), then an ADR isn't likely to be used. Frankly, if the odds of prevailing are good for you, then you'll be motivated toward litigating to the very, bitter end. That doesn't mean you should listen to your attorney in such cases, because spending your time in places other than court can be as valuable as battling over contested issues involving money.

Experts disagree whether ADRs are appropriate in complex cases. Unfortunately, this may largely result from the legal community's fears (and their greed) in using an unfamiliar process in an important case. For example, IBM's claims as to Fujitsu's illegal copying of its system software, a large and complex case, was resolved even in the early 1980s by mediation. A large, expensive 10-year-old dispute between Allied Corporation and Shell Oil was settled quickly after a minitrial. Texaco and Borden, involved in a years-long $200 million breach of contract and antitrust suit, settled using a 3-week minitrial.

Before walking down the rocky, litigation road, talk to an ADR firm in your area and listen to what they have to say. Contact your local bar association for a listing of the firms or attorneys in "dispute resolution," or look in the Yellow Pages under "mediation" or "arbitration" and begin calling. You might be surprised by what they say, and you'll probably sleep better at night.

Mediation

Mediation has had explosive growth and has the greatest potential of all the ADRs—in fact, industry estimates place the numbers of mediation in 1992 alone in excess of 100,000 when all nonaffiliated, private mediators are considered. This process has been used in every conceivable situation, ranging from divorce and child custody problems to automobile accidents, debt collection, medical malpractice, banking, real estate development, construction, personal injury, and business contract disputes. Employment cases, especially sexual harassment and American Disabilities Act problems, lend themselves well to mediation. Companies are now also using mediation in sexual harassment cases, expecially in those where the person bringing suit simply wants the behavior to cease.

Insurance companies frequently employ mediators to resolve their claim disputes with policyholders. General Motors is using mediation to resolve the problems that occur between it and its car dealers. Increasingly, HMOs are requiring their members to mediate first any quarrels over benefits and malpractice claims. Even personal injury lawyers with contingent fees are turning to mediators—they can save time, get their paychecks earlier, and save themselves large court costs. Florida and Texas require all civil suits to be mediated before returning to the courtroom, and other states are considering or have similar programs or variations on this approach.

Mediation doesn't impose a solution, as does arbitration, as its object is to assist the parties in resolving their dispute through the use of an impartial mediator. Its strength is that it's an informal proceeding, not requiring the services of lawyers, the judge, a court reporter, or anyone else other than the mediator. The power of mediation lies not in enforcing a solution—that's determined by the parties through the facilitator's assistance in determining what's important, what's not, and by focusing on common issues and solutions.

A mediator doesn't necessarily have to be an attorney, but should be someone the parties trust with experience in mediating such matters. A mediator can be a priest, rabbi, a business executive, retired judge, or anyone with experience. Lawyers in nearly every locality conduct mediations in divorce, child custody, landlord versus tenant disputes, and other matters, although lay people can and do this also.

The mediator assists the parties to understand other positions, to focus on alternatives in order to settle, and to impartially aid the parties in forming their own solutions. After a brief opening session with both sides, the facilitator generally conducts the mediation by shuttle diplomacy. The mediator moves back and forth between the opposing camps, pointing out the strengths and weaknesses in each party's position to encourage a final settlement. The mediator can propose any party's ideas without concern as to who's first "showing their hand."

Let's say Alice and Peter are running a successful, upscale restaurant as partners. Although both manage the business, they now don't want to work together any more, but they know a full-scale war would hurt the business. Rather than hiring lawyers to attack each other, they could instead retain a mediator. The mediator would first talk to Alice and Peter outlining what happens in mediation, then would talk with each one alone. The facilitator would see where the areas of agreement are.

If Alice felt she deserved more money for her share (although she hadn't said this to Peter) because she had started the business, the mediator would tell this to Peter (if Alice agreed to this). Both could be advised as to how likely it was that they would prevail in court on their viewpoint. The impartial party would go back and forth opening areas for discussion, trying to set the valuation of each person's share, and exploring who would buy out whom. Later, Peter and Alice would be brought back together in trying to gain a consensus. It is quickly apparent that this process emphasizes how you solve the problem, rather than proving that the other party is a liar and a jerk—a much better way to solve problems.

Or, suppose you were involved in a car accident and were injured. Rather than using arguing attorneys and taking years to reach a settlement, you could submit the matter to a mediator. If you had insurance and couldn't reach an agreement with the carrier, it's entirely possible you would be given mediation as an alternative for solving that dispute.

The mediation process can be used for large situations as well. One reported case involved a West Coast investor fraud case. The court gave the 60 parties in the case a 1-year trial schedule, and estimates of the legal costs for all involved ran as high as $60 million. The entire matter was settled by mediation in 12 days. The mediation fees for the entire case came to $25,000 (although not including the plaintiff lawyers' contingent fees).

Resolving your dispute by mediation requires one very important element—the agreement by both parties. Unless there's a provision in your contract to use an ADR, then if one party or the other can't be sold on mediation (or another nonbinding ADR), the process can't be used. But if you're interested and the other party is lukewarm or won't even respond, then contact an ADR firm or professional anyway. The firm or mediator will contact the other party, given your interest in doing this, with a much greater success rates in convincing the other party to participate given both their neutrality and experience.

Settlements can be tailored in ways not available in the courts. Rather than the judge awarding money damages that aren't collectible, a party may agree to work the damage off or give something else that's wanted in return. The proceedings are confidential—the mediator, representing neither side by law, is bound to keep everything private. This method is especially suitable for disputes that involve a long-term customer, business, or personal relationship (such as suing your friend over what's owed) and has been used for years in labor negotiations.

The primary goal of mediation, as with any of the ADRs, is to get the parties to the table—once there, the great numbers of mediations result in settlements. The parties nearly always split the costs of the mediation, whether it's successful or not, but the high success rate makes this ADR very attractive. Given that the average civil case in a state court takes nearly 1 1/2 years to reach some form of conclusion, the speed of mediation is another distinct advantage.

Mediation isn't particularly suitable when one party enjoys a strong case or is "stonewalling" the other. It generally is suited where the facts aren't one-sided or clear cut. Mediating when one party is simply shouting "You said you screwed me for the sheer hell of it in this letter," will be an uphill battle. The process is particularly beneficial when the parties are simply not able to understand or communicate with one another.

Mediators vary widely in their approaches with varying degrees of participation. Some see their function as that of a facilitator; others feel they should throw their opinions, at appropriate times, into the process.

This process is very suitable for any form of civil dispute you might have, whether it's your drunken friend breaking an expensive vase or the neighbor whose dog barks late at night. Mediation can be used when your car crashes, a will is disputed, debts need to be collected, or even when your kid bites another child in a fight.

A litigator who began mediating disputes instead on a full-time basis commented "It doesn't take much time before you realize the existing judicial system is a terrible way to solve disputes. The process tears up people as much, if not more, as the first arguments. Mediation is the only sane way to settle differences." Another experienced attorney said "The problem is educating people into using this process. They walk into an attorney's office not knowing what's available and find themselves in a legal process they wished they had never gotten into. It starts in the beginning as to looking into the best ways to solve a dispute rather than what seems to be available."

Again, attorneys will argue against using this approach, especially when the case is one that the lawyer could take. For example, when two of California's largest banks (Bank of America and Wells Fargo), announced they were adopting mandatory mediation and arbitration programs for certain account disputes, they were sued. The California Trial Lawyers Association was among the plaintiffs, arguing that this would deny customers the right to a trial by judge or jury as well as to equal access to the courts. This shouldn't have been too surprising.

As an attorney observed, "Despite the opposition of lawyers, mediation has and will continue to accelerate in being used to solve problems rather than solving them through the courts, especially in more important cases. There are more important things to do in life than committing several years of your life over a dispute that can bankrupt you. It's certainly worth a try to convince the other side to use it."

In addition to the for-profit ADR groups, various nonprofit community associations run mediation centers in larger cities as a public service. Although typically handling neighbor disputes and landlord-tenant problems, the mediators can handle other forms such as employer-employee and customer-manufacturer as well. Always talk first to some ADR service before seeing the attorneys.

Arbitration

This resolution process, as distinct from mediation, can impose a binding solution on the feuding parties. The parties typically select one arbitrator or a panel of three who hear the evidence and arguments of the attorneys, then render a judgment on the facts presented. The proceedings follow the rules and procedures of either a state arbitration act or those employed by the more commonly followed American Arbitration Association (AAA).

Arbitration is much less formal than litigation with typically no or limited pretrial discovery. The arbitrator isn't required to follow the rules of evidence, or required to have legal training, unless the parties have stipulated otherwise. It's more cost effective, private, can be tried faster, and results in a faster decision than in the courts, although it still isn't as inexpensive, flexible, or fast as mediation.

Arbitration is used frequently by parties who agree to use it by a contract provision in an agreement. For example, client complaints with stock exchange security brokers are typically handled by arbitration, including complaints by their employees against the firms, owing to standard provisions in the appropriate contracts. This ADR is used to solve consumer disputes without a lawsuit. Cases have included protests over sweepstakes printed on the back of cereal boxes, car sales, house purchases, and medical care. Arbitration is used contractually to settle disputes in the business contracts of numbers of large and small companies.

State laws also mandate that it be used at certain times (for example, civil actions up to a limited amount of damages), otherwise known as judicial arbitration. Some 20 states and 10 federal district courts at this time have mandated compulsory but non-binding arbitration as a prerequisite to litigating certain matters. The problem with nonbinding arbitration is that the attorneys might not take it seriously enough, using the process instead simply to see the other side's case, despite the admonition of judges. Parties can also stipulate (or agree) to use arbitration voluntarily after a dispute has occurred or a lawsuit had been filed.

Arbitrators are chosen from a list provided by the AAA, or as agreed between the parties and can have distinct experience in the disputed area. This expertise in a decision is a clear advantage over the courts, as judges can't be expected to have the necessary experience in all the matters coming before them.

Litigators typically complain there's no appeal from an arbitrator's decision in binding arbitration except on very limited grounds (such as improper conduct or bias by the arbitrator), there are no (or limited) punitive damages, that arbitrators tend to "split the difference," and that the process isn't appropriate if you have all the power enforceable in court. It's true that if you or your company usually backs out of deals or wears the "black hat," then you're probably better off to avoid arbitration and navigate instead through the courts in wearing out your opponents. This isn't a very cost-effective strategy, however, and there's always the risk you might lose big.

A clear trend has emerged in using mandatory arbitration of job discrimination complaints in numbers of industries. Owing to a 1991 U.S. Supreme Court decision, employment diisputes are permitted to be solved by mandatory arbitration when legally conditioned so by the employer. Although mediation can be an effective tool in solving these problems, requiring arbitration is a good backup, should mediation fail.

Private Judging

This ADR exists when the parties stipulate that a retired judge hear the case, utilizing normal trial court procedures and rules of evidence, and then render a binding judgment. The parties simply agree to use a "private" judge rather than waiting years for their case to wind its way through the normal court docket.

The advantages of using this method are obtaining a quick decision and retaining confidentiality as to the proceedings. Critics complain that private judging creates a two-tier system of justice that's available only to those who can afford it.

Private judging is different from the rent-a-judge concept. Retired judges can be employed ("rent-a-judge") in arbitrations, mediations, summary jury trials, and in any number of ADR hybrids, other than just private judging cases.

Summary Jury Trial

The summary jury trial ADR has all the normal attributes of a civil trial—counsel selects a small jury from the normal pool; preliminary instructions are given to the impaneled jury; the attorneys make short opening statements; each side presents its evidence with rebuttal from the other side; the judge charges the jury with final instructions; and the jury reaches its verdict. However, the summary jury trial differs in that only a short time is allowed for it (typically 1 day with each side's presentation limited to a few hours), rather than the weeks experienced in regular trials, and the jury's verdict is nonbinding. This ADR is usually limited to use in settling large business differences. Executives with settlement authority attend the proceedings, listen to the arguments presented, then enter immediately into settlement discussions after the informational verdict.

The parties see how a jury actually reacts to their position with time and money saved because of the short time period of the "trial." This method is often used when the parties haven't been able to reach an agreement and are on the courthouse steps. Parties reach settlements in 90% of these cases; if no agreement is reached, then none of the findings is admissible in court by prior agreement between the parties.

Minitrial

The minitrial differs from the summary jury trial in that there's no resemblance to court proceedings. It's an out-of-court, nonbinding, voluntary, and confidential method of dispute resolution, particularly useful when one side has taken an aggressive, uncompromising stance. It's a more expensive ADR than the others, given the need for a trial setting, a written detailed set of procedures and agreement, and all attorneys being present. However, it can be less expensive than having a long trial.

Generally the minitrial is used in large, important business disputes. Each side presents its case through attorneys to two executives (one representing each side) and a neutral facilitator (who may or may not have legal training). The three people are free to ask questions and explore the relative merits of the two positions. At the conclusion of the hearing, usually lasting one day, the parties may ask the neutral facilitator who would probably win.

The executives then meet together without the lawyers to negotiate a settlement. This approach can succeed as top-level executives see for the first time the weaknesses in their company's position, as well as the strengths of the other side. The decision makers meet eye to eye and are not isolated by the attorneys.

Negotiation and Settlement

This approach can't be overemphasized enough. It's an effective ADR, especially if the early settlement of the case is made your goal. Making the decision to negotiate and settle, even accepting less, is the first step to take in avoiding the large problems in litigation.

The Likelihood of an ADR Settlement

The chances of an ADR settlement depend entirely on the commitment of the parties and their attorneys to employing these alternative techniques in good faith. If owning your own business, then the first step is to institute a dispute resolution policy encouraging the use of ADRs by your managers.

Bungee Jumping and Orangutans

Employing ADRs requires the consent of both parties unless state law mandates arbitration or mediation to be used for a particular dispute. One southern law firm wanted aggressive, fearless attorneys working there, so the managing partner took all the lawyers bungee jumping to force them to conquer their fears. Depending on the particular survey, between 60% and 70% of the attorneys surveyed state that a lack of civility and "hard ball" tactics are increasing in the courtroom. Such

Provisions should be in your contracts requiring mediation and/or arbitration when there's a dispute. Agreements providing for ADRs in lieu of litigation have been universally upheld by the courts. A clause should be inserted in your contracts (especially with complex or large-dollar deals) requiring the disagreeing parties to first utilize nonbinding mediation, then another ADR if that's not successful. Arbitration is currently the most commonly agreed to ADR. Consult an ADR firm in your area for the wording as to what's best for your particular situation.

aggression and mauling tactics are avoided when you're using ADRs, and they have grown in use despite the attorneys.

Melvin Belli described the dilemma best. A federal court panel prescribed civility training for older attorneys and a pledge of good conduct for new members of the bar. The report for the Seventh U. S. Circuit Court of Appeals said rudeness was especially troublesome and present when the lawyers engaged in "Rambo-styled" discovery tactics only to find out what the other side knew. The report committee recommended "civility" training and a pledge of good conduct among other steps in its 38-step proposed code. "It's not reality," commented Belli. "To come in and say now they [the attorneys] are going to get a post-graduate course in civility is like going out in the jungle and teaching orangutans to use a knife and fork."

Several years ago, a group of law and journalism professors at a leading midwestern university announced an ADR program was available for libel lawsuits that had been brought against the media. The project was able to convince only five of the contacted 128 libel cases to bring their disputes into the program. The financial interests of the litigating attorneys and their resistance to trying the unknown were cited as the reasons for the project's failure.

Yet the definite trend is to use ADRs, and especially mediators, in settling disputes. They will be used more and more in replacing litigation, no matter how much the trial attorneys kick and scream. Lawyers will have to use ADRs more, if only because the costs of litigation are already so out of hand and are escalating. Lawyers need the business and will have no choice but to accept ADRs as the wave of the future. Clients, too, must insist on using them more than they currently do.

17

Can This Be Handled in Small Claims Court?

Small claims court has advantages not found in higher courts, such as municipal or superior courts. Here you can prepare and fight your own case without an attorney. The actions are simple and not complex, starting with the filling out a form available at that court. Procedures are inexpensive, and decisions are made quickly. The only drawback to these courts is the dollar limitation to how much you can sue over.

The Dollar Limits

The dollar limits on small claims court actions vary among the states. Although the highest dollar limit on such actions is in Tennessee with a $10,000 limitation presently, the dollar limits in most states are less than $4,000. Although small-claims actions have low dollar limits, the cases are tried quickly at little expense. The use of an attorney is either not necessary or not allowed in small claims courts, and the cases are resolved within 30 to 60 days after filing the complaint. Additionally, states are coming under increased pressure each year to raise their dollar limits, given the fact that small-claims courts are a cost effective way to litigate disputes. Information as to the maximum judgment amount allowed and procedures should be obtained from your local court. Be careful when reading a do-it-yourself book, as the numbers on judgment limits quickly become out of date.

Should You Sue if You're Owed More?

The speed and limited expense in a small claims court action means that a lawsuit in excess of the dollar limitation can still be the best valued approach in prosecuting a claim. For example, if the maximum amount one can be awarded in a small-claims court is $5,000 (as in some states), then any case with damages or amounts owing up to at least $7,500 may be appropriate to file there, including collection matters. Although you waive your ability to collect the addition $2,500, you can assume that an attorney would charge you at least $2,500 in fees before obtaining the $7,500.

Some individuals, and even more companies, choose to write off even higher amounts when considering whether to file in small claims court or in a court with higher limits. Small claims courts involve quick, informal proceedings with low filing fees and less stress. The process in regular courts presents much higher filing fees, legal expenses, formalities, complexities, and delays—it takes years in some states before a case comes to trial. If you feel that avoiding such delays is worth more, then additional dollar amounts can be considered when you decide whether to bring a case in small claims court.

What if You're Sued and Your Claim Is Much More?

If you feel that you have a claim against the plaintiff in a small claims action, then you can make that claim, if it arises out of the same occurrence or transaction. However, if you believe your claim is greater than the damage limits, then you have the right to bring that action in a higher court.

Some states require that claims over the limit be heard by the small claims judge to determine if the case has sufficient merit to be transferred to the higher court. In any event, you must begin a new action in the higher court, all in accordance with your state laws.

What Happens in Small Claims Court?

The action begins when either you or the other party files a complaint on the proper form and pays the required fee. These forms are available at the small claims court. Be sure to get a copy of the rules and procedures that govern your case at the same time and read them very carefully. As questions come up, then ask the clerk of the court who usually is very helpful.

It's necessary to fill out the complaint, or the answer, very carefully to be sure that all the important facts are listed. If you are suing, then you'll need to arrange for the complaint to be served. You can have someone else serve the lawsuit, other than a Marshall or the Sheriff's Office (as allowed by the court's rules), but you or anyone else connected with your case cannot serve the papers on the defendant.

You must give a certain time period, which time varies among the states, to allow the defendant time to prepare for the hearing date after serving the papers. During that time you will want to get your case in order.

Don't wait until the last moment to begin this preparation. On the date of the hearing, you will present your evidence to the judge, along with the other party. The judge will ask questions of everyone, including the witnesses, and review any documents or exhibits presented.

The judge will make the decision on your case in a matter of weeks after the hearing. If both parties agree with the decision, then the matter stops there (although there is the matter of collecting the judgment). If you don't agree, then you can appeal that decision to a higher court.

However, most states put limitations on this right to appeal. First, you will need to file the proper appeal papers within a short time period (including paying the required fee) after the date of the judgment. This time period can range anywhere from a few days to 1 month or more, depending on the particular state. Second, some states prohibit the plaintiff from making an appeal, reasoning that these parties had intended from the start to bring the action in that court.

States also limit the right of appeal to just those who showed up in court and argued their case. If you didn't, then you may not have the right to appeal. You can appeal if you think that the wrong law was applied, but you generally can't appeal based on the facts—as with any appeal, the appellate court will assume that the lower court had the best vantage point to determine what the facts were. Again, as with any other court, you'll need to pay close attention to the rules of procedure and regulations that govern such an appeal.

Preparing Your Case

The most important step, other than paying attention to the rules, is to prepare your case. It's not enough that you believe you're in the right. You have to *prove* to the judge's satisfaction that your position is what actually happened.

The judge doesn't know who's right when the parties argue what happened or who was responsible. Look at it from the judge's position. He or she doesn't know either one of you (if a judge does, then that person should let someone else hear the case) or what happened. Whichever case sounds best is the way the ruling will go.

Let's say you sued the defendant for selling you a rare bird that died only 3 weeks after you brought it home. Even though you took good care of it and followed all the directions, one morning the bird was dead. You remembered that the bird wasn't "acting right" only days after you bought it. In fact, you called the defendant to ask what the problem could be. Actually, it never was quite right, and you know the bird had been sick when you took it home. After you told the judge how sick the bird appeared to be a few days after the purchase, the defendant said the bird had died because you didn't take care of it. Who is the judge going to believe?

Unless there's evidence to prove your case (i.e., a witness was there when the seller said the price was lower because the bird wasn't "as good as the others"), then the judge will listen closely to decide who's telling the truth. But the judge doesn't really know who is or isn't fibbing. If the judge can't decide this, then he'll usually rule for the defendant. The rule that the plaintiff must prove its case by a preponderance of evidence gives the judge a way to make the decision when there's a tie.

In Chapter 15 we discussed a few principles that apply to any case, regardless of whether it's in small claims or a superior court. You must research the law to know what's on your side and prove that the facts are as you see them. You must prove the defendant's liability and the amount of damages caused.

How should you go about this? In this case, you would try to find other people who had the same problem with sick or dead birds bought from the defendant. If there were books dealing with the care of such birds, you would find the passages that supported your position and argue those points. You would obtain sworn statements from friends, or have them present, to testify that you took good care of the bird. Perhaps your vet would write a letter stating that the cause of the bird's death was due to a preexisting condition.

In short, you need to prove your case. However, if you can't and the damage or loss to you is small, then you might forget about it and save the wasted effort. Sometimes it makes more sense to not fight an uphill battle when your time is worth more spent somewhere else.

Talk to Someone Else

It's not enough to tell someone what you think happened, whether a friend or the judge. You might sit down with a friend and have that person play the devil's advocate with you. Have the person make all the possible arguments as if he or she were in the defendant's shoes.

Let's say you came out to your driveway just in time to see the defendant back into your car. He apologized, gave you his business card, then drove away. Later, you called and he denied ever hitting you, so you sued him in small claims court for the cost of the repairs.

We know it isn't enough to just say you saw him back into your car and break your taillight. You must *prove* to the court that: (1) the damage to your car was caused by another car; and (2) that the damage was done by the defendant driving his car. Then you have to prove how much it cost or would cost to repair that damage by submitting repair estimates or invoices.

Your friend, playing devil's advocate would say that there were no witnesses. Darn it, you would conclude, there were no witnesses. If there had been witnesses to the accident, they could testify in court or sign a statement in front of a notary that the defendant's car had backed into yours that day.

Your friend would then say "Prove that my car did it." You could take pictures of your car (and the defendant's when he wasn't around) showing that paint chips matching the defendant's car were on your broken taillight and bumper. You could measure that the height of the damage to your car was equal to the height of the damage or the bumper of the defendant's car. It might be possible to find someone who could say he or she saw the defendant's car by yours just before the accident. If the police had been called and at the time had made a report, this report could also be used in support of your case.

Evidence

Evidence can take several different forms. There's *direct* evidence that proves your case directly. For example, a witness saw the defendant hit your car, then exchange business cards with you. Having a credible witness on your side who saw what happened, whether in court or through a sworn written statement, is the best evidence in small claims cases.

Evidence is *circumstantial* when it proves a fact from which you can draw an inference supporting your case. Similar-looking paint chips from the defendant's car that match those on yours and are the same height of damage tend to show that the defendant was responsible for the damage. A police report could be helpful, if the defendant made incriminating statements or the investigator commented about who could have been responsible.

Evidence can be oral, written, physical, or in whatever form is available to help prove your case. If you're suing because the caterer didn't bring enough food for your guests, having a written contract indicating the number of guests to be served would help your case. If the defendant broke your prized vase, then a picture of that vase (both before and after) plus a written appraisal of its cost and value would be quite helpful on the issue of damages, after another guest testified in court that the defendant fell against it when drunk.

You should bring to court whatever you have that tends to prove your case. An advantage of small claims courts, as distinct from other courts, is that the judges will be more liberal in what they'll allow to be considered as evidence.

A Few Tips

1. *Don't wait to bring your case.* Every state has what's called a statute of limitations that bars you from bringing a lawsuit if you wait too long. For example, states limit your right to bring a personal injury action if that action isn't brought within 1 year (or some time period) after you discovered the injury. You should bring your lawsuit as soon as possible.

2. *Have some chance of collecting.* There's nothing more frustrating than going through the trouble to sue someone, prove the case, and win a judgment, only to find out later that the person has no money or is judgment-proof. You should have at least some way of getting that judgment paid, whether from the defendant's assets or earned income. If the defendant has no money and you discover that person is filing bankruptcy, then forget about it. Forgiveness is best when you can't get a dime.

3 *Serve the right parties.* If someone who's married borrowed money from you, then sue both the husband and the wife. If the driver of the car turned out to be the owner's brother, then sue both the driver and the owner. When in doubt, talk to the court clerk even if the defendant is living outside the state. This is your chance to imitate the attorneys.

4 *Get your story straight.* It makes sense to iron out any inconsistencies before you show up in court. If you're not sure what happened, then talk it over with your witnesses before court, not afterwards. Nothing is worse than to have witnesses and other evidence be inconsistent in front of the judge.

5 *Learn some law.* If your case involves more than, let's say $1,000, it may be worth the cost to buy an hour's worth of time from an attorney. You can ask what laws govern, the governing statutes or cases, and what should be done so that you'll win. If you want to save the money, then head to the local law library, ask the librarian how to find the law for your case, and research it from there. Also, there are a number of do-it-yourself books that can be browsed through at bookstores. If one seems to cover your problem well, buy it and save yourself the legal expense.

6 *Be prepared.* We've discussed the need to prove your case and to do your work before appearing in court. The one who generally wins in small claims court, especially since attorneys are either not allowed or too expensive, is the one who's best prepared. This is no different from what attorneys do (or should be doing) when they're in court.

7 *Don't tell a good story, just prove your case.* Small claims court judges are used to people who come in, try to act honest, and only tell their side of it. As we've discussed, this doesn't win cases. You need to prove your case by giving the judge something to hang a hat on in favor of your position. Witnesses, photographs, written statements, police reports, and written appraisals are more important than what you think happened.

8 *Fill in the gaps.* A judge needs to know the entire picture. When having your friend act as the devil's advocate, try to think about the questions a judge would have. Don't let the judge guess at any facts or the answers to any questions. For example, if your friend says the defendant could argue he wasn't driving the car then, try to find someone who can place the defendant as being in the area at that time. The judge shouldn't have to guess whether the defendant was driving the car, especially when the defendant is saying he wasn't.

9 *Don't ramble.* Once in court, you need to be brief, to the point, and not repeat the same thing over and over again. There will be many other cases to be heard, and you don't want to leave a bad impression on the judge. You want to offer only evidence and arguments that have to do with the case. Don't tell your life story or how you got a cold on the day your car was hit.

10 *Be courteous.* There's no need to argue heatedly with the other party or the judge. You should be firm and not agree with what the other person is saying, but there's no need to call that person a liar or a crook. That only makes you look bad.

You Now Have a Judgment

The celebration doesn't begin when you get a judgment. As we discussed before, your job has just started, because now you need to convert that piece of paper into hard, green cash. This is sometimes the toughest problem, especially when you're in small claims court. If you lost the decision, you still can negotiate with the winning party by saying you don't have any money, not going out of your way to pay the judgment, or just being evasive. Be prepared for this when you're on the other side.

The judgment creditor can use creditor's exams, negotiations, recording judgment liens, employing levies, and other collection efforts as discussed in Chapter 10. Remember that many types of property are considered exempt under various state laws, such as the equity in a house, the car, furniture, tools used in a trade, and other articles, all up to state-mandated levels. If the car is used in the defendant's business, then the entire car or a higher dollar level may be exempt, depending on the particular state. Thus, defendants can even have assets and be considered judgment-proof. This doesn't mean you shouldn't sue or undertake collection efforts, but it means that you should think about some way of collecting before you sue.

Some attorneys advise taking the judgment and simply recording it in the counties where the defendant owns real property and resides. The judgment sits as a lien on all such real property, needing to be paid off when the property is sold. If you feel that the defendant will eventually come into property, then recording that lien may make some sense. But don't forget to renew that judgment every 10 or 20 years, depending on your state's laws.

If the judgment debtor has severe money problems, then bankruptcy may be filed. Small claims court actions are almost always wiped out by a bankruptcy filing, because they usually are unsecured, everyday types of obligations— the type that are dischargeable. If your debtor will be filing bankruptcy, you would be better off to forget the entire matter.

This happens every day. The owner of a small commercial building had a real estate brokerage company break the lease. The broker was obnoxious about it and told the property owner, "Big deal about the lease, so sue me." The owner was tempted but had heard that the broker had financial difficulties and decided to wait, knowing the statute of limitations in that state was 4 years. One year later, the broker filed for corporate and individual bankruptcy, so the owner at least had the satisfaction of not being stiffed a second time by having gone through the legal process in vain.

No Attorneys Need Apply

Many states don't allow attorneys to appear in small claims court unless they're suing on their own behalf. In states that do, the limit on damages generally makes the use of an attorney not cost effective.

The beauty of small claims court is that you can be your own attorney in cases that shouldn't have an effect on your balance sheet. Suing or being sued is simple when there are no attorneys and the case isn't a "bet your house" type of problem.

However, one sentence to the wise: *If there's a chance that the defendant has a larger countersuit against you, then it may make sense not to stir up a hornet's nest that lands you in a higher court.*

When You've Been Sued (and How to Find the Right Attorney)

Find your litigation attorney, if at all possible, before you're served with the lawsuit when you believe something might happen. This is emphasized because it's so important. If a temporary restraining order or order to show cause is served with the complaint, you may only have days, sometimes hours, in which to respond. Don't wait until the last moment to try and find an attorney. It not only jeopardizes your case, but it also can result in a higher legal bill when your new attorney must stay up long hours to meet filing deadlines, rather than being able to work your case into the daily routine. This anticipation always pays a return.

Read the Complaint Thoroughly

After receiving the papers, take the time to read them over, once you've cooled down. Although you don't want to lose time finding an attorney, you want to see what's being alleged, the time by when you need to respond, the court that the lawsuit has been filed in, and how important the dispute seems to be. If you're still mad after reading the papers, put them down and read them again later. It's very important to keep your emotions under control, so that you can make good, objective decisions.

You need to think what leads you have to attorneys, how much you want to spend on the defense, and how much time you can give to the case. If the case is in small claims court or is a small matter, then at least it isn't a "bet your house" problem. If the case is more important, you'll want to consult with the lawyers right away.

Investigate at the Same Time

At the same time you're deciding on the leads to attorneys (see Chapter 5 again), start investigating the facts that are the reasons behind the controversy and problems. Don't put this off until the last moment either. Get the facts together quickly and organize them for presentation to the prospective lawyers. Presenting an organized synopsis of the facts makes it easier for both you and the attorney to determine if that lawyer is the right one for your case.

Contact Your Insurance Agent Quickly

You've been paying premiums for expensive homeowner, automobile, and other insurance policies. Given coverage by the policy, you won't be responsible for the costs of defense or the lawsuit if you've been injured.

Contact your insurance agent as soon as possible after the claim or lawsuit has been received. Many policies provide that if you don't contact the insurer within 30 days after the accident occurs (we aren't even talking about when an answer must be served), you lose this coverage and the right to the insurer paying for the costs of defense and damages. You have the additional duty to cooperate with the insurance company or their appointed counsel, with the insurance company in return having the duty to exercise good faith in its handling of your defense.

Given you have such coverage, it's the insurance company's responsibility to secure counsel. If you don't have coverage, then it's your responsibility—but don't take "no" for an answer when your agent says there's no coverage. Bring a copy of the applicable insurance policies to any meetings with prospective attorneys, asking them whether there's coverage. This cannot be emphasized more, given the huge expenses at stake in the litigation game. It may even be necessary to bring a separate action against the insurer over the company's failure to defend you.

If the insurance policy covers the lawsuit or claim, then the insurance company will hire a defense attorney at its cost to represent you. Generally, you don't have any say as to what attorney is retained, because the insurer is paying for this representation. The carrier typically has retained the law firm in advance to handle claims of this nature, already having negotiated in advance the contract rates and fees to be charged.

These lawyers actually represent the insurance company and to whom they bill their services. Although they must provide the best legal defense possible on your behalf, they usually won't advise you as to the extent of the policy's coverage. That is your responsibility, and you may have to consult a second attorney should you have questions on that. For example, the carrier might say it will pick up the costs of defense, but that the damages are your problem. When what you hear doesn't sound right, then check it out before accepting what's being told you.

Finding the Right Litigation Attorney

The basic criteria for choosing litigation attorneys over other lawyers are similar as those when you're looking for, let's say, a business attorney—overall experience in the field, familiarity with your type of problem, extent of defense or plaintiff work (depending on which side you are), availability, and cost. See Chapter 5 for a discussion of this, as well as additional considerations, such as costs, time availability, and the ability to work together.

The problem of securing the right litigation counsel is different depending on whether you plan to sue or have just been sued. As defense counsel typically isn't in place when the complaint is received, there can be extraordinary time pressure to find the right attorney with the deadline fast approaching to answer the complaint. The fee structures are also different.

If you've been sued, then your lawyer should be experienced in civil defense tactics and strategies. If you are suing, then you'll want what's called a plaintiff's attorney. Although it's true that litigation is litigation, at least in important or complex cases, you're better off with an attorney who specializes in the side you're on. The approach and strategies are quite different depending on whether you're the plaintiff or defendant.

The attorney should also be experienced in civil litigation matters, if at all possible, that deal with the subject matter of your case. Although this isn't always possible, especially in small towns and localities, defending a breach of contract action is different from defending a personal injury lawsuit, because of the subject matter alone.

If, on analyzing the case, it is determined that the matter must be judicially arbitrated, it would be better for your attorney to have had good experience in arbitrating matters rather than just trial experience. Needless to say, as the case's importance increases, you'll be looking for an attorney with more experience in your exact type of case.

In important cases involving your company, you will want to be as specific in your retention of the attorney, as well. For example, if you're defending a sexual harassment complaint, you will want an experienced defense attorney who has handled such cases, although not necessarily ones in your industry or with identical profiles. The problem accelerates when you've been sued without an attorney in place—you have a very short time in which to find, hire, and bring your attorney up to speed.

But you need to keep your emotions out of the way to be able to solve the problem. Further, any litigation attorney selected must be able to tell you both the upside and the downside of your position, including being willing and able to consult with the other side to try and settle the matter quickly without unnecessary expense.

When you telephone a prospective attorney, you're best off giving a quick sketch of the problem; then, to save time, ask if that attorney's available. Remember that it makes a difference whether you're a plaintiff or defendant as to the fee structure. If you're a plaintiff, you'll be interested in the lawyer taking your case on a contingent fee. If you're a defendant, you'll want to determine the hourly rate, retainer (if at all), and possibility of a fixed fee.

Don't Delay

If you think time flies, wait until you've been sued and don't have an attorney. Start looking for one the day you receive the summons and complaint. Holidays and vacations may intervene during the time period for answering the complaint. The action may have been filed out of state. It will take time, even after you have hired your attorney, for that person to clear the calendar, spend sufficient time on your case to understand it, and then draft and file the appropriate response. This can't be put off one day.

Determine the Response Date

It's critical that the date by when the complaint must be responded to is determined accurately, as well as the court in which you need to file your response. The time required to respond is different depending on the particular state or federal court. It will be anywhere up to 20 to 30 days from when you or your representative have accepted the service of process. Additionally, check the location of the court where the complaint was filed. If it's out of your town or state, then your search and hiring efforts become more difficult.

You may even call up attorneys you won't use and confirm the last day on which you can file a response and in which court. Although it's possible to set aside a default judgment owing to a tardy response, you shouldn't rely on this expensive, risky process. Ask any contacted attorneys who are unable to take on your case to recommend others.

If a temporary restraining order or order to show cause has been included, then you may only have days or hours in which to reply. This is why you should locate attorneys, if at all possible, before you are sued (and try to solve the problem before the lawsuit is filed). If you don't and can't locate someone in time, you'll have to appear in person and try as best you can to convince the judge to make some allowance for not finding an attorney. However, throwing yourself on the mercy of the court is never a workable solution.

Don't Panic and Forget about Expenses

Just because you've been sued unexpectedly doesn't mean you need to give your attorney a blank check. If you start in time, calling up several attorneys and discussing the case over the telephone, you can still use the negotiating and cost-control techniques that have been discussed. It is understandable that you want an attorney in place, but not one that you find out later does a terrible job or can't be afforded.

In addition to looking closely at Chapters 19 and 20, here are a few tips:

1 *Interview more than one firm.* You can't gain cost control or savings if you don't interview and compare different attorneys, whether looking in your area or out of state.

2 *Receive an extension to answer, then negotiate.* Whether you're under time pressures to find an attorney or not, ask for an extension from the answer date to explore settlement alternatives. It can take the heat off when you're running into problems finding a lawyer. But don't say the reason is you're having problems finding someone to represent you.

3 *Hire the attorney only for the initial response.* If you're not sure about the attorney you're hiring, and the time pressures are great, then simply hire that lawyer only to file the answer. This is easy to do—just say, you want an answer filed and will look at the case after that.

4 *Look for the fixed fee.* Whether you're under time pressures or not, always ask for a fixed fee or at least a cost estimate.

5 *Think early settlement.* Settling your case begins when you first begin thinking about it.

When Sued Out of State

If the court is located out of state, you should retain counsel who practices in that state. An attorney in your state isn't licensed to practice law in another state. It's not cost effective, even when an attorney is so licensed, for counsel in one state to travel and litigate in another. It's better to have an attorney who knows the judges, rules of procedure, and opposing lawyers where your action will be tried.

Call up friends, attorneys, and business associates for recommendations. If your company has been sued, then see if your chamber of commerce or trade association has recommendations on leads to out-of-state attorneys. Talk to anyone you think has a connection to one.

Consult the *Martindale-Hubbell* legal directory in your local law library for the city and state where the lawsuit was filed. Check out the size of the firms. The listings in this directory indicate the type of legal work firms engage in and their representative clients. If your business has been sued, look to see if any companies in your field are listed as clients. You need to be watchful as the law firm may not be able to represent you due to a conflict of interest, especially when one of their clients is a direct competitor. However, let the law firm determine whether there's such a conflict after you have disclosed all the facts.

If there are several firms with experience in your type of litigation, you will have the luxury of not needing to use the biggest law firm (which usually will be the most expensive). Read the biographies of the attorneys at these firms and review their education, bar associations, background information, age, and try to assess how much experience they have had.

While you are at the county or federal law library, ask the librarian if there's a copy of the *Prentice Hall Law & Business Directory of Litigation Attorneys*. It lists the attorneys in litigation (although not all of them), and you can compare this information with what's in *Martindale-Hubbell*. Ask the librarian to suggest other regional reference ideas.

Start calling attorneys in the out-of-state area as soon as you have names, but don't be discouraged if you can't find one right away. Even with the numbers of attorneys looking for work, they sometimes are too busy, on vacation, or may not be able to return your calls quickly. Attorneys who can't accept your case should be able to refer you to others in that city.

Be specific when talking to these lawyers, advising them as to the names of the parties (for the purpose of the conflict check), the court, the type of case, and the day by when the response is due. You should specifically request a conflict check, if the attorney doesn't at first bring this up. You can't afford the luxury of later discovering that the lawyer can't take the case because 7 years ago the firm did work now deemed to be a conflict.

After going through the details of your case, be sure to discuss fees, even if that lawyer can't accept the case. You want to find out what fees and billing rates are generally charged in the area. Even if the attorney says he or she is available, you should still contact other attorneys—don't hire the first person who's available.

Be sure that any review of documentation is on a non-charge basis; you don't want to be billed when you're just trying to find the right attorney. *Know when the charges for your case begin.*

If possible, hold off retaining the first attorney if you feel another attorney is also available and similarly qualified. This makes it easier to negotiate more acceptable costs, although this may be a contradiction in terms. If this is a major "bet the house or company" lawsuit, you should arrange to fly out as soon as possible to meet the prospective attorneys. If you can set up more than one interview, you may be able to shift the problem from a panic situation into one that is more cost controllable.

If you can't visit, then conduct the final interviews by telephone, covering the considerations set forth before. Ask for a description of the trial attorney's experience, who will be staffing the case, and an estimate of the costs. Start the process for litigation cost control.

By this time, your deadline may be fast approaching, but still ask for a written fee agreement. Make it clear that you expect the firm to work with you in budgeting and controlling your legal costs, including presenting you a litigation plan and budget on major problems. If you have a backup law firm, take a firmer position on limiting your legal costs and budgeting considerations.

Remember that the law firm isn't doing you a favor by taking your case. They will be handsomely rewarded for their efforts. You should stay in touch with any backup law firms, whenever possible. If you don't like or feel uncomfortable about the approach of the first attorney, don't hesitate to switch to the second as soon as the answer is filed but before any major expenses have been incurred.

See What Settlement Possibilities Are Available

At the same time you're looking for lawyers, determine if there are any settlement options. Call up the opposing party directly (not their attorney) and see what can be done to settle the case. You're under little obligation to talk directly with the opposing party's attorney at this time (you don't have a lawyer) in most civil lawsuits.

Tell the plaintiff you would like to save both of you some money before too much is tied up with the attorneys. As always, be careful not to make any admissions against yourself or try to be conciliatory, such as saying, "I can see why you would be upset as I made the mistakes."

However, you will need to keep your cool and not make matters worse. Otherwise (or if the complaint and/or state law prohibits this), you'll need to deal directly with the attorney.

The standard approach, whether an attorney has been retained or not, is to ask for a 30-day extension before the answer or response date becomes due. This allows the two sides to discuss settlement options and is renewable if the parties feel they're approaching a settlement.

A Word about Attorney Fees

Each party pays for his or her attorney fees unless provided differently by statute or your agreement. Various contracts provide, as part of the standard boilerplate, that "the prevailing party in any litigation over this agreement is entitled to recover reasonable attorney fees and court costs, as set by the court." Sometimes, creative attorneys set this clause in the context that the "substantially prevailing party" or "any activities required to enforce the provisions of this agreement, whether resulting in litigation or not" are entitled to recover attorney fees and costs.

A provision for such fees in the written agreement (or by state statute in that situation) between the parties can be a bargaining chip in any negotiations. The threat of being awarded expensive attorney fees by the court, should the proceeding go to trial, is a real one. However, remember that this can cut both ways and that paying the fees of both attorneys can be a real killer should you lose.

Establish Early Settlement as a Goal, Right Away

This doesn't mean that parties cave in, as some litigators might argue. Rather, you should look at a lawsuit as another problem to be solved by common sense, not necessarily by what court procedures the lawyers want to use. Attorneys by their training aren't oriented toward settling disputes in a cost-effective way unless the client gives them specific directions that way. It seems incredulous to many that attorneys who fight one another in combat are viewed as best able to construct an agreeable settlement. There's little incentive for the litigator who looks at cases as either "wins or losses" to settle—unless the client makes it clear in the beginning that's what is wanted. It's also much easier if the attorney selected is one who believes settling disputes is more important than taking it to the jury.

The longer you're in the litigation game, the more difficult it becomes to settle, because of the high costs already expended by then. At some point, it can become too late to think about cost efficiencies. As one party said, "You can't be murdered more than once."

Another reason for encouraging early settlements is that the longer the attorneys have to beat the case up inside the system, the quicker the dispute becomes a legal problem, subject only to control by the judge and attorneys. The control of the dispute then passes entirely over to them.

The Dos and Don'ts for Settling Disputes

DO:

1. Recommend that your lawyers utilize ADRs. Litigation is only one, very expensive alternative to be used when settling a dispute. Remind the attorneys that early negotiation and settlement is as much an ADR as any other.

2. Try to be objective about the dispute, looking at it with a detached, cold eye, as if you were asked by others to advise them. Much of litigation is caused by emotion, when all it really involves is money, not whether you live or die. Ask people who have experienced litigation what they did.

3. Talk directly to the other side, if possible, about ways to settle the lawsuit. It's not necessary, nor always desirable, for the only settlement steps to be taken by the attorneys. You should talk first to your lawyer about such plans, if an attorney has already been retained. Then make up your own mind. However, *never* try to talk to the judge about your case.

4. Make the first offer to settle. If everyone waits to make the first offer, then the case simply continues to eat up money. Offers of settlement aren't allowed to be introduced into evidence as an admission of liability or to show that a particular position is weaker. Don't wait to make the first offer because "we need to see what the facts are first," but instead formulate it based upon what you can accept and the legal fees that won't be incurred.

5. Look at any litigation from the eyes of the other party. It's not possible to make a reasonable settlement offer based only on what you see. You need to consider how the other side views the case. Put yourself in their shoes.

DON'T:

1. Fight to conceal evidence, thinking you'll surprise your opponent at trial. Experienced litigators even view this as being foolish.

2. Wait until after discovery is completed before actively starting settlement probes and offers.

3. Look at early settlement offers as showing signs of weakness.

4. Encourage perjury, lying, or falsifying evidence to protect your position. Let your attorney figure out the best way to insulate or soften important adverse evidence. If a cost-effective way isn't possible, then let the evidence be discovered.

5. Hesitate to fight strongly and fiercely in court if your opponent is fighting with a "scorched earth" approach.

Avoiding Unpleasant Cost Surprises

The battle is always uphill when you're trying to control litigation expenses, and it starts when you walk into the attorney's office. Lawyers receive training in law schools that's adversarial by nature. Moot court (mock court trials), law school subjects, and the law itself creates a training in "doing battle." Laws and litigation are complex, easily subject to different interpretations from both sides. The need to win, at all costs, comes from both clients and attorneys—losers aren't very happy. Litigation brings about a blitzkrieg feeling that you must hole up inside a bunker and fight to the death. Alternative dispute resolution and early settlement are at odds with the litigator's training, instincts, and desire to earn a good living.

Facing this is your need to settle a legal problem before it bankrupts you. The process begins when interviewing attorneys to see who'll work with you in watching out for your wallet.

It Starts in the Attorney's Office

The attorney has said he or she is able to handle your case, and let's say you're not a plaintiff with a contingent fee case. You'll be concerned with whether this can be handled as a fixed fee, and, if not, what the costs will be regardless of which side you're on. Controlling the costs of your case doesn't end with talking about the attorney's hourly rate, the time to be spent traveling or in court, or even a ballpark estimate as to what the total costs could be. A statement that "it could cost up to $50,000, if we wind up in trial" isn't good enough.

Listen Carefully

You need to listen carefully to the attorney's response to your questions on cost and the handling of the case. As lawyers normally don't give references of satisfied clients that you can check, usually citing client confidences, you need to rely both on your checklist, the interview, and your instincts. If the attorney resists your attempts at fixing the fee or working on a good cost estimate, then be careful. Professional lawyers want to do a good job, have good communications with clients, and don't want disputes over bills. You'll have to listen carefully and decide if this attorney is one to stay away from.

The Fee Agreement

Considering what should be treated in your fee agreement (see Chapter 12) is a good start. Although the fee agreement is the written contract between you and the attorney that outlines what will be done, the way the services are to be billed, and the rates for these services (among other areas), there are still unanswered questions.

When in litigation, regardless as to the side, you need to pin down more specifically what the costs will be. It's not enough to negotiate hourly rates and billing procedures without discussing the amount of the lawyer's time that will be expended on your case.

> When the attorney has taken your case on a contingent fee basis or a fixed fee, this agreement by itself can be your protection. But you still will need to watch your responsibility for out-of pocket costs such as depositions and filing fees, if they are not included or limited. However, when such an agreement isn't present, then you always need to discuss a litigation plan and budget, along with the fee agreement. You will want to know specifically where the time will be spent and what it will cost, both by certain areas and in total. Ballpark, one-sentence estimates only cause huge problems later.

The Litigation Plan and Budget

The litigation plan and budget is a valuable tool with important, or potentially ruinous lawsuits, although they're applicable to any case not on an absolute fixed fee (including contingent fee lawsuits when you're responsible for the out-of pocket costs). Even routine lawsuits should be controlled or estimated by using this approach.

As discussed previously, each lawsuit follows the same path, starting with the complaint and answer, moving on to the discovery process, then eventually reaching arbitration and/or trial. The basic *components* or categories of litigation are the pleadings, motions, legal research, discovery, factual investigations, responses to opposing counsel, court conferences, trial preparation, trial, meetings, and out-of-pocket costs. These form the great bulk of the costs, with each category estimated in advance for the litigation budget, then added for the overall estimate.

But wait, some litigators argue, you can't do this. You don't know what's going to happen later, especially by the other side. As with anything, you start by making basic assumptions about your situation or case. The preparation of the litigation plan, or what your attorney is planning to do (holding aside for the moment the question about the other party's moves), forms the basis for the litigation budget or estimate.

The litigation plan sets down by specific litigation category what you and your attorney are planning to do with your case. It sets down your assumed moves in each litigation category to win or successfully defend your case. The litigation budget uses the plan in determining what the cost of that plan will be.

If the attorney has given only a verbal estimate of the cost, but didn't break that estimate down into its components, then it's nearly impossible to monitor and control your costs. However, if the litigation components have been estimated in advance, which additionally requires agreeing on your plan, then you have the beginnings of an effective cost-control device.

Lawyers can be reluctant to spend time preparing such plans and estimates. When pressed, some may agree to do this only if you pay for their time. That should be refused. There are attorneys who prepare litigation plans and budgets routinely without charge to their clients.

A successful litigator with 15 years experience put it this way:

> I always use litigation plans and estimates. It forces the client and attorney to communicate as to what's done and the cost impact—we can avoid the later problems. If we're going off budget, then we sit down and talk about why it's happening and what to do about it. We might question if the next deposition is that important or if a motion should be done. The attorney should have at least a rough idea of what's going on—are we talking about $5,000, $15,000, or $50,000—and put it down in a plan and budget. If they can't, then they should send it over to a specialist who knows how much it will cost and can do that.

Preparing a plan and budget doesn't mean you discard the fee agreement. It still forms your basic agreement. You'll still need to review all bills as received, both against your budget and to guard against any mistakes in billing.

An Example

Let's say George and you were sued over the sale of your house as in our Chapter 2 example. but there was no insurance coverage. You had just received the complaint last week, ran around talking to attorneys, and now were with the attorney you wanted to use.

While discussing the case and the attorney's billing procedures, you asked what the costs could be. The attorney threw out the $50,000 figure. After you had gotten over your coughing fit, you asked how it could possibly be this high and are told:

> "I think that the complaint can be attacked for not stating a legal cause of action. If they get past that, then we need to move into the depositions. My associate and I need to depose your real estate agent, their agent, both the husband and wife who bought your property, the inspector who walked through the property before they bought it, and the engineer whose report you gave me. I think we can attack them on the issue of damages—it's a little different in this state. We might think about a motion for summary judgment. I think that the facts and law are on your side. Then..."

The attorney went on. Afterwards you sat back in his plush chair and asked, "Do we need to do all that? I don't want to spend money I don't have."

"Trust me," he said. Your response should be different.

"It's not about trust. If I didn't have that, I wouldn't be here. Remember when I said we needed to work together on the costs?"

"Yes. But what's done on this case to win is different. After all, I've been in this gig for years." He then gave a little chuckle.

"I need your experience. But I also don't have a blank check to write out to you and that SOB. I want to be sure I can pay your bill."

"That's always a good idea," he said good-naturedly.

"I don't know if we need to take the deposition of all those people. Do we really have to make that motion for... "

"For summary judgment," he added. "I'll think about that."

"What will that add to the case?"

As you begin to discuss the legal details of your case, you're thinking about the $50,000 cost.

"I can't afford $50,000," you say flatly. "What can we do to keep it down?"

"What can you afford?"

"Not that much."

"Winning means doing what you have to, even if you don't want to."

"I don't want to go broke in the process."

"You may lose your case," the attorney warned.

"I'll take that risk."

"Hmmm...," he said scratching his head. "Well, I'd like to file a motion for summary judgment. But that's always an uphill battle. Judge Wilson doesn't like them, so perhaps we can forget about that. My associate might not need to attend the depositions. We could trim one or two of the depositions, and let the other side notice them. Perhaps, I'd only send my associate over for them. He's cheaper." He then continued on about the case and his strategy.

"I would like to put this down in writing, if possible," you said later.

"What do you mean?" he replied, his eyebrows beginning to rise.

"Well, we've talked a lot about what we can do and what the other party might do. I need an idea as to how much the answer, depositions, and required settlement discussions with the judge will cost. Then come up with a total."

"That's hard to do. Judy Jones is a tough attorney. She fights tooth and nail."

"I understand. May be we can make an allowance for the extra fights she gets us into. It doesn't have to be anything fancy. I just need an idea as to what we're doing and what that will cost. This is the only way to be sure I can pay you for what's done"

"Well, let's see." He took out his yellow, legal pad, and began scribbling down numbers.

This is what a litigation plan and budget is about. The litigation plan and budget is more than getting something down in writing broken down into areas; it's about getting your attorney involved in deciding what's important in the case and what's not. The lawyer needs to know that you're watching your costs. You, the client, are taking responsibility for the case along with the lawyer. If you and the attorney decide it's not worth the time or money to prepare a formal, written plan and budget, then at least you're talking about the specifics of the case *before* you get the bill for the actions taken.

The Attorneys' Reactions

Whether it's the first time an attorney is presented with a detailed planning and budgeting approach or not, you should expect resistance from some attorneys. If you or your company incurs repetitive litigation, or six-figure costs annually, you can certainly require your existing attorneys to prepare these plans and budgets. It's no different than what you do with any other supplier or vendor.

If you don't have the clout, then attorneys may try to get by with a simple estimated range and a discussion of alternative legal strategies. They will say such a plan or budget isn't possible for any number of reasons, whether no one knows what evidence will be found or what the other attorney is going to do. This is true,

> The real reasons are simple for attorneys resisting litigation plans and budgets. Most attorneys are trained to do everything possible to win and not to think in terms of trading off the importance of a legal step versus its cost.

but it doesn't mean budgeting shouldn't be done. In fact, attorneys across the country already are doing this, even with their smaller clients.

These objections can be met by telling your lawyers to simply make assumptions. Your attorneys should assume that the facts you have given are true—a basic reason for being brutally honest in the first place. Tell your attorneys that this is a planning device, not a guarantee as to what the costs in fact will be.

You should politely decline to pay for the attorney's time in preparing a formal litigation plan and budget. Argue that there are advantages for the lawyer when thinking about a plan and budget. This opens up communications between attorney and client over costs and fees before there's a problem. It forces lawyers to think about the facts, laws, liabilities, and damages ahead of the game, enabling them to establish a strategy that's more likely to win. They should be doing this anyway.

As you focus on this approach, try to secure a "not to exceed" limit on the total costs. It also doesn't hurt to try for a fixed fee. After all, it's only your money.

The Written Plan and Budget

However, the attorneys you contact may resist preparing a written litigation plan and budget for your specific case. There are alternatives to having the attorney prepare a specific, itemized, blow-by-blow plan and estimate.

> The attorney can write down the plan and costs in the format shown below. It can be as formal or as informal as needed. The importance is the process, not necessarily having a word-processed, 20 page document.

If time is short, you may even have the answer or motion to dismiss filed before discussing overall plans and budgets. But you should have a planning and budgeting session before any further work is done.

The following table shows an example of a litigation plan and budget form:

Original Litigation Plan and Budget
(To be revised every 3 months with written consent of client)
PRIVILEGED AND CONFIDENTIAL

Category:	Description of Specific Action in Each Category*	Estimated Cost of Each Action in the Category	
		Low	High
Pleadings:			
Motions:			
Legal Research:			
Discovery:			
Factual Investigations:			
Responses to Opposing Counsel:			
Court Conferences:			
Trial Preparation:			
Meetings:			
Trial:			
Other Costs:			
Total Expenses:			

*Includes the attorney responsible for completing the function, as well as the estimated beginning and completion dates. Each category and cost is further broken down. All intended motions, depositions, interrogatories, admissions, and moves should be specifically identified by name. For example, "Depositions (all taken by TK)—Mr. Toms (by 3/15); Miss Simms (by 4/1); Mr. Pike (by 4/10); and Mrs. Toms (by 4/15). Cost, all except Mrs. Toms (low—$500 each; high—$1,000 each). Mrs. Toms (low—$1,000; high—$2,000). These are estimates only, and actual costs will be higher or lower from what is presented here.

Filling in the Form

Creating and filling in the form is not necessarily difficult. The assumptions and planning constitute the hard part. The attorney needs to decide what pleadings and motions will be made, extent of any legal research, amount of discovery, court conferences, meetings before trial, and other legal action considerations.

A very brief description of these categories follows, and additional information is included in Chapter 20. If you need to refresh yourself on the terms, take another look at Chapter 16 on the litigation process.

✔ *Pleadings*: The attorney must estimate the costs of the complaint or answer, depending on which side you're on. If the response has already been filed, then the time and cost to prepare is already known.

✔ *Motions*: The motions intended to be brought should be assumed, identified, and costed on both a low and high estimate. If the attorney thinks a motion for dismissal for failure to state a cause of action should be brought, then that should be identified. Any other motions, unless intended for discovery purposes, should be put down in this category. However, it isn't as important that the attorney put a response in any particular category— just that it is readily identifiable and can be understood for comparison purposes.

✔ *Legal Research*: Legal research will be needed for complex litigation. Attorneys seem to forget this, but if you've hired a specialist for a simple case, then you shouldn't be seeing costly, legal research. Although this is a difficult area for the lawyer to estimate, he or she should be able to know whether "a lot" or "not much" is required, and then make an educated guess. We're looking for a "good feel" as to what's entailed, not for exact numbers.

✔ *Discovery:* This is the big one. The numbers of parties to be deposed, examined, questioned, or investigated need to be decided, including an estimate of when those examinations will be given. Any admissions, interrogatories, and other motions or documents need to specifically identified. Additionally, the costs of transcripts, court reporters, court costs, expert witnesses, and travel time and costs would be included here if they have to do with discovery.

✔ *Factual Investigations:* The costs of expert witnesses, accident investigators, reconstructions, private investigators, and other fact-determination costs would be included in this category.

✔ *Responses to Opposing Counsel:* This category covers the objections of counsel that you don't know what the other party will be doing. Attorneys can estimate a range between "the other attorney does nothing out-of-the-ordinary" category to "the other attorney is scorching the earth." All that's necessary is a best guess as to whether the opposing lawyer will or will not file a lot of papers in response. Again, we're not as much interested in an exact number as in discussing what's more likely to happen as the case progresses.

✔ *Court Conferences:* Any preliminary or mandatory settlement conferences would be included in this category, as well as anything else identified by your attorney.

✔ *Trial Preparation:* Anything to do with preparing for trial should be included in this category. Preparing witnesses (this wouldn't include taking depositions), creating exhibits for the jury, and the time of the attorney to bring the case (and the lawyer) to where it can be tried are included. The lawyer's time when reading depositions, doing necessary legal research, and other activities motivated by the upcoming trial are contained here. The attorney should also estimate the additional time required if the trial date is reset, thus requiring the re-reading of depositions and preparing of witnesses again.

This category, as well as the following ones, would be used if an arbitration or other procedure were being used instead of trial. Any thought of using the arbitration solely to see the case of the other party, to be followed by a trial de novo, should be estimated and discussed with you.

✔ *Trial:* As the attorney's day rate for court appearances is known, this estimate depends primarily on how much time the trial or arbitration is thought to take. Attorneys should know, if experienced enough, whether this is a simple case (requiring days) or a complex case (requiring weeks). Any uncertainty as to the length simply is reflected in the "low" and "high" estimates. Additionally, the trial costs of expert witnesses, jury fees, meals, travel, and the like would be included.

✔ *Meetings:* Meetings between you and your attorney, your attorney and the opposing attorney, and inside the law firm would be included here.

✔ *Other Costs:* Specific costs and actions that don't fit in any of the above categories would be set down here. However, this is not intended to be a contingency or "plush" category. There already are ample provisions made for contingencies in the use of "low" and "high" estimates, as well as the categories that have already been established.

If the lawyer still argues this is too speculative, then respond you're only interested in using this method to gain a handle on costs. The lawyer is perfectly free, you would say, to add a big disclaimer at the end—for example, "This is an estimate only. No guarantee is given that the costs will occur in fact as presented here. This plan and budget is for planning purposes only and isn't intended to be a warranty, guaranty, or contract between attorney and client." Or use whatever wording makes the lawyer comfortable as to malpractice concerns. What's essential is to discuss the legal strategies and approaches before getting the bill.

Although the attorney will first prepare this form depending on the facts of your case, analyzing the plan and budget requires that both of you work together. There aren't many facts that need to be proved in any given case—the issues turn on proving only several pivotal facts and/or conclusions. The proving or denying of these particular facts is your case strategy. The elements of proof needed to carry your case are your attorney's responsibility; making determinations as to what should be done in meeting this burden should be both of yours.

As each task is reviewed, the two of you must determine if that task (i.e., deposing Roberts, the interrogatories to Sam, or the motion to dismiss) is in keeping with the general strategy for your case. *Always ask, will doing this further my case?*

Your attorney can be expected to argue that nearly everything he or she wants is necessary for a win. However, be warned that when attorneys say "you can't take that risk," they really might be saying that *they* can't take the risk. Their concern is being sued for malpractice, unless everything, including the kitchen sink, is thrown in. If this is a major concern to your attorney, then tell the lawyer

> The time spent by the attorney to prepare or discuss the plan and budget shouldn't be charged (although some do). How this is treated should be understood before proceeding further. However, spending adequate time in the beginning of a case to analyze it and the strategies is crucial. A decision can be made in 10 minutes that saves you $1,000 just by deciding if one deposition is necessary or not. Do this five times in a 3-hour conference, and you will realize the secret of effective legal cost control.

to send you a short letter covering themselves, but not to bill you for it.

The estimated time for completion of each task needs to be made, as well as the low and high estimate of these costs. The "high" estimate is to be used for those unexpected motions, meetings, opponent's actions, legal research, and the like that the attorney says can't be planned for.

Another reason for using low and high estimates is that attorneys usually underestimate the time it takes to complete anything, whether it's a motion, deposition, or a settlement position paper. It always seems to take more time for an attorney to notice a deposition, prepare the witness, take the deposition, and read the transcript twice (once after the deposition and then just before trial years later) when actually doing it, then when the estimate first was made.

Before being able to compare actual expenses to your budget and plan, however, you will need to be sure that the lawyer's billings will be "task based" or able to be compared against your budget categories. Lawyers do bill chronologically as time is spent on your case and may lump various activities into the same time entry. Although this may be more of a problem with large or complex cases, you should ask about this.

Routine versus More Complex Matters

For routine matters, such as simple divorces, collections, and low-damage personal injury defense matters, it's more than likely you'll get a fixed fee. If not, then the planning and budgeting process should be fairly simple and straightforward. Costs that vary in such matters typically result from unexpected defenses, factual problems, or the actions of the attorney.

Although the argument is heard that no case is routine, an experienced

> The larger the case, the higher the costs and greater the need for control. This approach forces you to view the case in the beginning in assessing what alternatives exist and your strategies. If you're being sued and the costs of defense are especially high, you may conclude it's better to attempt settlement first or to use ADRs.
>
> A well-thought litigation plan should result in more control over what happens, whether expected or not. The budget results in controlling the costs associated with that plan. This process allows you to determine the importance of the case versus the legal costs required and the decisions that must be made in settling or further prosecuting the case.

attorney should have a good idea as to what problems do occur. This planning process is especially successful with complex cases, even when more facts aren't known and there's more exposure.

Updating and Using the Plan

The budget, as with any other planning device, is the map first drawn when deciding what road to take. However, the initial budget will need to be revised as the case progresses and costs are incurred. A revised budget or estimate should be prepared when appropriate, but retain the original one for comparative purposes.

Although revised estimates are needed as actual expenses become available, the work isn't completed when the revised budget is done. The plan should be discussed from time to time in deciding whether it should be changed. As part of this, the attorney should agree that no additional motions, pleadings, or discovery work not listed in the original plan will be made without your consent.

It's absolutely essential you monitor the litigation plan and budget on a continuing basis. This system is worthless if only used in the beginning and then only paid lip service to over time. Timely changes to the budget and plan should be made as facts become available, and both must be continually monitored.

As costs are incurred, you should sit down with your attorney and revise the budget to take into account these actual expenses. Where estimates had been given before, you now can discuss actual costs. By sitting down and going over how the expenses are running based on your initial expectations, you now can see the trends of these costs. Be sure to determine in advance whether you'll be charged for these sessions. Some attorneys do (or try to).

By focusing on particular categories, you can make decisions based on the overall cost trends. Let's say you estimated the costs of depositions and transcripts to be $10,000. If it turns out that the case is taking more of your money than initially thought (as usually happens), you can decide not to take the depositions of minor players, using less expensive admissions and interrogatories.

Large companies fine-tune the litigation budget to an initial budget, actual costs, a revised estimate based on those costs, and how much of each category has been spent to date, all by cost component and added to a total. However, for the average person, it's sufficient to substitute actual costs into a revised number and narrow the range between the low and high estimates. It may not be necessary with your case to prepare formal, word-processed, revised estimates and budgets. What's important is to track these costs against what you first thought, then revise the expected costs to a closer range of numbers, even if done by hand.

A popular attorney with clients said:

> I view my role as a financial advisor. I tell my clients what's at stake, the risks, and ask what do they want to do. I go over what the range of costs could be and the likelihood of success, again asking what do they want. I give them my recommendations. We work together, even though I'm the expert telling them how much the future could cost them. People want to know what their case means in dollars, including the liability and risks. If the lawyer doesn't know this, then that attorney shouldn't be taking on the case.

Ask Why?

As the legal bills roll in, using the plan and budget allows you to ask "why?" in an informed way. Why is the motion category getting out of line from what was first thought? Is it really due to the other side or are we filing too many motions? Why are discovery costs getting out of line? What can we do to control this? When costs bounce out of line, you might decide to change your "scorched earth" or "first class" approach to a "tourist" approach—before receiving even larger bills.

Making Decisions

An important benefit of looking ahead and projecting your expected legal costs is the ability to make important decisions on your case. For example, a financially strapped greeting card company shipped original works of art back to the artist. These paintings had a market value at the time of $250,000, although there was disagreement afterwards as to how long it would take to sell the paintings (anywhere from 1 to 4 years). The greeting card company mistakenly sent the art to the wrong address, and the uninsured works of art were lost or stolen.

The artist's attorneys immediately sued the card company over the value of the lost art work. The attorneys convinced the artist that their fees would be reimbursed by the judgment or eventual settlement. A settlement offer of $150,000 was turned down, the attorneys and artist feeling that there was more money to be gained by continuing the litigation. The artist never sat down with her attorneys to estimate how much the legal fees would be, although she became uncomfortable later at their size. At the time, she was more upset about losing her original paintings.

The attorney fees generated amounted to $125,000 before a judgment for $250,000 was secured 3 years later. However, the greeting card company declared bankruptcy immediately after the judgment was awarded. Two years after that, and $25,000 more in legal fees, the artist received 20¢ on the dollar on the judgment, or $50,000, from the trustee in the bankruptcy court.

Forgetting about the value of the lost art, the artist lost $100,000 in cold cash, all of which went to the attorneys (the artist received $50,000 but paid $150,000 in legal fees). If she had taken the original settlement offer, the artist would have had $150,000 in the bank for 5 years with no legal expenses to mention. The decision would have been easier if a realistic estimate as to the lawsuit's costs had been made—the artist shouldn't pay $125,000 of legal fees to get the judgment plus $150,000 in cash, or a $275,000 swing versus winning a $250,000 judgment against a financially struggling company.

Factoring in the Fees

This process focuses on important decisions sooner. Let's say that your attorney says you have a "no lose" case to win $50,000, but the legal costs will be $25,000. If you can't get back your legal costs (either by law or agreement) and each side bears their own, then you should look at any settlement offer of $25,000 or more. Why? You win a judgment of $50,000, then have to collect it, in order to pay the attorney $25,000, then receive back only a net of $25,000. We said the system wasn't perfect.

If you can be awarded your attorney fees and court costs, then the situation becomes different. You can win $50,000 with all your legal fees reimbursed. But be very careful with this. If the defendant doesn't have the assets or is judgment-proof, then what you can get means nothing. But let's say that the defendant has a lot of money. You would be motivated to demand being reimbursed all your attorney fees plus the $50,000. In this case, that would amount to a settlement offer of $75,000 late in the case. There can be a wide swing in the amount of money you should accept in settlement, depending on the legal costs and whether they are collectible.

If you were the defendant, then the same reasoning applies. The value to the plaintiff depends on the amount of legal costs and who assumes them. If each were responsible for his own, and assuming you were completely at fault (which is usually not the case, but it makes the example easier), then you would offer less money to the plaintiff since each is assuming his own legal costs. If there were the chance you would end up with the other party's legal fees, then you would offer more.

If you were the defendant in our $50,000 example, having signed a note for that sum with no offsetting defenses, the situation with legal fees would be the same. Assuming you had assets the plaintiff could reach (which makes a big difference), then you would want to settle the problem as soon as possible. Why pay attorney fees when you owe the money? If the note provided that the borrower was liable for the costs of collection, then there's no reason to be liable for both.

However, cases are rarely clear-cut. There is never a 100% likelihood for anything. The best case can go out the window when the witness dies, the note is destroyed in a fire, or you get a lousy attorney. For looking at how you factor in attorney fees when assessing cases in the gray area, we must turn to probabilities and "expected value" concepts.

Probabilities

Legal consultants for years have been assessing the likelihood of different results in large damage trials for their large corporate clients. The range of damage verdicts (or exposures), the probabilities of those verdicts occurring, and then the weighted average (or the expected value) are calculated in deciding what's most likely to happen. It's not necessary to go into a detailed discussion of quantitative risk analysis, other than if you have the interest, it's possible to computerize the likelihood of winning or losing a given lawsuit. That doesn't mean that the calculations will hold true—only that the result is more likely to occur.

If You Have a "Good" Case

The same approach can be used without employing a computer simply by determining the expected value of a case. After discussing the litigation plan and budget, ask your attorney what's the likelihood that you'll win. The attorney should have some familiarity with the case because of the work already done. As settlement offers are either made or received, the same approach would be used.

Since lawyers aren't trained in risk analysis or probability theory, you will need to translate what they say in response. You need to reduce into percentages what the attorney means by saying there's an "excellent chance," "good chance," "average chance," "mediocre chance," "poor chance," or whatever other terms that lawyer uses. Remember that what a "good case" means to one attorney isn't necessarily the same thing to another. For example, does a "poor chance" to win the case mean that its less than a 25% chance for you to win (i.e., you would win only one out of four times)? Does an "average chance" equate to 50/50?

For example, if the lawyer feels you have a "good chance" to win $100,000, then ask what the term "good" means. If this means there's a 60% chance to win at that level, then you'll use that number. Assume that the same attorney feels you have a "poor" chance at winning $200,000; this means a 10% probability after the subject is discussed further. Ask then if there is any chance that you might lose and be assessed damages. Let's say the attorney, after your coaching, tells you there's a 30% chance you'll lose $50,000.

The expected value of the jury's verdict would be the summation of the product of the various probabilities and awards, given that all the probabilities were estimated (they have to add up to 100%). The expected value in this example would be $65,000 as shown below:

$$
\begin{aligned}
0.6 \times \$100,000 &= \$60,000 \\
0.1 \times \$200,000 &= \$20,000 \\
\underline{0.3 \times -\$50,000} &= \underline{-\$15,000} \\
100\% \qquad\qquad & \quad\; \$65,000
\end{aligned}
$$

The "expected value" of this case, or $65,000, can't be received until the judgment is received. If there are the typical court delays, then it may be 2 or 3 years before you get into court. Receiving $65,000 in the future isn't as valuable as receiving money now. Thus, this amount must be discounted to its present value in today's dollars. If it's assumed that this money could be invested at an interest rate of 10%, then the present value of $65,000 in the future, but received now, is $50,000—$50,000 invested at 10% interest compounds to $65,000 in 3 years.

Let's say that the legal expenses are expected to be $35,000 and that each side bears its own attorney fees. Thus, the expected value recovery would be a net $30,000 ($65,000 less the $35,000 legal fees), assuming that the jury's nearly one in three chance of assessing you a $50,000 hit doesn't come in. Also, what's received now is more valuable then it would be after you've waited for 3 years.

Your attorney has informed you there's a $25,000 settlement offer. Do you take it? Based on this analysis, most plaintiffs would negotiate further and not reject the offer out of hand.

This also shows why litigation as a method of solving disputes has fallen into disfavor when compared against the less costly and more efficient ADRs in settling problems.

However, if the attorney simply told you there was a "good" chance at getting $60,000 and "they'll settle before trial—90% of them do" without a litigation estimate, you would probably turn down the $25,000 offer, not centering on the one in three chance of losing $50,000 plus your attorney fees.

Unfortunately, this is the reason why many people have bad results in litigation. They don't analyze their case in the beginning in detail, waiting to make such decisions after their legal expenses have mounted. Attorneys seem to recommend that their clients wait until the important depositions are over, wanting to wait until the Holy Grail of the "smoking gun" statement or fact is discovered. That can be a mistake, as decisions aren't any easier to make even with all the facts laid out. No one knows for sure how a judge or jury will rule, no matter what your attorney hears in a deposition.

A 50/50 Chance to Win

Let's say your law firm states you have a "50/50 chance" to be awarded damages of $300,000, and the costs of litigation were expected to be $100,000. If you're on a contingent fee basis, then you wouldn't worry too much about expected values or probabilities. Your decision is increasing the amount of cash in hand, and the more the better.

However, if we assume that you bear your legal expenses, then the decision is different. If it's 50/50 that you'll win $300,000 (the remaining 50% being no recovery), then your "expected value" is $150,000 (50% times $300,000). If each side bears its own legal fees (you'll need a reading from your attorney on that), then any settlement giving you more than $50,000 should be reviewed. Your expected value of $150,000, less the expected legal costs of $100,000, is $50,000.

If you're able to collect your legal fees, then the decision swings more. If the other person or company has "deep pockets" and this collectibility is assured, then you have a 50% chance to win $300,000 (the expected value of $150,000) without any offset for legal fees (assuming you can recover them). This means that any settlement offer would need to approach (or be "in the neighborhood" of) $150,000 in order for you to consider accepting it. These are sizable swings.

Rethink What You Want to Do

It takes a clear mind to rethink what you want to do when the legal costs will be too much. No one likes to change directions simply because someone else is fighting back and calling you names. Pride can be a problem unless you stand back and look at what's really important.

You need to balance the costs against the likelihood of winning, the time, and what you get back by continuing the battle. For example, a developer had received a building permit and was about to start building a shopping center. Environmentalists protested and filed a lawsuit, arguing noncompliance with various laws governing the obtaining of the building permit. With the legal costs shooting up, the developer reversed directions. The company asked the city to withdraw the prior approval and resubmitted an application for a new permit. It would take 6 months and much lower costs to obtain a new building permit, complying with any possible objections, than fighting it out with much higher costs and years until being resolved. As basically the same shopping center would be built under the new permit, the developer simply chose the least expensive route.

"Looking back, I'd rather have taken what was first offered in settlement, instead of continuing on, and spent that $20,000 of extra legal fees on a new car," said one person who had gone through this decision. Solving your problem is more important than how you do it.

Specific Litigation Cost-Control Tips

As over 90% of all cases settle before trial, most individuals at the end of the dispute end up paying substantial attorney fees and costs that could have been avoided. As each side typically pays its own legal fees in such settlements, these expenses are deducted from any settlement proceeds coming to the plaintiff or added onto the settlement amount assumed by the defendant.

Additionally, the costs of depositions, transcripts, court reporters, court costs, and expert witnesses are added to the final bill presented to each side. It is common for neither plaintiff nor defendant to come out ahead after paying these expenses. What was fighting for a principle before has now become a major economic headache. It's unfortunate that many people are unaware of this, having had little or no prior court experience. It's learned afterwards.

The previous chapter developed the use of a litigation plan and budget in controlling your overall litigation expenses. First, you need to use different approaches with each case. Then, there are specific items that need watching to continue the control of your case and legal expenses.

Litigation Cost Components

Understanding the basic components of litigation costs is important in being able to control them and taking the necessary steps in this direction. The cost-control areas to be discussed are in the areas of pleadings, motions, legal research, factual investigations, discovery, responses to opposing counsel, court conferences and trial preparation, meetings, out-of-pocket expenses, and trial expenditures.

Use Different Approaches Depending on the Case

Claims for small amounts of money or "low damage" cases should either be handled in small claims court, by paralegals doing most of the work, or by employing new attorneys who would enter into a low, fixed-price contract for the experience. Claims for midrange damage cases may be handled by attorneys or associates in law firms charging lower rates (even by yourself, but be very careful and talk this over with a lawyer first). Claims involving high-exposure or the "bet the house" lawsuit should be given to experienced trial counsel. Evaluate the type of approach, and its cost, in determining a cost/benefit value for each case. You must not use the same approach for every dispute or allow your attorney to talk you into one that is not appropriate for the value of your case.

Pleadings

Clients should be careful that the lawyer doesn't spend too much time drafting any pleading (the complaint or answer to the complaint). This may build in advance a "win at all costs" mentality, regardless of the original estimate. A critical assessment at first is seeing how close the attorney comes to any initial estimates or "wild guesses" as to the costs required in preparing a pleading.

Although the trend is to use fixed fees in simple "cookie cutter" lawsuits such as collection efforts, uncontested divorces, and evictions, the more complex or larger cases normally don't. The client should first ask the attorney how much it will cost for the pleading. This estimate gives the individual an immediate fix as to the direction of the costs. The cost overruns in many cases are unintentional—the lawyer simply underestimated the time needed.

A client can take steps ahead of receiving the bill to control these costs. Working with the attorney so that important facts are quickly understood is particularly important. The individual should write down a complete and detailed description of the facts that can be handed to the lawyer. All information should be set down in chronological order, all papers separated with files organized, and duplicate copies made whenever possible to leave with the attorney. This saves time in drafting pleadings, as the information can be dictated directly by the attorney without having to search through disorganized notes or needing to have more meetings.

Be sure to make a list of the questions that you want answered in your meetings. Once one is answered, go directly to the next question. One trial attorney observed "Don't waste time venting feelings, emotions, and telling all the reasons why the other person is an SOB. You're being charged for that." Watching the time spent in meetings and not wasting the attorney's time with unnecessary phone calls is advisable—whatever can be done to make the lawyer more efficient translates into cost savings for you.

Motions

Drafting and filing motions (applications made to the court to obtain a favorable ruling) to attack an adversary's complaint or answer should be carefully evaluated as to the likelihood of success. Given that judges permit a seemingly endless series of amendments to pleadings, in order to avoid having cases dismissed due to technicalities, early motions can be a waste of time and money. The attorney should agree in advance that any motions to be filed will be discussed with you prior to any work being done on them.

> The cost of a half-hour telephone call is quite small when balanced against the thousands of dollars that can be wasted in an unsuccessful motion against the complaint, answer, or another filing. Attorneys always seem to push for such motions, but the client should ask the attorney each time "What are the chances we will succeed? Is it better than 50/50? *How does this advance my case?*"

Judges rarely grant a motion for summary judgment, as it takes the case away from the jury, applying the rule that "judges rule on the law and juries on the facts." This motion is granted only in the clearest of cases when there's no dispute in law or in fact as to the requested ruling. It's very difficult to find a case where there isn't something in dispute. One judge simply ruled on a motion for summary judgment by saying, "This motion is 1-inch thick. Something that thick must have something in dispute. Motion denied."

This doesn't mean that all motions for summary judgment should be eliminated. What it means is that these motions should be discussed with you before any work is started. If the attorney doesn't discuss it with you before performing the work, given this understanding, don't pay for those services.

Although large corporations have much greater bargaining power with their lawyers, their approach to summary judgments can give an idea as to how they're viewed. One general counsel for a large, publicly traded bank told his outside attorneys that the bank would go along with a summary judgment motion only on the following grounds: if the judge doesn't grant the motion, then the attorneys receive nothing for their time; if the judge grants the motion, then the attorneys receive *twice* their bill. There have been no takers on this offer yet.

Various motions can be avoided simply by the attorneys talking with one another, then writing confirming letters. For example, if a complaint is unclear on a point, rather than filing a demurrer (a motion objecting to ambiguities or other "technical" defects), the attorney should pick up the telephone and work it out with the opposing lawyer. Judges nearly always allow the losing party to amend pleading so that these defects are cured. Again, why pay for a more expensive way to do it?

Legal Research

The key to controlling this expense, as with motions, is for the attorney to secure your permission in advance prior to commencing any *extensive* legal research work.

You have this right. Legal research should not be necessary in simple or average cases, given that the attorney has tried similar cases before. It is rarely ever needed for the average collection or divorce case, for example, but listen to the attorney's reasons—then make your decision.

Factual Investigations

Unless this is a personal injury or other case requiring expert recreations, you can conduct your own factual investigations in simple cases. You know where your papers and files are, and you don't charge for your time by the minute as attorneys do.

Lawyers sometimes tell clients to bring everything in, arguing they know what to look for. However, if you have masses of files to be reviewed, you should ask what's *actually* needed, then do it yourself or arrange for someone else at a lower cost to do this work. If necessary, the lawyer can scan the files at your office or home, then determine what documents are needed and the type of search to be conducted. You can conduct the initial search and review or ask if a paralegal from the law office staff can do it instead at a lower billing rate.

Discovery

The area of discovery is the largest cost component of an average case's expense with the greatest potential for savings. Lawyers unfortunately feel they have to discover everything *before* the trial begins, with some attorneys even believing this before settlement discussions begin. They'll spend much time, effort, and expense to find out *all* the facts imaginable about a case, whether real or even necessary to prove a position. Attorneys and judges alike agree that much of the fact-finding conducted for any given case aren't necessary. In fact, some have seen cases where one-half of the time spent (and even more) in discovery wasn't necessary. This area needs to be controlled, no matter what's being litigated.

Hiring investigators, expert witnesses, and the like is a different matter, especially in complex cases. You must tell the attorney that any hiring and costs of experts, consultants, or securing witnesses to testify, other than what was agreed previously, must be discussed with you in advance prior to that action. Be sure that the use of any particular expert or witness is necessary for your case.

Take an active role in the hiring of any expert witnesses; meet with the expert or consultant, along with the attorney, before that firm or person is hired. You should be comfortable that the expert has the background and experience to be as much a value to your case as the extra expense. It is important that any expert witness or consultant has had sufficient trial and testifying experience, so that the person is not learning this at your expense. The expert's billing practices should be determined in advance, as should a written estimate or fixed fee for those services. Remember that in any meetings of this expert, that you will be paying for both the time of the expert witness and the attorney, thereby raising the hourly rate of this process by another 50% to 100%.

A great problem area between attorneys and clients alike is the totally unanticipated high cost of expert witnesses. It always seems to turn out that more hours were required than thought—the case was more complex, the other attorney's demands made more preparation necessary, the deposition was continued to another day, and any number of reasons. What makes matters worse is when the expert isn't used as the case settles or you lose anyway. Any use of experts needs to be discussed extensively at first and then closely monitored.

The Resistance Your attorney will argue that the plaintiff has the burden to go forward in proving certain duties or responsibilities were owed by the defendant and that they were breached. If this isn't done, then the plaintiff loses. After the plaintiff has argued its case, then the defendant must prove its version— losing if it doesn't. The argument is if your case isn't proved, then the case is lost, regardless of side.

One litigator with nearly 75 trials and arbitrations under his belt, argued "You can't be perceived as weak. You get out of trial by preparing for them. Have everything ready to go, no matter what." This is true but misses the point. It's both how and the bulk of evidence that is found that balloons costs way beyond where they should be. This litigator was also known for his streamlining of depositions, getting in and out quickly with what was needed, in addition to using less expensive discovery methods when appropriate.

Expensive depositions shouldn't be taken as a matter of course; these should be kept as short as possible, and should be streamlined in advance. Too many attorneys don't have an overall discovery plan and "overlawyer" the discovery process. They will prepare more than necessary or not at all, ask more questions in examinations than required (thus wasting time and money), take more depositions than necessary, and use depositions to the exclusion of less expensive alternatives. This isn't because of the attorney's wish to run up costs, but results more from the desire to find the "smoking gun" or ultimate fact from all possible facts that wins the case. You should be firm, but polite, to ask if what's being done is really necessary or meets an element of proof for your case.

If friction develops with your attorney over this process, then say you intend to pay the bill as agreed, but you need to keep expenses down so you can meet this obligation. If friction continues, don't give in. If it still continues, tell the attorney you'll need to consider a replacement, although you don't want to—remember you're paying the bills and have your rights. Paying clients do have strong rights.

Avoid engaging in fights over the opposing party's requests for document production, interrogatory responses, and other discovery matters, unless a benefit is clearly seen. In the end, the great bulk of documents and desired facts are eventually produced and disclosed, given the liberal policy in both federal and state courts to enforce the production of all documents and information that may decide a dispute.

On the other hand, opposing counsel can be a problem by being evasive, always fighting, or not fully meeting your requests. And people don't always do what they say they'll do and may lie in the process. "If you ask for documents, then sometimes you'll only get one-half of what's requested, observed one trial attorney.

You'll have to decide if the fight to get those documents is worth the expense, especially given the numbers of lawsuits that settle before trial.

The Problem with Depositions Taking a deposition doesn't mean that the witness won't testify at trial—quite to the contrary, the great majority do. When the witness testifies at trial, the deposition serves to verify the given testimony, can be used to attack the witness's testimony, or can be read into evidence if the witness becomes unavailable. It's used primarily to determine the facts in the case before trial.

Using expensive depositions doesn't make sense to prove minor facts, those not in issue, or facts that can be proven by other means. A person further can change any testimony at trial, even though the attorney can and will use the deposition to "impeach the witness" (or attack the credibility of that person because of the changes in testimony).

The problem is compounded by the fact that trials are many months or years away from when the depositions first were taken. Even the best of attorneys can forget the importance of facts over time. What seemed to be so important at one time becomes less so as the months pass. Reading thousands of pages of depositions again much later when preparing for trial changes these priorities, not to mention that this duplication is very expensive.

One Attorney at a Time Only one attorney from your side should attend a deposition, regardless of what is argued. Even if the other side has slipped in 3 attorneys to the other party's cost equation, that doesn't mean you have to endure the same trauma. If your attorney is experienced in depositions, that lawyer should know how to handle an uncooperative witness or opposing attorney. Ask whether a junior associate, rather than the senior partner, should be taking it. Further, if the other side has requested the deposition, it may not be necessary for your attorney to attend one that involves an unimportant witness. The attorney simply can order a copy of the transcript of the proceeding and review it later. This isn't a rare occurrence.

Limit the Number of Depositions Taken The attorney needs to develop a theme or story through discovery that proves your position. You should ask if it's really necessary to take the deposition of everyone to do this—it won't be in the majority of cases. As one trial lawyer said flatly, "I've never seen a case where you have to depose every party and potential witness to prove the case." Rather than deposing minor witnesses, the lawyer can talk to them over the telephone or have an investigator question them, among other steps. If their testimony appears to be important, then take the deposition.

Consider using less expensive interrogatories (see Chapter 16 for definitions and concepts as to these terms) in place of depositions for nonimportant parties. Use requests for admissions, typically a lower cost than even interrogatories, when possible in place of both interrogatories and depositions. Although the answers to interrogatories and admission requests can be evasive, this doesn't mean that taking the person's deposition will be any better.

Attorneys use depositions more than they should for several reasons—the desire to find all the available evidence; the hope of finding the "smoking gun" fact that turns the case; and unless the attorney has paralegals or junior associates available to do the work: the wish to avoid drafting written interrogatories and requests for admissions, which can be tedious work compared to taking a deposition.

Requests for admissions should be utilized more extensively than most attorneys do. Such requests can be drafted to force the other side into admitting facts, identifying documents, and laying the foundation necessary to meet your burden of proof. If the opponent doesn't answer these requests in a timely way, then the requests are deemed admitted. Denials to such requests can be accompanied with interrogatories asking for an explanation to the given answers.

Requests for admissions should be submitted early in the case to narrow down the need for depositions as the case proceeds. Stipulate (an agreement that is filed with the court) to facts not in dispute as early as possible. Many federal courts require parties to stipulate to uncontested facts prior to trial. An agreement on such facts allows the parties to focus on the more important issues, thus narrowing the scope of discovery, as well as the costs on both sides.

Each party needs to secure the most cost-effective way to find the evidence that supports its case, and it makes no difference whether you are suing or defending. For example, if a fact is easy to prove, why take a deposition to prove it? Ask if your attorney will consider using instead a request for an admission. If the fact is difficult to prove and important to the case, then use the deposition to find the evidence leading to it, and if possible use interrogatories and admissions from that point on. Try not to spend a lot of time in an endless search for that one pivotal fact that's only believed to exist.

Consider serving interrogatories with your answer. This can lead to more information in a timely and cost-effective manner. It can get your case off to a good start if you begin seeing the other side's facts and positions early. This can lead to earlier settlement if one party sees its case isn't as strong as first thought.

In addition, the experienced, efficient trial attorney saves money by preparing in advance and knowing what needs to be found in any deposition. That lawyer gets in and out of depositions quickly, searching for the evidence that needs to prove your position, not spending hours in a shotgun approach to learn everything possible about that witness's life. When other potential witnesses are discovered in a deposition, the efficient lawyer will decide on the best way to obtain that relevant

---

Some attorneys will resist questioning over whether certain depositions need to be taken. However, their explanations must be understandable, make sense, and be consistent within an overall plan or story as to the elements needing to be proved. The attorney's answer should be more than just "that's the way it's done" or "it puts them to a lot of trouble and we'll win eventually." Your question should be: "Will this deposition or information yield new information relevant to my case? Does its value exceed the cost? Does it advance my case?"

information, not necessarily using depositions. Plan to attend the first depositions (if a party to the case, you'll probably be doing this anyway) and see how efficiently your lawyer performs.

Don't Destroy Evidence Everything and anything that anyone connected with your case says, writes, does, or gets involved in, whether before or after the lawsuit has been filed, *is* evidence that can be brought before the court. Don't conceal, hide, or destroy evidence at any time. The ensuing fights over this conduct, the risks to your case, and the increased costs aren't worth it.

If Files Are Subpoenaed, Provide Them Not complying with a subpoena for information (a court order requiring the party to supply the information requested) can subject you to stiff sanctions, contempt-of-court proceedings (penalty or punishment proceedings held by the judge for not complying with a court order), extra costs, and headaches. This doesn't mean confidential or sensitive material not relevant to the case must be handed over to the other side, but it does mean a red flag is raised when your law firm says they're planning to disregard the subpoena. In any event, don't resist reasonable requests for documents and information.

If the order requires the release of what are considered to be confidential or sensitive materials, your attorney will need to go to court and obtain a protective or exclusion order for these materials. A factor considered by a judge in this determination, in addition to balancing the needs of the parties, is whether the requested files are kept in a secure and separate location away from the rest of the files, thus indicating the intent that these files were to be kept confidential.

Responses to Opposing Counsel

Aggressive responses by the opponent's attorney can result from a variety of reasons—the other party wants (or the attorney has solely adopted) a "Rambo" or "scorched earth" approach; it's a "bet your house" problem for the other side; or the two attorneys aren't getting along. Your attorney must be able to maintain communications with the opposing lawyer, no matter what. If they can't get along, then the costs associated with your lawsuit simply increase.

When the attorneys are fighting over personal differences or minor matters, you need to determine who's at fault—your attorney, opposing counsel, or some combination. This can be a difficult choice, since lawyers are paid to win, not necessarily hired for their winning personalities. For example, one exasperated attorney said about another "He hasn't had his head handed him enough times to become humble." However, remember that the problems have occurred because the opposing parties couldn't work out their differences in the first place—the attorneys simply could be mirroring their clients' behavior.

Constantly engaging in fights over document production, interrogatory responses, and other discovery matters, unless some benefit is clearly seen, should be discouraged. In the end, the great amount of documents being fought over end up being turned over to the requesting party. The lawyers should discuss all requests for information by telephone and try to agree without requiring a judge to rule over their differences in contested, expensive hearings.

Motions for sanctions against opposing counsel should be taken only in the case of the litigation terrorist or where your case is being severely and unnecessarily delayed. You rarely receive enough in fines to offset the legal costs incurred in making and arguing such motions.

A different story exists when opposing counsel continues to make unreasonable requests for information. It could be that they're trying to win by making your life as miserable as possible. In that event, as one litigator observed, "If opposing counsel if taking a pure tactical approach in papering you with motions, or misquoting facts in them, then you have to go for sanctions when they're there. That law firm might think twice after paying a fine out of its pocket."

Court Conferences and Trial Preparation

The prime control technique is to obtain a litigation plan and budget beforehand, then hold the attorney to that. However, if there is no overall fixed fee or a litigation line-item budget in place, ask the attorney what it will cost to prepare for the mandatory court conferences and/or trial. These costs (as with all others before being incurred) should be compared to what additional amounts are required to settle the case *before* the costs are incurred. What's maddening is to settle the lawsuit on the court's steps for that amount *after* you paid for all the expenses of discovery, court conferences, and trial preparation.

Meetings

Telephoning rather than meeting still is the best rule—phone calls are shorter, less expensive, and take less time taken from your day. Further, determine what the attorney wants if you need a face-to-face meeting, and be prepared so you don't waste time. Experienced clients tell their attorney they only have 1 hour on the day that the attorney is free. If the lawyer responds that there isn't enough time to go over the matters in that time period, then simply say you want to see what can be done in the shorter time period. You may be surprised at how much can be accomplished. If you need more legitimate time, simply set another meeting.

Trial

This is the tricky area. The attorney, with everything riding on the trial, wants to spend whatever time's required to win as the trial date approaches; therefore, he or she is certainly not as interested as you are in controlling expenses. This forces every client into a trade-off. As discussed throughout, value doesn't necessarily mean what's cheapest. You need to balance the costs of the work against the value of what's received in return. The unfortunate problem is that trials are expensive, no matter what is discussed or the attorneys and clients try to do.

As the trial date looms closer, it's easier to estimate how long the trial will take. However, that doesn't mean that it will take less time. A day of trial usually isn't very long. "If you start at 9:00 a.m., are given a lunch break, and have a 4:30 p.m. end, you only have five to six hours of trial each day," commented one trial attorney. It is possible for this to be balanced by the attorneys agreeing to a "bare bones" trial in simple cases where the numbers of witnesses called to testify are reduced, and the extent of examination and cross-examination, exhibits, and types of presentations limited.

Your attorney can discuss this with opposing counsel, and this may lead, in turn, into settlement discussions. Be prepared for the argument that your side can't appear weak by calling up opposing counsel simply to cut down the costs of the trial. It's better to argue that a simpler trial will be easier for the judge or jury to understand. "The cardinal rule is to keep the trial simple. If you don't keep it simple for the judge and jury, then you'll lose," commented the same attorney. "Anything we can stipulate over by agreeing as to evidence or streamlining facts is in both parties' interest," said another.

It is more difficult in complex cases to cut the number of days spent by your side in the trial battle. The simplest of cases are tried based on estimates in days; in complex trials, you are talking about multiples of weeks. It is usually this projected cost that persuades the parties that now is the time to settle, although the previous costs of discovery, among other expenditures, have already been lost.

In addition to keeping it simple, winning litigators know that their case must have an understandable theme to win. "You need a story that's easily understood and that the jury or judge can warm up to. There has to be a rhythm to the case, and the attorney must be totally prepared and able to conduct that music," said one litigator. "Knowing the judge and what's liked or not is helpful," observed another. "How experienced and good the other attorney is makes a difference, of course. But sometimes even the good ones have off-days," reflected a third, adding, "You never really know who's going to win."

Other Strategies to Control Litigation Costs

There are additional strategies that can be employed to control litigation expenses other than reviewing the specific stages of a case.

Use a Litigation Plan and Budget, Whenever Possible

The litigation plan and budget discussed before must be used in your decisions on the case. You probably worked hard to get one; once in place, it should be used. Whether the case is fought to the bitter end or those monies, to be spent anyway, should be used for an early settlement offer is an important decision. This planning forces both you and your attorney to estimate how likely you are to prevail and what the costs may be. This analysis can be used to decide whether ADRs should be used and when. Be sure that any deviations from the plan and budget are discussed, and this time shouldn't be charged to you by the lawyer (but be sure to talk about it first).

Review All Bills Closely

Law firms should submit bills that are understandable and allow you to compare how expensive the case is now to what had been estimated before. As discussed extensively in Chapter 13, reviewing all bills in detail gives good information as to what's going on, in addition as to how the costs are tracking against your budget. Ask "Why?" on all important expense items. If any item appears outrageous or excessive, ask for an explanation. If that doesn't make any sense, ask for a credit.

The process of reviewing bills can be used in lieu of a litigation plan and budget in centering on areas that are susceptible to the lowering of costs. The problem with this approach is that the costs have already been incurred and you have less negotiating room.

Use Other Legal Personnel

Discuss the proper use of the lawyer's paralegal, at a lower hourly rate, instead of the attorney for various tasks. Preparation of motions, interrogatories, various notices, and even legal research, are areas that can be handled by experienced paralegals, subject to the lawyer's final review. If the firm doesn't have an available paralegal and the case is large enough, consider hiring an outside paralegal to work underneath the lead attorney in performing these tasks.

Additionally, contract attorneys can be retained apart from the lead law firm at a lower cost to conduct specific jobs such as conducting depositions, completing important legal research, drafting motions, and even appearing in court on nonessential matters. A contract attorney is a lawyer, typically a sole practitioner, who performs specific aspects of a case for a fee usually lower than what the lead law firm would charge. Contracting out depositions to contract attorneys and using paralegals (whether on the law firm's staff or hired by you separately) to grind out motions and interrogatories are strategies that can be used at times in more complex, expensive cases.

While at the Proceedings

While you're in court or at a deposition, evaluate the abilities of the attorneys and listen closely to what the other party is really saying. Don't dismiss what's said just because it doesn't agree with what you think. Try to determine if the other side has a case—it's better to try settling differences than continuing to fight and losing a disastrous judgment.

Don't make rude gestures or remarks to the opposing party when they're seen in court. Try to be civil, even to the extent of approaching the other person and saying "You know, this is costing both of us a lot of money. How can we get this behind us?" You can't end or settle a case if you only look at the other side as the enemy.

Make a Checklist

Make a checklist to discuss with your attorney how you can control your expenses. This checklist would be used to ensure that the cost implications of any legal decision are always considered before doing the work. You should ascertain, for example, the following:

1 Filing successive demurrers or motions to dismiss isn't to be done without discussing it first with you.

2 Preparing and filing motions for summary judgment also must be discussed first and are to be discouraged.

3 The law firm doesn't need to have more than one attorney attend any deposition, or more than one attorney prepare any motion, without prior approval.

4 Successive reviews of the same document over time is subject to not being paid.

5 Changing of attorneys who work on the case must first receive your prior approval.

6 The case should be staffed in a large firm from the bottom up—an *experienced* associate does the work with the partner supervising. Down-pyramiding of work isn't authorized and will be compensated only at the rate such work is usually paid. For example, a senior partner performing junior associate work will be compensated at the junior associate level and not at senior partner levels. Interoffice discussions by attorneys on your case should be kept to a minimum.

7 Stipulate to facts not in dispute as early as possible.

8 Depositions should not be taken as a matter of course, must be justified, kept as short as possible, and streamlined in advance.

9 The use of consultants, such as jury-picking consultants and expert witnesses, must be discussed before these people are hired. If you have the time, you'll meet with them before the decision to hire is made.

10 ADR and settlement approaches will always be used to encourage a fast resolution of the case.

11 To the fullest extent possible, you or your company will do work, such as finding documents, copying, and providing other cost-effective measures.

12 Motions for sanctions against opposing counsel shall be used sparingly, only when it will advance your case, and then only with your prior consent.

13 Legal research in areas where the partner or an attorney is an expert is to be held to a minimum.

14 No fee will be paid for unnecessary letters to you or excessive meetings between attorneys in the same firm.

When Your Cash Flow Goes South and the Fees North

Legal fees owed to attorneys, unless you gave security such as a second mortgage on your house, enjoy no more legal protection than those of any other unsecured creditor. Don't pay the law firm over other creditors, especially if you owe federal or state income, payroll, or sales taxes. These should always be paid first.

Stretch out fees owed, if possible, and arrange to make affordable installment payments. There's no question you'll spend your money first on utilities, food, medical bills, and the mortgage before paying your attorney. There's no need to treat your lawyer any differently from other creditors.

This isn't to say you should "stiff" your attorneys—just don't treat them any differently because they're lawyers. Although they can sue without incurring legal costs (but they do lose billable time), there are laws protecting clients in this regard. Any lawsuit filed over unpaid fees usually is countered by the client's claim for an offset or damages due to legal malpractice, and attorneys know that suing over fees brings about such counterclaims.

However, this doesn't mean an attorney must continue to represent you when the services aren't being paid. Although most states have statutes protecting clients from the unauthorized or arbitrary withdrawal from representation that would impair a client's legal rights (such as just before trial), judges can be sympathetic toward releasing lawyers from representing you when they're not being paid.

A Word about Confidentiality

The general rule is that conversations you have with your lawyer, but with no other person, will be held confidential and not be permitted to be disclosed in court. The purpose of the attorney-client privilege is to encourage the full and honest disclosure of facts to an attorney without concern that such disclosure will be used against you later. However, this protection can be lost if certain conditions aren't understood, and it could cost you money.

The disclosures must be made when you're talking to an attorney, either to see if your case will be taken or after accepting the representation. The attorney must be a bona fide lawyer who's licensed to practice law. The facts or communications must be intended to be confidential, can't involve the commission of a crime or fraud, and the privilege must be claimed in court at the proper time by the lawyer.

Be careful not to waive this, as the attorney-client privilege in these cases can't be used later to prevent the other side from using it as evidence. For example, suppose you admitted "We did it" to a friend or in front of the lawyer's secretary (who later was fired). Or the notes from your meetings were thrown into the garbage, and a private investigator or someone from the other side discovered them. This evidence won't be protected.

The attorney's notes, documents, and opinions regarding the case generally are protected under federal law and most state laws by so-called "work product" statutes or decisions. This protection can be lost also if you or the attorney carelessly discard copies of evidence or things discovered later by the other party.

Lawyers rarely abuse the privilege by telling the other side what was told to them in confidence—they're too motivated to win. The problem is when they use the privelege to withhold facts not covered by it; those fights are a waste of time and money. This occurs, for example, when what was told to them was also told by you to others. Problems also arise when attorneys use confidential information for their own benefit, such as buying the stock of a client when working on a corporate merger. Or they may buy real estate next to your development without your knowledge, only to sell it back at a higher price when you go to the next stage. This not only violates conflict of interest, security, and other laws, but it is also malpractice.

Don't Necessarily Change Attorneys in Midstream

Clients are frequently upset with their litigation attorneys, as much because of the process itself and lack of communication as they are with any mistakes made by the law firm. If you're upset with the work because of a bad result or miscommunications, talk to the attorney about correcting the problems. However, only approach changing attorneys in midstream with caution, as this maneuver can greatly increase your expenses. See the Chapter 21 for additional details.

What to Do about Excessive Fees or a Lousy Job

Taking the time to talk to several lawyers about your case in the beginning is the best defense against excessive fees or a lousy job. When you compare one against the other, check the state bar association as to pending grievances, become knowledgeable about the process, and hire experienced attorneys who'll work with you on costs, the likelihood of having a problem is less. It all starts with finding the right lawyer.

Even with an attorney carefully checked before hiring, you still need to be careful. It's easy for an attorney to charge off and create a bill excessively higher than expected, if there was any miscommunication as to what type of job you wanted. Clients who let their emotions run, such as saying "I'd rather give my money to you than that S.O.B.," or "that lousy good-for-nothing is going to get what's deserved," will end up with costs they can't stand. While you were stewing angrily about the injustice, the attorney was doing no more than what you wanted—getting even with every legal weapon possible. Unfortunately, it's much later before you wake up and decide those bills are now the worse problem of the two.

It's more difficult to prove legal fees were excessive when you didn't take the time to know exactly how or for what you would be billed. You substantially narrow down substantially the risks of being overcharged when you have a written fee agreement, know what's in that agreement, and go through the process of a litigation estimate, plan, or budget. Of course, if you have negotiated a fixed-fee or not-to-exceed agreement, then the likelihood of a dispute over fees is substantially lowered. Whatever agreement you have, whether the fee is fixed or not, should be written and agreed to in a clear, easily understood way.

Be alert to what's being billed. If the attorneys haven't provided sufficiently detailed bills, then have them bill with the necessary detail. If you feel too many meetings between partners and associates are occurring over your work, for example, see if a senior associate alone can perform the work rather than that junior associate who's working directly with a senior partner.

Talk directly with the attorney over any questioned bill. Don't sit back and stew, receiving one high bill after another, before you blow up and call that person every name in the book. A few attorneys are dishonest (such individuals are found in every profession) and these people need to be caught before you're terribly overbilled. Once you catch an attorney billing in excess of what you feel is fair or against your agreement, immediately complain and ask what happened.

Upon seeing the mistake, many attorneys try to rectify the problem. However, if they don't or the fees stay excessive, then what do you do?

The Strong Consumer Rights

Another well-kept secret in the legal profession are the strong, consumer rights that clients enjoy when they fire their attorney or have a dispute over excessive fees. These rights include state bar investigations, malpractice litigation, and mandatory fee arbitration, among others provided primarily by state law. Check your local or state bar association for the details.

Before embarking on any action, it makes sense first to see if the matter can be worked out with the attorney. Experienced, professional attorneys know that there's much downtime when a client begins pressing them over a bad job or high fees. Professionals would rather spend the time to fix a mistake or reduce a bill that's higher than expected than waste negative time in a fee dispute or malpractice action—they have better uses for their time.

However, attorneys can also think that they did a good job and deserve the fees, even if the client lost the case. There's nothing worse than for someone to lose a case, or pay monies in an out-of-court settlement in addition to having a high legal bill on top of that. Yet, such occurences happen every day, and for every case there has to be a loser when there's a winner. One litigator reflected "I can't think of a time when an attorney lost a case and didn't believe that he or she shouldn't be paid for his or her efforts. You try as hard as you can for your clients, but—win, lose, or draw—if you put the time in, then you get paid."

However, when you have come to an impasse with your attorney and feel you've been had, then it's time to exercise your strong consumer rights.

Client Consumer Rights

It's well established in law that legal fees must be reasonable under the circumstances. Rule 1.5 of the American Bar Association's Model Rules of Professional Conduct, as just one example, provides that any legal fees charged must be reasonable and ethical. The ABA, as well as state bar associations, have enacted specific codes of ethics and laws regulating the conduct of their attorney members. State laws regulate the conduct of lawyers, ranging from when written fee contracts are required to the penalizing of attorneys for unethical conduct.

Although remedies vary from state to state, clients today enjoy numerous rights in the event of bona fide complaints against their attorney or law firm. This wasn't so true years ago. However, the consumer revolution in product liability and medical malpractice has continued on unabated into the legal profession. Some feel that this is only justice being served, because if the attorneys could attack everyone else, then it was only fair play for them also to become vulnerable.

The complaints over the power attorneys had when fighting client claims at no cost brought about these significant changes. Further, attorneys are always looking for new business, no matter who is to be sued. Lawyers love to sue other attorneys, just as they like to sue anyone else on behalf of their clients. It's a very profitable business, especially when the attorney has a malpractice carrier.

Clients have the ability to complain to the state bar, hire a legal malpractice specialist on a contingency basis, refuse to pay a bill, and force the attorney to go through mandatory arbitration, among other state-granted rights.

State Bar Investigations

State bar associations typically have formed grievance committees empowered to investigate client complaints, order a hearing on the matter, and discipline the attorney. The powers of such committees generally include the right to order restitution of monies, conditions as to the attorney's continued practice of law, and even the suspension or removal of that attorney from the practice of law in that state. Such investigations can be quite forceful proceedings, causing the attorney to take your grievances very seriously.

An advantage of this process is that the system works for you at no cost. You make the complaint, an investigator talks to you about the facts, then the bar association takes it from there. Lawyers take it seriously when they receive a call from the state bar saying a complaint has been made against them. Although the powers and results of these investigations differ among the states, the consumer cries for change are being heard.

Be careful when your attorney is talking about bringing a grievance against the opposing attorney. Although there are times when this is warranted, it's also true that some lawyers in the heat of battle will use them to gain a tactical advantage over the other attorney. When this is discussed, determine whether it's fair and advances your case and who pays for this.

Information about grievance procedures is available from your local or state bar association, including how complaints are brought. Making a state bar complaint doesn't mean you can't talk to another attorney to file a malpractice suit over mistakes or excessive fees. In fact, both a malpractice action and a state bar complaint can be filed.

Malpractice Litigation

Perhaps it was fitting that the attorneys who made life so miserable for doctors, accountants, manufacturers, and others would turn against their own kind in the same way. An attorney who makes a mistake today has significant cause for concern. If the error resulted in damages, or your new attorney feels that punitive damages can be obtained, then your case will be taken on a contingency fee basis. This is the best of all worlds, as you're on an equal footing—both attorneys aren't being paid on an hourly basis.

It's estimated that one out of every three attorneys will have at least one malpractice claim during his or her professional career, and the number of such claims is steadily increasing each year. Malpractice litigation can be brought against an attorney for reasons other than a professional mistake, such as conflicts of interest, fraud, misrepresentation, and misapplication of trust funds.

An attorney with malpractice insurance is required by the carrier to turn any claims made in a timely manner over to the insurance company or lose the defense by the carrier. Approximately three out of every four attorneys carry some form of malpractice insurance, although the cost of this insurance is excessively high because of the numbers and severity of previous claims made by dissatisfied clients. Most attorneys, therefore, have deep pockets through malpractice insurance and assets to pay for the damages they cause.

> Lawyers who are in such surplus today don't protect their own—they don't even think about it. Even if your new attorney doesn't handle malpractice lawsuit, he or she can earn a referral fee up to 25% of the total award won by the malpractice attorney referred the business. Attorneys will write off small fees entirely, or give a credit to a large fee, rather than risk a malpractice claim over a bad job.

Attorneys understandably will defend malpractice claims strongly. One of the most frequent defenses used is that the lawyer made a business judgment rather than a legal error. A business judgment that doesn't work out isn't malpractice.

For example, a lawyer representing the seller was negotiating the sale of a business. During the discussions the attorney agreed, in return for other concessions, to allow an "offset clause" to be inserted by the buyer's attorney into a $250,000 promissory note. This clause allowed the buyer to offset the costs of remedying problems, if not disclosed by the seller but discovered after the sale, directly against the promissory note without it being a default under the note.

The computer system later crashed, causing havoc with the company's customers and suppliers. The buyer offset $125,000 against the principal, then stopped making payments entirely because of the damages incurred to correct the problems. The seller was out of luck. This wasn't legal malpractice, as it was caused by the negotiations or business decisions made by the seller's attorney over what should or shouldn't be in that particular note. The agreement was legal whether the clause was in or not. Although this wasn't legal malpractice, the law firm worked for free on behalf of the seller in an ensuing lawsuit brought against the buyer for not making any further payments on the note. The lawsuit was later settled with concessions made by both parties on the terms of the note.

However, a real estate attorney was asked by a client if she should worry about a lawsuit filed against her personally in the state of Hawaii. The attorney wrote back to the client, telling her not to worry about that lawsuit because she had no assets in Hawaii, although the attorney knew she had assets in other states. The happy client followed the lawyer's advice and allowed the default judgment to be taken. Later, the judgment creditor took the judgment, then discovered to its glee that the judgment debtor owned assets in other states.

The plaintiff filed a judgment lien on the properties in the other states and forced their sale in satisfaction of the judgment. As "sister state" judgments are recognized under the U.S. Constitution, a judgment received in Hawaii will be recognized by all other states. The attorney was clearly guilty of malpractice by not recognizing that as a matter of law judgment liens are recognized by other states, including those where the client still owned property.

Legal malpractice is a specialty just as product liability and medical malpractice are—you need to secure the services of a specialist. Attorneys who don't specialize in this are happy to take your case, whether they joint venture it with another who does or keep it themselves. For assistance in the techniques of finding the "right" attorney, see Chapter 5.

Deciding whether to bring a malpractice action or not can be difficult. These can be nasty lawsuits, and again you're going into the courts. Such action can be used as a negotiating threat if the fees are excessive. You will need to decide this in the same way other decisions have been made concerning litigation—time, expense, and attorney fees versus the return. Don't make the decision when you're mad, but wait until you have had the chance to decide this with a clear mind.

Mandatory Fee Arbitration

Many states provide for mandatory fee arbitration at no or limited expense to the client in the event of a fee dispute with an attorney. If the client has such a dispute and desires arbitration on the matter, then it's mandatory in these states that the attorney must have the case decided by arbitration; thus he loses the right to litigate the matter in the courts. What's interesting is that the legal profession recognized that an ADR, such as arbitration, would be one way to curb the inequities inherent with attorneys and the court system.

By not being able to litigate in court, the attorney loses the advantage to defend at no cost—both parties are placed on a more equal footing. Generally, the arbitrator is another attorney who does this as a professional service to the community. The states provide varying rights of appeal, and clients may retain an attorney at their expense to represent their interests in the arbitration. There is a small filing fee, the proceedings are informal, and the services of the arbitrator generally are provided at no charge.

Information about the extent of these and other programs can be obtained by contacting your local or state bar association.

For Whom Does Your Attorney Work?

Determining for whom an attorney works can be confusing, even for lawyers, and this creates malpractice conflict-of-interest situations. It's easy to see that lawyers who worked for a competitor or someone with an interest adverse to your case shouldn't take your case. In litigation, attorneys can't take cases with such prior adverse representations; however, they can in nonlitigation matters, such as contract negotiations, provided the conflict is disclosed and both parties agree (usually in writing).

Let's say you sued your landlord; then you discovered your attorney had represented the landlord previously in court. You wouldn't be comfortable. If you lost, you might blame the lawyer for being biased due to the prior representation. Even if you won, you might feel the fees were too high and still complain about the conflict of interest. The lawyer shouldn't have taken your case.

Businesses present particular conflict-of-interest problems for the attorney. The company is the client, regardless of who pays or authorizes the bills. The individual shareholders, officers, directors, and employees of the organization aren't the client. The authorization for retaining that attorney must have come from a corporate officer who has the power to hire such counsel.

This doesn't present problems in sole proprietorships where the owner hires and pays for the lawyer's services, but it can become complicated in situations involving partnerships or corporations. Should an attorney perform work on behalf of one, that entity is the client, regardless of who has the power or control.

For example, an attorney who represents a partnership has a conflict of interest when the partners begin feuding among themselves. If the dispute is bad enough, the attorney representing the partnership must resign in favor of lawyers who will represent all of the partners or shareholders individually with respect to the disagreed matters. To favor one partner over another, whether intentionally or not, subjects both the partnership and the attorney to a malpractice suit.

A company with shareholders, regardless of who controls the board of directors, presents a classic conflict situation. The attorney, even when hired directly by the president, must view the entire company as the client. Although this may result in the attorney's bills not being paid, that lawyer can't take sides in any dispute among the shareholders. Nor may the attorney represent any officer or director individually in the same subject matter, if that attorney is representing or has represented the company previously. Separate counsel needs to be retained.

Should any attorney fall into the trap of these situations, which isn't a rare occasion, then there's the risk of a malpractice suit. Should a shareholder or partner be frozen out, whether the lawyer is at fault or not, that attorney may become the "deep pockets" for that dissatisfied party. This situation can be used also as a negotiating weapon when legal fees are excessive or even still owed.

Start Interviewing Others

If you're dissatisfied with your lawyer's work, you should start talking to other attorneys, whether your case has been completed or not. They can be a good sounding board as to whether the lawyer committed malpractice, excessively overcharged, or didn't. If you decide later that your attorney isn't as bad as you first thought, then you do have backups in case you change your mind. You also can recheck the competitiveness of your present attorney's fees and billing.

Be careful not to come across as a whiner or complainer. Attorneys whom you consult don't want to inherit the same problems as the old one. They will be on the lookout for any signs that you simply don't like attorneys, the process, or paying reasonable fees (although to you the fees are excessive).

Replace only for Good Reason

If you're still dissatisfied with the present law firm after these meetings, then decide before making any changes that the problems aren't in part due to your actions. You could be part of the problem by not communicating, waiting until the last moment to make decisions, or not providing the necessary information. Be honest with yourself because if the problem is also your fault, then the problems simply continue on with a new law firm.

Whether changing firms will improve matters depends on the facts. If the delays and extra costs you had incurred were due to be continued, last minute changes and demands on your part, then simply changing law firms won't be the answer. If instead they resulted from the attorney's lack of communication and follow-through, despite your telephone calls and complaining letters, then the lawyer is at fault. If both of you are dragging your feet on items, or misfiring in communications, you should first try to work it out together. It's your call.

But remember that changing firms can be quite expensive. If you change in the middle of litigation, then the new law firm will charge you for the time required to review the file and to be brought current in the proceedings. It will take time for the new firm to know you as well as the old one, no matter how slow it appeared your old law firm was. Sometimes keeping the old attorney who's known is better than taking chances with a new one who could be worse. Spend time thinking about this problem before making a decision.

Give Them a Second Chance

Before changing law firms, warn the firm you're considering replacing it, give the specific reasons, and set a time limit by when the changes need to be made. There are two reasons for doing this. First, you have no assurances that another firm will meet your requirements any better. Second, law firms clearly want to retain business in today's market and not have malpractice claims.

Be sure you have been talking to the right person with your complaints and suggestions. If you are dealing with a small firm, then you know that person. In a large firm, however, the person doing the work may not be the person who has the most to lose should you become upset. The salesman or "rain maker" who brought you into the firm at first may be the decision maker with the most to lose. Be sure you have talked to that person, as well as the one doing the work.

Giving the old firm a second chance doesn't mean you should be "soft" with them. Give them 30 to 60 days to "shape up or be shipped out." It takes time to bring a second law firm up to speed and malpractice lawsuits are always there. If the reason for transferring is due to serious overbilling, malpractice, or a breach of ethics, don't pay any bills still owed, and transfer the business immediately.

Replacing the Law Firm

It could be you retained the wrong-sized firm. A large law firm may be neglecting your problems in favor of much larger "flag ship" clients. A smaller-sized law firm may not have the ability to handle all of your complex problems, if you have a variety of requirements, although they may be trying with mixed results.

If at all possible, retain your new law firm before discharging the old one. If the reasons for changing law firms aren't related to overcharging or a fundamentally serious reason, then handle the transfer with grace. The cooperation of the old law firm in moving files and cooperating with your new attorneys can be helpful. The new firm will always have questions.

The Question of Remaining Fees

Attorneys know that any owing fees are clearly at risk when they have overcharged or done a bad job. Given the strong consumer rights enjoyed by clients, even normal fees billed by law firms for work not involving malpractice can also be at risk, especially when the fees are relatively small. It's usually not worth it for a law firm to take action to collect small fees. Some attorneys will turn these over to a bill collector when permitted by state law. However, should the client enjoy a right to mandatory fee arbitration, such acts usually don't deny the client that right to a fee arbitration.

Should the fees be suspiciously high, you might consider hiring a legal audit firm. Although legal audits are conducted usually to determine how efficiently the law firm is when doing voluminous work requirements for a larger corporation, and not fraud, they do have a place. Generally, the client pays for these services, but is reimbursed by the law firm through reduced billing levels or credits to fees. Overstaffing, incorrect levels of staffing, and work done by people at the wrong level (i.e., a partner doing work that a junior associate should be doing or too many "discussion" meetings on your case) are typical problems spotted by such audits.

Assuming you don't use any outside accounting or legal audit firms (they have to be paid, as well), there are several ways to treat high bills—you can do nothing, negotiate with the law firm, put it in the hands of your new attorneys, call up the state bar association for an investigation, or call up the local bar association regarding your rights as a client over disputed fees.

Your consumer rights don't extend to not paying legitimate or reasonable fees, no matter how high they appear to be. Attorneys have been collecting owing bills for centuries, and they understand their rights well. If you have questions about any fees or work performed, first contact that firm. Follow up any telephone call with a letter stating specifically what problems exist. And then negotiate strongly.

Should you negotiate a lower, acceptable bill, then consider that you've done a good job. Should their offers or demands not be acceptable, then don't just forget about the bills. Contact your local or state bar association for advice before being sued over what's owed. Although excessive billings are at risk these days, this doesn't mean that lawyers won't take action to collect what's needed to pay their mortgages.

You should talk, as well, to malpractice attorneys as to whether they'll take your case. Take your time when deciding to make a malpractice claim and litigate. The lawyer who neglected your case won't be ignoring this one, and it will be another battle. This doesn't mean you should avoid this type of litigation, but it does mean knowing what you're getting into.

What if You Win (or Lose)?

You now know that a judgment for or against you, whether large or small, doesn't necessarily mean that the award will be paid. Defendants have the ability to: move or transfer assets, regardless of legality; appeal an adverse judgment; negotiate when there's a limited ability to pay (or simply give that appearance); threaten or in fact file for bankruptcy; move out of state or country; and record exemptions, such as the homestead exemption, among other moves. The losing party even can file bankruptcy.

At the same time, the judgment creditor is trying to collect that judgment—recording a judgment lien, conducting an asset search, using a creditor's exam, obtaining writs of execution and garnishment, levying on real property, or simply sitting on the judgment. If the judgment debtor ducks into bankruptcy, then the judgment creditor looks for ways to attack that proceeding on grounds of fraud or some loophole in the law. See Chapter 10 for further details.

It's all a game. The same laws apply, but each side is taking steps to protect or further its position, depending on whether it's the winner or the loser. At the same time, there's is only one guaranteed winner—the attorney on either side who gets paid, no matter what, provided the client doesn' firstt run out of money.

What Really Happens

Let's look at one example to see what can really happen before and after getting a judgment. A reoccurring situation occurs when two people live together, buy things and mix up their finances, then break up. Or they start a business together, then run into problems getting along. It's no different than getting a divorce.

Tom and Kathy fell in love and lived together. They began importing fine sculptures from overseas, selling them to interior decorators, then to the general public, and the business prospered. Nothing was set down in writing, because they loved and trusted one another. The business was very profitable.

Five years later, Tom and Kathy started fighting over business policy—Tom wanted to add other products and Kathy didn't. One thing led to another, and they broke up. Tom moved out, and neither spoke to the other at the business. At this time, the company was selling imported fine products in excess of $500,000 annually and growing rapidly.

Kathy met someone else and approached Tom on selling out, but they couldn't agree on the price. Kathy's best friend told her the business was worth "hundreds of thousands of dollars." It wasn't, but Kathy didn't know what the true value was. Tom, upset over Kathy's new boyfriend, marched in to attorney Anne Tone and told her that Kathy wanted too much for the business (which was true). Tom's attorney understood that with everything commingled, nothing in writing, and what was basically a divorce situation, litigation would be a mess. She advised that both parties use mediation. In fact, Anne knew a good mediator who understood business and had conducted divorce mediations with excellent results.

Kathy's attorney, Bill Bates, didn't like the idea of mediation, never having tried it before, and advised her against it. Kathy had never heard about mediation, but she went along with her attorney's suggestions. Settlement discussions didn't work out, and Bill filed a lawsuit on behalf of Kathy. Neither Tom nor Kathy had ever been in a lawsuit before, and Kathy left the business to work for someone else.

The depositions became nasty when Tom accused Kathy of having affairs behind his back (not true, but he now believed it) and Kathy accused Tom of hiding assets and taking advantage of her (not true, but she now believed that). Two years later, the business was beginning to decline, primarily because of the time Tom was spending on the lawsuit.

The trial lasted for 5 days, resulting in a jury judgment for Kathy in the amount of $100,000. Since nothing was in writing regarding attorney fees, or by statute, both were responsible for their legal and court costs under their state's laws. Kathy owed Bill Bates $50,000, whereas Tom owed Anne $35,000 (yes, there is this difference between attorneys).

Tom fired Anne, feeling she had done a lousy job defending him, and refused to pay Kathy. Anne hadn't done a bad job. It was difficult because nothing had been in writing, and the jury had believed Kathy.

Kathy's Conversation with Her Attorney

Kathy marched into Bill Bates' office, saying "He won't pay the judgment?"

"No problem. The business is still here, and we'll move against everything else. You have a judgment against him personally for a hundred grand," he said.

"Less what I owe you."

"True, but I can wait for what you owe until we get it from him. He's also paying me, you see."

"In a way, I guess."

Tell me again what he has that's valuable."

"There's the business, two cars, the furniture, and his coin collection,"responded Kathy.

"Tell me about the cars and everything."

"One car is the Mercedes that's used for work. The other is a Bronco. We both bought the furniture. It's beautiful—old antiques and a few original paintings. His coin collection is worth tens of thousands of dollars alone. Everything together's worth over $100,000. Then, there's the business."

"We'll get going on it right away. The 30-day appeal period has expired, so that's behind us. We'll record the judgment in the county. That will protect us especially if he owns real property, now or later."

"He doesn't own any. Image was more important."

"Okay. We'll prepare an immediate order for the Marshall to go and seize the Bronco, the coin collection, and some of the furniture. I'll put a levy on his checking and savings accounts, but if he's been smart, they've already been moved."

"What about the Mercedes?," asked Kathy

"We have a little difficulty there. As I remember it's used entirely in the business for driving the customers around, and that car can't be seized in this state. I know his attorney will argue that one, if we go after it, and there's no need to add to your bill."

"That's fine by me."

"I'll argue that the furniture is actually an investment to try and get around that exemption. I'll also see about a court order to direct the bookkeeper to garnish any wages or payments to Tom over the business's bills and what's exempt."

"Will there ever be an end to this?"

"We're almost there."

Tom's Conversation with His Attorney

Tom had now retained attorney Jim Jones who demanded, and received, a $5,000 retainer of which $2,000 had been charged in getting up to speed. Tom had been paying Anne in monthly installments but had listened to Jones's advice to save his money for the upcoming battles—he had stopped paying her. Jim and Anne were negotiating that, at least from what he could see of the last bill.

"So what do you want to do?" Jones said, looking up from his desk.

"I don't know. That's why I'm here."

"The appeal period expired before you got into my office. We could have used that threat to work out a better deal on the judgment. Who wants to wait for their money, especially after that kind of trial?"

"Lousy experience," Tom agreed. "What about Anne Tone?"

"She'll wait another month or two. I told her you had no money."

"That's true. I can't pay any of this off. In fact, it takes everything I take from the business to meet my living expenses."

"You don't live poor," Jones deadpanned.

"It's been a good life....Except for the last year or two."

"I've been thinking about your problem," Jones said, ignoring Tom's point. "You have two choices. First, work out a payment plan, including selling off your coin collection and a few of the paintings. Second, you can fight them."

"What do you prefer?"

"That's up to you. You didn't hear this from me, understand? But the coin collection and the Bronco simply disappear. Let them fight over the furniture. That's probably worth ten or twenty grand. Then, we throw you into bankruptcy."

"Including the business?"

"Of course. But you've already moved your best accounts into another corporation. All the money goes there, the other stuff stays in the old company. You might even lease another place, maybe even in another state, and operate the good business from there."

"Can you do that?" Tom asked.

"It's a problem if you're caught. But at some time, the people just give up trying to collect and lick their wounds."

"How much does this cost?"

"As you know, I charge $200 an hour. I don't see this work being any greater than $10,000, max." Tom simply shook his head in disbelief.

"I better start trying to keep something, especially with these costs...I love that coin collection, and Kathy has no right to it. It was always mine. And my brother sure could use the Bronco."

"Don't tell me what you do from here," warned Jones. "What do you want to do about the business?"

"I do owe Kathy something for starting up the business with me. But I still don't agree that was worth $100,000. It really burned me up when her friends lied on the witness stand as to what she did and how much she owned of my business."

"That's over now. Nothing you can do about spilled milk."

"I can't move to another state. All the accounts are in the city, and Kathy knows who all the customers are. I can't file bankruptcy. That would hurt my standing with my customers. Image is important here."

"We could threaten it and say you're having problems keeping the business afloat. That could get you a better deal." Jones gave a little smile.

"And what happens if there's no deal?"

"They'll move to attach money from the business. But I've done this before, You could have customers mail their checks directly to you...Incidentally, did you move all your checking and savings accounts to a bank in another city, like I said?"

"Yes. That's been done."

"Well, let's stonewall them a bit. If they have problems finding assets and getting money out of you, then we can get a better deal for you. That's only fair. You know, I went through something like this with my ex-wife. I learned a lot..."

One Year Later

Some months after that discussion, Tom had to file personal bankruptcy. A general business recession had begun to swing into full force at the time of the trial. He hadn't taken any response to the sales slowdown, as his time had been preoccupied with the trial and later collection activities. He did hide his coin collection, but decided to give the Bronco to Kathy when his brother didn't want it. Fair was fair, he thought, although he was beginning to dislike Jones's approach.

Kathy had received $5,000 from "tapping the till" at Tom's business until he filed bankruptcy and then liquidated the business. She also received $15,000 from selling the old antiques that Bill successfully argued was Tom's investment, and thus were able to be attached and not exempt from collection. All this money went to pay the legal bills, but she kept the Bronco.

Tom wiped out all his legal obligations by the bankruptcy, whereas Kathy began negotiating another payment plan with Bill, now owing $40,000 in legal fees. She sold off what she had and raised another $10,000 for the fees. Unable to pay anything more, the $30,000 still sits owing on the books of Bill's law firm, but he's not doing anything about it, knowing she doesn't have the money. If and when she does, then he figures she's good for it.

Having something in writing and trying mediation would have been advantageous. However, these types of cases aren't rare. Having a judgment doesn't mean you collect the monies. It depends on what assets can be located that aren't exempt and whether there's enough around to satisfy everyone. It also depends on the attorneys and how everyone decides to approach the separate collection procedures. The hassles, uncertainties, and high legal fees don't end with the judgment.

If There Are Assets

If you're the judgment creditor, you will begin your steps immediately to collect on the award, assuming there isn't an appeal. By this stage, unless the judgment is large or clearly in error, appeals normally aren't taken. The parties want it all to end.

However, in large judgment cases when the loser has assets to protect, appeals can be threatened or even taken to place additional pressures for a settlement amount less than the judgment. The threat of further litigation and expense, coupled with an appealable issue, can result in a judgment creditor accepting less. Even if the defendant has won, a plaintiff can make similar threats of an appeal to pry out some form of a payment. In smaller cases, the other side, knowing this is less likely, will say go ahead and wait and see.

Collecting on any judgment depends on the amount of the judgment, the assets that the judgment debtor has, and what relationship the judgment has to those assets. Let's say that the judgment is for $50,000, plus interest at 10% until paid, and attorney fees of $30,000 (the loser is paying for the winner's). If the loser had assets of $25,000, then clearly the judgment won't be paid off. It would make sense for the loser to file bankruptcy, given a dischargeable judgment, and start over again. The winner still owes its side's attorney fees and now would become a loser.

However, if the loser had nonexempt assets of $250,000, then there's a different case. The judgment will either be paid off or appealed. If the judgment debtor wants to get on with life, the attorneys or parties will negotiate over the terms of payment, either in full or in installments. The judgment will become subject to an agreement whereby the creditor won't undertake further collection activities, as long as payments are made as agreed. Once all the payments have been made, then a satisfaction of judgment is usually filed, all in accordance with local law.

Having assets to protect doesn't mean that a bankruptcy filing won't be necessary. If the winner presses the loser for full payment, and there's not enough cash, then the loser may consider a Chapter 11 (if a business) or a Chapter 13 (if an individual) and have the payment plan established in the bankruptcy proceedings. The winner usually understands that bankruptcy can mean losing control over the process, and a reasonable threat of bankruptcy will help bring the parties to the bargaining table. Depending on the judgment creditor's actions, it may even become necessary to make the bankruptcy filing.

Look Closely at What's Available

It is always better to see how any judgment will be paid off before suing, rather than waiting until after you receive the judgment. This can make a big difference. Similarly, if you're the one being sued, it's better to determine what assets are exempt or can be protected before the decision, even better when this planning is done before you've been sued.

It's possible to apply for a writ of attachment, seizing property prior to the judgment, when a plaintiff believes that the defendant is selling off assets to avoid an expected judgment. State laws usually mandate that a bond be obtained by the

If you *might* be sued in a large damage situation, then you should consult an attorney over the moves to take *then* to protect your assets. People also hide assets, whether following their attorneys' advice or not.

When suing, you want to know that your defendant has assets and can't dispose of them during the litigation. Attorneys usually conduct an asset search by hiring one of the many firms that locate them, and this should be done *before* the decision to sue is made.

plaintiff in such a case, insuring against loss in case the judgment isn't obtained. Such writs are governed by state law, and you'll need to follow them strictly. Writs of attachment should be distinguished from the writs of execution that are used to seize personal property after receiving a judgment. Attorneys don't use writs of attachment as often as you might think.

It's hard to stop a motivated defendant from hiding assets when he or she is willing to lie about it. Contempt of court and criminal charges require a separate hearing, but even using this approach doesn't mean that the assets will be found.

How Liquid?

The more liquid an asset, the easier it is to apply against a judgment—real estate, cars, furniture, and even jewelry aren't liquid and must be sold to be converted into cash. This requires complying with the state laws on such sales, netting out the costs of collection and sale, and deciding to what extent they are exempt under state law.

The more liquid an asset, however, the easier it is also to transfer and hide. Switching savings and checking accounts can be done easily, not to mention hiding cash, stocks, and bonds with family, friends, or even out of the country. The missing loot is explained easily away as having been spent on living expenses and attorneys, which may or may not be correct.

If a defendant, you'll be motivated to converting assets into cash. If the creditor, you'll be just trying to get your hands on as many assets as possible.

How Movable?

Although cash, stocks, and bonds are preferred when you are the judgment creditor, more than likely you will be finding the less movable assets. Real estate is a prime target, because all the creditor needs to do is record the judgment in the county where any real estate is found. The creditor then takes the steps to force the property to be sold, applying the proceeds against what's owing. Or the creditor can sit back and do nothing, knowing the debtor can't sell or refinance the property without paying off the lien. Meanwhile, the interest continues to run.

Cars, trucks, boats, motorcycles, and even airplanes can be moved about, making life difficult for the judgment creditor. However, this can be as much a drag on the judgment debtor—you must hide it far enough away so it can't be located, but that makes it as difficult for you to enjoy its use, especially when you're being followed by a private investigator.

Diamonds, jewelry, silverware, small antiques, and even Rolex watches can be hidden more easily than cars and trucks. For that reason, debtors prefer liquidating their possessions down to smaller sizes.

This doesn't mean that all is lost for the judgment creditor. Any sources of income, to the extent not exempt, are good targets. Salaries, commissions, and even bonuses can be garnished. Owning a business, given that it's financially solvent, provides a readily identifiable source of cash that can be targeted.

It's All in Your Attitude

Some defendants convert property into cash and assets that can be easily hidden and spent. They'll even spin off a business into another company, liquidate the one that's known, and continue as before. People have been known to quit their jobs and go underground rather than pay off a judgment.

On the other hand, a nice solid corporation always makes a tempting target because it's always there. Whether the officers like it or not, they don't have the flexibility to avoid judgments as individuals can. However, an executive with 20 years spent working for a company usually doesn't quit, and that salary offers a steady way of repaying someone.

If a judgment has been rendered against you, and you've been a sterling member of the community, then there's less flexibility. However, if you just lost your job and want to see the world, then the judgment creditor has the problems.

> It's the differences in how people react to a judgment that determine who gets paid or doesn't. If it so happens that the debtor wants to do things the "right way," then the creditor gets paid. If he or she doesn't give a damn or hates that person, then the creditor has problems, whether or not there are assets.

A Perspective

We have seen even with the explosion in lawsuits and out-of-control disputes that there are steps you can take—steps within your control. As one defendant said, "Like anything else new, you don't begin understanding what to do until you've begun experiencing it. Then you look backwards at what could have been done, but it's too late when you're already in court. The trick is doing this before you're there and getting burned. I would now get more information about what to do first, before letting the legal process blindly take over. I had more control than I first thought, but I didn't know it then." Some of these areas include the following:

Preventive Steps

A number of areas can be anticipated and are within the control of every person, even in these times. Taking preventive steps begins when you ask common-sense questions about your home, business, and volunteer activities. Many times it's just what you're doing as part of everyday life, such as fixing your front steps, incorporating your business, or calling a lawyer about a problem before there's a lawsuit. Taking preventive steps isn't being slightly paranoid—you have a better case if you do land in court. It's simply trying to win ahead of time.

Cost-Effective Insurance

The insurance coverage on your home, cars, rentals, business, and volunteer activities, as well as excess liability or "umbrella" coverage, should be reviewed with your insurance agent. You should know what is or isn't covered before there's a claim.

Any specialized insurance coverage for areas not covered by general policies should be checked out for your specific situation. The cost effectiveness of any insurance needs to be reviewed as to the best mix for amount, deductibles, exclusions, and overall coverage. You may decide even to self-insure, but these decisions need to be chosen carefully, not fallen into because of inaction or simply not knowing better.

Hire Your Attorney First

The telephone call to an attorney about potential problems is the most cost-effective tool available. Avoiding a $25,000 legal bill to defend an avoidable legal problem covers many telephone calls, meetings, and buying that new car. There are ways to find the right attorney; these, in turn, depend on your knowing what you specifically need. Getting the right attorney for you is the most important step, and there are ways to do this.

Put Everything in Writing
(and Understand It before Signing)

Failing to put understandings into writing is a great cause of misunderstandings, disputes, and lawsuits—many of which are totally avoidable. You need to understand ahead of time your rights and duties before signing any documents, especially those supplied by banks, insurance companies, and real estate agents with their pages of preprinted language. There are rules to follow concerning when the attorney should review any documents before signing, or when you should do it yourself. You can use releases not only for settling disputes, but also as a defense in case something happens later.

On Death and Taxes

Everyone has to face them, and you can minimize the financial problems ahead of time. By planning in advance for the proper handling of taxes (regardless as to the type) and your estate (such as properly using powers of attorney, trusts, and wills), you can have assets to enjoy and pass on to your loved ones. And there are concepts as to when you should or shouldn't hire a lawyer in these areas in keeping the legal fees down.

The Tough Times

Should you fall unexpectedly into a cash squeeze, it's possible to keep personal assets from being attacked. Knowing how to deal with creditors and knowing when to file bankruptcy (or even threaten it) are part of this. It is the knowledge of your legal rights when the creditors call that can help you survive the tough times.

Your Business

As in your personal areas, there are specific ways to practice preventive law and defenses, regardless of the business area involved. Whether it's your product or employees, you can run your business profitably and with fewer problems by making common-sense decisions. You should treat your lawyer as you would any other supplier, holding that person to cost and value considerations. There may be a time when you'll want to take your legal work inside the company, and there are ways to do this. Managing your business involves managing its legal function, and this is no different than any other area such as handling marketing, production, or finance.

Managing Your Attorney and Costs

Managing lawyers and their costs when legal work must be performed is a little known area to most of us. However, these areas are straightforward with the proper use of the fee agreement being as important as knowing the specific techniques of such cost control. Although this can be intimidating to some, just remember that it is your money and assets at stake. With the large numbers of attorneys looking for business, you have a better chance for a lawyer agreeing to a fixed fee or other value billing approach, in place of the straight, "the hours times my hourly rate," approach used previously.

What if There's a Problem?

What a person does when a problem occurs determines how easily it can be solved. You should try not to overreact, realizing that every action taken from there becomes a permanent part of the "court record" and can be brought up in court. The facts and case should be looked at closely before you decide to retain any lawyer.

Part of this is deciding whether there's a real problem, not just an illusory one where you will only be throwing money and time away. You should try to solve problems by ADRs and mediation, rather than through the more expensive, time-consuming process of litigation. As the general public becomes more aware of these alternatives, there can only be less stress, more time, and more money to enjoy the finer things of life.

Finding the Right Litigation Attorney

There are ways to find the right litigation attorney, especially when you've been sued and when there isn't much time to respond. At the same time, the basic steps that need to be taken are understandable, as well. But you should remember that all disputes eventually settle with the need to focus continually on keeping your costs in line until that time.

Controlling the Costs of Litigation

Protecting yourself and your assets means also safeguarding everything from the excessive fees of attorneys when you are forced to hire them for litigated matters. In many cases the hit on your property can be greater from your attorney than it is from the other party. As the steps to the courtroom are strange to most, even for players going through it again, you must know the strategies and tips to avoid becoming another casualty of this war. There are direct ways to handle this, including when and how to focus on settling your dispute. Remember that ADRs and mediation are a better way to solve legal disputes than the courts with their poor way of handling them. And in case you have a lawyer who does a lousy job or bills excessive fees, you have strong consumer rights that can be enjoyed.

But What if You Lose?

The same problems present when a judgment creditor tries to collect on an award are strengths for the debtor. Losers have the ability to appeal a judgment, file for bankruptcy, move assets around, and leave the state, among other frustrating tactics. The winner is taking steps to collect on the judgment, such as conducting creditor examinations, asset searches, and executing on the judgment, all at the same time. It's all a game, and the true winner puts this into proper perspective.

The Winners and Losers

Protecting assets today is a game of winners and losers. You can lose them by any number of events that are difficult to avoid, whether because of a hurricane, losing your job, or a lawsuit. A lawsuit is no different than any other major problem in life—you try to do your best and go on from there.

With our present way of solving disputes through the courts, winners can be losers and losers may turn out to be the winners. You can be wronged and have the best case, but still lose in court over a technicality. A judgment turns out to be uncollectable, or the case costs you more in legal fees than the award. The loser declares bankruptcy while you continue to pay your attorney.

Regardless of what happens, win, lose, or draw, the real winner is the one who can put that dispute, settlement, or judgment into a proper perspective and enjoy the rest of life. Attorneys look at their cases very simply—you win some and you lose some. It's better to win, but there's always another case. As an experienced litigator said, "It's all a big game. I don't take it that seriously....Never have. There's more to life."

You need to do the same thing. Suing or being sued is another game in life. You want to do your best and know the rules, but there's always what you can't control. After you've played the game, then go onto a different one, vowing to avoid the court game the next time.

The winner isn't always who gets the most or loses the least in this game. The actual winner is whoever can step back, laughing heartedly at what has happened, and can still know that life is enjoyable. Whatever happened needs to be put totally behind you, whether the money's won or lost. It's all within your control.

Index

Note: A listing in this Index does not guarantee that the subject is treated in its entirety or that any text discussion covers your particular problem or situation.

Biographical Statement

DENNIS M. POWERS, B. A., J. D., M. B. A., has over twenty years experience in legal matters advising clients on how to solve legal problems cost-effectively, avoid court, and control their legal expenses during litigation.

He has lectured at universities, written newspaper and magazine articles, conducted seminars, and participated in television programs dealing with these areas.

He is a graduate of the University of Denver Law School and the Harvard Business School. Mr. Powers resides in Kenwood, California, with his wife, Judy.